The
Glory Way

Bruce Hyatt

New Wine Press

New Wine Press
PO Box 17
Chichester
England PO20 6YB

Unless otherwise stated, Scripture quotations are taken from the King
James Version of the Bible. Crown copyright.

NKJV – the New King James Version, copyright © 1983 by Thomas
Nelson, Inc.

Sheet music: Used by permission. Copyright © Roy Turner.

ISBN: 1 903725 02 X

Typeset by CRB Associates, Reepham, Norfolk.
Printed in England by Clays Ltd, St Ives plc.

Acknowledgements

We are grateful for permission to use the following quotations:

Page 18 – Rick Joyner: from *The World Aflame*, pp. 7, 11, © 1993. Used by permission of MorningStar Publications and Ministry

Page 18 – Colin Whittaker: from *Seven Pentecostal Pioneers*, p. 10, © Marshall Pickering 1986. Used by permission of Colin Whittaker

Page 19 – Edward Jeffreys: from *Stephen Jeffreys*, p. 92. Used by permission of Elim Pentecostal Church/Rev. Wynne Lewis

Page 19 – Jack Hywel-Davies: from *The Kensington Temple Story*, p. 48, © Monarch Books 1998. Used by permission of Dr Jack Hywel-Davies

Page 248 – J.I. Packer: from *Keep In Step With The Spirit*, p. 253–4, © 1984 InterVarsity Press. Used by permission of Dr J.I. Packer

Page 282 – Watchman Nee: from *A Table in the Wilderness*, page for 28 November, © Kingsway 1969/1983. Used by permission of Kingsway Publications, Eastbourne

Page 334 – Richard Wurmbrand: from *Reaching Toward The Heights*, page for 15 July, © Zondervan Corporation. Used by permission of Michael Wurmbrand

Page 362 – Izzie Waller for her chorus, *Our God is the God of much more*. Used with her permission.

Page 366 – Charles Stevens for his chorus, *He set me free*. Used with his permission.

Page 408 – F.W. Bourne: from *Billy Bray, the King's Son* pp. 17, 16, 19–20, 21, 28, 46, 47, 20, 44, 121, © 1877 Epworth Press. Used by permission of the Methodist Publishing House

Roy Turner – All quotations of his choruses are used with his permission

Our thanks go to Pearl Dryhurst for lending many copies of the *Glory News* (a good number of which had been collected and handed on to her by Joyce Walter). When amalgamating these copies with those at the Basildon office it was possible to compile a complete set. This was invaluable.

There are many quotations, particularly in the first half of the book, which have no reference. This means that they have been taken verbatim off cassettes of recorded conversations, or copied from letters. Others are scribbled notes from telephone conversations or quite simply from chatting to people. So I am grateful to all those who so willingly gave of their time, and who openly shared so many reminiscences. It would have been totally impossible to write the book without this input.

It was at the initiative of Alan and Shirley Churchill that the task was ever started. They began by asking Margaret and me to interview Connie Staples. It was absolutely fascinating hearing her memories of a lifetime. Alan lent us cassettes of further conversations he had had with her. We then interviewed a number of other folk who were in at the beginning. This got the whole thing off the ground.

My thanks also go to Alan Churchill, Doug Aistrup, Roy Turner, Andrew Churchill, Angela Woolmore and Bridget Greenfield for reading the text. Their corrections and additions were essential. At this stage too more information came pouring in from several directions. In the final analysis this book has been a communal effort.

I must give a tribute to my dear wife and helper, Margaret. After we had together interviewed the folk in Newark, she did much work in unscrambling this information and typing it out in a basic draft. Then as the book gathered momentum, she shrewdly combined forbearance and chivvying. In her general reading, too, she proved to be an excellent finder of unusual quotations.

When it comes to discussing Christian music she exhibits a fine sensibility. She can just about play by ear any hymn in any key, a rare ability she dismisses as common or garden. A great deal of what I have written in the chapter on Glory Choruses has come through the sieve of her discernment.

Lastly, Margaret's daughter, Ruth, has done the bulk of the typing on computer. This was a task fraught with unseen snags, but she tackled it undaunted. We are all very grateful to her.

Contents

Foreword

T his is the untold story of the link between the Pentecostal and present-day Charismatic movements. It is the Glory Way – the forerunner, bringing great change and liberty to the Church as a whole.

The book contains testimony by but a fraction of the many thousands who were and still are being touched by this Glory Way. Its great expression is one of much joy pouring forth from within God's people, assisting them to cope with the experience of this great adventure we call *life*. Many have been touched by His nail-pierced hand, having their body, soul and spirit healed, cleansed and awakened, glimpsing the truth of the Christ within and being transported to realms far beyond time and space.

The moving of the Holy Spirit in the early nineties spawned a number of books about the twentieth-century revivals. These neither referred to nor took account of the tremendous impact of the Glory Way. I felt at that time, if only for the historical record, mention should be made to set the record straight. Then I heard on the grapevine that an attempt was being made to write a book. 'What a task for somebody to undertake!' I thought. However, undertaken it was with Bruce Hyatt, daring to take on the mammoth task of interviewing, writing to and telephoning so many people and piecing together this wonderful story of the Glory Way. It has taken Bruce and Margaret six years to bring this book into being and I for one feel that it will be an inspiration and a tremendous blessing to those who read its pages. The thread that runs through it is one of Love. It was the Love which touched me some thirty years ago when I came into contact with the Glory people. I am convinced that as these pages are read, as Henri Staples used to say, 'You will never be the same again'. I believe this, because the story lifts up our wonderful Saviour **Jesus Christ**.

Douglas Aistrup

Introduction

This story of the Glory Way is about a group of people touched by the finger of God. It centres on Newark in Nottinghamshire, the home of a most unusual couple, Henri and Connie Staples. The narrative begins in 1948, although its roots go back very much further. They are Pentecostal. Beyond that they cannot be pigeon-holed.

Henri was not a church planter or founder of a denomination. 'Perish the thought!' he would have said. He did not pen his sheep. It may be very necessary for others to do this, but it was not his mission to aim at that. With both their hands Henri and Connie liberally cast good seed around them on every side and the wind of the Spirit blew this wherever He willed.

The Apostle Paul talks about Christian believers 'as unknown, and yet well known' (2 Corinthians 6:9). Henri was not averse to publicity. He certainly had an eye for seizing an opportunity, for catching the attention of a town and filling its town hall. It did not come his way to hire a football ground or sports stadium, though he certainly would not have shirked it if he felt the Lord had wanted him to go for it. Yet wherever they went Henri and Connie and their enthusiastic friends did create a stir and make an impact. Opposition was inevitable and their critics tried to pass them off as a freak fringe group, and barely orthodox at that.

The fact of the matter is, the Glory Way has been a sovereign work of God. In the Glory Way the Holy Spirit rejuvenated the flagging energies of the Pentecostal assemblies of Britain. The Glory Way has been an unseen leaven (or yeast) working in the midst of God's people. Through the Glory Way the Holy Spirit has carved out fresh channels to bring spontaneous living spiritual water to many thirsty souls. Its influence has been primarily in Britain; but has also spread out to northern Europe, the United States and to other countries in Africa, the Far East and Australasia.

Before going any further, you may well ask, Why the name 'the Glory Way'? This is quickly answered by Connie Staples: 'We never attached the word "Glory" to ourselves when we started out for God. Other people did that. They came and observed, and said: "This is the Glory of God". That's a true testimony. We don't call ourselves anything, we just let God have His way and labour to please Him.'

God delights to do the surprising thing. The supernatural interacts with the natural far more than we might imagine. The ordinary course of nature is full of marvel, wonder and mystery. Almighty God takes the initiative in it all. The most stunning and undreamed of thing that God ever planned to do was to enter His own creation as one of His own creatures, to become a tiny human being, in the Person of the Lord Jesus Christ. This Jesus, carpenter of Nazareth, is nobody less than God Himself; *'without controversy great is the mystery of godliness'* (1 Timothy 3:16). In doing this God took His human race completely by surprise. Who could have imagined such a thing? So often with God things are upside down, back to front, 'the first shall be last', a stable rather than a palace. And so, in the ongoing flow of the history of His people, the Church, Jesus Christ delights in the unconventional, the despised. It is His way of continually pricking the bubble of pomp and hypocrisy. He takes *'the things which are not, to bring to nought the things that are'* (1 Corinthians 1:28). In its day the Glory Way has been despised, laughed at and warned against. With a shrug of their shoulders people have turned their backs on it. They have criticised it for going too far, for going over the top, for getting things out of proportion, for not doing things 'decently and in order'. Two-and-a-half centuries ago people poked fun at George Whitefield and the Wesleys for being 'enthusiastic' or 'fanatical'. They would say the same about the Glory Way. But what about Jesus Himself? *'His friends . . . went out to lay hold on Him; for they said He is beside Himself'* (Mark 3:21). And when He drove the corrupt and greedy moneychangers from the Temple court *'His disciples remembered that it was written, The zeal of Thine house hath eaten me up'* (John 2:17).

The truth of the matter is this: the Glory Way may well have been criticised for being unbalanced, but in actual fact, it has played its part in redressing a balance. Its supposed lack of balance has proved to be a balance! How does this work out? A friend of Henri Staples pointed out to him that God has a three-legged stool of *'righteousness and peace and joy in the Holy Ghost'* (Romans 14:17). So often the Christian Church has majored on righteousness and peace and has thought that this was enough; but it has lacked a clear expression of joy. The Lord raised up the Glory Way to put the joy leg back. I have heard a man exclaim after a meeting, 'Well, whatever else you might say, there's no doubt about it, these people really know how to praise the Lord!' That is the legacy that Henri has left.

There's another point. In this twenty-first century one of the criticisms levelled at the churches in Britain and much of the Western world is that they have been middle class. And yet we read of Jesus that *'the common people heard Him gladly'* (Mark 12:37). Why has Christianity, seemingly, become out of touch with so many working class people? This accusation may well be overdrawn. However, be that as it may, Henri and Connie Staples in their own sphere have given the lie to this. With unerring touch they have got alongside ordinary men and women, whoever they may be. In the middle of a meeting Henri would stop and point to someone in the sea of people in front of him, 'The woman in the green jumper there has been blessing me. Yes you, love. I can see by your face that God has been doing something special for you. Come up here, sister, and tell us about it.' Henri had burning in his heart this scriptural conviction that absolutely everybody is infinitely valuable and important in God's sight, and that they should be given the opportunity to express what they feel, however halting and inarticulate they might be. 'It's in you brother, it's in you sister,' he would cry encouragingly. This was infinitely helpful in bringing a person out of his or her shell and of boosting their confidence. It is a vital quality of Christian leadership and a precious one.

Here, in a nutshell, is the special character of the Glory Way, the contribution of the Glory people to the great and wonderfully varied kaleidoscope of the life of God's people. Their task and role has been to redress a balance, to put the joy leg back on the three legged stool; and they link hands with all those world-wide who do the same. Jesus is building His church *'and the gates of hell shall not prevail against it'* (Matthew 16:18), and this universal church by now is a mighty army of believers reflecting in its ranks the enormous diversity of gifts, quality and nature of humanity at large. Besides evangelists, missionary pioneers, pastors and teachers in plenty, it has needed thinkers, imaginative writers, linguists, Bible translators and scholars, publishers and printers, communicators, doctors and nurses, administrators, aviators and engineers, scientists, artists, architects and musicians. This great family of God has also needed anointed leaders of spiritual shock troops like Henri and Connie Staples.

Chapter 1

Beginnings

Here We Are Again

We are in Newark, Nottinghamshire, one of England's historic towns. With its weekly markets and its ancient castle on the banks of the River Trent, it is a haven for tourists and sight-seers. It is August bank holiday, about 1960, and a crowd, cheerful and eager, streams into the assembly hall of the local Technical College. They greet one another warmly with a hug. The hall is colourful with bunting, and at the back of the platform is a large draped banner inscribed 'Praise the Lord for goodness' sake', and then another, 'You'll feel better for coming here!' This is the annual gathering of the Glory Way. There are several hundred people. Folk have come from all over the Midlands; a good number of them are Jamaicans and other West Indians. There are some in kilts from Peterhead in Aberdeenshire. Others have trekked up from Dorset and Cornwall. A few have come over from Scandinavia and Germany. Perhaps a couple of Americans or South Africans are also there and two Dutch lads who have crossed over from the Hook of Holland and cycled up from Harwich.

On the platform at the front are several people with accordions and guitars, together with banjo and piano accompaniment and, without any formality, the music starts. One of the accordionists, standing centre stage, is an energetic little man with an infectious smile and laughter in his eyes. This is Henri Staples. Voices are uplifted. They sing,

Here we are again, Hallelujah, here we are again,
By His love and mercy, here we are again.

It is a kind of signature tune, sung to the melody of an old hymn, 'Bringing in the Sheaves'. What is perhaps startling initially is the clash and tinkle of tambourines on every hand, even some cymbals, which certainly help to keep the rhythm and movement. The Caribbean folk look thoroughly at home, their eyes dancing, their smiling teeth flashing. All over the hall many lift up their hands or clap as they praise God.

There is a pause and Henri comes in with a prayer speaking quickly and colloquially with his strong Nottinghamshire accent, and he adds, 'In the Name of Jesus I bind every hindering spirit. In the Name of Jesus I loose the spirit of salvation, the spirit of joy, the spirit of healing, the spirit of deliverance. Heavenly Father, I pray that you will quicken every man and every woman and boy and girl in this meeting...' Then the musicians and everyone launch into another chorus, 'It is joy unspeakable and full of glory.' Suddenly the aisles are full of dancing people; it is natural, spontaneous, unchoreographed. Then they begin to swirl round the room; newcomers are taken by surprise; old-stagers give them the nod and sweep them into the praising throng.

Folk are back in their seats once more and quiet descends. Henri reads a passage from the Bible and earnestly exhorts everybody to present their bodies as a living sacrifice to God, to get alone with God and to wait on God more. Then he spots a person here and there, inviting them to come up to the microphone at the front to give a testimony. Some come reluctantly, others are eager. Often the hesitant ones surprise everyone, including themselves, with the words they find coming out of their mouths. There can be an amusing moment when Henri asks them, 'Have you ever jumped for Jesus?' But after an instant's slight embarrassment they enter wholeheartedly into the spirit of the request, others joining in, all leaping up and down. 'Now', he says, 'tell everybody to raise their hands and praise the Lord!' They laughingly obey and are amazed at the electric response. By now everyone is thoroughly loosened up and receptive to the Word; testimonies or exhortations follow.

Sick folk may be present, one with an ulcer, another with a crippled back or leg, someone critically ill. Henri prays for them while brothers and sisters gather round in support. There have been some very remarkable cases of complete restoration to health as we will see later in the book.

'This gospel works!' Henri cries, 'You'll never be the same again!' He opens his Bible and starts reading and explaining a passage of Scripture: ⸻

The Spirit of the Lord God is upon me; because the Lord hath anointed me to preach good tidings unto the meek; He hath sent me to bind up the broken-hearted, to proclaim liberty to the captives, and the opening of the prison to them that are bound.

(Isaiah 61:1)

Then he says, 'Come on, Con,' and his wife strides on, handkerchief in hand, from one side of the platform. She is a bonnie woman with a shock of light brown hair and a laughing ring in her voice. 'Are you well shod?' she cries, 'These shoes were given me by my Heavenly Father and they have only been worn by one person before and that is the Lord Jesus Christ. I have got my feet shod with the Gospel of Peace. Hallelujah!' With a confident step, she walks up and down looking her audience in the eye. So the meeting continues, orderly, but unpredictably, until that majestic verse from a hymn is struck up:

Hail Saviour, Prince of Peace,
Thy kingdom shall increase
Till all the world Thy glory see.
And righteousness abound
As the great deep profound,
And fill the earth with purity.

Henri picks up his tambourine and conducts everyone as though it was the last night of the Proms. It is repeated time and again. No one wants to stop. Banjo and guitars strum, tambourines and cymbals clash, a sea of hands reach up to heaven. The Glory folk are just so glad to be there, to be enjoying the presence of God together, the blessing of the 'latter rain'. Eventually with shining faces they drift away to their caravans and lodgings, eager to meet up again the next day to resume their praises of God.

Revival and Pentecost

One of the spin-offs of knowing the Lord Jesus Christ as your living Saviour is an understanding of yourself and where you stand in the flow of time. God gives you a new sense of dignity. You know where you've come from and where you're going to. You are no longer a meaningless number on a computer or a piece of flotsam or jetsam floating aimlessly around on the wide ocean. You have a wonderful destiny. You may begin to wonder how many people have gone ahead of you on the same route. This is the history of the Church, the body of Christ, with its ups and downs, dark alleys and wonderful horizons of advance. God has moved steadily on with His purposes.

Where then, in this flow of events, does the Glory Way stand? It was born out of the great Welsh revival of 1904–5 and the Pentecostal Movement. The two come together in the work of the remarkable Jeffreys brothers. Concerning the revival in Wales, Rick Joyner highlights its significance in this way:

> There is no other example in either Biblical or church history in which a region was so quickly or radically transformed for righteousness, or the world so impacted, as happened during this revival ... There have been a few spiritual awakenings in history to span the globe and touch millions, but it can be argued that none had as much concentrated power and impact as the Welsh Revival. It seems that the Lord looked down upon Wales and said, 'I am going to show the church and the world what I can do with just a handful of faithful saints who will yield themselves to Me.' The results of that demonstration still send shock waves of conviction and hope to all who hear the story.[1]

The mining region of the valleys of South Wales was particularly affected and transformed. Even the pit ponies were at a loss how to obey their masters' commands because the miners had stopped swearing.

In Maesteg, three mining brothers were converted to Christ: Stephen, George and William Jeffreys. And in 1907, when folk came south from Sunderland in the power of Pentecostal blessing, they received a great baptism of the Holy Spirit, with speaking in tongues. More than ever they felt themselves emboldened and empowered to witness for their Lord. They were to be used greatly. Dr Martyn Lloyd-Jones has said that in his opinion the greatest evangelists in Britain in the twenties and thirties were the Jeffreys brothers.[2] George founded the Elim Pentecostal churches. Stephen first worked with him and then with the Assemblies of God. Stephen was an outstanding preacher, a burning and a shining light, always breaking new ground, riveting his hearers. People would squirm in their seats under conviction of sin till at length they accepted Jesus as Saviour and were filled with joy. His son Edward wrote of him:

One could see that the secret of his power over men and women to whom he ministered ... was the enshrined love-passion which possessed and energised him ... They could not resist the flood of lava-like zeal and enthusiasm of this glowing son of Wales, for when the Spirit was upon him there was something definitely volcanic about his ministry. [3]

His preaching was authenticated by very remarkable cases of healing. The blind were given sight, the deaf heard, twisted and crippled bodies were made straight and whole. These cases have been well attested by his devoted friend J.W. Adams, vicar of Wall near Lichfield. Furthermore, in more recent years when Kensington Temple was completely refurbished, willing workers found under the floor of the main church 'numerous crutches, wheelchairs, leg-braces and other medical aids that had been discarded following the campaigns of Stephen and George Jeffreys during their revival meetings in 1920 and 1930.' [4]

This dynamic heralding of the gospel stirred up the churches and assemblies of the land. Donald Gee, the Pentecostal thinker and writer, commented,

But one significant and fruitful result of Stephen Jeffreys's memorable and impressive ministry throughout the British Assemblies was the way it inspired so many other men to attempt big things for God. A veritable wave of evangelism and evangelists followed in his train – New assemblies were being opened continuously, and a new urge to public testimony of a bolder order swept like fresh air through little faithful groups of believers who for years had seemed content to lie hidden in odd corners and back streets. [5]

This thumbnail sketch of the Welsh Revival, the beginnings of the Pentecostal movement and the evangelism of Stephen Jeffreys give some idea of what led up to the Glory Way. The work of Henri and Connie Staples, for all its spontaneity, did not come out of a vacuum. These were the great influences behind them. *'The wind bloweth where it listeth'* (John 3:8).

Express Trains

'D'yer hear that whistle down the line? I guess it's engine number forty nine.' Diddly dum, diddly dum, diddly dum, rattle, rattle rattle! The spoons, knives, forks, plates and cups on the supper table of the railwayman's cottage danced and jingled. The little brick building shook with the violent vibrations. An express train dashed past, several hundred tons of steel, glass, wood, water and coal, a controlled projectile thundering down the track, the last word in state-of-the-art steam technology. Grey smoke and white steam erupted into the air, blotting out the sunlight for a moment, seeping through little cracks in the windows in thin wisps, bringing with it an acrid, tangy, thrilling smell. The three children, Henry, Eric and Agnes, dashed to the window and gasped. 'Wow! Mum, did you see that? Going faster than ever! It must be!' This was a common daily occurrence, yet it never failed to excite the two boys and their sister and fill them with wonder.

Their father, William Staples, came down the wooden staircase from the signal box with a nod to his colleague who was climbing it to take over the next shift. He walked the few paces to the house and turned into the living room. He was rubbing his hands and smiling.

'Bye, lads,' he wagged his head, 'that were a good'un, weren't it? Them new Mogul two-six-oh's are quite summat. Must 'a bin doin' seventy mile an hour if it was doin' twenty. Little bit faster than old Puffin' Billy!'

Railwayman William Staples had the responsibility of controlling the Balderton signal box near Claypole, a few miles south of Newark, on the express East Coast Main Line which ran between London and Edinburgh. This was part of the Great Northern Railway, which in 1922 became the London and North Eastern Railway. As we have seen, the little brick house the family lived in was very close to the railway line. The rail company economised by buying only the bare minimum of building land! Their mother (later known as Gran Staples) recalled, 'When the trains passed by, the little home seemed to shake on its foundations, and many a visitor was startled by the unearthly din which filled the room.' Their three children were born there: Henry the eldest in 1908, Eric in 1910 and then Agnes six years later.

These were stirring days in the annals of British railway history. The year 1932 was to be critical. Up until then there was a gentleman's agreement between the LNER and the LMS (the London Midland and Scottish, which ran to Glasgow) not to outdo one another. But this was now put to one side, ushering in a period of fierce competition, with each railway company cutting down their time to capture the passenger market. Both streamlined their locomotives to gain a few valuable minutes. Nigel Gresley's 4–6–2 Pacifics were really beautiful engines and had the edge on the LMS. Dad Staples must have often looked with pride at the Flying Scotsman, the Silver Jubilee and other express trains as they thundered down the line below his signal box, the locomotives with their distinctive swept back lines, painted silver and light blue. A train spotter today would give his right arm to have had such a job, particularly on that never to be forgotten day, 3rd July 1938, when the Mallard flashed by with its seven silver coaches on its record-breaking run to top 126 mph just twenty-five miles to the south of Claypole at Essendine, near Stamford. This world record for a steam train still stands today. One cannot help wondering whether something of the dash and impetus of those express trains gave character to the spiritual impetus of the railway signalman's son, Henry.

Some years earlier William Staples averted a tragedy, here recounted by his grandson David Willows. At Newark there is a strange crossing, one of only two in the whole country, where the LMS line from Nottingham to Lincoln crosses the main LNER line. It has always been an obvious hazard, though no doubt great pains were taken from the very start to avoid danger. Now Mr Staples was manning a signal box several hundred yards to the north of this crossing, and on this occasion a train on the Nottingham to Lincoln line was about to go across the crossing just as an express LNER train, speeding down from Edinburgh on its way to London, came into view. Mr Staples would have been looking up the line and watching its plume of smoke on the horizon. Then sudden alarm must have gripped him. He would know by experience that the distant funnel was puffing out smoke at far too quick a rate. Immediately he sprang into action and clamped three detonators on the line to warn for an emergency stop. As the train came charging on, these exploded under the pounding wheels, the brakes went full on and the whole thing screeched to a halt in the nick of time, thus avoiding a nasty collision with the other train. Mopping their brows with relief, the guard, fireman, engine driver and Mr Staples had a long cool talk about what action should be taken, but came to the conclusion that it would be better to say nothing. However, on the train's arrival at Kings Cross station in London, the guard decided to report the incident. A few days later an inspector visited Henry's dad at his signal box to check up on the event. He was full of admiration for the swift action which had saved the day, but Mr Staples was determined to shield the engine driver from blame and so disqualified himself from promotion which would have been offered him. A spiritual parallel springs to mind here: that Henry and Connie, through their prompt obedience to God and their Spirit-filled warnings and pleading with people, put many gospel detonators on life's line and averted many a spiritual disaster.

The Staples' home was a Christian home. The parents were true believers, Methodists. William Staples proved his worth as a preacher on the local circuit. Then, as we shall see, in the early thirties they left the Methodists and linked up with the Pentecostal Assembly at Sherwood Avenue in Newark. Henry, Eric and Agnes in due time all trusted the Lord for salvation. Young Henry gave his heart to the Lord when he was nine or ten years old, which would be at the end of the First World War.

William and Sarah Jane Staples were a hospitable couple and were only too willing to have visiting preachers to stay. We have a fascinating incident told by Arthur Burt, who in himself is a living link with the past. (More of him anon.) Some time in the 1930s, when a young man, he preached in Newark, at the Pentecostal Assembly, Sherwood Avenue. He was invited to stay the night by brother and sister Staples and they drove him to their railwayman's house in the dark. It never occurred to them to tell Arthur their house was beside the railway. His bedroom window on the ground floor was on a level with the wheels and the firebox of any passing engine. At dead of night one of these monsters suddenly rushed past, scaring Arthur out of his wits. He involuntarily sprang out of bed and found himself standing in the middle of the room in his pyjamas, shaking from top to toe.

A Back Alley in Rock Valley

Where was the first spark of the Glory Way ignited? The answer is in Janie Marshall, Connie's mother. Her conversion to the Lord Jesus started a chain reaction of consequences which is immeasurable. The Marshall family lived in Mansfield. Connie reminisces,

> There was all forests and trees around. You see, Mansfield was in a hollow and you always had to go up to get out of Mansfield. Whichever way you went, you had to go up a hill. You can see some of those rock dwellings now on the right-hand side down Skerry Hill as you go into Mansfield from here, from Southwell Road. If you look on the right there are some railings and there are some boarded up caves there. Ours was like that. They're still on show there. So,

that's how it was. But then, you see, Mansfield started to blossom out with the mines. My grandma used to go – before there was coal – just down the road for a mile and there was a big quarry there as well. She was a very strong woman. She used to carry great loads of sticks on her head back home for fires, open fires like in these old fashioned grates. That's how they had to cook in those days. Primitive really!

Connie's grandfather, born in the middle of the nineteenth century at the height of the industrial revolution, worked at one of the foundries in Mansfield. 'He was a very clever engineer,' explains Connie. 'It didn't matter what we wanted, he'd got it at his fingertips.' He invented a particular sewing machine modification, but a man he used to work with stole the idea from him and got it patented. 'So my poor old grandad didn't get any benefit out of it at all. It was a shame.' He was a real character, 'a marvellous man, gentle, very sprightly and young looking.' When old age pensions were brought in, her grandfather was near retirement, and the firm kept asking him, 'How old are you, Billy?' 'Oh, I'm all right yet', he would reply, 'I can't remember when I were born.'

Connie's grandparents kept a public house in Rock Valley. It was one of the oldest pubs in Mansfield. It was there, in fact, that Connie herself was born. She says she does not know much about it as a pub, because about that time it ceased to be one and became simply the private house where her parents and grandparents lived. It was built on the slope of a hill by the side of a sandstone quarry, right into the face of the rock. Above them, on top of the cliff, was another street of houses with the road winding down to them. There was a big metal box factory down at the bottom of the road, a rough road. In front of their house were gardens of miners whose cottages were also built into the rock. 'Our pantry was where the barrels used to stand.' Connie said. 'They took them out of the rock. It was cool, you see. They had got these square things cut out of this rock and the barrels used to stand there. Up above there was a big room, it looked out onto some gardens. There used to be spinning wheels for making material. That was the spinning shop.'

Connie's father, brought up in Rock Valley, was a plumber and he went up to Barrow-in-Furness for a particular job of work. There he met Janie, a Lancashire Lake District lass who came from Ulverston on Morecambe Bay. Her dad also had a pub and the rest of her relatives were farmers. 'Their home was in very pleasant countryside,' Connie remembers, 'about a mile from the sea. Nearby was a monument on a big hill; at Easter and other holiday times they used to make paste eggs, colouring them brightly and rolling them down the slope in a competition for first prize.'

Connie's father brought her mother to Mansfield where they set up home with his parents in Rock Valley. There Connie first saw the light of day or as she puts it, 'born in a back alley', three years before the outbreak of the First World War. She remembers the jubilation at the Armistice in Mansfield Market Place when she was seven. This market-place was to play a significant part in her future.

The Ragged Mission

Connie's father had an old school pal, a cobbler called Mr Brown. This Christian brother was deeply concerned about the plight of the miners' children who were running about with no shoes on, and were hungry too, with barely a crust of bread. Connie explained,

> It was a terrible time round us, in a poorish quarter of the town. Mr Brown had a plot of land, and he said to my dad, 'Albert, my heart goes out to these poor ragged kiddies. We've got to do something for 'em, running about. They haven't any fires or anything at home. If I start to put up a mission, a chapel, will you help me?' 'Yes,' replied Albert, 'I'll do everything I can and I shan't charge you anything at all. I'll do it in my spare time.'

This was a generous offer, because plumbers were not well paid. Connie's dad was only earning about £2.10 shillings a week. Anyhow, he rolled his sleeves up and went at it, and in time they had the Ragged Mission built. Then Mr Brown said, 'Albert, put this great big copper in. Not in the chapel itself. Build a place at the back with a couple of toilets, and make a kind of wash house for the copper to go in.'

So in this way compassionate Mr Brown and those with him met this crying need in the area, and to these mining people he preached the gospel. In time the name Ragged Mission was changed to Gospel Mission, and each Sunday Connie's father started going to this mission hall which he had helped to build, and after a time gave his heart to the Lord.

Also during this time he fell ill with lupus, which is a tuberculosis of the skin, a disfiguring and most painful disease. It was eating his flesh away; he lost an eye and an ear. It took away his nose and began to eat away his upper lip. He could get no relief from the pain. There were not many drugs in those days to kill the pain. He was in agony and often used to run up the wall with his head to try to get relief. He never went to bed, but just lay on a couch.

Now it so happened that Mr Brown had invited a certain Welsh evangelist, William Davies, to preach at the Gospel Mission; a preacher with real fire in him, who had been converted in the Welsh revival twenty-one years earlier. He came with his wife for a fortnight and was a great blessing, but he was concerned that the Christians there only knew about salvation. They knew nothing about the baptism in the Holy Spirit. He felt there was something more to be done there, so his wife said she would pray about it.

Janie's Conversion

While Connie's father had been going to the Gospel Mission, her mother used to get the wash tub out and do her washing on a Sunday, just to annoy him.

'You religious lot!' she grumbled, 'I'm Church of England. That's good enough for me and my kids.' She got really mad with him. She was not going to get mixed up in any religious stuff.

Mr and Mrs Davies advised Connie's dad, 'Leave your wife alone. We'll pray. She's fighting you. She likes the high life, doesn't she?'

That was quite true. During the First World War she had taken a job at Boots the Chemists. She would go to all the fancy dress balls and she loved horse racing too. She certainly liked life. So she really went for her husband about his salvation. 'She played him up, I can't begin to tell you,' continues Connie. 'She wasn't really like that. The enemy was having a go. You could cut the atmosphere.' Mr Davies realised that Janie would make a marvellous Christian if she once got saved. They would make her an object of special prayer. He commented, 'She's been a good'un in the world and she'll be a good'un for God, when she gets it real. Don't say a word.'

The Welsh evangelist was most concerned about Mr Marshall's chronic ailment. He said, 'We're coming to pray for you Albert.'

Thinking of Janie's opposition, Mr Marshall replied, 'I don't know what your reception will be but I'll be pleased for you to pray for me.'

When she heard of Pastor Davies's impending visit, Connie's mum said they could do as they liked but she wouldn't be there. However, she just went out and sat on the stairs listening. There was a slight improvement in her dad which her mother had to admit, so Mr Davies said he would keep on coming to pray for him.

Then she seemed to get worse after this and one night she stomped off to the cinema to try and get away from the atmosphere at home. It was one of the best films they had had for months, but in half-an-hour she came out in disgust. What happened next she could not recall, except that she found herself on the back row of the Mission. She was handed a hymn book which she held upside down. When someone leant over to her and pointed out that she would get on better if she held it the right way up, she was livid and immediately left, nearly throwing the book at him.

Next day the usual prayer meeting was to be held in their house, so Janie said, 'I'm off out,' but she didn't go out; she again sat on the stairs with the door shut. Presently the door opened while they were praying, and she found herself in the meeting and she just sat and listened.

After a while Mr Davies went over to her and said, 'Now my dear, won't you surrender and give your heart to the Lord, even if it's only for the sake of your husband?'

She didn't reply and never said a word for about twenty-four hours, which was totally out of character. But she was changed from that moment. When she went to bed God gave her a vision of Heaven, and she talked to Him. She could not fully describe it, but said she met Him coming down the path through a beautiful garden, where all the flowers were fluorescent and very big. She was weeping and she asked Him if she could stay there.

He said, 'Not yet, you are not ready. I've got something for you to do. I want you to go down to that black patch and listen to Me.'

The next night Janie was in the meeting at their home and they could see that something had happened to her. She found herself on her knees in front of the old-fashioned grate and she started to speak in tongues, which no one but Mr Davies could understand. She asked what it was, as she felt so on fire inside.

'I'm on fire. It isn't *that* fire', pointing to the grate. 'It's in here. I'm on fire!'

It was the fire of the Holy Ghost (Acts 2:3). Mr Davies put his hand on her shoulder and said,

> God has done a wonderful thing for you. Now you didn't know this but we were supposed to go back to Wales next week and I said to my wife, 'If God wants me here in Mansfield to start up Full Gospel Meetings, may He baptise someone in the Holy Ghost without me having to preach it, and I'll take that as a sign that He wants me here'.

So they were all overjoyed at this as Janie in particular wanted everyone to know about this wonderful Holy Ghost which she had just received. Mr Davies said it was the quickest conversion he'd ever seen in his life. It was terrific! Her neighbours said, 'Oh, give her a week. She'll be back, going to the balls, backing horses and swearing like a trooper' (which had been her habit). Said Connie, 'She used to swear at us kids. It was terrible, because you see we lived where the miners lived and it was like pit talk.' She was absolutely changed. She couldn't swear any more: 'God washed my mouth out,' she said, 'and I don't want nothing else.'

Connie's dad got better. His face still remained very disfigured but he was completely relieved of the frightful pain. Connie is sure that the turning point came with her mother getting right with God. Mr Davies knew now that he must extend his stay to teach about the Holy Ghost, as there was a real spiritual hunger in Mansfield, but he needed another building to hold the meetings in. Once again, Connie's dad played his part in preparing and decorating an upstairs derelict printing room. It had previously been used to print Mansfield's local newspaper and was situated through an old archway with cobblestones where horses and traps used to go in and out.

Connie's Conversion

During the time of her mother's conversion Connie was an onlooker. She was still preparing to be confirmed in the Church of England. She had been enjoying her confirmation classes and respected her Bible teacher there. But she went to the first meeting in the old printing room and Mr Davies preached in the Spirit and it touched her. It was the first meeting, with the anointing of the Holy Spirit ministering openly. Connie said,

It really got me, but I kept resisting it. I thought, 'Well, I'm C of E, and I'm interested in what *they* are telling me.' Mr Davies explained that there would be no manifestation when *they* put their hands on me. It was just C of E dogma. I was a bit up in arms about that and replied, 'Well, I'm *there* at the moment!' I was stubborn.

Mr Davies got one of his friends to come down from Wales. He was a lovely old man but, 'Bye,' Connie related, 'you could feel the presence of God. He was like a father.' There was a row of young people there and he called them all out to the front so that he could pray for them, and then he gave his talk. He preached a gospel message of salvation. He talked about being filled with the Spirit. Connie found Mr Davies kneeling by her side pleading with her, 'Now my dear, are you ready to yield to the Lord? Because He wants you.' Connie just nodded her head. He asked her if she would pray after him, but she refused. She couldn't say a word. She felt quite dumb. However, he prayed. She didn't feel anything then, and she thought, 'Well, now I've done it. And I don't feel any different from what I did in church.' Although she felt nothing at the time, the next morning she said that she felt as if she was walking on air. It was a delayed reaction. She thought how beautiful the trees and flowers were.

Everything around her, as she went to work, looked beautiful. She had never seen anything like it and realised that she was saved. Mr Davies faithfully preached to the new converts the need to be filled with the Holy Ghost to keep them from backsliding, so Connie went for prayer for this baptism and did actually speak in tongues, but she never got the real joy in her soul for some years. They had some wonderful times with visiting preachers from France who were really on fire for God. The power of God was so strong in those meetings that people threw away their cigarettes, racing cards and papers. However, it didn't match up to what God gave Henri and Connie later.

Stephen Jeffreys

With their thriving meetings, the hall in the old printing room was crammed with people. It was too small. 'I tell you what', said Mr Davies, 'We'll have a campaign and we'll take the Co-op Hall in the middle of Mansfield. We'll take that for a fortnight.' They invited none other than the dynamic evangelist Stephen Jeffreys.

These were great times. There were long queues to get in. People were healed and many were challenged with the gospel and saved. Here again we can trace the direct flow of revival from South Wales to the English Midlands. It is interesting too that the Welsh revival was born in a mining area, and it was taken by the Jeffreys mining family to the mining town of Mansfield.

Connie and Henri had not yet met, but the coming of Stephen Jeffreys to Mansfield changed that. The big, but not big enough, Co-op Hall was hired for his meetings which were held in the afternoons and evenings. Henri had a half-day on Wednesdays and there he was queuing half-way down to the market to get in. Connie and her friends came after work finished at five o'clock and got themselves up in the balcony for the seven o'clock meeting. It was so powerful that they all got lost in what was going on. Henri, who was manager of Curry's, was downstairs on the front row with an assistant of his who said, 'Hey up, look up on that balcony at those young folk, there are some nice bits of stuff up there, Henri.' The meeting was so absorbing that Henri told his friend he was not interested in the balcony, but that he wanted to bring his mum and dad along to enjoy it too. His dad was off work with an ulcerated leg, and Henri hoped he would come to be prayed for. Well, his pal kept on urging Henri to look up at the girls but he flatly refused.

After the meeting, Henri's pal was so insistent. He got hold of Henri and determined to get acquainted with Connie and her friend. Besides this, Connie's friend fell for Henri straight away and was anxious to meet up with the men, but Connie refused and said she was going home. Eventually her friend brought the men over and introduced Henri Staples to Connie. The girls were offered a lift home in Henri's second-hand Ford car which he had just acquired, but once again Connie stalled saying she did not usually accept lifts from young men whom she did not know. As there were four in the party she was eventually persuaded but was a little apprehensive as to her mother's reaction to it. Her fears were groundless, as her mother welcomed them with open arms. As soon as they arrived Henri got on their piano and her mother bought fish and chips for everyone and they all had a jolly good sing. This formed the pattern each evening for the rest of the campaign.

Henri managed to get his mum and dad to the meetings and his mother got filled with the Spirit straight away. She was rolling on the floor.

Henri's dad asked, 'Is she all right? Does she need a drink of water?'

Henri assured him she would be all right and that it was the best thing she had ever had! His poor dad was not at all sure about it, for they had to take her home 'drunk'. As for the ulcers on his leg, the outcome was very wonderful. Folk came round and put their hands on him and prayed for him. He was instantly healed. Instantly! And next day he went straight back to work. So they were won over to this Pentecostal way, and eventually left the Methodist Chapel in Claypole, joining the new Pentecostal Assembly in Sherwood Avenue at Newark.

There was also a sad incident at this time. Connie's mother had a brother, Joe, who from early years had been crippled with rheumatoid arthritis. Janie and Albert witnessed to him and persuaded him to go to Mansfield to hear Stephen Jeffreys.

'Now, Joe', Janie said, 'we'll help you to the front. You just give your heart to the Lord, because He can do a lot for you.'

He did! For this crippled man suddenly stood straight up, like a rocket! Uncle Joe was perfectly whole in every limb and finger. But when he went home he met an atheist friend who talked and talked to him, until he had totally undermined him with unbelief, and within two days he was back a cripple, as bad as he had ever been. Unbelief is so dangerous.

Empire Street Chapel, Mansfield

With the impact of the Jeffreys mission, the meeting place in the old printing room proved to be much too small. Mr Davies asked the Co-op if he could hire the hall for a little longer. Meanwhile Connie's father found that there was a piece of land in Empire Street for sale, so they bought it. Now it so happened that a big hall or mansion was being pulled down outside Mansfield; it was near the famous Elizabethan house Hardwick Hall. Mr Marshall had to go over there for something and he could see that there were piles of demolished house lying around with no one bothering about getting rid of them. So, quite simply, for the trouble of carting it away, he got nearly everything free which they needed for building the new chapel. He got windows, doors, bricks, floorboards, tiles, everything. Several of his friends helped him and in next to no time they had it built. All the seats and chairs were given them as well. It was a miracle of God's provision.

William Davies had had very little to do with the Assemblies of God, but he decided that the new chapel should belong to the denomination, if only to ensure a good supply of other preachers if he happened to be away.

There was a sad irony that Mr Davies through compromise lost the fellowship of the person who had been God's sign to him to stay in Mansfield, Janie Marshall.

'Mr Davies,' she said, 'you're not preaching Pentecost any more. Why?'

The reason was that a group of Anglicans had been attracted to the meetings, and he was soft-pedalling distinctive Pentecostal teaching. Janie decided to have meetings in her own home. Mr Davies was upset and she was upset. He continued to talk about her and her testimony in his preaching; he missed her in every way.

Janie said sadly, 'I'm not compromising on that. It was my experience. It happened to me. How could I go back on that?'

This was certainly true to her character. She would always tell people straight. Once after a meeting the pastor shook her hand and asked her if she had enjoyed it. She replied, 'Enjoyed the meeting? If I had to endure any more of that, I'd go back to my pint of bitter!'

Marriage

After their initial meeting, Henri asked Connie if she would go home with him. Her mother encouraged her, saying she might be able to talk to him on spiritual matters. But it wasn't as simple as all that. Wires were getting crossed. Just before the Jeffreys campaign Connie had packed up a relationship with one young man and had vowed she would never get unnecessarily entangled again. Then along came someone else, a Welsh pastor at Newark, who was greatly attracted to Connie and wanted to go out with her. She told him about her recent upset. Then, when he brought up the subject of Henri, she explained that she was only a friend of his through attending the meetings together. However, the Welsh pastor gave Henri's mother the idea that Connie was playing fast and loose with them both. Because he was a pastor, Henri's mother believed him and she would not welcome Connie home after that, which naturally stopped everything dead for the moment.

Nevertheless, inspite of all this, Henri's courtship with Connie – given time – took its own course. They were meant for each other. It so happened, that there were plenty of evangelistic meetings to go to. In fact one can say that at the end of the 1920s and into the 1930s, there was a spate of evangelism in the Midlands. The Jeffreys brothers had set the pace and many people were boldly proclaiming the gospel. Evangelism was in the air. It was breaking out everywhere.

All of a sudden, one day, Henri said to Connie, 'We keep going to all these meetings. Can I take you out?'

Connie replied, 'Aye, friendship?'

'Yes,' Henri said, 'friendship!'

And things progressed from there. They were courting about three years. Henri once said, 'I don't want any other young woman.'

And Connie said, 'I don't want any other young man either! This is my life.'

They were married in Mansfield on 1st June 1933 in the new Pentecostal chapel in Empire Street. Theirs was the first wedding in the building. Connie says,

> God put us together. The way we met and the way God engineered it for us to be together. It was Him! It was made in Heaven, that marriage. It was the will of God definitely. When we came to realise it, we both had no doubts that it was all right, the assurance that we fitted in with one another. Henri said to me, 'Well, I like you because you're adventurous, not timid!'

A Witness

About that time a visiting missionary from India came. It was then that the Holy Spirit impressed upon Connie that she must go and tell people who were in darkness the message of salvation. The brother had been speaking on the Second Coming of Christ and she clearly remembers him saying, 'It's five minutes to twelve.' The presence of God was so with this man that she and several others began to weep and weep and the desire, which she had never had before, was born in her to tell others this Good News. She felt like shouting it from the roof tops because she wanted everybody to know, it was so wonderful. Connie feels now that this was God's seal on their union.

Connie knew what it meant to witness to the saving grace of Jesus Christ in her life. She recalls how real God was to her in those days. She had such a hunger and desire for Him. It was as though God gave her an immediate anointing as she lived day by day and witnessed for Him. She described it later like this:

When Jesus told His disciples to go, He said, 'You are My witnesses.' That's all they wanted to be. No fancy names, nothing! He wants you as you are, as a witness. 'You are My witnesses,' and that's enough; that will do. It works. I used to witness in the factory. I used to work at Barringer's Metal Box factory and I used to be witnessing all the time, talking and working.

On one occasion Connie was working with a girl in the factory and gossiping the gospel to her. She relates how they were behind some stacks of tins conversing while they worked and apparently one of the forewomen was the other side of the stack listening, intrigued by what she heard. It was no tittle tattle about lipstick or fashion, but about how to be saved and really know it. Concerning another person Connie said,

I witnessed to a girl and she was an atheist, a very bitter atheist. She could be so sarcastic. She'd swipe you off your feet. Anyway I thought, 'I'll have a go, I'll tell her what's happened to me.' So I says, 'All right, you come with me tomorrow night to the meeting and then see what you believe.' So she says, 'Oh, yes, I will, seeing it's you. I value your friendship.' (Because we used to pop off to different things together.) So she came with me, and I'll never forget it. She was puvverduffed! It hit her. She changed.

Chapter 2

Transformation

Business! Business!

H enri was a born salesman. For him selling things was fun. It was an essential part of the cut and thrust of life. With his natural warmth of character and ready smile he loved to charm people into buying his goods, into convincing them that he had precisely the one thing that they were looking for, and at a bargain price. Connie explains,

> You see, business was his god. It didn't matter if we dropped in our tracks as long as we were making money and doing business. Yet he wasn't really worried about the money. Rather, he loved the business, to get out and do it, to meet people and do business with them. Honestly, he could sell you a load of muck, if he was so minded. He could! He'd go out on the knocker when we first started up and he'd go round and collect all the old bikes and take them down the cellar and make them new ones. There were no new bikes then because of the War, and, as he was collecting these bikes, he'd talk to folk and he'd sell 'em summat.

In fact Henri delighted in playing salesman's games, in seeing just how far he could go in persuading people to buy things. He would say to himself, 'Well, man, you don't really want it, yet you'll have it, you'll buy it.'

As a very young man Henri worked in Mansfield at a branch of Curry's cycle shops. The staff worked hard, from eight thirty in the morning until nine at night, except for Wednesday afternoon. Henri was ambitious and drove himself, and at a young age was made manager. It was really amazing how he increased the turnover of the shop. He would walk up the streets of the miners and factory workers, pushing an old pram with a gramophone in it playing records. He would stop the gramophone a moment and shout about his wares. It was unusual but it worked.

Henri however was unhappy in his job, because the firm was never satisfied. They were asking too much of him. He was wearing himself out. Connie said he used to wear a bowler hat and horn-rimmed spectacles and, to see his face then, he looked about forty years old when he was only a young man. This was before they were married. After her day at Barringer's she would go and help him every night, because she hardly saw him otherwise. She would go down to the store and give him a hand. In particular he would give her the job of window dressing, of making the shop front really attractive. She soon discovered that she had a flair for it. Then the inspectors would come round and still they were not satisfied.

Soon after they were married Henri was offered the job of manager over four or five Curry's shops centred on Burton-on-Trent. They moved house and went to live there. Henri built the business up well. He had some good managers, but unfortunately he had to work with his boss's son, who was just out of college, a know-all, who didn't have a clue about selling bikes. Henri stuck it out until one day he could stand it no longer.

'It's no good,' he told the boss, 'I can't work with your son. He's inexperienced; he doesn't know anything about the trade at all. But he wants to do what *he* wants to do. So, I'm sorry, I'll have to find somewhere else.'

At that point Eric, Henri's brother, came over from Newark. Connie said to him, 'They're killing him.'

Eric replied, 'I can see that. I tell you what: I work for Pratt and Gelsthorpe's. They generate electricity as a private company for Newark, to augment the national grid.'

He himself did repairs for them on the side, and he explained how the boss had recently been looking round a big empty shop in Balderton Gate in Newark. Eric told them that his brother who was a manager at Curry's was not happy and that he could make this a real going concern, selling new bikes. The upshot was that Henri went to see Mr Gelsthorpe, who took to him straight away. He said, 'Well, I can see you're a good salesman, and that's enough. I'll set you up on £3 a week and commission.' Henri agreed to that, left Curry's and moved to Newark to take on this new venture.

Henri was determined to make an impact. He said, 'It's no good. We've got to put a good show on here. I'm going to sell musical instruments.' The boss agreed. They whitewashed and blanked out all the windows so that you could not see in for a fortnight or more. Then they rolled up their sleeves and set to work. They cleared the floor and Connie cleaned it thoroughly. They painted it dark blue and put a stand in the middle. They set up large coloured photos of Radio Luxembourg and the various other radio stations. They put five or six bicycles on show and they decorated all the walls with gold and silver tinsel paper and made attractive flower arrangements. Connie remarks, 'Although I say it myself, it looked a real picture.'

Henri got to know a few musicians to buy in instruments. They asked him, 'Why don't you set up carnival bands?' This was a real need in the Midlands. Well, it went like wildfire. On a certain day he had a special opening. Henri gave it a name; he was very clever at advertising. The blanked out windows were cleaned. He got an advertiser to take pictures. They opened up and everyone came to see it. It was such a surprise to look inside. It was like fairyland.

Henri had invited a band to come over and play on a Saturday morning. When they started to play the streets were filled with people and the traffic came to a standstill. It was a right carry-on, a terrific success. There was a tea-shop next door and they could not keep pace with serving their customers. So Henri drew the people and business really got off the ground. He sold accordions, pianos, violins and trumpets. He worked all hours; Connie never knew when he was coming home. But she was working flat out too. Her heart was with him to help him. The shop had created a stir and business built up steadily. Travellers came from Nottingham to say, 'Henri, there isn't a show like this in the city! Congratulations!'

Henri loved bright lights. Eric tells the story how once his brother had the window of this shop lit up by a mass of lights; there were far too many. They were much too hot and the merchandise on show in the window with the dressing and decorations all caught fire. Everything! (Ironically it was Pratt and Gelsthorpe's who supplied the electricity.)

Besides the musical instruments, they had a show of bikes at the side. They also sold radios. The firm Philco put on a competition to see who could sell the most radios. Henri won two tickets for a trip to Luxembourg for a week.

His boss went with him, and he said, 'Henri, I don't know what to say to you.'

'What do you mean?' Henri replied.

'Well, you're earning more than I am!'

When chatting things over at home with Connie, she said to him, 'You know what. It's no good. You'll never be satisfied until you get your own business going.'

'Yes,' mused Henri, 'everyone wants to hold me back.' He knew he had the ideas and could make money.

'Oh, it's in yer!' Connie insisted, thinking, 'Yes, and God will use that one of these days. He'll get a hold of you, my lad, and gi'yer summat that will knock yer back.' She decided to get fasting and praying for him.

Henri went to his boss, Mr Gelsthorpe, and said quite simply, 'It's time for me to go.'

But the firm didn't want him to leave. He was too useful to them; they had taken him on business trips to Sweden and other places and had found his imaginative drive invaluable.

He said to his boss, 'It's no good, Bert, I can't be with you any longer. I've got to progress. I can't stand still and just have a wage'.

The firm then tried to make him a partner. Henri appreciated that but said,

'No, that won't work, because I know it won't. I've got to have my own head.' He was restless and progressive.

At this point his brother Eric told him about a little shop in Appleton Gate. He said, 'It's filthy. It's three storeys high, with a cellar. There's actually quite a bit of room. It's smack opposite the Police Station.'

Henri decided to go for it. The shop was in fact owned by a Methodist businessman, a chemist. Henri went to see him, and because the shop was in a derelict state, he was able to take it initially for six months rent free. The next step worked out like this. Henri served a month's notice with Pratt and Gelsthorpe's, and then took a temporary job in the Uttoxeter area of Derbyshire as a manager and organiser of seventeen shops. It was a challenge and he built the business up. Meantime, Connie and her dad tackled the derelict shop with Henri helping when he came home in the evenings. To begin with they had to have a corporation cart to shift all the rubbish and debris. Once that was done, they cleaned the whole building from top to bottom. On the three floors above the shop there were the living rooms and five bedrooms, one of which they made into a bathroom. They used about a hundred rolls of wallpaper. Connie and her father worked like skivvies. It was a miracle that Mr Marshall was able to do what he did; the terrible pain of the lupus disease had left him and he had considerable energy.

Henri finished his work in and around Uttoxeter just in time for the opening of their shop at Appleton Gate. It was spick and span but they had very little to sell – just a few bikes. 'Imagine opening a shop with hardly any goods to sell!' comments Connie. They had a large photograph, which they put on a turnstile in the window.

With that done Henri said, 'I'll have to pray for someone to come and loan me some stock till I can sell it.'

The words were barely out of his mouth when, lo and behold, a traveller from Firs of Nottingham, a big electrical firm, came and said, 'Look here, Henri, we'll stock your shop for you and we'll give you six months credit, because we know what you can do. You're a born salesman. You're a high-pressure salesman. It'll not be long before you're paying it back.'

What a miracle! It didn't cost them anything to stock the shop. Henri went out on the knocker selling bikes. He also fitted the cellar up as a workshop and, as much as he could, he went round picking up all the bicycles that wanted mending, working down in the cellar till twelve o'clock at night. He was selling bicycles in his sleep.

The Second World War

Their shop had only been going for six months when war broke out. Connie said, 'Folks'll think we're barmy starting up business at a time like this.' In the event they were able to keep going.

Involvement in the armed forces in time of war is a matter of conscience. Neither John the Baptist nor Jesus told centurions and other soldiers to get demobilised. In the Second World War there were military commanders like General Dobbie, the defender of Malta, who were fine Christians. The French Protestant Christian, Jacques Ellul, fought against Hitler in the French Resistance, yet was highly exercised over the ethics of fighting. Len Moules, the future leader of WEC* was a 'desert rat' in the Tank Corps in North Africa; he prayed fervently to God that he might not be involved in killing the enemy and the Lord honoured this. Some Christians refused to join the armed forces

---

* now Worldwide Evangelisation for Christ International

and preferred the scorn and ill-treatment of those who would call them cowards, even imprisonment, rather than be guilty of killing others.

Henri was one of these. He said, 'I'm sorry, I'll do anything to save life but I'm not going to take life.'

The government officials replied, 'Well, you'll have to be a conscientious objector.'

Henri said, 'Ah well, I will be. Yet I'm not really. But that's up to you.'

So he was put on call-up for the fire brigade, and allowed to get on with life. In fact, Henri's business quickly extended. Another shop next door became vacant, so he took it. Then three more came empty and he took them. Eventually he had five shops in Appleton Gate, and they went very well. There was certainly plenty of scope for Connie's skill in window dressing.

Early on in the War an amusing thing happened. The papers were saying that the air-raid sirens would sound the alarm when the Luftwaffe came over. (There had already been a bit of bombing in the Midlands.) When the first air-raid siren went off Henri was so startled, he shot downstairs, in his pyjamas! He fetched all the cash and put it down in the cellar in a steel box, then he sat on the cold cellar steps and wouldn't come out. Connie opened the door and doubled up with laughter.

'Look at that! Look at yer! You'll catch your death of cold!'

'Not likely!' he protested. Then she took pity on him and got him some clothes and tea.

There was a little bombing in the Newark area, but once the Spitfires and Hurricanes were established in the area it ceased. However, one day the shop door opened, and in stepped an official.

'Have you got any bedrooms?' he asked.

'I hope so', replied Connie. 'We've got three storeys.'

'Can we have them?'

'What for?' she queried.

'Well, we'd like you to take four airmen and look after them,' he explained.

'That's a tall order, having a shop and all, isn't it?'

'Well,' he persisted, 'do you think you can do it?'

'All right, send 'em,' Connie agreed.

So Connie and Henri certainly did valuable war effort by hosting these service men. There was Mr Chell, a builder who had been in the reserves. 'He was a lovely old man. You had to laugh when he got his uniform; he looked too old to be in it.' He told them he was glad they had put him with them. 'It's more homely and you do feed us well.' There was a Yarmouth man too, who unfortunately got killed when the train he was going home in was bombed. Horace, number three, was a bachelor whose home was the other side of Nottingham. He had a fatal accident when a vehicle ran into the back of the lorry where he was sitting. The last one was Bill, from Leeds, a nice homely lad, a workman, who with a hint of wartime romance 'gets a fancy woman at Newark.'

In the middle of the War, in 1942, Henri's father died. He had not yet retired and was still working on the railway. It seems his life was shortened by grief at losing his daughter Agnes who had died shortly after the birth of her first child. (This child was David Willows, who has had a fruitful life for God as an evangelist.)

When Henri's father died this meant that his mother, Gran Staples, had to move from the little railway home near Claypole. Henri found her a cottage near them in Newark, in Emminsons Row, where she opened her doors to all in need. Like her son and daughter-in-law she was very hospitable, and had a heart for reaching people for the Lord. She had something real and wanted to share it. In fact, all three of them welcomed people from the services to a cup of tea or a meal, when they were at a loose end. The records of heaven alone will reveal how many people were welcomed into their homes and introduced to the Lord Jesus. It was a very considerable number. Henri used to talk of a turnover of about two thousand soldiers and airmen. You never know how God may work in a person's life. Here is one instance, that of Les Atkinson:

> I was brought up a Roman Catholic. My first fourteen years I lived in a strict family, went through college and spent seven years in a monastery training to be a priest. Three months before taking the ordination World War II broke out. I asked to be released from my vows and joined the army. It was 1942. I was stationed at Newark, where I met brother Henri, who used to meet us out of the pubs and take us to Gran Staples, who sobered us up and sent us back to camp. That is where the seed was sown. It was not until 1966, when I went to Sheffield to a rally, for a night out, that I was hit with such force that I had to go back and give my life to Jesus. Since then I've been going to Glory meetings, conventions and getting greatly blessed, doing what

He calls me to do, ministering to others, telling them of His greatness. It is never too late to accept Him.[1]

Running a retail business during the War had its own peculiar hazards and opportunities. The whole of the country's industry was geared to the single aim of the War effort. Generally speaking commodities were scarce; often they were totally unobtainable. However, because of the black-out everybody had a great need for torches or flash lights and their batteries. Everyone was after them. Philco were very good to Henri, sending him stock. They came to his shop to supply him with torches and batteries when no one else in Newark had any. Then, when he found he was running particularly low on them, he got his little car going (with an allocation of petrol from somewhere) and went round the whole of the Midlands scrounging torches and batteries from everywhere he could. That certainly helped to keep the shops going.

Then they branched into children's toys. This may well have seemed madness, for the supply of most toys had dried up. Before the War, when he had been manager at Curry's, they had always sold toys at Christmas, so Henri decided to do the same. He travelled to a big factory in the Midlands.

The manager said to him, 'Henri, I can't show you much, but I've got a warehouse full of heads and arms and legs and bodies, all stacked up.'

With an impulsive decision Henri replied, 'I'll take 'em.'

'What, the lot?'

'Yes!' Henri affirmed and immediately filled up his van with them. Once back in Newark they set to work, fitting the dolls together. Connie had women helpers and they made lots of pretty dresses. (Desperate for clothing material they ingeniously used bleached sacking.) They put them in the shop windows and they sold like hot cakes.

We couldn't keep pace. We'd got one big what's-its-name about four foot high. It was a really beautiful bride doll, Italian, with a wonderful face for colouring (provided by a friend of Henri) plus all her little bridesmaids. There was nowt like it. So I thought, 'I'm going to have a go here, in the window.' We put a little church behind it with some fancy stuff and a little gate, and I'd got these to look as if they were coming out right across the window. It drew crowds from everywhere. In fact the police came to Henri and said, 'What do you think you've done?' Henri asked, 'What *have* I done?' 'Stopped the traffic!' The street outside was packed with folk.

That incident created a little diversion from the austerity of the War with its rationing and blackouts.

Sowing in Tears

God really touched Connie's life and got hold of her in reality, when she was about seventeen. And then a few years later at about the time of her wedding, when she heard the missionary from India at the Gospel Mission, saying, 'It's five minutes to twelve before Jesus comes,' God impressed further truth on her heart. He used to sing, 'Everybody should know.' Until then she knew she was born again 'in a measure like, but it was a matter of will worship, you know.' She went to all the meetings, the Breaking of Bread, the prayer meetings, the Bible studies, but she never felt any excitement or anything, that is until she heard this missionary. His message really gripped her; it got hold of her. God was suddenly so real to her. She says, 'I wasn't myself for weeks.' It was like Psalm 126:1–2 re-enacted: *'When the Lord turned again the captivity of Zion, we were like them that dream. Then was our mouth filled with laughter, and our tongue with singing.'*

But then something else began to happen to her: she began to weep. It seemed to be deep inside her. She could not understand it. The sense of the presence of God was still as strong as ever; but it was as though she was mourning for something or somebody, she did not know what. She and Henri were growing in grace and faith together as a married couple. Connie said, 'God started to work with us when we were first married. It was in His will and we knew it was. But we'd only just started to realise the power of God, and what it could do.' Strangely this weeping would come on her. It was during the wartime; and then she felt it particularly strong a couple of years after the War. She began to realise that the Pentecostal Meeting was not really Pentecostal, but was merely a form, so she decided to use her one free day to pray and fast. She recalled,

I'd never heard anybody preach about it. The young people still came to our house in the evenings after the shops had shut and Henri would talk to them and they would have a sing. I asked them if any of them would like to meet at the chapel on Sunday mornings in the vestry for prayer. So they came faithfully each week and that was the time when God really started working with us two. After a time I started to go to meetings again, but all we could do was weep. We thought it was strange, and yet felt it was so right. The carpet was drenched with tears. I didn't know in those days that it was travail, which God had put on us for something that was going to be born. [2]

I had a great weight on me and was constantly weeping, unable to stop. Even when I was serving a customer I had to turn away and burst out crying. Henri told me I must pull myself together or I would have to go into a mental home. I was like that for about a year, wherever I went, even in meetings. Once I was at the Skegness Assemblies of God conference. John Carter and Smith Wigglesworth* were there and we enjoyed their ministry. But I wept and wept, even on arriving at the boarding house.

Dissatisfaction

Henri Staples gave his heart to the Lord and was saved at the age of nine or ten in the Methodist Chapel at Claypole. Then, as a young man at the age of twenty-two, he again consciously committed his life to God in a Methodist meeting. In fact, while giving his testimony in the First Issue of the *Glory News* in 1956, he speaks of this as his conversion, and he says, 'This was my first experience of the wonderful power of God in my heart. [3] I was so happy, I remember skipping home.' [4] It is interesting that John Wesley dated his conversion at the age of 35 when at a meeting in Aldersgate Street Church in London he felt his heart 'strangely warmed'. Yet other people, weighing up his life, consider perhaps that he was converted when much younger and that his experience at the age of 35 was one of assurance of salvation. This could have been the same with Henri.

It was very shortly after this that he heard the preaching of the great Stephen Jeffreys at Mansfield. Of this evangelistic campaign he wrote,

---

* John Carter – Principle of the AoG Bible School. Smith Wigglesworth (1859–1947) – Yorkshire plumber, powerfully used by God world-wide in a healing ministry, even to the point of raising people from the dead.

> I went along to these revival meetings and I was amazed and thrilled to see marvellous miracles taking place before my eyes, and I surrendered my life afresh to God. [3]

God was meeting with Henri and leading him on. Connie, however, seems always to have been way ahead of him spiritually in those earlier years. Soon after they met he had announced that he was a Methodist, but Connie wryly thought, 'You might not be a Methodist much longer!'

Before the War they used to go most years to Blackpool and then on to Pentecostal conventions at Preston. Connie recalls,

> That's where Henri began to be convinced that God had more for him. I think it was Smith Wigglesworth who prayed for him, and he started to speak in tongues. The meeting finished. He should have got it then, but he didn't. He was balked; he didn't wait long enough. But at least he had started to speak in tongues. That's when God began to give him a hunger, I believe.

Writing in 1988 and looking back half a century Henri wrote,

> I thought, if only I could get back to the joy I had, when Smith Wigglesworth was at Preston and I was down on my knees and the power of God was coming down and I was prayed for and it came on me and I couldn't stop. It was time for us to come home from Preston to Mansfield and they pulled me away. I've never forgiven them for it, because it was so lovely, so real and I was tasting something of heaven ... Brothers and sisters, how I longed to get back to that place for years and years. I had blessings, little ones, but not the lot. The joy came into my soul on occasions, but the people around me didn't encourage me, because they didn't know what was happening. [5]

In the late summer of 1945, just before the final end of the Second World War, Connie took a week off from their business in Newark along with Gertie one of their shop assistants, and together the two of them went to a Pentecostal convention in South Wales. They were joined later by Henri. The whole experience is worth recounting extensively, as told by Connie:

> It was a week of Bible study, with the Assemblies of God. Smith Wigglesworth came for one or two nights: Archie

Friday was there, and all the pastors. We got lodgings not far off with a Methodist family. There was a man in the lodgings who wasn't saved, called Davies. He said, 'My wife's a Methodist. If I could have what you lot's got, I'd have it.' He was responding to the way we had been singing up in the mountains when he was showing us various walks and the singing was affecting him.

Well, we were going to have a young people's 'open air'. There were people stood at their cottage doors all the way round. We were singing and a lovely old man who was leading it said, 'Why don't I take you into a meeting to sing for us?' I replied that I had never sung in public in my life and would be scared stiff. He disagreed. But soon, as the meeting progressed I said to Gert who was with me, 'Gert, I'm going out there, in the middle. I've got summat to say. It's only a line, but I'm going to start.' I went boldly out into the middle and the Lord gave me, *'Man shall not live by bread alone but by every word that proceedeth out of the mouth of God'* (Matthew 4:4). I continued, 'There's a lot coming out of a lot of mouths, but I don't know where they're going to.' The chap who was leading said, 'We could do with some more of that.' I didn't realise it, but the anointing was beginning to come. Can you see? I was hungry.

Henri came at the end of the week. But the trouble was, all his salesman's business was in his mind. The funny thing was, we at the convention were in the Spirit. The meetings were in the Spirit. It was lovely being right with it. And I knew he weren't with it. 'Oh come on,' he says, 'we're going sight-seeing.' We hadn't had a car all week, so we were glad to get a ride. We came to a very high suspension bridge, and got out of the car to walk over it. But I didn't want to. (She had a sudden attack of vertigo.) 'It vexes me,' I protested, 'I'm drawn; I want to throw myself over.' I didn't want to go. 'Oh, come on, don't be soft,' Henri said, 'I'll hold your arm.' Do you know, I've never had such an experience in my life. I wanted to throw myself over down there, and I thought about the Lord. The enemy tempted Him. 'Throw Yourself down. God will give His angels charge over You.' I thought, 'I'm going to do it. I'm going to do it.' You see, Henri didn't know what was going on in me. I said, 'I can't go any further, Henri.' He says, 'Come on!' and he dragged me across there.

I was poorly all next day. I was trembling and trembling. I lost my joy. I lost everything. And God taught me never to trust your nearest and dearest. He taught me it was more essential to be in the Spirit than going with them. I'd had such a lesson. I didn't say it, but I wished Henri had never come. I knew he hadn't 'arrived' (spiritually) – only in a measure.

Back home in Newark, some time later Henri and Connie had the biggest argument. He argued from the natural. He had just had a little touch of speaking in tongues, but he never got through. Connie continued,

We were on the same level in our work. We worked together in every other way. We fitted like a glove with material things. But when it came to the Spirit, we couldn't agree. Whatever he said, I was the opposite, pleading, 'You haven't got what you can have, that's what's upsetting me. You're in a fool's paradise. You think you've received the Holy Ghost, but you haven't received the fullness. Henri, there's something more.' 'Oh you,' he says, 'you're never satisfied!' And I replied, 'I'm not going to be either!' 'By guy,' I thought, 'Lord, You get hold of him!' [6]

On another occasion about this time Connie was really blunt with him. 'It's business, business, business!' she said, 'Your business is your god. I'm second and everybody else is second.' Henri had no answer to that. He could only bite his lip, and in his heart there was such an aching void that only God could fill. One Sunday morning in their assembly at Newark a woman gave a prophecy; she was a teacher. Her word was brief and simple, but it came with power: 'God is about to do a new thing. Even now it is springing forth.'

The Piano Stool

In 1948, the year Israel became a nation, God gave a special anointing to a number of chosen vessels. Henri was one of them. He was forty years old at the time, and he writes,

A spiritual dearth had settled on the churches of our beloved land. I myself seemed to be pouring all my strength and power into my business when God moved in a new way in my life. He showed me that I was not a hundred per cent with Him, but among those spoken of in Revelation chapter 3 verses 14–19, who were neither hot nor cold. I sought God in a new spirit of repentance and I do thank Him that He met me in all my needs. [7]

'God really got hold of him,' Connie continued. 'Turned him inside out, which I was longing for.' It happened like this. Henri fell ill with overwork; he had ulcers. They had been working eighteen hours a day towards Christmas. The doctor said, 'Rest! You're burning yourself out.' 'Oh, I can't,' protested Henri. But the doctor insisted that he must, and there he was for a week. While Henri was ill, he picked up his Bible. He had never had time for his Bible, except at chapel, because he was a salesman. He was selling bikes in his sleep. Anyhow he read and read the Scriptures. God started to deal with him in that bed. Connie later wrote,

> As he read it he began to weep. He didn't let me see him, but I knew he was weeping and weeping. He wept for a week. I firmly believe that was true repentance. He didn't know what was happening to him. Inside I had been weeping too, but there was such a joy in me, I could have jumped over the moon. There Henri was crying and weeping with a mouthful of blistering ulcers as big as your thumbnail. His tongue was a mass of them; the doctor put caustic pencil on them to burn them out. [8]

After a week of this intense illness Henri recovered. One afternoon he got up just as their shop assistant Gertie came in from Peterborough market. Henri asked, 'Gert, have you had a good day?'

'Aye,' she replied, 'I've had a marvellous day. We've taken a lot of money. But I'm pleased to see you up.'

It was Thursday, the evening of the weekly prayer meeting, and he said, 'Well, I'm going to the meeting tonight and I'm going to get drunk!'

He had read Acts chapter two and he believed it. Connie heard him say this and she thought he really meant it, as it clearly came right from the heart. Connie decided to go as well. 'I'm not going to miss this,' she said to herself.

At this moment Connie's days of weeping and travail ended. 'It was a funny thing, but suddenly I stopped crying and stopped feeling heavy and there was such a joy that started bubbling up inside me.'

The meeting was routine, anything but lively. In fact it could not have been more dead. They all prayed round in a circle and then the pastor said, 'Come on Henri, get on the piano. Play a hymn and I will close the meeting.'

At that a remarkable thing happened. The supernatural took over. Henri fell off the piano stool. It was as though a strong heavenly hand knocked him off it. He rolled across the floor and back again, speaking in tongues as clear as a bell, at the top of his voice. God took hold of him at that moment and gave him a mighty new anointing. God had clearly said, 'I will do a new thing'. Now it had started.

The pastor exclaimed, 'What's up with him? Is he having a fit?'

'No,' said Connie, 'he's not having a fit! He's never been so right in his life. It's the best thing he'll ever have. Leave him where he is.'

She could see the pastor didn't believe it. Religion kills. He didn't know what to make of it, even though he was supposed to be a Pentecostal minister.

Well, Henri could not stop speaking in tongues. He did so all the way home and he never spoke English for about a week. When Connie asked, 'What'll you have for breakfast?' he wrote on the frying pan, 'I'll have some bacon and eggs and tomatoes.' Connie's brother and those who were helping to run the business could not get any sense out of him.

'What's he talking about?' they asked. 'What's up with him? There are travellers queuing up to talk to him, and they can't talk to him.'

Connie told them he would be all right in a bit adding, 'He's never been so right in his life.' At this her brother looked up in bewilderment. Gazing at Henri, Connie had never seen anyone so saturated in the Spirit; he was living in heaven.

He used to go to the top of their house and spend hours with the Lord. One day Connie found him praying, 'Please, Lord, don't take it away'. She reassured him, 'Now me duck, what the Lord has given you He will never take away.' (*'For the gifts and calling of God are irrevocable'* – Romans 11:29.)

After he started speaking English again, he would get up in the morning and say, concerning one of his customers, 'I'll pray for so-and-so. Summat's a matter.' Off he would go and his visit was always effective: he brought a word of encouragement, fitly spoken, *'like apples of gold in pictures of silver'* (Proverbs 25:11), that solved a problem, or brought some deliverance. He also discovered that he had the gift of healing. Things began to happen.

There was the striking example of Gladys Black, who lived a little way down their road. She belonged to the Brethren; her husband was a Pentecostal preacher and she had been seeking the baptism of the Holy Ghost for fifteen years. Henri said one day, 'I'm going to pray for Gladys.' There she was, helping Henri's sister-in-law put some washing on the line. He did not have to touch her. He put his hand on the latch of the garden gate, and as he was walking up the path she flung her hands in the air and started to speak in tongues as if she had been born to it. It was as though she was drunk. When she popped back home again, her husband Stephen was astonished.

He said later, 'Well, Henri, I don't agree with what you're doing with your praising the Lord and singing and all this. But you have put the Holy Ghost the other side of my fireplace and I shall always be grateful!'

Another way in which God dealt directly with him was over the matter of smoking. At that time it was a very usual adult habit. Besides, it helped him at work with his customers. He smoked about forty cigarettes a day. Then he came to the point when he wanted to give it up and knew he must, but found in his own strength it was extremely hard to do so. However, the Lord had now put this great joy in his heart and this overwhelming desire and impetus to praise Him, and so he stumbled on the solution to this problem. Praise! As Henri thanked and worshipped and praised God, the habit dropped away.

The Assemblies of God Tribunal

Henri and Connie had been in the Pentecostal Assembly in Newark, at Sherwood Avenue, for quite some years. When God so anointed Henri and filled him with the Holy Spirit, one would have thought the pastor, Ernest Foster, would have been happy; but he was not. He wanted to quieten Henri down, but the joyful man could not sit still and was praising God at every opportunity. He could not stop shouting. He could not stop playing choruses and hymns on the piano and his accordion. He was so overflowing with joy and praise. Altogether he was too much of a disturbance for the assembly, and quite simply, they did not want to know. Henri told them that if everyone praised God more there would be more power in the meetings.

Connie soon noticed that they were being cold-shouldered. They had planned to give hospitality to a visiting preacher, a very able man, and his wife, with whom Connie had a close friendship. She had prepared a really nice tea, when to her amazement they walked past the door and on to another home. They never said anything; no apology. It gave Connie a stab, but then God made Nehemiah 8:10 real to her: *'The joy of the Lord is your strength.'*

Before long Henri was asked to travel to London to appear before an Assemblies of God committee or tribunal. His nephew, David Willows, points out that this is a most unusual procedure, because this sort of thing is usually sorted out locally. It was, in fact, a most interesting occasion; Henri's case, in its way, was dealt with openly and fairly. It was very good that the whole matter was not swept under the carpet.

For a start there were a number of really seasoned experienced Pentecostal Christians present, those who had been in the front line of the spiritual battlefield, and had even hazarded their lives. There was that man of faith, Howard Carter, who had travelled extensively round the world, preaching and sharing the gospel wherever he went, at every step trusting God to provide his travelling and day-to-day living expenses. He was the author of a classic exposition on the gifts of the Holy Spirit. His brother John Carter was there, one time Principal of the AoG Bible School. Also present was Jimmy Salter,* just retired from a lifetime's work as a pioneer missionary to the Congo. There were a number of other fair-minded discerning men present, as well as the Newark pastor, Ernest Foster.

Henri was invited to give his testimony, and he made a very considerable impression. John and Howard Carter then tried to reconcile the situation with Ernest Foster. 'What happened next', related Connie, 'just made you cry.'

Jimmy Salter went to Ernest Foster and said, 'Brother, you know I witness that this brother has had something very real. Now then, you're a shepherd of the sheep and a shepherd has to die for his sheep. Come on, brother, shake hands with him and let there be peace.'

---

* Prior to the outbreak of the First World War he travelled with William Burton into the heart of the bush and jungle (of which some of the inhabitants were cannibals and witchdoctors) to bring the light of the gospel of Christ to villages which had never heard it. It was a spearhead of evangelism, which the Lord had wonderfully honoured. Salter was also son-in-law of the Smith Wigglesworths.

But he would not; he refused.

Henri then spoke, 'I can't compromise with what God has done. If they had what I've got they wouldn't be able to sit still and be quiet. He can't bear me in his own meetings. Sorry, but I can't sit still. God has given me this gift for music. These choruses are coming to me all new. I've never heard them before. I can play them straight away. I can't just sit down to an ordinary meeting. If they want that, that's it.'

At that Henri came out and he got on his knees and he asked the pastor to pray for him. (Connie felt it deeply.) 'It would have broken your heart, you know. If that couldn't touch people and move people, I don't know what would. Because they could see the reality of Henri, you see.'

When he got up off his knees he said to Ernest Foster, 'Look brother, I am not going to cause any disruption in your meetings again. I'll never knowingly ask anybody to come with me unless God is going to use me; and I won't take anyone from your fellowship in any way. I'm going out on the streets, I'm going to my customers, I'm going to the sick. Wherever God leads me I'm going. I have a job to do; I know I have. That's what I'll do.' (One can almost hear an echo of Martin Luther's 'Here I stand. I can do no other. So help me God, Amen.')

At that the tribunal said, 'Very commendable, brother, very commendable.'[9]

As a sequel to this a couple of strange things happened. Some years later Ernest Foster left the assembly at Newark and went north to become a pastor in Scotland. He was never able to settle there; he found he was not on the wavelength of the people. Unbelievably he then contacted Henri to ask him if he could find him a little house and a job, and Henri managed to fix up both for him. As the proverb (Proverbs 16:7) says, *'When a man's ways please the Lord, He maketh even his enemies to be at peace with him.'* However, poor Ernest could not settle into the clerical job that Henri found for him, either, so he went to pastor a work at Blidworth, near Mansfield for a short time until his death. (Ironically, this was the very assembly where Roy Turner was baptised in the Holy Spirit shortly before coming into contact with the Glory people. Roy played a significant part in spreading the Glory blessing, as will be related later.)

Secondly, years later, right at the end of Henri's life, he and Connie had a visit from the man who handled all the correspondence at this tribunal. His wife accompanied him. He was about to start a pastorate in Mansfield with the Assemblies of

God, but he wanted to get this matter cleared up first. He came to say that he was sorry that he had not stood with Henri at that time, but frankly he had found himself in a very awkward position. So also had the other stalwarts on the tribunal. Altogether there were three older members who knew exactly what Henri was talking about, but the official line of the Assemblies was that in such cases of controversy they would always stand by the pastor.

He told Henri, 'We knew you were right. But because of the ruling of the Assemblies and for the sake of the work we had to agree. It wasn't right. I could get no peace of mind. So before going to be the pastor of this church in Mansfield I had to see you.'

Connie comments, 'He had come to say how sorry he was, and I admire him for coming to see us. So God vindicates you if you're right, even if it's after thirty or forty years.'

Chapter 3

Standing for God

The Next Step

A t this point Henri and Connie suddenly found themselves wonderfully free to make their own decisions and to serve the Lord in a new way, no strings attached. But this amazingly unstructured moment had its own peculiar difficulties. In a sense they did not have anything to go on; it was experimental. Roy Hollingworth, one of Henri's future young helpers, puts it like this: 'Henri had had this anointing in about 1948, but he didn't know what to do with it or how to harness it. Henri was not a public speaker sort of person. In fact Connie was more like that. But as Henri had said to the Pentecostal tribunal: 'Wherever God leads me I'm going. I have a job to do.'

Looking back on this time Connie has this to say,

> When we first went out Henri couldn't use his gift. We had tried to stay within the denominations, but they wouldn't let him use his gift. They wouldn't let him play his accordion. 'You're not to play choruses, you're not to shout and praise God,' they said. Henri told them, 'That's me finished.' So out we came. Then he said, 'I shall not die, but live and declare the Glory of God' similar to Psalm 118:17. There was just the two of us, and after that all the people at the church cut us off dead, but it didn't bother us at all. Henri said, 'The Lord's not given me all this joy, and charged me inside for nothing. If I have no joy I can't witness.' [1]

When the Lord commissioned Moses to rescue the Israelites from Egypt, He asked him, *'What is that in thine hand?'* (Exodus

4:2) Henri and Connie didn't have to look further than their immediate circumstances, at what came to hand. To begin with they had their contacts at work. Connie says,

> When some of Henri's business colleagues got to know, he felt about that big (indicating very small). You can imagine. But he witnessed to them. He didn't draw back. He never held anything back. They thought he'd gone bonkers. But he continued to witness to them. And then God showed us that it wasn't people's faces we had to bother about, whatever they were registering – it was pleasing Him! If you please Him, it doesn't matter. They can all be against you, but it makes no difference. God is with you. And people said about Henri, about both of us, 'We witness the presence of God with you.' And that was that. We realised it was the anointing that was breaking the yoke, I tell you.

Together, Henri and Connie felt a wonderful liberty to go where the Master would lead them, to be at His beck and call. The first Sunday after the Tribunal they did not go to the mission at Sherwood Avenue. Henri said he was going to Lincoln, so they both went. Once there, they made for the river, and lo and behold they met a man called Bob who owned a large barge that carried gravel. Henri also had a boat – he had had one for years – and while cruising around on the Trent at Newark he had got to know this large warm-hearted man, who now suddenly popped up on deck, and catching sight of them cried, 'Henri! Come and have some tea.'

Afterwards, Bob took them to a Pentecostal Assembly in Lincoln. He was most enthusiastic to have them there. He told them the pastor was away and that there was to be an after-meeting for the young people. At this meeting, Bob whispered to the leader, 'Get that young man up at the back, will you, and his wife.'

So Henri and Connie were invited onto the platform. While they were singing some choruses, the power of God fell. Henri had never before been on a platform to speak. 'Well, it just poured out of him and the place was in an uproar!' Connie recalls. 'It was marvellous what happened, marvellous! They saw a side of things they'd never seen before and neither had anybody else.'[2]

Bob said, 'I'm glad you've come, Henri. The pastor wouldn't have allowed that, you know.'

Connie felt that it was 'a kind of confirmation that we were being led!'

With Gran Staples nearby and their combined hospitable disposition, it naturally led to their having meetings in the room above the shops when the cups of tea had been pushed away. Henri and Connie never had to be concerned about being left high and dry, cut off in a backwater. Henri pointed out that God brought people to them:

> Now the first thing that I found was that I no longer had to go looking for people to take to the mission. I was so full of joy that they came to me and it was so infectious that they caught it. I had no longer to take people to the mission to get them saved, they so much wanted what I had got, that I just prayed for them and they got it – a real born-again experience from God. Hallelujah!
>
> One day I went over to the Assemblies of God church at Grantham and was asked to say a few words. I just told them how God had blessed me and, when we started singing, the people came out of their seats dancing, and some stood on their seats waving their handkerchiefs. I had never seen such a carry-on before and when I went home I said to my wife, 'Con, I wished you'd been with me tonight and you could've told me whether this thing was right,' and I told her all that had happened. I was new to all this and not knowing much of the Bible at that time, I looked to Con to help me, as she was well versed in the Scriptures.
>
> A week after this event we went over to Grantham again and we made it our business to be late so that we could see what was going on. When we arrived at the church, I looked through the keyhole and, praise the Lord, there was a sister testifying about the great blessing she had received the previous week. This encouraged me to go on. [3]

Santa Claus

The year of 1948 was certainly a critical turning point in Henri's life. The next thing which took place was again most unusual.

> It was in the year 1948, the Christmas season was creeping up on us and competition was keen. At that time I was in the toy business and as my shops were situated on the fringe of the shopping centre at Newark, I had to think of

some means whereby I would attract customers to them. Of course there is no greater attraction for the children than a toy fair, a magic chimney, and a Santa Claus and that is what I decided upon, but I must put it over different to the way it had ever been done before. It must be something out of the ordinary. I've always been a man like that, for I believe variety is the spice of life. Our God is a God of variety and since He is my Father and I am His son, it is not surprising that the same spirit is in me.

Yes, we must have a Santa Claus, but how could I arrange it different? As I thought about it, I had a great idea. I had a Cyclemaster powered bicycle, so I would get a man dressed as Santa Claus. He could ride through Newark with his bag on his back, eventually arriving at the shop to open the toy fair. I would have a ladder set for him to climb up through the third storey window, from where he could throw small Christmas gifts to the crowd below and then take charge of the magic chimney.

Plans were made and notices inserted in the local press, so that many looked forward with eager anticipation to the forthcoming event. It was then that God met with me, and filled me with His Holy Spirit. I had been baptised with the Holy Ghost before, but this was something even greater. As I look back today I realise that God was doing a new thing. It was about this time or a little earlier that the great deliverance move began in America, and many were raised up and anointed of God to heal the sick and set the captives free. I was so much under the anointing of God, that I wished with all my heart that I could cancel the toy fair and the Santa episode, but it had gone too far and so I had to see it through.

When the great day arrived the town was full of excited parents and eager-faced children. The crowd gathered so thick outside the shop, that the traffic came to a standstill in the street and extra police came on the scene to keep the crowd under control. I stood surveying the scene as they awaited the arrival of Santa Claus. It was a huge success and everyone seemed delighted but I found no joy in it. It was then that God spoke to me. As I looked at the huge crowd of eager excited faces watching Santa climb the ladder, the Lord said to me, 'Henri, you're lifting a false man up. I, if I be lifted up, I will draw all men unto Me.' Believe me, folks, it just broke my heart. I turned from the scene and just wept before the Lord. I told the Lord that I thought He was being lifted up. But He showed me how so many were lifting a denomination up, or a creed or doctrine and such like. He told me, if I would only lift up Jesus, He would draw the crowds and hundreds would be set free. I promised God there and then, if it was the last thing I did, I would do all in my power to lift Him up, and ever since that day I have sought to magnify the Lord and exalt His great Name. I have lifted Him up in my business, often amidst ridicule and opposition. I have lifted Him up in our meetings. I have lifted Him up in testimony and I have lifted Him up in praise and believe me, brothers and sisters, it works wonders. Hallelujah.

The crowds have come all right and what is more they keep coming. My Jesus is real and He can meet every need. Many today are preaching condemnation but God has given me the ministry of reconciliation and it is my greatest joy to lead men and women to Christ. He has put love in my heart for everybody and what He has done for me He can do for you. God has got no favourites. This is the Latter Rain outpouring, and it's for all who will seek Him with all their hearts.

Later, when I saw the photographs of that Christmas event, I said to my manager, 'One day I will show these pictures to thousands of people,' not knowing then how it would be done; but here they are, folks, and may God bless everyone of you and fill you with all the fullness of God. [4]

Opportunities

Life flowed on. At the beginning of 1949 Henri kept a diary and it is worth quoting some extracts from them, showing how packed full with usefulness his days were:

Saturday 1 January, 1949
Prayed with Nellie, read John 14. Nellie confirmed that she had given her heart to the Lord on Thursday. Told Reg and Lilly about my experience of being filled with the Spirit. Reg asked what was going to happen next. I told him I was 'going up'. Glory.

2 January, 1949
Went to Brenda's for supper. Had a good chat about the Lord. We all had a wonderful time in prayer. I wept in the

Spirit for the first time. It was a wonderful experience. I want more of it. All I could think about was that souls are going to hell and they don't know it. I feel I want more power from the Lord to be able to tell them. Oh help me and give me more and more power.

6 January, 1949
Called at Mum's. Had a grand chat about the Lord. Went to Mrs Winfield's. Told them about the signs of the times and the second coming. Played some choruses, read scriptures and had a word of prayer. I believe this was a victory. Glory.

7 January, 1949
Full of Joy. I felt the Lord was turning our business. Proof soon came. Arthur gave his notice in. I weep for Arthur's conversion. While I am weeping Mrs Pegg comes in broken-hearted to tell us she is to have major operation. We ask her to come back to the Lord. She weeps and prays to the Lord. We pray for her and she goes on her way rejoicing. Glory. Went to see Arthur at home. I have proof of something he has done wrong but also talk about his soul. Some of his friends arrive so I leave. Soon after Arthur comes to see me. I have a further chat with him and he wants to go to the police. After more talking Arthur starts to cry and gives his heart to the Lord. Glory. Thank you Lord.

8 January, 1949
Still full of joy. Mrs Pegg came back to say she is much better in her spirit. She has told her husband what I had said. Glory. She is not going into hospital until April. I ask her to witness while she is in there. Arthur confesses the wrong he has done. Had a grand time of blessing at Brenda's. Jeff is filled again. God bless him.

9 January, 1949
Still full of joy. Arthur tells Con I was right. He does feel a lot better since he got saved. I feel a heavy burden to speak at meeting and call on the Lord for help. I speak at the meeting with tears and plead with them to really get to grips with God because time is short. Mrs Blenden and Mrs Black in tears, others really moved. Praise the Lord. Bob and Mary come back to the Lord with tears after they pray for the Lord to forgive them.

10 January, 1949
Still full of joy. Urge Ian to go for the full blessing. He feels so full of joy he nearly kissed the insurance man. Glory! Reg comes to see me at about 9.30 pm. We chat about business and the Lord's coming.

12 January, 1949
Still full of joy. Jack told Albert about a dream where he picks up the paper and it keeps turning into a Bible. Believe the Lord will save him. Steve spoke about liberty at meeting. A very good meeting indeed. A big change in Steve, praise the Lord. Witness to Brown Brothers' traveller.

13 January, 1949
Anglican priest comes to see me. I tell him my testimony. It upsets him so much he nearly loses his false teeth. Glad when he's gone. Went to see bank manager. Told him about the gospel and signs of the times. Told him that it is up to us to be ready to meet the Lord. He agrees and we part good friends. Lord save him. [5]

On another occasion a travelling salesman came to their office, 'and Henri had him on his knees and was praying for him before he had a chance to say what he was there for! He got deliverance and was never the same again. God changed him.' [6] At some point he had the joy of leading a friend to the Lord, Ken Robinson, the son of a colleague of his father's who manned the Claypole signal box.

Yet another morning he was upstairs in his office trying to do his books when he suddenly said, 'It's no good. I've got to go and see a customer of mine. He's broken his arm, and he only lives down here. I'll be back in a bit.'

So he went and prayed for him and straight away God healed that arm. The chap was frightened to death. He could not believe it.

Henri said, 'I've come to tell you about Jesus, I've come to tell you about the Lord. It's Him that healed you. Yes, I've come to pray for you.'

And the startled man exclaimed, 'Don't do any more!'

Mansfield Market

It was at this moment that Henri and Connie saw a particular need, and instinctively knew within themselves, by the grace of

God, that they could meet it. Here was an opportunity to be seized and they went for it. This was their Sunday evening open-air witness for the Lord in Mansfield Market. One could say that by walking through this particular door of obedience their work for God fanned out from that point in ever increasing usefulness.

One week-end in September 1949 Henri said, 'It's Sunday night. I'm going on Mansfield Market to see what's going on.' He later described how:

> I was driving through a market square. The place was teeming with people, standing aimlessly about, and I was fired with a desire to start an open-air work among them. It was a noted meeting place for many of the local inhabitants, and God had put a love in my heart for every one of them and I longed that they might have a share of this wonderful love and joy that the Lord had given to me. [7]

These Sunday evenings in Mansfield were moments of convivial relaxation for the townspeople. They came to the pubs to meet their friends and have a natter in the market place.

There were three other groups who had meetings there: an evangelical free church centred on Hardy's hat shop, who were evangelical and effective in winning people for Christ, also the Salvation Army and the Assemblies of God. Each would have an hour before the next group took over. As Henri and Connie watched, they were standing next to a group from the Assemblies, one of whom was playing a harp and Henri realised that these folk in particular were getting nowhere at all with the people. 'We need something here,' he said to Connie.

> We're coming here next week. Look at all those miners. They're not even listening. I'm going to bring my accordion. I'm going to play and you're going to sing. I'll get my staff to fix a loud speaker on my car.

During the week they had the equipment fixed up and next Sunday evening found them in the market place again. The police came round and asked what they were doing. Henri told them and they said it would be all right, but they must wait until nine o'clock when the others had had their innings and must finish at ten, so that the publicans would not complain about losing their custom. Henri readily agreed to this. And so they began, standing at the back of their car. As they started to sing and really get going, folk began to gather round. The miners loved singing and were soon heartily joining in. They were thrilled to bits. They squashed in so close that they were right on top of the couple. They gave Henri no elbow-room at all; he could hardly play the accordion. It was not long before God's power came down in a wonderful way. The late summer night was warm and balmy, and as they packed round everyone sang and sang until Connie was thoroughly exhausted and Henri came to the end of all the choruses he knew.

Connie gasped, 'I'm going to have a drink'.

Henri took no notice. 'Say summat!' he said.

Taken aback she replied, 'Such as?'

Henri insisted, 'I dunno, but say summat!'

Connie thought, 'Say summat?' She had only once before spoken in the open air, on that occasion in Wales. She said to the Lord, 'You did say, "Open your mouth wide and I will fill it."' And her mind fixed on that same text as before, *'Man shall not live by bread alone, but by every word that procedeth out of the mouth of God'* (Matthew 4:4). 'That's what He gave me,' Connie commented 'and I went from there. It just opened up, it was wonderful.'

Back in the car, when it was over, Henri said with a glint in his eye, 'Bye, summat's in this 'ere. I'm going for this. This is the place where God wants me.' So back they came each Sunday evening regularly at nine o'clock, and soon they came on Saturdays as well. Henri would produce his accordion and with Connie beside him they would cheerily strike up 'Here we are again!' Week after week the miners and others would crowd around. Their evangelistic effort really took off. No doubt about that. They were right in the middle of where the need was. It was not a question of handing out leaflets and inviting people into a building, or even a stadium, at a publicised time and then hoping people would turn up. No, the beauty of an open-air meeting is that you are in direct contact with people just where they are, and their response is immediate.

Once Henri and Connie had made their stand and forged ahead, they did not remain isolated. Before long, the Lord gathered round them a faithful little band who caught their enthusiasm and wanted to join in. Roy and Betty Hollingworth, a young couple who had recently come to know the Lord Jesus as their Saviour, were the very first two. Roy had come to his spiritual senses when he had fallen gravely ill, and Betty had been saved whilst going to cottage meetings in the home of Janie, Connie's mother. Violet Lowe was the next one to join them. She had become a Christian some little while before, as we shall read about later. This was her first impression:

> It was one Sunday evening, when I walked away from the hat shop, that I heard music on the Market. There, standing in the middle of the Market, were Henri and Connie. Henri was playing an accordion and Connie was singing; I was amazed. It seemed crazy what they were doing, simply singing hymns and choruses without anything else going on; no back-up, no support. But what joy of the Lord was radiating out from them! After the meeting he came over and encouraged me. Well, I couldn't wait until the next week. When I arrived the second time there were others with them.

Roy Hollingworth and another young man, Albert Sleigh from Shirebrook about five miles north of Mansfield, were the two extra folk on this occasion, making five in all.

In time Violet was joined by her fiancé Peter Cowling, who used to drive up from London bringing four others with him. In 1951 Norman and Olive Parsons came over from a farm in Derbyshire. Gran Staples, Henri's mother used to come over with Henri and Connie from Newark, plus Joan Chadwick, a young seamstress who lodged with her. Olive's sister Hilda Nicholls and her husband Bob would drive up together from Stafford. Then there was Jean Guiteri from Bristol, who threw herself into it. As did the Jamaicans Linnette and Tom, who brought some Caribbean rhythm with them. Margaret Pailing, who had been brought up in the Salvation Army, also joined in; and Steve Hollingworth, the brother of Roy. There were also Albert Foottit and his wife Mary, who was blind. In autumn 1952 Joyce Hare (later Walter) was walking home from her Brethren meeting across the Market when she heard singing all around the streets. She had had a keen interest in opera and she was attracted by the singing of Connie and Roy Hollingworth. She relates,

> Roy was wearing a green jumper with 'Hallelujah' in red on one side and 'Jesus Saves' on the other. He was so outstanding with it and his face was radiant, but I soon realised it was nothing to do with opera, but was a gospel meeting.

Once the open-air meetings became known, folk from the churches would enjoy coming along too.

It is interesting that there was also another young man, recently saved, who was already witnessing on Mansfield Market at this time. This was Peter Scothern. He knew Connie's parents well, and for some time he and Henri were to share preaching at a mission in Mansfield. Subsequently Peter Scothern was used greatly of the Lord in Africa and India, as well as in Wales and southern England in remarkable cases of healing and deliverance from demon possession.

To begin with, Henri and Connie simply drove to Mansfield in their Rover, rigged up with a loudspeaker. Then Henri's brother Eric brought over a van from their shops, and they would hang a loudspeaker on the railings of a monument in the middle of the square. The number plate of the Rover happened to be JHN 316. (This was long before people other than royalty could have personalised numbers.) That number plate often came in handy for emphasising John 3:16, *'For God so loved the world, that He gave His only begotten Son, that whosoever believes in Him should not perish, but have everlasting life.'* The young people stood in a group by the car and van. Violet recalled,

> We never had a platform or anything like that; we just stood on Mansfield Market. Henri used to shout out, 'Come on Policeman! It doesn't mean to say because you are a bobby Jesus doesn't love you!' Even the bobbies laughed at it. Then, instead of 'everybody', he would start singing,
>
> > *Every bobby should know,*
> > *Every bobby should know*
> > *I have such a wonderful Saviour that*
> > *Every bobby should know!*
>
> The police used to thank Henri for being there on a Saturday and Sunday night, because they said the people were so intent on listening that their job was halved.

Certainly Henri and Connie went at it heart and soul. In fact, Henri was putting so much of himself into these open-air meetings one dear soul had a real concern for his health! This was Mrs Hardy who ran the evangelistic hat shop.

'I've been listening to Henri,' she told Connie. 'Now, don't let him wear himself out. With what he's got he'll burn out. Be careful. Don't let him overdo it.'

She fully recognised the anointing of God on him. One can hear in this remark echoes of Whitefield's and Spurgeon's quip, 'I'd rather wear out than rust out.'

After about eighteen months of these meetings Henri had the growing conviction that he needed a special caravan built. The problem was that they had no money. They were just in the process of building up their business in Newark. They were tight times financially. All profits had to be ploughed back. Connie had never taken any wages for what she was doing, working six days a week in the shops, from ten in the morning till about seven or eight o'clock in the evening, sometimes all night around Christmas time. So about a couple of years before, their friend Arthur Hampshire (who later printed the *Glory News*) said to Henri, 'Bye! You never pay your wife anything.'

'No,' he replied, 'I can't afford to.'

Arthur looked him in the eye and told him straight, 'When you get back home, get yourself to the bank and put £500 in her name. I demand it. Honestly Henri, it's not right. She's been working, working, working all her life. I think you should do that, and you will!' And he did. It amazed Connie.

Anyhow, as soon as Henri had the bright idea of having a caravan built, he came to Connie with the words, 'Please, can I have that £500?' As Connie told the anecdote forty-five years later, she laughed her head off. 'Well,' she thought, 'I wouldn't let him have it for anything else.' But seeing it was for this caravan, she relented, and gave it back to him. So they went to Peterborough to a man that built special caravans. Henri told him what he wanted:

> I'd like all the front oakwood, a nice platform and a bit of a desk of some sort to put a Bible on and my hymn books.

Asked if he wanted any words on the outside, he said:

> I'd like a big long text, *'And they went forth, and preached everywhere, the Lord working with them, and confirming the Word with signs following'* (Mark 16:20).

In other places on the caravan he also had written, *'With His stripes we are healed'* (Isaiah 53:5), *'Let us be glad and rejoice'* (Revelation 19:7) and 'Praise the Lord.' The side of the caravan was cut out to make a stage, so that it was like an open air theatre, with striped curtains and bright lights which came on. As well as the desk, there was a blackboard. Altogether it was a novel idea.

However, when Henri came to collect the caravan, he was horrified. The man had put a big cross on the top of it!

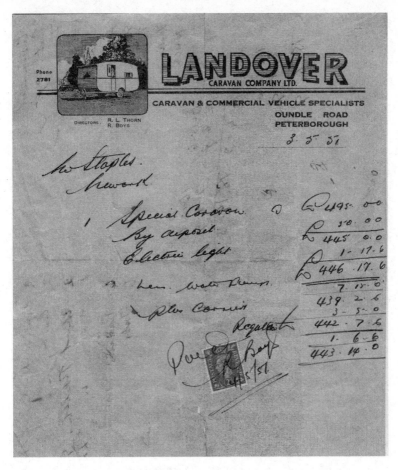

Receipt for caravan

'It isn't like that!' Henri cried.

'Like what?' came the reply.

'That's finished,' Henri continued.

'It was necessary once, but now it's finished. It doesn't go that way any more. Now, if you had put a crown on it, that would have been all right!'

The caravan builder was flabbergasted. 'Well,' he said, 'I told my foreman it were different. And I can see it is different!' So down the cross came.

The caravan was brought to Newark, and an amusing thing happened. Henri's row of shops in Appleton Gate were opposite the Police Station. As Henri drove into the road he had an amplified tape recorder playing some choruses; and he went and parked the caravan by the back of the Police Station. A police officer came across to him and said, 'I say Henri, you mustn't come past here playing them there hymns.'

'Sorry', said Henri, 'but they weren't that loud.'

'No perhaps not,' replied the officer, 'but the thing is, there was a court case on and they were just sentencing the fellow and you were playing, 'With arms wide open He'll pardon you!'

With the special caravan Henri and Connie and their helpers were now fully equipped to meet the opportunity confronting them in the market place. Each Saturday and Sunday evening Henri would drive down Leeming Street and onto the Market. The Mansfield folk looked forward to their coming so much; they would be watching for them in eager anticipation. The Rover car and caravan would park, the team of youngsters would form a group and at nine o'clock sharp the striped curtains would be swept back on the stage; the lights would come on to reveal Henri and his accordion cheerily striking up, 'Here we are again!' The miners and others would crowd round yet again, and everyone heartily join in the singing. As someone has put it, 'Henri jazzes them in!' Roy and Betty Hollingworth remember these days so well:

> Henri also had what he called his 'chorus girls' who took part in these open airs, Betty, Olive and Jean being the first ones. The young people loved it. Sometimes in the winter they could not get to Mansfield, but once when the weather was bad they decided to go anyway to hold their usual meeting. When they arrived there was not a soul in sight, because everyone was sheltering from the rain. Henri's folk were in the caravan with the front open, so they were dry and Henri shouted out, 'God bless you brothers and sisters, I know you're there, standing in the shop doorways.' When anyone got saved Henri would send them to the Elim Church. He was not interested in building a congregation himself. On one occasion they were invited into a working men's club, so they agreed to go. They were put over in a corner where there was a small podium, and had to do their singing in a smoky room that stank of beer against a background of Bingo numbers being called out. It was not very satisfactory but it gave them another opportunity to have a go for Jesus.

With the group of young Christians who gathered round Henri and Connie, life got into a new routine. On Sunday afternoons folk used to gather in their home above the shop in Newark for prayer and praise followed by tea and sandwiches. Then it was off to Mansfield to join in with the six thirty meeting at the Gospel Mission. (After twenty years the rift over the lack of Pentecostal witness there had been healed, and the elders were only too glad to welcome a group who brought a breath of revival with them.) As an alternative they also went to a meeting at Janie Marshall's. After that it was on to the Market for the much anticipated stirring hour with choruses, preaching, testimonies and what the miners endearingly called 'Connie's hot pot'. Come ten o'clock and the little team would stand around for as long as was needed, talking about the Lord Jesus to all who lingered, sharing Scriptures, leading some to the Lord, praying over the sick, seeking deliverance from sinful habits, phobias and fears. Often it was the early hours before they got home. Altogether they would go to Mansfield four times a week. There were two midweek meetings on Tuesday and Thursday at the Gospel Mission or Janie Marshall's with the two week-end stints on the Market.

From the team of young Christians Albert Sleigh was an exceptional speaker. 'He was a lovely lad,' Connie said. He was filled with the Holy Ghost while on the Market. 'And when he spoke in the open air you could hear a pin drop, he was so anointed.' Another young man was Stephen Hollingworth, who used to praise God in tongues. One evening he was speaking in tongues in the Hungarian language, in Magyar, and three Hungarians happened to be standing by. They perfectly understood his message. This pointed them to Christ and they were saved.

People were helped in a number of ways. A dear elderly Salvationist exclaimed, 'Bye, Henri, this is real. I've been in the Salvation Army all my life, but I've never felt so happy as when I come and stand here. This is my church out here.'

Once he asked Henri to pray for him: 'When I don't come here I'm lonely. Will you pray for a nice Christian wife for me?' Henri prayed there and then, and a couple of weeks later he came up smiling with a lady on his arm.

'He's done it, Henri. He's found her for me!'

Connie explained that they were an exact match and they both had the joy of the Lord. [8]

Henri used to refer to the singing as their secret weapon: 'They don't realise it's anointed of God. They'll never be the same again if they're listening.' Singing the truths of the gospel has a penetrating effect. The Apostle Paul in his letter to the Colossians (3:16) talks about 'teaching and admonishing one another in psalms and hymns and spiritual songs', and admonish means warn, reprove, urge, advise, remind. This is why General Booth made hymn singing to the accompaniment of brass bands such a vital arm of the Salvation Army's work. With firm conviction he said, 'Give them some songs. It will drop in their hearts.' His son-in-law, Mr Booth Clibborn, used to say, 'Come on, it's always a right time to praise God wherever you are.' (As it happens, he came down to the Gospel Mission in Mansfield and almost certainly joined in one of their open air meetings.) In so far as people are singing God's truths they are wielding the sword of the Spirit in the power of the Spirit. One favourite was:

> *Grant us Thy truth to make us free,*
> *And kindling hearts that burn for Thee,*
> *Till all Thy living altars claim*
> *One holy light, one heavenly flame.*

This verse of a hymn really set folk on fire. But it was only one of many. Choruses came to them from all over the world. Somebody would ask, 'Have you heard this one, Henri?' He would soon pick it up by ear and they would be well away. When they sang them, people would learn them easily, 'because the rhythm and the anointing was helping them,' Connie explained. They only had to sing them twice and everyone else caught on. It was lovely to hear them all singing together. Connie would strike up with an old favourite, 'It is no secret what God can do.' She often used to sing it and it got right through to people, speaking to their very hearts. The miners and everyone pleaded, 'Don't go home yet, Henri,' but the Police insisted, 'I'm sorry, my lad, the pubs are complaining. Their customers are dropping their pints and coming out here to listen. We can't allow that.' Henri assured him he would definitely finish at 10 pm.

Before Henri started his meetings there used to be so much drinking and fighting that the Police would have to bring six Black Marias to take care of the trouble-makers in the market place. Now, they confessed to Henri they didn't understand why, 'but we only have to bring one now. We hardly see any trouble. You come with a few choruses and a few hymns and you've cleaned up the Market.' Connie later commented in the *Glory News*:

It was the Spirit of God taking over and the miners would say, 'We were singing all these down the pits the other night, Henri, and it was grand'. To me that's the reality of the baptism of fire. [9]

Also there was terrible language down the pits, but after three or four weeks of Glory open-airs the miners said, 'You *never* hear anyone swear down the mine.' 'That's what the Spirit of God can do,' said Connie. 'We know it breaks the yoke on them. There's many, many got saved we shall never know about.' Some years later Henri wrote about these Mansfield Market days:

It was a difficult environment but, hallelujah! He that was for us was greater than all that was against us. We stood fast however and won the day. The Gospel that I preach really works, hallelujah! They had heard it before in the religious way with no effect, but when it was put over in the Glory way they began to listen and take notice. They soon realised that there was nothing miserable about this but that it was joy unspeakable and full of glory. As soon as the singing went forth over the loud speaker people flocked around to listen as if drawn by a magnet. It was said of Jesus that the common people heard him gladly, and I have found the same, so much so, that if we fail to turn up on a Sunday night the phone is ringing the very next day, and people are writing in, wanting to know the reason why.

Many are the souls who have been delivered and set free in these gatherings. Among the first converts was a Communist who had been in jail. I praise God that we have the answer to Communism. On another occasion a man was found weeping by the caravan door after the meeting was over. As I talked with him, I discovered that he had served time for attempted murder, and he wondered if God could save a man like him. I was able to tell him that Jesus came to seek and to save that which was lost, and that God loved him as much as he loved me. He took Jesus into his heart and was wonderfully converted. A BBC singer happened to be passing one day and was arrested by the spiritual singing. He asked to be allowed to sing along with my wife Connie. We were pleased to grant his request knowing that the Spirit of God was working on his heart. When the meeting drew to a close he asked us to pray for him. [10]

There was an unusual instance of the power of their singing. It was not unlike the case of a certain Scotswoman trying to listen to George Whitefield. She was right out of earshot on the edge of a huge crowd, and yet was deeply affected by 'the holy wag of his head'. In this case Connie's voice was far too far away for the words she was singing to be understood. But that did not matter. An elderly couple, George and Mary Robinson, were sitting in their back garden up on the Ravensdale estate, and they could hear the music and the singing floating up on the still night air from the loudspeakers in the market place down in the hollow over a mile away. George described it like this:

> As I sat outside my house on that September night I heard the singing. Me and my wife, we just sat there spellbound. It was like a bit of heaven. We couldn't hear what you was singing. Something happened to us Henri. Don't know what it is.

Henri replied, 'I can tell you what it is. It's the presence of God and He wants you two.' So he led them to the Lord. Connie was thrilled:

> I remember the day when I prayed, 'Lord, I don't want just to sing. I want You to give me a voice to wake the dead.' And He did. [11]

That night those two passed from death unto life.

Not surprisingly Henri and Connie came in for real opposition. To begin with they had plenty of heckling and verbal abuse. Then tomatoes and rotten fruit were hurled at them, and oddly enough sometimes money! It only needed one or two to start it and then others would join in. One night they hit Henri in the face. Really, he and Connie got a lot of stick, but they just carried on playing and singing. Suddenly, one night, a large thick-set man got up. His name was Jock. He said to Henri, 'You don't know me and I don't mean any harm. I'm just straight out of prison. I've been stood here and I've enjoyed it. Can I speak a few words? I'm not going to say anything aggressive.' Henri agreed and gave him two minutes. So Jock addressed the crowd, 'Now then, you lot. You all know me here. I'm a boxer and you've seen me fight. But what I want to tell you is, if one more person throws anything more at these folk again, you'll have me to deal with!' Jock eventually became one of them, putting his trust in the Lord Jesus.

God has His own ways of dealing with opposition. Walter Boyes from Boughton, a dozen miles north east of Mansfield, wrote later in a *Glory News*:

> Some years ago I used to stand in Mansfield Market Square and laugh my socks off at Henri's crowd having an open-air meeting. I was expecting the yellow van to come at any time and take them all away, but never thought that one day I would be one of them. But, glory to God, I've got it myself now. I sing, I shout, I dance. I praise the Lord and I really feel grand. [12]

There was also the very sad case of a woman who lived four or five doors away from the Gospel Mission. They were having a good meeting there, with a real sense of the presence of God with them. All of a sudden this woman came bursting in at the back of the hall. She ranted on at them, using such awful language. Henri put up his hand and said, 'Now, my love, you don't know what you're saying and you don't know what you're touching. Be careful!' When she left the building Henri prayed for her. But that night she dropped dead, and when the doctors examined her they were puzzled, because they could find nothing wrong with her. All the Christians on Mansfield Market testified about it. Connie commented, 'Don't touch God's anointed. Don't touch anything to do with God. It's dangerous. Anyway, I tell you what, it made a subdued silence on the Market when we went next week.'

The prophet Daniel said, *'the people that do know their God shall be strong and do exploits.'* In Proverbs we read, *'the righteous are bold as a lion.'* The Apostle Paul exhorts us, *'be strong in the Lord, and in the power of His might,'* and *'quit you like men, be strong.'* As this valiant couple pressed on with their exploits, they felt consciously upheld by God and empowered. Connie expressed it thus:

> If you're right within, it doesn't matter what they say. We stood, because God was talking to us. He brought us more into an awareness in the Spirit.

She described how they would be in bed talking and suddenly a scripture would come to her, *'Go to the lost sheep of the house of Israel.'* She wondered, 'Well, where's the house of Israel?' Then on another occasion God gave them the reassuring promise, 'My presence shall go with you.' And yet again some verses from the book of Revelation came vividly to their minds, *'You hate the deeds of the Nicolaitans which I also hate,'* and *'the blasphemy of them which say they are Jews, and are not,'* to which they could add again, *'which thing I hate.'* Yes, they were finding that they could well recognise whether people were real with the Lord or not. They said, 'Yes, Lord we know what you mean.' They found that God was revealing these scriptures by the Holy Spirit to them and quickening them. That gave them strength. It is true that *'the joy of the Lord is your strength.'* Connie added, 'By gum, it was them scriptures lived with us. They were so real. We acted on it.' (Daniel 11:32; Proverbs 28:1; Ephesians 6:10; 1 Corinthians 16:13; Matthew 10:6; Exodus 33:14; Revelation 2:6, 2:9, 2:15; Nehemiah 8:10) Smith Wigglesworth was wont to say: 'One day lived as a lion is better than years as a dumb sheep.'

The House of Henri

Back in Newark the home of Henri and Connie was becoming a centre of Christian activity. It was literally a house church. It was a natural growth, spontaneously springing up, from a seed which God had planted. People were coming and going all the time, their neighbours, contacts from the Mansfield Market meetings and business colleagues. So it was not surprising that they started meetings in the flat above their main shop. Connie protested, 'We didn't want to start meetings in our house. It started itself.' Their home was an open house. People would just drop in, phone up, come round and there was the sheer fun and joy of being together. Cups of tea, snacks and meals together would flow into moments of praise and thanksgiving. Henri would be seated at the piano, his hands rippling over the keyboard. Out came the tambourines and other musical accompaniments such as a violin and a mouth organ and away they went in songs of joyful praise, dancing around the furniture.

'There's no respect for time and place is there with God?' Connie said. 'It's a way of life, isn't it? Our house was an open house for the Lord for donkey's years.' She described how one night they were nicely tucked up in bed, tired out. Very likely they had been carol singing. Suddenly they heard a rumpus on the stairs, and before they knew what was happening there were about a dozen people round their bed. It was astonishing. There was such joy between them they could not keep away. They came up specifically because they wanted to know how to be filled with the Holy Spirit.

Their Christian walk was not all icing on the cake either. They knew what it was to endure persecution. They had their shop windows broken. People shouted abuse; there was vile language. Jesus Himself said His disciples would have tribulation.

Henri always instinctively knew the tremendous importance of getting time alone with God. There was so much going on around them and it was very easy for him to be rushed off his feet. His favourite place of retreat was their airing cupboard. It was his 'trysting place' with the Lord. Whatever else was happening, whatever pressures there were from needy people and business, he could escape into the airing cupboard and know for certain that he would not be disturbed there.

Before long Connie and Henri made two rooms above their shop into one by knocking down a partition. They called it the 'Glory Room' where they could hold meetings. Their nephew David Willows gives us a glimpse of the atmosphere there when he came to one of the meetings at the age of sixteen:

> It wasn't too long before I plucked up courage to go along to my first Glory meeting, which was up in the Glory Room. I remember going up the stairs and there were people sitting on them. I found the door was off (the Glory Room door) to get more people in. The room was absolutely solid with people. Somebody was playing the violin; someone else was playing the piano and claveline. The place was absolutely electric. It was alive. As soon as I walked through the door people would hug me. I suppose being Henri's nephew and Gran's grandson I was particularly earmarked, I don't know. But I remember that it was so absolutely full of life. I just loved it. There was this tremendous love and joy that came across. I was used to meetings that lasted an hour. But this meeting went on for several hours. I didn't want it to stop. It was wonderful.

Many people at that time and since have been struck by the power of the love of God in Glory meetings. Pastor Hadley of Birmingham wrote of Henri: 'Love simply flows out of his heart as he speaks, and it is love that can be felt by all.' His wife Olga added, 'I realised that this love Henri and Connie had was not a casual love, but a Jesus love.' [13]

Behind Henri's shops there were two rows of cottages with a courtyard in between called Jallands Row. The owner of the cottages told Henri that he could have them at a bargain price, because they needed repairing. Henri snapped up the opportunity, and in time they were lived in by a string of Glory people, the only exception being one of Henri's employees. At the top of

Jallands Road today drawn by Bruce Hyatt

Jallands Row was Henri's mother, Gran Staples. She moved there from Emminsons Row when she came back from Bristol. Her house was always open for hospitality and for about four years Joan Chadwick, one of the witnessing team on Mansfield Market, lived with her and greatly helped her. Other families who lived in the row of cottages were Joyce from Mansfield and her husband Les Walter (Laughing Les) who had come up from Worthing, Violet also from Mansfield and her husband Peter who worked for Henri as a television engineer. Then there was an elderly lady who had a bird that called out 'Get the Glory!' There was Elizabeth Clark the mother-in-law of Eddy Johnson, who as a wheelchair cripple was wonderfully healed, and also Margaret and Mick Pailing (Margaret's parents were among Henri's early supporters). Jallands Row was a joyful place. These Glory neighbours were in and out of one another's houses with outbursts of singing and praise, particularly at the weekends.

As we have seen, the story of the Glory Way started with one family. In the *Glory News* of 1997 Connie quaintly called this the House of Henri. She got the idea from Psalm 115 where it speaks of *'the house of Aaron'* explaining:

> God chose Aaron for that day, and I thought, 'Yes, and God has anointed vessels for every age. Yes, Aaron, you were anointed for your day.' Jesus had not yet come. Pentecost had not yet been given. They were still under the law and had not the freedom we have, but Aaron carried the anointing. The Lord started a house with us, the House of Henri. It's not a boast, it's what God did with the anointing He gave us both. I didn't realise I'd got an anointing until I got going!

This then was the beginning, one husband and one wife with their parents united behind them. Before long God added and wedded to them a band of loyal supporters. We shall call them Glory Warriors and the next chapter will give us a glimpse of their lives.

Chapter 4

Young Glory Warriors

Roy and Betty Hollingworth

Roy was born of Christian parents in Mansfield:

> I was made to go to Sunday school twice every Sunday, but I
> hated every minute of it, and decided as soon as possible
> that I would get away from it all. At the age of eighteen my
> opportunity came and I left home for life in the big city.
> Whilst living in London I tried most of the things that this
> world has to offer, but after five years I began to think that
> there was something better to be had in life than what I had
> then found. [1]

Betty came from Dover in Kent, but during the War her family
became evacuees in Wales, and then moved to West Harrow on
the outskirts of London. There she met Roy and they were
married.

> In those days I didn't know the meaning of the word
> salvation. Roy's family were Pentecostals but mine did not
> attend church at all. When I was fourteen I was confirmed
> in the Church of England, the bishop laying his hands on
> my head for me to receive the Holy Spirit. Who was I to
> argue with that? I thought that was all there was to it!
> After living in London for six months, we moved to
> Mansfield to live with Roy's family. His parents were good
> Christians but I didn't really want to get mixed up with
> their type of religion. It seemed a bit eccentric to me. My
> father-in-law was always laughing in the Spirit and to me
> this seemed very unholy and irreverent; he thought I was

very worldly because I used make-up on my face and went out to the pictures about twice a week. He called me 'Jezebel'.

As time went on, Roy and I became friendly with a Pentecostal woman who had meetings at her house on Wednesdays and Sundays. Her name was Janie Marshall, and we would go along to these get-togethers to please her because she was very kind to us when we were finding it a bit hard to make a go of our life. Roy was working very hard at the pit in those days and would always be very tired, so Janie Marshall said she was going to pray that the Lord would find Roy another job and a house of our own. [2]

They were unhappy in their marriage and, to make matters worse, Roy, in the middle of his work as a miner, fell extremely ill.

I felt so ill that I wanted to die out of the way, for I just couldn't be bothered with anything. When my dad came and told me that if I gave my heart to Jesus, He would heal me, I thought it was nothing short of blackmail and it was a very doubtful Roy who said 'yes'. Nevertheless, it was the beginning of great things for me, whereof I am glad. Oh, glory to God! The very next day when the doctor called, I was up and about and was able to go almost at once for a week's convalescence. From that day our marriage began to mend. My wife got saved and Jesus became so real to us. [3]

Betty describes her experience:

It was around that time, too, that God started to work on my heart. They were praying for the sick in one of the meetings and I began to weep. My father-in-law asked me if I would like to get saved and ask Jesus to take over my life. I said 'yes', and he prayed for me, but I didn't really feel much difference there and then. It was about two days later that I realised that something had happened to me. I know the exact place in Mansfield where I really began to feel God in my life. I was walking back to work, when I stopped and looked up. At that moment I felt such a wonderful joy flooding my soul. Even as I write about it I can feel the thrill of that moment. I knew then that I was a new creature in Christ Jesus and would never be the same again!

A few weeks afterwards, God answered prayer. Roy got a job at a power station near Newark and we were given a house that went with it. It was wonderful! We were so thrilled! Praise the Lord! And so we moved to Newark where we met Henri who was being wonderfully blessed of God. We started to help him in the work he was doing, spreading this love, joy and peace wherever folks were hungry.

The open-air meetings in Mansfield Market of course were the main thing, but there were also cottage meetings:

We were so full of enthusiasm! You couldn't keep us away from the meetings. Having God in our lives really meant something to us and we were very sincere in what we thought God wanted us to do. We worked very hard at it!

We were always trying to please God, fasting for weeks, praying often, and spending nearly every night of the week at some meeting. Even though I realise today that, no matter how hard we try to please God in all our works, He loves us for what we are. I truly believe that those early days with Henri and Connie helped us a great deal. We really sought after God's will for our lives as we fellowshipped in the Glory Room above Henri's shops. It was lovely to feel the spirit of love which flowed in each one and it was no wonder we were called the Love Family. [4]

Henri was a lot of fun; he was quite audacious. One must remember that he was young and his adherents were even younger. He had a lot of narrow cards printed with 'Get right with God' on one side, and 'It's later than you think' on the other. All the young folk had got their pockets stuffed with them. On the way home from one of their evening forages Henri pulled up outside a church and together they stuck the cards all round the door. This kind of thing appealed to the young. His approach was different. He also made all sorts of signs which he put up in his car. One was a reminder to people to pay their instalments for the bikes they were buying; it was a picture of a hand holding a hammer hitting someone on the head with the caption 'I haven't heard from you for a fortnight. Just to remind you!'

They travelled about all over the place in a couple of Henri's Bedford vans which held about eight on the benches at the back.

Eric drove one of them and played his mouth organ while they all sang. The few choruses that they knew were sung over and over again every week and included ones like, 'Oh you can't go to Heaven in an old Ford car, 'cos an old Ford car won't go that far,' and 'We'll ask brother Albert to help us along.' Every Tuesday night they went to Sleaford, picking up two old ladies on the way, to have a meeting in the home of Mr and Mrs Peacock, a lovely elderly Christian couple whom we will meet later. One of their favourite hymns, 'I will sing the wondrous story,' was sung fervently with the chorus variation of 'Sing it with Mrs Peacock in glory.'

'We didn't have any other life,' said Betty. 'It was such an exciting time full of activity.' Another of her special memories was of the time she was in hospital giving birth to her son Pete. Henri went to see her after he had been vaccinated against diphtheria, and he gave her a kiss in the good old Glory fashion, but she caught it from him and had to be put in quarantine. The doctor asked her, 'Do you kiss in your religion?' This was probably the origin of Henri's saying that the Glory was more catching than diphtheria. Another of his sayings was 'Serves you right,' meaning it didn't serve you wrong! He had many sayings which he repeated time and again during his forty years of ministry. But they stuck more than many sermons would have done. 'This gospel works,' and 'It rubs off on you,' were two more. Some of the young students playfully quoted them as if they were quoting scripture, missing out one of the words in a saying which others had to fill in, e.g. 'This gospel ------'

Youthful enthusiasm was encouraged. Philip Anstey of Leamington Spa had tackled the mammoth task of going round every house in his home town, giving a tract or talking to the occupants. He occasionally stayed with Roy and Betty and told them about this, which inspired them to do the same in a little village nearby. They set off on their bike with its sidecar and baby Pete inside, texts painted all over it, and went round to everyone. They met farmer George who, when Roy talked to him about Jesus, started to cry. Once when they were there, the parson came along and chased them out of the village saying that they were stealing his flock. But farmer George stuck up for them saying his life had been changed since they had come, which was more than he could say for the parson.

Henri had procured a lot of large tracts which had WARNING! printed across the top in red. Underneath there were things like, 'Flee from the wrath to come.' Once on a visit to Scunthorpe they held an open-air meeting and after they had finished singing they all went round the crowds giving out these tracts. It was a happy occasion because people stood around listening.

Peter and Violet Cowling

Violet came from a Christian home where her father and mother had faithfully taught her about Jesus. Then one Christmas Eve, when she was in her mid-teens, she got fished off the Market and taken to the hat shop where she heard spontaneous testimonies from people whose lives had been transformed by meeting with Jesus. This affected her and she gave her life to Christ. So when she saw Henri and Connie on the Market she was drawn to them. 'They can't have been there on more than one or two occasions previously, or I would have seen them,' recalls Violet,

> The third time I went they invited me over to their flat to have some fellowship, and that's when it all happened for me. I was brought into the kitchen and up there (pointing) you would have had SMILE, and, JESUS LOVES YOU on there, and KEEP SWEET and all these different things. So imagine as a young person going in and seeing all that; it was so unusual. When I picked my cup of tea up it would have said, *Violet, you have never had a cup of tea with so much joy on it*. When I picked my fork up it would say, *Praise the Lord at all times*, and you would pick your plate up and it would say, *His praise shall continually be in my mouth*. I was so overawed with it, but not afraid, because when I had first met them on Mansfield Market I felt the love. There was such a warmth; I felt as if it was wrapping itself around me. I stayed the night and had breakfast with them, but everything I touched had got GLORY on it. Connie had a lie-in so Henri said, 'Come on lass, we'll go to a Breaking of Bread service.' I don't know where he took me but it was full of all these coloured people.
>
> We had a bit of lunch when we got back and Connie was sat on one side of the fender. It was one of those fenders with a box on either side, and she was there reading the Word and Henri was playing the organ ever so quietly, 'Blessed quietness, What assurance to my soul.' I sat in this chair and I thought, 'Something's happening to me,' and I didn't know what to do, whether to sit in the chair or to get on my knees. So I got on my knees and I was immediately

filled with the Spirit. Afterwards when we had tea, everyone was laughing and Henri said, 'You've never had trifle with so much Glory on it.' We went out to the open-air after that and had a wonderful time. That was really where it first started on me and it was in Henri's old arm chair, where I was sitting, so when I go to see Connie now she says, 'Go on, sit in father's chair.'

As she looks back on events in her life, Violet did not feel that she had had a 'Glory' experience as such, but that it had come in stages. She had been really saved before she met Henri and Connie, but when she did meet them she felt this spontaneous love for people oozing out of them. Their ministry was a real asset in her Christian life, and before it was dubbed The Glory Way by someone, it was known as The Love Family. In Violet's case it was not a question of throwing in her lot completely with Henri and Connie:

As a young person you need to be with young people and I didn't dissociate myself from the church where I was going. They had a choir and we used to go round different places, which I found was very necessary; so I carried on going there and I found that I was able to combine the two.

As a young Lancashire engineer, Peter found work in South London, and it was there that God changed his life.

I give praise and thanks to Jesus my Saviour who paid my debt on the Cross and set me gloriously free. He did this because He loved me. Why, I shall never cease to wonder but praise be to His Name it is so.

He did a miracle in my life when I asked Him to come in and to take control, for I had reached the point where life to me was just a senseless roundabout and there really didn't seem much reason for it. Everything had become a farce and it was just a case of putting on a brave face and living in a world of pretence.

Through reading His precious Word, God gave me a desire to seek the truth and also made me conscious of my sinful and unworthy condition. One morning I rose from my bed with conviction (of sin) so strong upon me that I was compelled to walk from Balham, where I was living, right into the district of Bloomsbury in the centre of

London, a good six miles walk, and through the open doors of a church where I met Pentecost for the first time.

I was most impressed with the whole meeting. It was completely new to me and for the first time in my life the meaning of a risen Christ and an empty tomb hit me. This was what I'd been looking for. Jesus said, *'Seek and ye shall find.'* Praise His Name! That day I accepted Jesus as my Saviour and it worked. Hallelujah! He completely changed my life and every problem was solved and He put within me His peace. Shortly afterwards I received the baptism of the Holy Ghost in a prayer meeting at my local assembly.

Peter then went to a house meeting in South Norwood, where he heard a tape of a Glory meeting being played. The whole group were very affected by the tape, and the leader of the meeting said, 'I think we ought to get down on our knees and pray and see if we ought to go up to Newark.' They all felt that they should, and Peter was the first to get there. It was an August Bank Holiday Convention. He felt so strongly drawn to the meeting, yet what was he really going to?

The opinions were so diverse that quite truthfully I went prepared for just about anything, but what I received, praise God, was not just anything but something – something real, right from God, a new deeper experience. [5]

When I first came up from London in 1958 these types of meetings were unheard of; the things that you now see in churches where they get up and clap. Henri started it really, giving someone a clap when they came up to the platform, and it offended many people. Nowadays it isn't (usually) frowned on.

Peter and Violet met each other at the meetings. Peter would hire a dormobile and get four people, drive up to the Saturday meeting and stay with some kind person and go to the Sunday meeting in the afternoon and then drive back to London.

They married in 1959, and lived in Mansfield where Peter got a job. After a while he was employed by Henri and they came to live in one of the terrace cottages in Jallands Row. In their friendship with Henri, Violet recalls,

He used to do such unusual things to you in the meetings you know. I remember when we were in Bristol once and there was a minister there with his dog collar on, and I was just walking past when Henri called me over and said, 'Come here, Violet, come here, Don't you think this is a lovely lad? Give him a kiss and show him what a hug's like.' The thing is, you did it. If anybody else had said it you wouldn't do it, but it was natural to him. If you met him in Newark you had to be hugged, no matter who saw you. There are things that stick in your mind and when you're young they do register, so that all through your life you're aware that they're there and eventually you appreciate who started it. When from the age of sixteen or seventeen every time you met him he would encourage you and say the same things and you would have heard them sixty times, you remembered them. For instance, he would say, 'God will always be as big as you want Him to be, and bigger if you want Him to be bigger, and bigger if you want Him to be bigger.' 'And I'll tell you something else, madam, never ever have a critical spirit. It will rob you, it's a robber you know, duck, it's a robber.' At the time I didn't realise how very true that is. Another thing he would say was, 'If you can't say anything good about anyone, don't say anything bad. Just say nothing.' It had an enormous impact on me in my early Christian life, because he would tell you again and again and again.

Norman and Olive Parsons

Norman was born and brought up in Stafford, whereas Olive and her two sisters, Hilda the eldest and Frances the youngest, were Shropshire girls from Westbury in the Welsh Marches. All three girls came up to Stafford: first Hilda arrived to do nursing, to be followed by Olive and Frances at the beginning of the War, when they shared a terrace house. Olive was seventeen at that time, and worked in the Post Office. She later worked on a farm as a land girl; so did Frances. It was on this farm that Olive met a farm hand, Norman.

They got married in 1950 and went to work on a farm near Bletchley (Milton Keynes) in Buckinghamshire, living in a tied cottage. They did not get on well with the farmer there; he was an ex-army major and expected to be addressed as Sir, and only surnames were used. It was like being in the army. Norman says he never prayed in those days, but he did kneel down by his bed and say thank you to God for looking after him each day. That was his Christian life at that time; it was as far as they went in the Church of England.

He looked in the *Farmer's Weekly* to find a job somewhere else and applied for one in Derbyshire. It was a shot in the dark going from Buckinghamshire to Derbyshire. That was in 1951. They were due to have a new council house, but it was not ready, so for about six weeks they went to live in the farmhouse with the farmer he was working for, in the hamlet of Biggin. This was not far from the little town of Hartington above the River Dove. It is in splendid Peak District countryside with upland pastures, solid stone farm buildings and dry stone walls. The picturesque Dovedale gorge is only four miles to the south. The farmer's wife was a friend of Connie's brother. She was, as Norman says, 'a bit Pentecostalish,' and used to visit a man in Newark in the Faith Home and then invite him back to their farm in Biggin. He frightened them to death because he was on about the tribulation and the terrible things that were coming on the earth and he really put the wind up Norman who was only a nominal Christian and had not heard about Pentecost and salvation, or anything like that. But on another occasion while this lady was in Newark, Henri happened to pop into the Faith Home, which he did from time to time, and she invited him over. His visit coincided with Norman's and Olive's short stay in the farmhouse and he led them both to the Lord. Two weeks later they left the farm and they would never have seen him had he not gone then. 'This emphasises God's timing,' they said, 'the way He moved us from one end of the country to the other, took Henri over there and enabled us to meet him at least twice while we were there.' One occasion was a Sunday and he found them reading the Bible. 'I am pleased, lad, you've got The Book out!' he said because he realised they were on the right road. Henri put a lot of effort into keeping in touch with people and also made sure, as much as possible, that they kept in touch with one another.

Norman bought an old banger while in Derbyshire, (£100, '34 model). This gave them the freedom to travel all over the country, but more importantly it enabled them to get over to Newark for fellowship. Their next move was to Burton-on-Trent, then in 1953 they moved to Newark and have been there ever since.

Norman and Olive quickly became an integral part of the team of young people surrounding Henri and Connie. They joined in enthusiastically with the Mansfield Market witness. Henri whimsically called a number of the young women his 'chorus girls'; they sang so well together. Olive and her sister Hilda were amongst them, as well as Betty, Jean, Margaret, Mavis and Gladys.

As time went by they had three of their own children and adopted two more. In the role of young mother and helper amongst the Glory folk, there was something special about Olive's character. Laurie and Margaret James, who came into the picture in the mid-1950s, said that Olive was

> a lovely and a very spiritual person who loved the moving of the Spirit, often crying throughout the meeting. She danced gracefully (she was no light-weight), and she would often bring precious teaching from the Word. If we had to say who had the greatest impact on our young lives, in pressing on in liberty in those days, we would say it had been Olive Parsons.

Norman, the practical farmer, became the group's bus driver. He was a veritable right hand man. The original coach which Henri produced from somewhere was a Bedford 29-seater, a rather lethal vehicle with unreliable cable brakes. They used this for the Mansfield Market run. For more distant trips from 1961 onwards Norman drove an old ambulance that had been bought from a friend in Kent, Archie Friday. It was a three-litre Bedford and was one of the old type with the engine out front. It was unstable in cross winds.

Other Bedford coaches followed with Norman taking them on trips all over the country from County Durham to Devon. There was a real community spirit evident on these outings as Norman points out. A sense of togetherness has been lost to us who travel in our private cars. He says,

> We had good fellowship during our travels. Sometimes the singing was so noisy, I had to change gear by the speeds as I couldn't hear the engine, especially when we had a load of Jamaicans before most of them moved to Nottingham.

Bob and Hilda Nicholls

At the beginning of the War Winston Churchill gathered round himself a powerhouse of men who galvanised the nation when Britain's back was against the wall. There was Lord Beaverbrook who forced the Spitfire through the aero factory production lines.

Another was Ernest Bevin who was the energetic Minister of Labour and National Service. 'No minister played a greater part in organising the country's resources to win the war. Under Bevin's direction, Great Britain most effectively mobilised men and women for the armed forces and war industry.' [6]

Bob Nicholls was one of the nation's Bevin Boys. He, like Norman Parsons, came from Stafford. He had started his working life with Eastern Electricity, but then the War came and down he went into the mines to labour for Hitler's defeat. When German U-boats in a sinister way were sinking our ships bringing in a vital supply line of food and raw materials, Britain was dramatically thrown back on its own resources, and every blow of the coal miner's needy pick was a blow for survival and freedom.

During those strenuous years Bob had met Hilda, Olive's sister, and they married at the end of the War. His first peacetime job was as a salesman for the firm Betterware in Ruskington, near Sleaford in Lincolnshire, when he teamed up with and worked under Chris Wingfield, who was later to take a lead in Glory meetings. In due time God worked in his life in a radical way. It is best told in his own words:

> It is a good thing sometimes to let our thoughts wander over the years gone by and discern the over-ruling hand of God in our lives. How amazing it is to see that the Lord has caused all things to work together for our good and what confidence it builds into our hearts when we realise that He is still in control and will never leave nor forsake us but will perfect that which concerneth us.
>
> It was in the year 1951 that God first began a real work on my heart. I had been converted for about twelve years and had become an elder in a local Pentecostal Assembly. Preaching was like a hobby to me and I got quite a kick out of it, but the day came when the Lord began to show me that my presentation of the gospel didn't work.
>
> We often prayed for the sick and the afflicted but I never saw anybody healed or set free. The meetings we held used to go on week by week in the same old rut and nothing ever happened of any account.
>
> However, the year of 1951 saw a great change, for a man who was full of the Holy Ghost came our way. He had come over from the church in America and his ministry was so anointed that it had a lasting effect upon myself and many others and we began to seek the Lord in prayer and fasting

for something real and practical, and for the first time for a very long time some of us began to taste the blessings of the Holy Ghost.

My own wife had been quick to grasp the new thing that God was doing in the midst of His people. She had never had much change for the way of Pentecost that men had tried to teach and demonstrate to her, but immediately the Holy Ghost began to work in reality she entered straight in and was mightily blessed.

During the October of 1951, my wife was brought to Newark by her sister Olive, who had recently been saved through Henri's ministry, in a meeting held in a farm house. When Hilda returned home from Newark she was bubbling over with joy and blessing and was anxious to tell what a wonderful time she had experienced. The effect it had on me was like showing a bull a red rag. I was absolutely mad about it. If revival was to come at all then it must be through the denomination to which I belonged and that would be the only revival acceptable to me. O how bigoted I was. How I needed to be delivered and set free from it all. I felt very bitter against Henri and forbade my wife to ever mention the name of Henri in our home. However, I continued to seek the Lord for I strongly desired all that God had for me and whenever there was any anointed ministry I would go forward to be prayed for, but somehow it availed nothing.

The time came when I was laid aside on a bed of sickness and it was there that God spoke to me and said, 'My son, give me thine heart.' Of course it never dawned on me that the Lord meant my heart, as anything I received from God or gleaned through studying was always for the one purpose and that was to pass on to others through the medium of preaching. I meditated upon this text for some time but as nothing seemed to develop from it, I mentioned the matter to my wife. 'God wants you to give Him *your heart*,' she said, 'He has only had your head until now.' It was then that the penny dropped and I got on my knees and asked Him to take possession of my whole heart and being.

Shortly after this experience I went to a big convention, full of great expectations, but as the meetings progressed I became very disappointed, and I realised that the desire of my heart would never be satisfied there, but where else could I turn? Slowly the realisation gripped me. I must go to

Newark and when my wife voiced the same thing I reluctantly replied that there appeared no other way. We packed
our bags at once and set off for Newark. I wasn't feeling very
sweet about it, I can tell you, and as we entered the home of
Roy and Betty, I must have presented a sorry spectacle, full
of lumbago and miserable religion. Betty remarked to Hilda,
'Another bundle of bondage,' and she never spoke a truer
word for I think I had about touched rock bottom.

I went to the meetings but didn't enjoy them one bit, as
I seemed to be right outside the fellowship although I had
been made welcome. On the Sunday night was the Mansfield open-air meeting and Hilda and I were invited to travel
in Henri's car. There were five of us in the car but I felt the
loneliest person in the world and by the time we were
nearing Mansfield I was becoming quite desperate and
decided to do something about it.

The opportunity was soon forthcoming and I humbly
confessed to Henri and Connie how I had been so bitter and
prejudiced against them and asked their forgiveness, and,
oh, what peace and blessing filled my soul as they prayed
and wept over me. The very next day God sent a deluge of
the Holy Ghost and filled my heart to overflowing with joy
and gladness. There is no need to say that when I returned
home I was a different man.

Of course this wonderful blessing from God was only the
beginning. The Holy Ghost took me in hand and began to
purge out all the old teaching that I had received over
the past years and to set me free from the stiffness and
mortification of the dead-letter religion. The Holy Ghost
certainly knows his job and doesn't require any assistance
from us except that we yield ourselves to Him as clay in the
Potter's hands. Praise the Lord. I went through some very
dark experiences but the Lord brought me through. To God
be the glory. In the early part of 1956 we came to live at
Newark and hit another rough patch, but praise God, all
things work together for good to them that love God. [7]

Bob and Hilda lived temporarily with Norman and Olive on
the Derbyshire farm, while a flat above one of Henri's shops was
renovated for them. Later they moved into 31 Appleton Gate and
Bob became Henri's right-hand man, working full-time for the
Glory Way. This gave them the opportunity to produce the Glory
reel-to-reel tapes and the *Glory News* magazine, which Bob edited.

Hilda was regular pianist in many of the Glory meetings, bringing her unique rhythmic style to the praise and worship.

Joan Chadwick

Born and brought up in Stoke-on-Trent, Joan describes how in 1948 she gave her heart to the Lord in a Pentecostal meeting:

> What a wonderful experience it is to have Jesus as a real personal Saviour, and I do thank Him for the joy and peace with which He fills my soul. Hallelujah! After my first taste of the goodness of God in salvation, I went along fine until I began to feel the hardness of the way. It was then that doubts crept into my heart and I got into such a state of self-pity that I came to a standstill in my spiritual life. I found myself in a dilemma. The world had lost all its attraction as far as I was concerned but somehow I had lost the joy and blessing that salvation brings, and it seemed to hold very little for me. However, I cried unto God and asked Him to do something for me, and thanks be to God who giveth us the victory, He heard and answered my cry.

The answer to this heart cry was contact with the Glory Way. Henri and Connie came to Stafford and then took several meetings in Silverdale and Burslem, on the outskirts of Stoke-on-Trent. Joan went to them all. She followed this up with a visit to Newark.

> The Holy Ghost gave me such a wonderful blessing and it was then that I really understood what this glory was all about. Oh! Hallelujah. I'd never seen it like this before. Here were men and women, filled with the joy of the Lord, and daring to have a 'go' for Jesus. The love of God just flowed from their hearts. It was wonderful. I returned home full of gratitude to the Lord for ever leading me into this glory way. Thank God this is real – Christ in me the hope of glory, living out His own sweet life in me as I yield to Him every moment of the day. [8]

Henri was tireless in keeping in personal contact with many people. In a characteristic scrawled note to Joan, written in capitals with glory sparks bursting out of words, he wrote:

IT WAS GRAND TO MEET YOU LAST WEEK AT BURSLEM AND TO HEAR YOUR LOVELY TESTIMONY. KEEP TRUSTING IN JESUS, JOAN. LET HIM HAVE FULL CONTROL OF YOUR LIFE. JESUS IS WANTING REAL MEN AND REAL WOMEN IN THESE LAST DAYS, WHO WILL DARE TO GO ALL OUT FOR GOD! WE ARE PRAYING FOR YOU SO YOU JUST DARE TO LET GOD LOOSE IN YOU, AND TELL YOUR FRIENDS AND YOUR PALS ABOUT THIS WONDERFUL THRILLING GOSPEL! ASK THEM TO COME ON TO THIS WONDERFUL JOYRIDE BEFORE IT'S TOO LATE. TIME IS SHORT! IT'S LATER THAN YOU THINK. JESUS IS COMING SOON. GET BUSY FOR JESUS. THERE'S A GOOD LASS. ALL OUR LOVE IN JESUS.

No wonder God touched the hearts of many young people like Joan, showing them the Christian life as an adventure. Joan loved joining in the Mansfield Market open-air meetings, and in the many trips taking meetings around the country.

In 1958 she moved to Newark and for four years shared Gran Staples's cottage in Jallands Row, and worked in the town as a skilled seamstress. Of her time with Gran, Joan says:

Yes, it was a continuous stream of people; hectic but never dull. Gran never liked turning anyone away. We very often had to go elsewhere to sleep. One such time comes to mind. Henri put a bed up in a derelict cottage in Emminsons Row. (It was situated at the back of his shops.) The first time we slept there it felt strange, to say the least. But we finished up having a good laugh.

A few years after Olive Parsons went to be with the Lord Norman married another long-standing member of the Glory team, none other than Joan Chadwick.

Les and Joyce Walter

Like Connie, Roy and Violet, Joyce Hare was born and brought up in Mansfield. She was thirteen in 1952 when she got saved in the Brethren Gospel Hall where she also learnt the fundamentals of the faith:

In fact, I was sure that I was so rooted and grounded in the truth that nothing would shake me or ever make me think otherwise. I steered well clear of anything dubious. Praise God, I have realised since that all my preconceived ideas had to go whenever I opened up my heart to receive deeper truths. Hallelujah! In those early years ... I was always so stubborn, always weighing up things and treading so carefully...[9]

After a time Joyce discovered the Glory revival meetings in Mansfield Market.

As I was walking home from church through the Market I heard singing all around the streets, and it attracted me. The crowds gathered round; all sorts of people from all walks of life. The joy radiated from within those people on the van. It drew me and others like a big magnet; in my case it was a gradual process. Henri, having had this new anointing, ministered love, joy and peace in a vastly different way from what we were used to.

She added, 'Though I couldn't understand it, I had to admit it was very real, as I could feel the love of God emanating from their very beings!'[10]

Joyce had always been interested in opera which is why she was so strongly affected by the singing, particularly the ringing voices of Connie and Roy. She was so struck by the affect on the listeners when Connie sang, as she often did, 'It is no secret what God can do!' Many a night, when she lay awake, she could hear the singing going over in her mind.

Joyce started to go to the Glory meetings in Newark, and she was full of questions. Then bit by bit she found the Lord putting her through a loosening up process. With the grounding in the Word of God given her by the Brethren, she then went on to experience freedom in her spirit and to learn to stand on her own two feet.

What it means to be set gloriously free! Set free from sin first, then from the traditions of men which are like a rut or a routine that you're in, to be delivered from them so that you can enjoy freedom of expression from within for what God has done in you. That is the sort of freedom and liberty I mean. We young folk didn't like it when Henri got us out to the front to testify, and we thought it was crazy when he made us jump for Jesus, but he was doing it to set us free, and it worked. We also used to fall down in the Spirit, but not backwards; we went forwards on our faces in reverence and an attitude of worship.

I was cautious about the baptism in the Holy Ghost having been brought up in the Brethren. I'd got it all in my head, and I was very set in my ways, but then it dropped a foot lower into my heart and I began to relax and enter in. Eventually I was excommunicated from the Brethren who did not agree with this move of the Holy Spirit. They told me to either stay with them and behave myself or get out altogether. A scripture came to me, *'Come out from among them and be ye separate.'* But I hadn't quite got the nerve to, so they did it for me. I was trying to compromise: if I went to the Brethren I would try to be like them and if I went to the Glory meetings I was like them. It was a tremendous relief when they made the decision. I had been happy there at the start, but once I got used to the Glory I found I couldn't mix it.

As Joyce went on with the Lord she found that fellowship with the Glory folk was practical and had its very real satisfaction.

This is real and it works out daily in each of our lives. It incorporates a body ministry, whereby we all take part as the Holy Spirit moves us to share, to encourage one another in the faith to grow. We are set gloriously free from bondages and traditions of men. It's all in Jesus, the rock of our salvation. We all used to go out to the front a lot to be prayed for at Kings Road meetings in Newark, and we were always putting things right with one another and hugging; we always felt we had to put things right before we could get free in the scriptural way.

They came to prove that it was not only love, joy and peace that the folks needed then, but longsuffering too.

Oh, it's such a thrilling life to be going on with God and reaching out into the unknown realms of His being. 'Still praying, as I onward bound, Lord, plant my feet on higher ground!' [11]

The *Glory News* magazine did not start until 1956, so in the early days Henri used to get the young folk to write to their friends and various contacts. It was in this way that Joyce gained a pen friend down in Worthing by the name of Leslie Walter. He took the trouble to answer her many questions on the things of God. He belonged to the Apostolic Church and first came to Newark at Christmas 1952 joining in one of the Mansfield Market meetings where, amongst other people, he saw Joyce.

I did not make her acquaintance on this occasion, but soon after my return home to Worthing I received a glory letter from her. Apparently Henri had given her a number of addresses, among which was mine. From then on we continued to correspond on spiritual lines. In May 1953 we met each other for the first time, but the thought of courtship never entered our minds. However, as we continued writing to each other, our friendship grew deeper until we realised that we were in love with one another which resulted in our marriage in Mansfield.

Joyce describes it thus:

a friendship sprang up between us which later ripened to love. We believed that God had brought us together for a purpose, and, as we put the Lord first in our lives and prayed about it, He opened up the way for us to be united in marriage. [12]

This took place on 18th May 1957 and was the first Glory wedding. One of the cottages in Jallands Row was available for them and they quickly settled in there with other Glory folk as close neighbours. Like Gran Staples and others they had an open home and, over the years, had no end of folk, who came to the meetings stay with them for the night. Although many were people they didn't know, 'we just blended in as if we had known them years,' Joyce explained.

'Laughing Les,' as he was known, had what Henri called an infectious laugh and would set the whole place laughing with him. Both Les and Bob Nicholls were from the Apostolic Church, and initially it was Bob who told Les about the Glory meetings. As a result of contact with Henri and Connie, both men had a new experience of God, entering into 'the latter rain anointing'. The Lord brought them close together geographically too. As widely spaced as Worthing on the Sussex coast and Stafford in the west Midlands, both ended up in Newark, only a few doors from each other, both in property owned by Henri.

Jean Guiteri

One of the Air Force men whom Henri and Connie took to their assembly in Newark was an Italian, Luigi Guiteri. This was in 1947. A friend of Henri's had warned him not to see Lui because he was violent. This was a simple fact; Lui had a furious temper. He was a strong family man with six children. His wife had left him and he was filled with bitter resentment against her. Anyhow, Henri was not deterred from trying to speak to him. He invited him to come to an evangelistic meeting and with his invitation held out the carrot that there would be good singing. Lui was a fine Italian tenor and this attracted him, so he went. He heard the gospel there that evening and accepted Jesus Christ as his Saviour.

Not long after this Lui was demobilised from the RAF and took his family to Bristol. He had worked there before the War as a skilled craftsman in laying tiles. He now wanted to return and get his old job back, which he managed to do. For the time being he had his children cared for in one kind of a home or another. The eldest of them, Jean, was temporarily put in a Roman Catholic convent remand home. Then after some months he was able to get them all together again under his own roof. But life was extremely difficult for him; he was obviously very preoccupied with making a go of his new work and the children were a handful, particularly Jean who had developed into a real trouble maker. Gran Staples made the brave decision to shut up her little cottage in Emminsons Row and move down to Bristol to look after them. While Lui was in Newark he had often had a meal with Gran Staples; this is why she now felt a particular concern for him. She was not young and it was hard work. She was capable and a good manager; the younger children responded to her care, though Jean remained an undisciplined thorn in Gran's side. No one could tame her.

However, the situation took a sudden turn for the better when Jean accepted the Lord as her Saviour. Jean had what she calls 'a flighty friend', and she used to go around with her just to annoy Gran. But it so happened that there was an evangelistic campaign somewhere just south of Bristol. Gran invited Jean to one of the meetings but, little monkey that she was, she said she would not go unless Gran bought her a long coat of the kind then in fashion. She was aged sixteen. Anyhow, Gran took a deep breath and bought her the coat, and to the meeting both these worldly girls went. In his message the preacher threw out the challenge, 'It takes a man to be a Christian. You have to be tough! You're going to be really for it, as far as the world is concerned.' This really appealed to rebellious Jean and her friend. They walked out to the front, the only two in this big meeting. The extraordinary thing is that Jean was not saying sorry to God. She had no spirit of repentance. But she wanted to show others that she meant business. Really she wanted to shock other people, to prove to them that she could do the difficult, unpopular thing. For whatever reason, she came to the Lord, and He graciously accepted her. It was the turning point of her life.

In fact, that evening might have been her last. The two girls lived about fifteen minutes walk from each other. Jean saw her friend home first, and as she was making her way to her own home, she was knocked over by a vehicle and was very badly injured. The driver never stopped; he just carried on, leaving her unconscious on the kerb, looking like a crumpled bundle. Some men walking by thought she was some old woman who had somehow collapsed. They got her to hospital, and straight away she had 24 stitches in her head. The doctors found that her spine was badly hurt and that she was paralysed down one side. They said that she would never walk again. But she did!

In the meantime, Gran Staples kept looking after the family. Altogether, she was there in Bristol for three or four years. But finally the great effort she was making began to tell on her. She was ready to drop. So down from Newark came Connie to relieve her, and had a stint of about six weeks caring for them all.

Jean, recovering from the trauma of her accident, asked if she might go north to Newark and stay with Gran Staples. Having given her so much trouble in the past, she was now devoted to her. Back in her little cottage Gran recovered from the strain of the last four years and after a while she was able to send for Jean to join her. With her coming to Newark, this boisterous half-Italian, half-English, teenager found herself in the thick of Glory activity centred around Henri and Connie. She joined in with the free coming and going of enthusiastic visitors and the meetings held in various places. On one occasion, when Gran's house was full Jean was sent to sleep at Connie and Henri's.

While she was there two young airmen were invited for a meal. They were born again Christians and they were seeking to be filled with the Holy Spirit. Henri began to play and sing to these two lads, and he talked to them and exhorted them. They so much wanted to know more and there was a wonderful spirit between them. It was the power and presence of God with them all in that room. Now Jean was also with them at the table and

she sat there listening intently. Then all at once the Holy Spirit
fell on her. Nobody touched her. Connie continues,

> She started to speak in tongues as I couldn't begin to tell
> you, at the top of her voice. You could have heard her down
> the street. She didn't stop at all. I said, 'We've got to go to
> bed. It's midnight. Neighbours will be going mad!' They
> were in the cottages nearby. But if we got her upstairs to the
> third floor, then they wouldn't hear her. So we got her up to
> bed, and we were in the next bedroom. The hullabaloo
> continued. We couldn't get any sleep. Yet it was amazing
> because she started to prophesy. She'd never read the Bible.
> They weren't allowed to read the Bible in this convent
> where she'd been. I knew she didn't know the Scriptures
> naturally. Anyhow, she started to prophesy out of Isaiah
> like I haven't heard anybody in my life. And it went on all
> night; she couldn't stop. So I went in to see her and told
> her, 'Stick a handkerchief into your mouth or summat.' But
> that didn't stop her. She'd speak in tongues; then she'd go
> off and she would be prophesying, and I've never heard
> anybody prophesy so exact from Isaiah and the prophets.
> Henri said, 'She doesn't know any Scripture.' I answered, 'I
> know. Hark at her!' Henri asserted, 'That's the Holy Ghost.'
> God just took her over. It was really wonderful what
> happened. Changed! She was never the same again. She
> had been a black sheep. By guy, she was a right sheep after
> that. She had something very real, had Jean.

She went on to become a trusted member of the Glory family,
pulling her weight in the Glory team. In 1952–3 she helped with
the open-air meetings at Mansfield Market, and when they got
invitations to take meetings in and around Nottingham Jean was
one of the number. Back in Newark she became involved in the
day-to-day life of the Glory folk in Jallands Row and the shops in
Appleton Gate. When in time the *Glory News* magazine was
brought out Jean took her turn at typing fair copies of articles.
In 1957 she married Jock, the tough boxer who had stood up
for Henri and Connie in the early days of the Mansfield Market
open-air meetings, and was consequently saved. This was where
she had first been attracted to him. Her friends warned her, 'He's
a rum character. He'll find a fight anywhere.' She replied that she
didn't care because she loved him. Connie reflected that Jean
'was a similar nature and dynamite.'

CONNIE AND HENRI

HENRI

CONNIE AND HENRI

CONNIE

HENRI'S SHOPS

LIFTING UP. THE WRONG MAN (SANTA)

MANSFIELD MARKET GLORY BUS

MANSFIELD MARKET OPEN-AIR MEETINGS

SOME OF THE CROWDS

GRAN STAPLES AND JANIE MARSHALL

SALLY AND ERIC BILLS

ROY, OLIVE AND MINNIE FRIDAY IN THE BEACON HILL OFFICE

PEARL DRYHURST

HENRI'S BROTHER ERIC

HENRI'S GLORY GIRLS CONNIE, OLIVE, BETTY, MARGARET, JEAN, MAVIS, HILDA, AND GLADYS

NEWARK AMBULANCE HALL

HORACE & WINNIE REDFERN MANSFIELD MARKET CONVERTS

ROY AND BETTY HOLLINGWORTH

LAUGHING LES AND JANIE

WILLIAM & GRAN STAPLES, HENRI AND HIS SISTER AGNES AT THEIR COTTAGE NEXT TO THE BALDERTON SIGNAL BOX

HENRI'S DAD WILLIAM

ROY AND GYDA SWEDISH INTERPRETER

BOBBY PASTOR ALWIN AND LEONARD

GLYN GREENOW

LEN AND GWYN
400 MILES FOR A MEETING

SISTER SMITH, AGNES AND JANIE

JEAN GUITERI

GROUP IN JALLANDS ROW FROM TOP LEFT
RAY HUBBARD, PEARL, JOAN, HENRI, MIRIAM,
LES DACRE, CECIL MORRIS, JOYCE, GRAN, LES,
PICCOLO PETE, COLIN BLACK

OH THE JOY

LEFT VICTOR AND CECIL STEWART, SIMON
CAMERON, DAVID GREENOW FAR RIGHT SAM
STEWART TAKEN AT A GLORY CRUSADE IN N.I.

HENRY ARCHER

BOB NICHOLLS AND THE TAPE MINISTRY

JANIE, CONNIE, HENRI, ALBERT, ROSE AND AGNES

ARCHIE FRIDAY

CHRIS, VERA, CONNIE AND RON

BOB AND HILDA NICHOLLS

ARTHUR BURT GIVES FORTH AT THE TECHNICAL COLLEGE NEWARK

THE GLORY ROOM
ABOVE HENRI'S SHOPS

Chris and Connie Wingfield

Chris was born and brought up in Scunthorpe in north Lincoln-shire. His parents were godly people. Chris recalls how close his mother was to the Lord. His father was one of twenty-six founder members of the Elim church in Scunthorpe. (He had fought in the First World War and had been wounded seven times, with pieces of shrapnel left in his body.) Pentecostal pioneers like Harold Horton and Donald Gee came to stay in their home.

There was no Elim Sunday School, so Chris was sent to a Methodist one, and it was in the Methodist church in the town that he was saved when a certain Pastor Broadbent from Cliff College spoke on the 'Burden Bearer'. He gave an appeal and Chris responded.

Scunthorpe is a steel town and during the war it was surrounded by anti-aircraft defensive gunsites. Young Chris used to cycle around on his bike and preach in the town, and particularly at these gunsites. He was also a Crusader leader, teaching boys in the top class, up to the age of fourteen. The blessing of the Lord came down on them. Chris remembers when one boy, moved on by the Holy Spirit, started spontaneously speaking in tongues. He was also involved in a separate children's work on weekdays and it was then that he met his future wife, Connie. (Having two Connies in the Glory Way has been slightly confusing!) That was in 1943.

Connie was musical, and at this time composed a chorus, *I met Jesus at the cross roads*, which was published in the Elim chorus book. In fact, this chorus went world-wide. She was invited to join John Woodhead's Revival Party, to play the piano for him when Elim took over a church in Southport. Chris went there at that time during his annual week's holiday to do the loud-speaker announcements for them. He worked as a door-to-door salesman and was promoted to be a branch manager at Newark in 1950 where he met Henri. They became close friends, and Chris very much enjoyed going to the Mansfield Market open-air meetings.

On one occasion they were packing everything away at the end of the meeting when they found that there was a flat tyre on the Gospel caravan. Chris took the wheel off and went to see if he could get it repaired. He found a taxi garage open. It was about midnight and all they could do was to inflate the tyre. Chris fitted it back on the caravan, and Henri was heard to say, 'Keep it up, Lord, until we get home.' On arrival at Newark, Henri pulled into the yard where the caravan was parked. When they unhitched it from the car, the tyre immediately went down. Connie (Henri's wife) said to him with a merry laugh, 'Well, you only asked the Lord to keep it up until we got home!'

Chris and his wife were caught up in the sudden expansion of the Glory Way in the many meetings up and down the country. He bought a Volkswagen Caravette and away they went to the Isle of Wight, London, Bradford, Leeds, Southend-on-Sea, Basildon, Thorpe Hesley, Lincoln, west to Wales and way up north to Peterhead. Connie played the piano for some meetings and also arranged some of the choruses printed in the *Glory News*.

When in Newark they had people to stay with them many weekends and particularly at Convention times. Soon after they moved to Newark their son was taken ill. They asked Henri if he would come and pray for him, which he did. After this, they sat having a cup of tea together in front of the fire. Characteristically, Henri exclaimed, 'Let's have a victory cup of tea!'

Chris was a Branch Manager of the company that he worked for and covered a wide area around Newark. He often called to see Henri and Connie when they were living in their caravan in their *Glory Field* at Little Carlton. One afternoon he called and all was quiet at their Gospel caravan. He was just getting into his car to leave, when Henri suddenly appeared at the door and invited him inside. They had a very good time waiting on the Lord. And so Chris had discovered one of Henri's secret places where he got alone with God.

During the nineties Chris has been largely responsible for leading the Saturday evening meetings at Fiskerton chapel. During this time he and Connie have weathered great personal discouragements, particularly when their daughter Sharon, wife of a young Spanish pastor in Majorca and mother of five, was tragically killed in a road accident.

Ron and Vera Wray

Ron was born and brought up in Hull, and it was just after the end of the War, on 14 April 1946, that he gave his life over to Jesus and was born again. He says that when he came out of the little mission hall that Sunday night he really danced with joy in the main shopping area of Hull. For him, dancing with joy was to be an oft-repeated experience.

It so happened that in his early months as a Christian, Ron mixed with some wonderful men of God who helped and encouraged him and steered him along the way. He felt the need to study the Bible and really get to grips with it, so he decided to become a student at the Assemblies of God Bible school at Hampstead, London. Soon after finishing his studies there he met Vera. She came from a good sound Christian background; her parents loved the Lord and sent her from a very young age to the Primitive Methodist Chapel in the village where they lived. Vera accepted Jesus as her Saviour in June 1945. Her father and mother were very hospitable. From her childhood years and long afterwards she remembers how they had open house to many a visiting evangelist and preacher.

While Ron and Vera were courting, they took meetings on a regular basis at a mission in Hull. They got married on 1 April 1950 and attended the Assemblies of God church in Hull for ten years. It was towards the end of these ten years that things began to change, and in a big way, too. There were five elderly people, members of this church for many years, who could vividly remember the things that happened in George Jeffreys's meetings. In short, they were used to meetings full of the Holy Ghost, and they were seeking for more than what they were experiencing at that time in their assembly. Vera and Ron were happy there and thought they were having lively fellowship. However, these five old folks knew differently. Moreover, they had been going to a number of meetings at Newark, and usually after the Sunday morning or evening service they would tell Ron and Vera what a wonderful time they had been having at the Glory meeting in Newark the day before.

One of the elders of the church was a man called Sidney Broughton. He was born in 1905, and still at the age of 95 rides his bicycle to several meetings a week. Ron and he took a train to Newark in December 1959 to find out for themselves what these meetings were like. It was snowy weather as they travelled there and made their way to Henri's shops and the Glory Office. They first met Bob Nicholls and Pearl Dryhurst. Bob explained how Henri would be seeing to the closing of the shops (as this was Saturday tea-time) and would then come to see them. Ron remembers how excited he felt at the thought of meeting with this man who encountered God in such a remarkable way. Eventually Henri arrived, and on seeing him and the greeting he gave them they knew immediately that this man was different. You knew something must have happened to him. He invited them to his flat and Connie gave them tea and biscuits. All the while Henri was talking to them about Jesus and what had happened to him. It was thrilling.

After talking to them for some time he opened his Bible and began to read John's Gospel chapter fifteen to them, dwelling particularly on verse sixteen. With tears streaming down his cheeks and kneeling down in front of them, he said he would pray for them. He laid his hands on each of them and prayed that they would be set free. He prayed thus: 'Brother, in the Name of Jesus I set you free!' And Ron exploded with a shout and says that he has never been the same since!

They were also invited to have tea at Gran Staples's cottage. They knocked at her door and were invited in. The first man they spoke to was Eric Bills. He had a radiant smile and greeted them with love and affection. They left Newark rather late that same night, boarding the train complete with a reel-to-reel tape recorder and tapes to listen to, which proved very useful in the days to follow. On arriving home in Hull in the early hours of the morning, Ron knocked on the door and Vera, on opening it, felt the impact of this wonderful sense of freedom in the Spirit. They both laughed so much and felt the excitement of this brand new experience with God. Henri told them to go back to their church, which they did, but found this wonderful liberty difficult to contain. They felt restricted and had to find a new direction, which meant in due time that they started having meetings in Hull. From a handful of people, about seven of them, the meetings grew until they had a congregation of 120.

Henri encouraged Ron to join the enthusiastic band which travelled up and down the country to hold meetings. They went to many places: Wales, Belfast, Peterhead and elsewhere in Scotland, the Isle of Wight, Southend-on-Sea, Blackpool, Leeds, Bradford, Thorpe Hesley (north of Sheffield), Willesden Revival Centre and elsewhere in London, and so many more. They would arrive home at four or five in the morning with a happy tiredness. Ron says,

> What precious times, what sweet memories! The joy that dear Henri manifested and the love which you felt issuing from this lovely man of God was just wonderful. What an experience to see him minister to all the needy people in any meeting. He was so in tune with the Holy Spirit. To know him and to be with him on so many occasions was to know joy unspeakable and full of glory.

On the level of simple friendship, Henri used to come over to Hull from time to time and Ron would help him to buy a boat.

They went around by car on various errands, and Vera and Ron had Henri and Connie to a meal from time to time. Once in Scarborough, Henri and Ron were contacted by a Christian brother called George from Fraserburgh, who had a trawler. He invited them to go for a night's fishing. They had to hang around for a few days until the weather was right, and then off they went. The conditions may have been pretty normal for George, but for ordinary land mortals like Ron and Henri the sea was still horribly rough. In fact, it was a terrifying experience. Clad in their sou'westers, Henri and Ron clung to the rail. They went green, and were very seasick. In fact, the fishing boat was a drifter. It simply bobbed up and down; it did not steam along under way. One moment they would be on a level with the next boat. Then up they would sweep and they would be poised thirty feet above the other boat. But only for a moment, and then the swell would give way from under them. Down they would swoop and their companion boat would be thirty feet above them!

After some time Ron and Vera left Hull and moved to Great Driffield in East Riding, Yorkshire, where Ron has practised as an osteopath and homeopathic doctor. Down the years until the present, Ron has played his part in the ministry of the meetings in Fiskerton chapel, as has Roland Steeper from Scunthorpe. The two men and their wives Vera and Josie forged a particular friendship, and Josie, as it happens is also the sister of Connie Wingfield.

Albert and Rose Chapman

When he was in the army at the end of the War, Albert found that he was under great conviction from the Holy Spirit to get right with God. He sent away for a New Testament, and as he read it he used to quake at the judgements of God, particularly those in the Book of Revelation. He was discharged from the army and started working in Mansfield. At this time he used to listen to Radio Monte Carlo, particularly to an American programme on a Thursday night at 11 pm. Then he would kneel down by his bed because he wanted salvation. He was searching, and he used to go from one church to another.

It so happened that Albert's parents were friendly with Janie and Albert Marshall, Connie's mum and dad. In fact, they had known one another for years. Both his father and her father worked for the Fire Service, in the days when fire engines had solid rubber tyres. The four of them enjoyed going to firemen's dances, where Janie would be the life and soul of the party. After she was saved, Albert's parents would joke with her if they met her in the market, 'Are you coming for a drink?' With a twinkle in her eye, she would reply, 'I don't need what's in that bottle!'

Albert was employed by Mansfield council as a driver of bulldozers and tractors. It was his job at 8 pm on a Saturday evening to drive a Ferguson tractor, pulling long six-wheel trailers which were then loaded up with market stalls and their equipment. He would then drive them a quarter of a mile away to the Cattlemarket. In this way he became aware of the activity of the market place. Albert describes what happened one evening:

> I first saw this dapper little man accompanied by his wife on Mansfield Market. Finding a small place cleared of garbage, he set up his desk and lamp, put on his accordion and began to play gospel songs, singing along with his wife. Happy and joyful in their singing, they soon attracted a small crowd of people. But there was something so different about the music and songs. What it was I didn't know then, but now I know Who it was, the Spirit of the Lord! The year was 1950 and I learnt this man with his wife were Con and Henri Staples, a man with vision, love and compassion for the lost, prepared to pay the cost in his life to win souls to the Lord.

There on Mansfield Market the miners were crowding around them. Albert listened intently to Henri and Connie and found that they were saying exactly the same thing as the Christian broadcasters on Radio Monte Carlo. That encouraged him. About this time too, he went to the Gospel Mission (the building built by Connie's dad and Mr Brown) and listened to an elderly man preaching about breaking up the fallow ground. This made a great impression on him.

In the summer of 1952 Albert had a riverbank maintenance job. He and other workmen had to make a firm barrier to a stretch of the River Trent and back-fill it with earth to prevent flood water from wearing it away. By coincidence, this was at Fiskerton, downstream from the village, two or three hundred yards from Riverside Bungalow, the eventual home of Henri and Connie. One glorious summer's day, on an off-duty moment, Albert drove out there with his parents. They parked the car and stretched their legs. He says,

Moving away from them I became aware of singing somewhere faintly, then a little louder, but so sweet and filling
the air all around. Within me came an urge, a desire, a
longing to be where the singing came from. Time, people
and places didn't seem to matter any more. Then I realised
this beautiful sound was coming from a boat moving on the
river. How I longed to join them as it passed by. Oh for a
pair of wings, I thought. These people were singing something so different from the current songs of the day. I heard
words of heaven, joy, love and peace in their singing. An
accordion playing, laughter and arms waving. It was a
wonderful unforgettable experience. Later I learnt it was
Con and Henri with some of the Glory folk singing on his
boat to the people on the river banks. The Holy Spirit came
that day and reached out to where I was.

Three weeks later (it was 19 August 1952) Albert was once again
standing amongst the crowds on Mansfield Market. There was
Henri, not with desk and lamp, but with their elegant Glory van,
which he called a Soul Clinic. A couple of people were singing:

In loving kindness Jesus came
My soul in mercy to reclaim . . .
   From sinking sand He lifted me;
   With tender hand He lifted me;
   From shades of night to plains of light,
   Oh, praise His name, He lifted me!

Once again, it was Spirit-filled singing which struck home to
Albert's heart. He so desperately wanted to get right with God. At
the end of the meeting Henri gave an invitation, asking if any
one there wanted to give their heart to the Lord Jesus, and if so to
put up their hand. Albert put up both his hands and came
forward, making himself known to them. He put his trust in the
Lord. It was a joy for Connie to speak with him, because of
the long-standing friendships of their parents. Then Albert was
introduced to the group of young people: Betty, Roy and his
brother Steve, Norman, Olive, Violet and others. Soon after this
he received a letter from Henri, who encouraged him characteristically with, 'You're born again. You're a son of God. Go flat out
for Jesus. We haven't got much time left!'
   Albert continued to go to the Gospel Mission and in September 1953, at a meeting when Peter Scothern was preaching, he

sought the baptism of the Holy Spirit. Scothern invited him and
another brother into the vestry. He was very patient with them,
laying his hands on both of them and saying, 'Don't do or say
anything.' After some time of quiet waiting on the Lord Albert
began to speak in tongues. At this moment he heard the Lord
speaking with an audible voice, 'My gifts are without repentance'
(are irrevocable: Romans 11:29).

A year later Henri and Connie were taking a meeting in the
same Gospel Mission and Albert was there. It was packed to
capacity. Henri began singing his favourite chorus, 'Here we are
again', encouraging the people to praise the Lord. 'Now close
your eyes,' he said, 'and ask the blessing and presence of the Lord
to come amongst us.' Albert recalled,

> As I closed my eyes there came before me a head with black
> hair and I saw a pair of hands holding a ring or crown of
> thorns and lowering it onto the head with much pressure.
> The thorns protruded in every direction, piercing the brow
> and the temples. Blood flowed freely down the face from
> the wounds and scratches. 'The thorns were four inches
> long, with the ends strong and needle-like,' said the Holy
> Spirit to me. I wept and wept as I thought on what I had
> just seen.

Some time after, that same year, Albert was employed in
laying a new sewage system in a village. An elderly man who
lived there frequently came to monitor the work and Albert got
to know him. One day he gave Albert some magazines to read. In
the centre pages of one was a photo and description of the type of
thorn tree from which a crown was made for the Lord. It stated
that the thorns were four inches long, strong and very sharp.
Then Albert had this to add:

> There came a day when I went to hear a visiting minister at
> a small local church speak on the hands that placed the
> crown of thorns on the Lord's head. He explained how
> the Roman soldier's hands were symbolic of all sinners'
> hands. God included all, for all have sinned and come short
> of the glory of God, everyone without exception. This was a
> revelation to me. Up till then I had considered the soldier's
> actions were entirely his own and had no spiritual signific-
> ance, but to demean and ridicule the Lord in front of
> others.

Albert had married after he was demobilised from the Army. But when he gave his heart to the Lord and was saved, his wife left him. 'She was a bad lot,' Albert said. On Boxing Day of that year (1952) he stood by the kitchen sink and he heard again, as it were, an audible voice saying, *'My grace is sufficient for thee: for My strength is made perfect in weakness'* (2 Corinthians 12:9). His wife did not want anything to do with the gospel, and after some time they were divorced.

Janie and her husband always made Albert very welcome at their home. Janie had known that he was seeking the Lord and she prayed him into the kingdom. She pointed out to him that he also must have been an answer to the prayers of his grandparents (on his father's side) who loved and followed the Lord. His father, when young, had made a profession of conversion. His two sisters, however, remained unbelievers. He used to go to the Marshalls' home most nights of the week. Young Roy Turner often used to pop in there too. They did not waste time on chit chat, but straight away they would get their Bibles out and start talking about the Lord. On Wednesdays and Sundays they had meetings. On one occasion, Albert arrived half-an-hour late. They were singing a hymn when he arrived. Suddenly the music stopped and Janie, who always called a spade a spade, said, 'Now, my lad, we start at 7 pm. The Lord was always on time and you must be so too!' It was a stern lesson which Albert never forgot. Some years later he got to know a brother who was editor of the magazine *Midnight Cry*, who gave him the unexpected compliment, 'You're a time-keeping man!'

Janie's husband took a Bible class of young men in the chapel at Empire Street. He was a faithful teacher, and was always known by the nickname of Sir Crow. He would emphasise accountability to God and say, 'Remember, you must give account of your stewardship.' Certainly, those who came under the influence of the Marshall household had good upbringing as children of the Lord. Strange little things stick in Albert's mind. Janie used to use an old-fashioned carving knife, which was getting very worn. So he decided to surprise her with a present of a super new modern serrated saw knife. Actually Janie was more than a bit puzzled by this. The upshot of it was that some days later he saw her straightening the edge of the lawn with his nice new knife! It was in the Marshall home that Albert met his Rose and after some time, in 1966, they were married. They have one daughter, Sharon.

Quite some years later, Henri and Connie with one or two friends used to visit the hospital in Mansfield on a Tuesday evening. They would sing to the patients and help to settle them down for the night. Albert began to go along and help them. They certainly got to know a good number of Mansfield people in this way. One evening, Albert came to the bed of an elderly lady, who gave him a wry wink. 'You don't know who I am?' she asked. It was Janie!

Going back to those friendships which Albert made with the other young Glory people, off they would go in their bus to Cleethorpes, Barnsley, Lancaster and north Yorkshire. The meetings at Thorpe Hesley, north of Sheffield, particularly stick in his mind. For about seven years there they were given a warm welcome by Jack and Claris Witham. Often Bob Nicholls would lead the meeting with Roy Turner as the chief musician. Then there were the Glory holidays on the Isle of Wight and elsewhere when Albert and Rose had hilarious times of fellowship. Albert remembers how they had such a happy relationship with Henri and Connie and everyone.

Some years later, in 1972, Albert worked at a colliery and one morning he was quietly waiting at seven o'clock for the siren to blow to start work, when the sound of music and singing filled the air around, so clear and plain. He felt the presence of the Lord with him, with peace and joy in his heart. 'Truly this is straight from heaven,' he thought. The words and music were sung over and over again. 'And now,' he said, 'I was singing the same words and music from my innermost being. Truly amazing. This was by the Holy Spirit.' Albert hurried to find pencil and paper as this angelic singing continued. He did not want to miss one word. He found a railwaggon weight ticket and began to write as he listened to the words around and within him:

> Behold My hands and see My feet,
> Do not doubt or faithless be,
> The mocking robe and crown of thorns
> Was not My own but worn for thee.

> *And when you stand before My Throne*
> *I'll see the Blood and claim My own.*
> *I shed My Blood and gave My all,*
> *Poured out love to ransom thee.*
> *Be washed today, My Word doth say,*
> *In the Blood of Calvary.*

As for the tune, he was scared of forgetting it and kept singing it all day. When he got home he played it on his accordion and recorded it on a tape. A little later, Hilda Nicholls arranged it for the piano. This chorus was soon sung at Thorpe Hesley and then at other Glory meetings. Albert also had a niece in the United States who had the words and music published.

Chapter 5

Wider Horizons

The New Jerusalem

I n weaving together all the strands that make up the Glory Way, we should step aside for a moment and look at a Christian group that settled in the area in the 1930s. These were the Faith Home people who lived at Farnsfield, a village half way between Newark and Mansfield. This was the headquarters of the Ceylon Pentecostal Mission, a large organisation led by a dynamic Indian evangelist, Pastor Alwin. He had the responsibility of directing no less than three thousand national full-time workers, Tamils and Sinhalese, in Ceylon (Sri Lanka) and India and also in Malaya (Malaysia). Altogether there were two hundred Faith Homes, the majority of them being in these three countries; and then in the west there were five in France, three in Britain and one in the United States. They were a very earnest and zealous band and attracted to their ranks folk who were determined to be all out for God, 'sold out for God,' or as Oswald Chambers expressed it, 'My utmost for His highest'.

In the outworking of their personal Christian lives the Faith Home people were faced with an oft-encountered spiritual problem. In aiming to be spiritual athletes, in trying always to tread with hinds' feet upon God's high mountain ranges, there is the continual danger of falling into legalism, of being bound by a set of almost unattainable rules. This is a paradox, because in a sense this kind of bondage is the last thing a true child of God expects to experience. *'If the Son therefore shall make you free, ye shall be free indeed'* (John 8:36). David Willows, Henri's nephew, was involved with the Faith Home for a good number of years when he was young. He described how their tight-knit fellowship gave him a great sense of security, of being cared for. This meant a lot to him because he had lost his mother as a young child. (She was Henri's sister Agnes.) But he found that the community stifled his initiative. He never had to make major decisions, as these were made for him. Furthermore, they believed in being *'eunuchs for the kingdom of heaven's sake'* (Matthew 19:12). Workers were not supposed to marry workers. The Faith Home also had unusual teaching on the expectancy of the return of Jesus Christ as described in 1 Thessalonians 4:16–18:

> *For the Lord Himself shall descend from heaven with a shout, with the voice of the archangel, and with the trump of God: and the dead in Christ shall rise first: then we which are alive and remain shall be caught up together with them in the clouds, to meet the Lord in the air: and so shall we ever be with the Lord.*

The leaders of the Faith Home taught that only those who 'love His appearing' (2 Timothy 4:1), only those who actively look for the 'glorious appearing' (Titus 2:13), only those whose faith has been truly tried and found praiseworthy (1 Peter 1:7) would qualify to be caught up in the air. The spiritually sleepy, unaware, complacent, will be left behind. It is the difference between being a wise or a foolish virgin (Matthew 25:1–13). Obviously, these dynamic exhortations of Jesus and His apostles are desperately relevant and true, but the danger lies in taking one's eyes off the counterbalancing truth of the finished work of Jesus Christ on the cross and in the rest and heart's ease of the knowledge and full assurance of salvation. Spiritual anxiety creeps in. As David Willows says,

> You were saved by grace, but you never really knew if you were going to make it to the Rapture. You were always living by works and so you were trying to attain to attain. The Faith Home people said, 'If we are wrong we haven't hurt anybody, because with this teaching people have lived holier lives.' That might be all right in one way. But in actual practice this teaching resulted in a lack of joy. It was a condemnatory ministry.

In contrast to this, on the positive side, the Faith Home people had a strong vision of the New Jerusalem. It was fresh and new, with the dew of heaven upon it; even overwhelming, ecstatic. The apostle John in Revelation 21:2 describes how he saw *'the holy city, new Jerusalem, coming down from God out of heaven, prepared as a bride adorned for her husband.'* There was an old lady in India, a very godly woman, who had a vision of this. God gave it to her. She saw it all so vividly. It was all so wonderful, marvellous, miraculous. She said, 'I've tried to tell you about it as I saw it, but really I don't think words will ever describe it.' She was at pains to emphasise that this New Jerusalem will not be at all like the Jerusalem that already exists. It will come down from God out of heaven, a golden city, of gold like clear glass, with walls of jasper, with its twelve foundations of precious stones and its gates of pearl, a city intensely beautiful and full of light (Revelation 2:10–21).

This visionary Indian lady then went on to say how God will prepare a people to fit this remarkable place. He will purify them and bring them up to His peerless standard. He will put sparkling shoes on their feet and dress them in shining, glistening clothes. They will go up to meet the Lord and He will come out to meet them. In fact, He will catch them up in heavenly embrace. This is the privilege of those who have received the Holy Spirit. What is more, they are chosen of God. Jesus said, *'Ye have not chosen Me, but I have chosen you'* (John 15:16).

In about 1948 Janie Marshall invited some of the Faith Home folk from Farnsfield over to her house in Mansfield to have a meeting. Henri and Connie were there; Henri was playing the piano. The main speaker was the head of the mission, Pastor Alwin. With him was an English missionary called Leonard Boon, who had worked with him out in India and had been his secretary. On this occasion, Pastor Alwin was led of the Lord to speak on the New Jerusalem. He spoke of the godly old lady's vision; he just poured it all out. Leonard also spoke along these lines. Henri was absolutely stunned by what they had to say. He was fascinated by this Indian brother; he could not leave him and talked to him for hours. That was it. He caught the vision of the New Jerusalem. He was not the same for days. He could not sleep for a week. He said, 'I can't get it out of my mind. It's marvellous, what he was saying. It's doing summat to me. I don't know what it is, but it's doing summat.' David Willows says that the impact of the New Jerusalem vision absolutely revolutionised Henri's life. Janie Marshall put it this way: that as Pastor Alwin 'described the wonders of that city, God so moved upon Henri that he determined in his heart, there and then, by God's grace, that he would reach that heavenly goal – Mount Zion – which cannot be moved but abideth for ever.' [1]

Meantime, Pastor Alwin went away to London and promised to come back. Henri sat at their bedroom window and watched the street for hours for his car returning, because he wanted him to pray for him. Henri said, 'He's got summat and I want it!' Eventually he arrived. Now Pastor Alwin had really taken to Henri, and he saw the potential in him. He wanted him to go back to India or Ceylon with him.

When Henri asked him to pray for him, Pastor Alwin replied, 'It's no good my praying for you for God to give you power, unless you are willing to use it.' By this he meant that Henri and Connie should sell up business, house and home and go out to India with him.

Henri dug his heels in. He said, 'I can't go that way. I've too much here.'

Pastor Alwin became emphatic, 'Give it all up for God. You'll find that God will make greater everything you've got.'

Henri answered back, 'I've heard that one before and I've seen folks giving up things for God and they've been left flat out. No go!' When Henri questioned Connie, she felt strongly the same way. She replied,

> No way. I'm not drawn to go abroad, because when I first started out with God – when He started to work with us two – He gave me the scripture, *'You are not sent to a people of a strange speech and of a hard language'* (Ezekiel 3:5). That was for me. God gave me that scripture and I thought, 'That's it. I'm not called to go to a foreign country.'

Anyhow, Pastor Alwin prayed for Henri, but he did not receive any blessing or power from it; nothing which satisfied his hunger for God. Looking back, Henri and Connie could see the hand of God in this, for when Henri received a real anointing it was something which came directly from heaven without the intervention of any person.

In 1948 or the next year the Ceylon Pentecostal Mission moved their Faith Home from Farnsfield to Newark. Henri made a house available for them in Emminsons Row, which backed onto Jallands Row. The missionary Leonard Boon contacted a friend of his, Leslie Bray, who was a pastor in London, and invited him and his wife Dorothy to come north to Newark and look after everyone in this house and lead the work. The Faith Home stayed there in Emminsons Row until about 1954 and then moved to a much larger building, not far away in

Lombard Street. They were based there until the late sixties, and then finally made their headquarters in Nottingham.

As can be imagined, once Henri and Connie had helped the Faith Home to move into Emminsons Row, they were keen to go to their meetings. But very soon, however, they found that there was a striking difference between them and the initial time when Pastor Alwin rhapsodised about the New Jerusalem. That occasion was full of joy, while these others were not. So for some years they had a very mixed experience with the Faith Home people. They went intermittently to their meetings and Pastor Alwin himself would visit from time to time. They had fellowship with him and thought, yes maybe, that this was going to be the place where they would worship. But there was always some element there which held them back from throwing in their lot with them. There was something in their teaching that Henri and Connie could not go with. They could not witness with it.

To illustrate this, Henri, once when he was meeting with them, sat on a broken chair and it nipped his bottom! He was told, 'Don't mend it. You have to accept things like that. Don't make them any better. To do otherwise is sin.'

That really got him mad. 'Rubbish!' said practical Henri. 'Give me that hammer. I've been born after the Creator and that Creator is in me and I'll create summat!'

The police in the Police Station opposite used to say to Henri, 'Hey, what's that strange noise we hear at nights?'

Henri replied, 'Oh, they're a group from India. But I can't explain to you.'

The point was that they were on their knees for hours and hours saying the same thing. The Glory folk just could not go along with it.

Without any doubt, to have the Faith Home as near neighbours created a certain tension. They were a spiritual challenge. The whole question came up again, for Henri and Connie, of throwing their lot in with them. They wanted Henri to sell up everything and give it to the work, for you were not supposed to have anything. One day Pastor Alwin came to see Henri and asked,

'Are you coming over to us? Because if you are, I want to take you straight back to India.'

Henri replied, 'I'll think about it, brother.'

So he thought about it and did not say anything to Connie. When Alwin later pressed him again, Henri clearly replied,

No! God's told me to preach the gospel on my own door-step in my own shops. That's what I'm going to do. You needn't fret about it. You needn't be sorry about it. Just thank God that one Englishman has got something real. I'm going to go and witness all over the place.

Connie for her part said to Alwin, 'How can I give everything up? Look at all the lodgers I've got. I just can't walk out.'

She reflected later, 'I can thank God we were never trapped. We could have been. God steered us away from it.'

The Faith Home fellowship, then, were a formative influence on the Glory folk. They brought an inspiring vision, that of the New Jerusalem, and they brought a testing challenge. The Lord used them to sort out Henri and Connie's priorities and calling. *'Iron sharpeneth iron; so a man sharpeneth the countenance of his friend'* (Proverbs 27:17).

The events recounted here were spread out over a good number of years. Returning to that meeting in Janie Marshall's house, it is very interesting to note how Janie herself, in thankfulness to the Lord, had this to say:

In those early days we could never have realised the great work God was planning when He united my daughter Connie and Henri in marriage. It was only as time went by that the Lord's purpose began to unfold. One night when Henri and Connie ... were gathered with us for fellowship, the Holy Ghost moved in a powerful way. A coloured brother who was present received a wonderful revelation and began to unfold the mysteries of the Second Coming and the glories of the New Jerusalem ... That night the Holy Ghost made a great impression upon Henri's soul and spirit and thus the seed was sown, which was to grow into a mighty harvest. A short time afterwards, God gave Henri this wonderful glory anointing and sent him forth to blaze the trail for a mighty revival. Together with Connie he has been faithful to the heavenly vision. Bless the Lord! [2]

David Willows

Mention has been made of David, the son of George Willows and Agnes, the young sister of Henri. George was an engineer drafts-man with a flair for building design; he helped to draw up the plans for the building of the Assembly of God church in Sherwood Avenue, Newark. For a while he was part of the fellowship of this assembly. Later he joined with the Exclusive Brethren. As we have seen, Agnes died tragically only a matter of a few weeks after David was born.

At the age of sixteen David left the Exclusive Brethren and joined the Ceylon Pentecostal Mission's Faith Home in Newark, where he did useful training. After two years he began full-time ministry with them. He had around him the influence of godly men. Also he experienced a direct anointing from the Lord – a tremendous experience, he says – which never left him. Altogether he stayed with the Faith Home until he was twenty-two, so he was with them during his formative years, where he learnt much which was to help in his future ministry.

At some point in his seventeenth year he spent six weeks with the Glory people. In fact, Gran Staples kept a watchful eye on David and fasted on his behalf, as she questioned whether he should be at the Faith Home.

As might be imagined, Henri made his own unique impact on David's life. As a young man he went round to see his uncle. David recalls,

> He sat with me and talked to me for about three hours. The main gist of what I remember him telling me was about reconciliation – yes, reconciliation, not a ministry of condemnation. That was something that got hold of me and really was what set me free, changing my direction. As described already, the Ceylon Pentecostal Mission had some odd practices, like making nearly all the decisions of what you should or should not do. I don't mean they were totally wrong, I mean that it held you. If you came out of it you were made to feel that you were like the man who was looking back after he had put his hand to the plough, and so was not fit for the kingdom of God. You would no longer be a worker with them. Because of that there was pressure put on me not to leave.
>
> So when I came out of the Faith Home I had to start making decisions again. I found this very difficult. Bob Nicholls was a great help. Also Henri ministered a tremendous amount into my life at that time.

Just after leaving the Faith Home David went to Peterhead, travelling there with Ron Wray and enjoying the warm fellowship of everyone. Around this time he joined the Glory move at Newark and began travelling around with the Glory teams.

Since those days he has ministered around this country and different parts of the world as an evangelist, spreading the message of new life in Jesus, with a very real anointing of love, joy and praise. Henri had prayed this very thing for him.

David and his wife Dorcas live near Northallerton in North Yorkshire and are part of the leadership of Hollybush Fellowship, the dynamic Christian Centre run by Jim and Cynthia Wilkinson.

Another member of the Staples family who loves and serves the Lord is Margaret the daughter of Eric, Henri's brother, and therefore David's first cousin. A trained nurse, she has worked for a good many years in South Africa. Back in Newark she is a member of the Assemblies of God fellowship in Sherwood Avenue. Her sister Julia and her husband live in Rutland and attend the Quakers' meeting; while their brother Philip and his wife Helen have a large cycle shop in Newark as his father and uncle before him.

Grace and Mercy

With the weekly routine of running a row of shops and taking weekend open-air meetings in Mansfield Market, Henri and Connie were quick to follow up any contacts which came to hand. They recognised any conversation at the shop counter, any note through the post, any answer to a ringing phone as a possible opportunity for extending the kingdom of God. They strove to make themselves available *'for the Master's use, and prepared unto every good work'* (2 Timothy 2:21).

Mr and Mrs Peacock
A man who came into the radio shop one day asked Henri if he would visit his parents in Sleaford, a market town about twenty miles away in south Lincolnshire. He explained that they were getting on in years and that his dad was ill. So Henri and Connie drove there, carefully eking out their rationed petrol. They came to a terrace of houses with a large field beyond them to one side. They knocked on the door of the end house and were given a welcome by the elderly couple, Mr and Mrs Peacock. The old lady sat in a rocking chair, and her husband was by her side, distinctive with a neat white pointed beard. They were a lovely couple; little old folk, spotlessly clean. Their life had not been at

all easy, as the husband had been an invalid for years, and his wife took in washing to make ends meet. She also now suffered from arthritis. But she was something of a comedienne; she would say the most ordinary normal things and then give them a funny twist and everyone would end up in stitches.

Henri talked to her, saying, 'I've come to pray for you Ma, and I've come to tell you about Jesus. And you can get born again and it'll help you.'

They had never heard anything like that before. The old lady sat there listening hard, rocking herself. Then she said, 'I'm going to make a cup of tea. Everybody has to have a cup of tea before they go.'

Henri replied, 'All right Ma. Listen to what I'm saying.'

'Yes, I'm listening.'

He did not know whether she was or not, but she reached up to a corner cupboard to get down a packet of tea and told him, 'Keep talking, Henri.' So he kept talking.

Then, when she took the packet of tea she threw her hands up in the air, crying, 'Say that again.' He repeated it, and she said, 'I've got it. I've got it. I know what you mean. We're not born again, but we're going to be!' She said it just like that, out of the blue, and her face was lit up.

As they drank their cup of tea they talked to the elderly couple. And soon Mrs Peacock was able to say, 'He's saved me, just me.'

Her husband professed salvation too. They were just like children, so simple. Then she asked Henri to pray for her arthritic hands. She was having a problem lifting the tea pot up and carrying it to the sink.

He prayed for her and added, 'Now Ma, when the pain comes on, just start praising the Lord, will you? It'll help.' That was the first of many visits.

When they returned the next week, Henri asked, 'Are you praising the Lord, Ma?'

She replied, 'Yes, it does come in handy!'

As she said this, she was sitting in her rocking chair. She suddenly exclaimed, 'Come here!' At this she grabbed Henri, put him on her knee and rocked him backwards and forwards. Then she continued,

> What do you think has happened, Henri? I says to Dad, 'What Henri's telling us is real and it's true. I tell you Dad, there's summat more we haven't got.' We went to bed

that night, Henri, I knew something had happened to me. In that field at the side of our house there were crowds of people. I saw Jesus coming and I saw all these people going up, but we weren't going up. I says to Dad, 'Wake up, wake up, Jesus is coming and we're not going. There must be something we don't know yet.' Henri, we've got to get nearer to Him, else we shan't go, shall we?

Connie remembers, 'She really got this fear of God and yet it was the beginning of her blessing with the Lord. It set the place going. You've never heard anything like it. And her face was lit up.'

From then on, Henri and Connie used to go to this cottage in Sleaford every Tuesday evening for quite some time. There was always a wonderful welcome. They invited other people; often Henri and Connie brought a car-load of people over from Newark. The sense of the power and presence of God in that little cottage was terrific. They praised and prayed; people were delivered from oppressions and depressions. The evening always ended with Henri asking Mr Peacock to 'Close in prayer, brother,' and he, sitting by the fire, without fail quoted 'Lead, kindly Light, amid the encircling gloom,' right through to the end.

Once, when Henri and Connie drove a car-load of young people over, a policeman stopped them and asked, 'Well, what have you got in there, then?'

'Oh, it's all right,' Henri replied, 'we're on the King's business. We're going to Sleaford.'

The policeman was a little rattled. 'King's business? What business? You're not supposed to travel like this. You know that! You've got about six or seven folks in here. It shouldn't hold them.'

'I know I have,' Henri replied disarmingly, 'but we're just going to cheer up an old lady and her husband.'

The policeman shrugged his shoulders, smiled and waved them on.

In the course of these cottage meetings they had a strange experience. Shortly after the Lord had saved and so blessed Mrs Peacock a district nurse in her late twenties came to a meeting. She was the daughter of a Pentecostal pastor in Bridgwater in Somerset, and she had been recently widowed; her young husband had died of tuberculosis. The old lady was talking to her before the meeting started, and she sensed there was something spiritually wrong with her. She challenged her, saying that she was not like Henri and Connie and the others. She felt she was not genuine. The nurse protested that she was, that she was a true Christian. But the fact of the matter was that she was harbouring an intense root of bitterness against God for the early death of her husband.

When the meeting got under way, the joy and power and liberty that they had enjoyed there disappeared. The little gathering laboured under a great spirit of heaviness. The heavens were like brass. They could not get through to God. Henri said, 'I don't know what's happening. This has got to be broken.' He did not connect this with the visiting nurse. No one knew her or anything about her. Henri told everyone to get down on their knees and sing a hymn about the Blood of Jesus. This restored a certain degree of liberty.

A little later, the nurse acted in an odd way when she invited to a meal about six men whom Henri and Connie had brought over from Newark. She pointedly did not want any of the women. She also asked Henri to stay the night, which he did but with Connie most certainly with him and they were both very glad to get away after breakfast. Furthermore, at another of the meetings at the Peacocks, when again the heavens were as brass, Connie burst out in an impassioned prayer to the Lord. Unbeknown to Connie the nurse stood up behind her, raised her hands with the obvious intention of hitting her hard on the head. Suddenly she thought better of it and rushed out of the room.

The cottage meeting group earnestly prayed that God would take her away from the area; and in a short while she left for South Africa. Two or three years later the Glory folk had a large praise meeting in Cheltenham Town Hall. As they were clearing everything away afterwards a lone woman stayed behind, waiting for them. It was the Sleaford district nurse. She told with some feeling how in South Africa the Lord really sorted her out. She had to get right with Him, and she was now on her way to somewhere in the Americas as a medical missionary. In her travels, she happened to go briefly to Cheltenham and saw this Glory meeting advertised. She said she simply had to see Henri and Connie to apologise with all her heart for the trouble she had given them. She had to put things right. This opportunity was clearly of God, she said. Of course, they willingly forgave her, and were most moved that the Lord in turn had so moved in her heart. They, too, clearly saw His hand in this turn of events.

It hardly need be pointed out that one person out of the will of God can wreck a meeting. It only takes one person who is badly out of sorts with God to block the very blessing of heaven. The presence of Jonah on board the ship bound for Tarshish brought a storm. When they threw him overboard there was a calm.

George and Mary Robinson

It is a wonderful thing when people in their last illness and on their deathbed have a sense of overwhelming certainty that they are bound for heaven; that when they die they are going to be gladly welcomed by the Lord Jesus. It is not wishful thinking; it is something beyond doubt, beyond dispute. At the end of John Bunyan's *Pilgrim's Progress*, Mr Standfast says:

> I am going now to see that Head that was crowned with thorns, and that Face that was spit upon for me. I ... shall be with him in whose company I delight myself.

In the open-air witness on Mansfield Market, Connie's singing voice was carried over the rooftops to the ears of George and Mary Robinson on the Ravensdale housing estate, a considerable distance away. They heard the singing and were drawn to a saving knowledge of Jesus. Over a time they became real friends of Henri and Connie. They were a couple with honest and good hearts.

They once went over to see their daughter Doreen at Blidworth, a few miles south east of Mansfield. George had some things in his car that he had picked up to give to Henri. They were continuing their journey to Newark, bringing these things over, when George said, 'I don't feel too good, Mary.' He just had time to pull the car over into a lay-by when he died at her side, of a heart attack. It was obviously a great shock to her.

After all this, Mary then went to Blidworth, where she lived next door to her daughter. Henri and Connie went over to see her and pray with her, and then about a year later they went to see her again. Meantime, she had contracted a tumour on the brain. She was ever so poorly and in awful pain; in fact, she was clearly dying. And yet she had the most amazing joy, the true joy of the Lord. She was fantastic.

When they arrived, her daughter was weeping. She said, 'We can't understand our Mum. She keeps saying, "I'm ready. I'm longing to meet Him."'

Henri said to Mary, 'Now then, ma duck, what is it?'

She replied, 'I'm just waiting to go, Henri. They don't know what they're missing.'

Doreen broke in, 'Mum, don't talk like that.'

Her mother reassured her, 'Doreen, you've not to cry. I've never felt so happy in my life. I don't want to stay here. Although you're my daughter, I don't want to stay.'

'Mum! Mum!' Doreen cried, 'Don't! We don't want to lose you.'

Mary said, 'You don't know what you're talking about. If you saw what I saw and felt like I felt, you'd be longing to go. Don't worry about me. Don't fret over me. Doreen, you don't know what you're missing. I'm going to be with the Lord and it's wonderful. I want to go now, this minute.'

A Derbyshire Farm

In April 1951 Henri and Connie had an interesting weekend in Derbyshire's Dovedale, at Biggin near Hartington, as guests of the farmer and his wife where Norman and Olive worked. As mentioned, they had a particular link with the farm because the farmer's wife was a friend of Connie's brother. While they were staying there they took a meeting. The farmer's wife also asked them to go to see a neighbouring farm. The family there were very concerned about their son who had some disability, and they wanted very much for Henri to pray for him. This second farmer was not a believer, but his wife was and she wanted Henri to talk to her husband about the Lord. She said, 'If Henri talks to him he will be saved.' This farmer was a very friendly and sincere man and he really took to Henri. They talked together about the farm and various problems on it, concerning the cattle and one or two fields. There was one particular field which was unproductive. They would sow it, but it produced a miserable harvest. So the farmer asked Henri to pray for it and God gave a wonderful answer to prayer. Next year they had a bumper crop. This really spoke to the farmer. In fact, the field continued with wonderful harvests year after year.

Now it so happens that a young Italian called Bruno helped on the farm. He had been a prisoner of war, and after returning to Italy he had come back again to this farm for further training and experience. While he was there in Derbyshire he had to leave his wife and family behind in Italy. His English was not very good; he could just about get by with the language. Also, he was a Roman Catholic. However, he listened very hard to the conversation at the table. Henri and Connie were talking about the Lord and what it meant to be a Christian, and he was drinking it all in.

One morning, however, at breakfast, he looked sad. Henri asked, 'Now then, why are you looking down, my lad?' Bruno explained in his broken English how he always got a letter from home once a week. Now two weeks had passed and he had not received one. He was longing for a word from his wife and was very worried. Henri was most concerned and replied, 'Right, my lad, we'll take it to the Lord.' And they prayed about it. When they had gone to bed that night, God gave Bruno a vision. He described how an angel stood at the foot of his bed. The angel raised his hand and told him not to worry. 'Everything's all right.' He felt such a peace and fell into a deep sleep.

Well, the next morning, as Connie describes it, 'there was such a hullabaloo!' It was Bruno. He'd got a letter and he was jumping up and down. The amazing thing is that he became a true believer at the same time! All at once he said, 'Me want salvation. Me want to get saved. Me want this.' No doubt he had had an intense longing in his heart to be right with God. There he had been, quietly sitting at the meal table listening to every word that Henri and Connie had been sharing. Now he suddenly came out in the open, and he was wonderfully saved and born again. God changed him. He really had 'summat real'. And he wanted to tell others about the Lord. He said with feeling, 'Me go back home after my time here and me never forget what I've got here!'

What happy conversations they had with Bruno. Once Henri said, 'Come on, let's go through the garden and have a talk.' He and Connie walked with him down the garden path and out into a field. There were some cows grazing there. Then they came to a pasture with a bull. Henri and Connie were not at all bothered by it and simply walked calmly on. Bruno went pale and looked agitated.

Henri asked, 'Well, what's the matter with you?'

Bruno stuttered, 'It's a bull. We shouldn't be here. It's ferocious.'

Henri and Connie did not look all that worried. They had taken the animal for granted and not realised it was a bull. Now that they did know, they still did not turn a hair. Bruno was amazed at their fearless calm behaviour. God spoke to him through this experience, too. 'When God's with you,' said Connie, 'it makes a witness, doesn't it?'

Bristol

Towards the end of the time when Gran Staples was in Bristol, looking after Lui Guiteri's children, Henri and Connie went for the weekend. It was not long after Henri had experienced his anointing and filling with the Holy Spirit.

Gran had said, 'I wish you'd come to Bristol, Henri, and pay us a visit. There's a little Pentecostal fellowship. The pastor there is very free. He's a Holy Ghost man and he lets the meetings go in a measure. I'm sure you could do him some good.'

Lui's house was full, what with his six children and Gran. But there was room in a nearby Bible college. The pastor of the Assemblies of God fellowship in Newark knew the staff there and asked if Henri and Connie could stay there; they were only too happy to let them, though Henri and Connie on their part felt reluctant. This sixth sense they had about the place was vindicated when they found jealousies and tensions amongst the teachers and those who ran it. They felt a strange atmosphere there, as though 'there was something trapped,' said Connie, 'which couldn't get released.'

What a relief it was on the Sunday morning to get to the Pentecostal meeting with Lui and his six children and Gran. What immediate liberty they felt. The pastor was full of life and such a genuine person. The Spirit of God was on him. Once the meeting had got going he warmly invited Henri to speak. 'Come on, brother Henri,' he said, 'Get up here and tell them what God has done amongst you and is still doing.' Soon the power of God fell on the meeting. There was a woman with very bad arthritis. She was a nice old lady, an old Pentecostal, and there she was sitting in the front row. Well, she shot into the air, crying, 'I'm healed!' The power of God was electric.

After the meeting the pastor pleaded, 'Henri, you say you've only come for the weekend. Don't rush away. This is God. I know the Holy Ghost and I know a Holy Ghost man when I see one. Do stop longer.'

'Brother,' answered Henri, 'I've never taken over a meeting myself. We haven't got that far yet. We just minister to folks round about us and go in the open air.'

The pastor persisted, 'Can you start?'

'Well,' Henri said, 'I can try. I like the accordion, you see.'

So the pastor got one for him and he and Connie stayed on ten days, taking about another thirteen meetings. Things really happened. The place was packed. Several people were saved. Some of the students from the Bible college came and got filled with the Holy Spirit. This brought friction with the college; after a few meetings the staff prevented the students coming.

At the end of the series, Lui Guiteri was over the moon. 'Oh, Henri,' he said, 'I wish you'd stop down here.'

'Well,', he replied, 'I simply can't. I'm tied up with the business at the moment. Anyway, God is working up there. If I can, I'll come again.'

And so it turned out. Henri and Connie travelled back to Bristol a second time for more meetings, and they took Betty and Roy Hollingworth with them. On this occasion they stayed with a landlady only a few doors away from Lui, Gran and the family.

One day Lui said to Henri, 'I've got a pal down the road. He's bed-ridden and ever so poorly. He's a Christian. Would you come and pray for him?'

'Of course we will,' Henri replied.

They went in, trooped up the stairs and came round the bed. Now there was another man already there.

The patient introduced them, 'This is an elder from an Assemblies of God church. He's come to pray.'

Henri greeted him, shook hands with him and said, 'Well, we'll pray then. Will you pray, brother?'

They all shut their eyes and there was dead silence. So Henri asked him again, 'Would you pray openly for our sick brother, and we'll be with you?'

Sometimes we catch a glimpse of God's sense of humour. This fellow walked over to the window, opened it and prayed openly out into the air outside! The others could not believe it, and were in stitches. Roy and Connie somehow managed to creep out of the room, down the stairs and out in to the street, where they just exploded with laughter and giggles. They did not know what to do with themselves.

That night when they all went to bed they just could not stop laughing. An almost desperate spirit of heavenly Holy Ghost laughter was on them. The whole incident just seemed so unbearably funny. There was only a thin partition between the two rooms where they slept. For a little while there would be silence for a bit and they would try to get some sleep. Then all at once Roy would burst out laughing again. He would set off Betty. Then Henri would catch it. Then Connie. They laughed themselves silly. As for the patient, the prayer must have done him some real good; he seemed to be a lot better. *'A merry heart doeth good like a medicine'* (Proverbs 17:22).

Growth of a Fellowship

'Henri was led of the Spirit,' Connie said of her husband. 'I never knew of anybody that acted on being led of the Spirit like him.' And so it was. Whether on their home ground in Newark and Mansfield or further afield, God led Henri and Connie on from step to step. They were at the Master's beck and call, 'ready for every good work.'

To take one example – a rather unusual one – when Henri was leading a meeting he would often find that God showed him what to do in the palms of his hands supernaturally; the anointing came on his hands and somehow he was led by the Spirit to call people out of the congregation to be prayed for and set free.

There are always many people who need to hear the gospel of Jesus, who need to hear the truth in terms that are meaningful to them. There was ample room for the Glory Way to expand and bring the message of joy, salvation and deliverance to Notting-hamshire, the Midlands and then further afield. Henri took his little team of spiritual shock troops wherever the Holy Spirit directed!

Certainly there were folk scattered around the country who were hungering and thirsting for this kind of ministry. Pearl Dryhurst in Birmingham, for instance, tells how she had been praying for some time, 'Lord, please show me if there is true revival happening anywhere. If so, please put me right in the middle of it, so I can be part of it!' She was so hungry for more of God, but she did not really know what she wanted. One day she was invited to hear a Glory tape, in the old reel-to-reel days. 'Whatever's that?' she wondered. Directly she heard it, she knew, 'That's it. That's what I've been looking for!' There and then she determined somehow to get to Newark. Out of the blue someone sent her a leaflet about Glory meetings with their address. Even now she does not know who sent it to her. So she got there; God met her desire. Years later, looking back she recalled the intense hunger that drove her on to find the Glory Way, or rather the hunger that drew her.

A young man doing his military service caught sight of a *Glory News* in 1956. Laurie James was a young Christian, enthusiastic, searching for more. This magazine made a deep impression on him. 'Here appeared people who were enjoying being Christians. Something in me quickened when I read of dancing and joyful praise and saw pictures of happy faces, tambourines and so on.'

In the early 1950s invitations started coming in for Henri and Connie to take meetings here and there. They fitted these in as best they could around the demands of the shops and the week-end meetings at Mansfield. By the later 1950s, about every alternate Saturday, the Glory Way would fill up a coach, driven by Norman Parsons or Eric Staples, Henri's younger brother, and take off for another town, often at quite a distance. Henri called this 'blazing the trail!' They went to places as far afield as West Auckland on the Pennine edge of County Durham, Bolton and Manchester over in Lancashire, the spa town of Cheltenham in Gloucestershire and Brixton in London's south bank. They had meetings at Evesham in its fruitful vale, at Banbury in the north of the Cotswolds, at Kettering and Irchester in Northamptonshire and Baldock in Hertfordshire, eastwards in that fine medieval city of Norwich, at flowery Spalding in the heart of the Fens, at Scunthorpe and the port of Hull on the Humber, at Stafford, Uttoxeter, Derby and twisty-spired Chesterfield in the north Midlands, at Thorpe Hesley just north of Sheffield, and at Huddersfield, Bradford and Leeds, the hub of the old West Riding of Yorkshire. In particular, many were their calls north to Bradford and south to the Northamptonshire Midlands, to Irchester.

It is not only footballers and sports teams that enjoy a sense of camaraderie by travelling to a distant town. The Glory folk felt banded together as the Lord's shock troops, with their praising exuberance and joyful faith, daring to be Daniels and getting back home to Newark at two in the morning. 'An important feature of Henri's meetings,' Joyce Walter adds, 'was the display-ing of banners which he used to put up beforehand such as, 'You will feel better for coming here,' 'Jerusalem Joy,' 'Praise the Lord for goodness sake,' as well as the large stars that bore the words LOVE, JOY, PEACE, HEALTH. Strings of coloured flags festooned the walls to make everything look as cheerful as possible. If Billy Butlin could do it in his holiday camps, so could Henri. He had some sayings which he said over and over again. You could never forget them:

> You'll never be the same again (his favourite).
> Fill up and feel the difference.
>   (He likened the meetings to filling stations.)
> This gospel works.
> It's more infectious than diphtheria.
> God has no favourites.

It's in you brother, it's in you sister.
  (Christ in you the hope of glory.)
You'll feel better for coming here.
You can't mix it.
Get right with God: it's later than you think!

The Glory folk had a number of meeting places in Newark itself. At the very beginning, people met together in Henri and Connie's kitchen at the back of their flat to talk about the Lord. In those days they were involved with the Faith Home, but before long they realised that they were not in agreement with them. At that point they decided to knock two upstairs rooms together in their flat above two of the shops. This was known as the Glory Room. In the early days, they sometimes had people sleeping there. They met to fast and pray there. Strangely, at that time they did not read the Bible together. 'In most of the meetings there,' Betty Hollingworth says, 'we would cry the whole way through.' Connie comments,

> There was a bond of love which made everyone want to be together. The movement was born in tears, they didn't know why, but when they gathered together they began to weep. It was then that they experienced having all things in common when they passed round the only hanky to wipe their eyes on. God was laying the foundations of a work that would bring thousands into the joy of the Lord!

Jean Tourle, formerly Guiteri, recalls how folk would come into the Glory Room, sit down on the floor and get straight onto their knees. When Henri came in he would shut the door and not let anyone in. He realised that they needed concentration and must not be disturbed. (As mentioned before, when left to himself he would hide away in the airing cupboard.)

The Glory Room was also a place of energetic praise and rejoicing, as nephew David Willows found when he stayed with Gran Staples. Gladys Black dryly comments, 'When everyone started dancing people used to wonder how the glass in the windows stayed in; there was such a vibration.' And she adds interestingly, 'Henri had a sign which said *Soul Clinic* at the bottom of the stairs, and many a soul was stirred in those meetings.'

People really crowded into the flat and the Glory Room. Connie said, 'Talk about, "If I be lifted up, I will draw all men unto Me".' As they lifted up Jesus in their talking and singing, folk came, cramming into their home and sitting all the way down the stairs. Before long they needed a bigger place and they were able to hire a wooden Ambulance Hut nearby, which they used for their Sunday afternoon meetings. National Serviceman Laurie James remembers how he found it one Sunday in September 1956, as he broke his train journey between Edinburgh and London:

> Arriving in Newark, it seemed a quiet place. Wandering around I saw a Salvation Army couple and asked if they knew where the Glory meetings were. They instructed me to carry on down this road, passing several shops which had Henri's name over, and behind a brick wall on my left I would hear them. Sure enough, behind the brick wall, I could hear the singing. It was the Ambulance Hut where the early meetings took place. I was rather a nervous person then, and it took me a great deal of courage to enter the hall, for it was indeed rather noisy, but having come all that way I was determined. So in I went. It was a happy, joyful fellowship, totally different from anything I had ever seen. I never knew who Henri was, so assumed he was there. In fact, he was away ministering and it was Bob Nicholls leading, but I was not aware of any individuals at this time. There were about a hundred people there, including a few coloured people who, I believe, came over from Nottingham. I was never the same again. Something had been born in me and to this day that joy, which was imparted to me when Bob and others prayed for me, wells up within.

Once again the Ambulance Hut became too small, and when they were wondering where to go next their attention was drawn to a large Victorian gothic hall in Kings Road. Initially, Henri was reluctant to take it, but he had contact with one of the bosses of the Power Station who greeted him: 'I say Henri, we've got this place for a recreation hall for Staythorpe Social Club. We don't want them to have it on a Sunday, because they're rowdy. This hall has been a chapel and I've got a bit of respect for the place. Would you take it? And we shan't charge anything.' So Henri took it, sharing the building with the social club. Laurie James remembers helping Eric on Sunday mornings preparing the hall, and this included opening the windows to let the beer smell out!

They used this hall until 1967. Eventually, the club wanted the hall on a Sunday afternoon, so Henri had to look round for somewhere else. He hired a very large room over three corner shops opposite Newark Hospital. Both the Saturday evening and Sunday afternoon meetings were transferred there. It was for their exclusive use. However, it was much smaller than the Kings Road Hall. Laurie James says, 'Personally, I feel it was not a good move and Newark meetings were never quite the same after that to me. The peak days at Newark were whilst at Kings Road.'

Bob Nicholls went ahead with the support of the Glory Folk at Newark and found a disused chapel on Beacon Hill, on the eastern outskirts of the town. He was convinced that the Glory Way needed a more permanent meeting place. Henri never liked the thought of being pinned down by property; his passion was for evangelism, that people would be touched by God and take the Glory back to their local church. (Like the Wycliffe Bible Translator, Joe Boot, fresh from his Brazilian tribe, who exclaimed to me with some passion, 'I've done with building-centred Christianity!')

Anyhow, all the fellowship countrywide raised funds together and bought Beacon Hill Chapel. Violet Cowling comments,

> When people get set free, especially when they've been in other churches, they've got to have somewhere to go. Beacon Hill was derelict when they got it, and the members went in and did it up.

It was thoroughly cleaned and decorated, and eventually they got central heating and chairs. It was finished by the end of June 1969 in time for the reception of the wedding of Bob and Hilda's daughter Anne to Roy Turner. (The marriage ceremony itself took place in the church of the Anglican vicar Charles Widdowson, well known in the town for his Pentecostal witness.)

Bob's method of leading the meetings was quite different from Henri's. God does not mean our personalities to be stereo-typed, however charismatic and worthy of imitation a particular leader may be. Bob usually led when Henri was away, which was quite often. His wife Hilda, still at the Beacon Hill Chapel, was a great blessing. She was musically gifted, and she flowed in the Spirit.

As the Glory meetings were becoming more widely known, folk were prepared to come considerable distances on special occasions to enjoy fellowship together. Laurie James comments:

However, throughout this period, it was the early August Bank Holiday Convention, held for a number of years in Newark Technical College over the bank holiday weekend, that really drew the crowds to Newark. Visitors were boarded out in guest houses and caravans. There must have been several hundred visitors to these. Usually on the Monday morning there would be a baptismal service in the River Trent alongside the castle. Henri would be in the water in his trunks and numerous people were baptised, much to the interest and amazement of passers by.

David Willows, Henri's nephew, has a boyhood memory of one of the early conventions. A group of Glory folk were marching round the Friary Gardens. After this an open-air meeting was held in the village of Farndon, a mile or two west of Newark. They took the gospel van, opened it up and there was preaching and singing. This was so characteristic of Glory meetings at that time; the spontaneous impetus for outreach. 'It was absolutely life-changing,' David says with conviction, 'no doubt about that!' And that was it, dynamic spiritual life.

In a *Glory News*, Dorothy McBroom of Armagh wrote: 'If there is anyone who sometimes wonders if there is a God or not, the advice I would give you is, Go to Henri's in Newark and you won't be in any doubt after that. Praise God. Amen.'[3]

Chapter 6

Rhythm and Song

Joyful Jamaicans

After the end of the Second World War, West Indians began to travel eastwards across the Atlantic to Britain. The first ship, *Windrush*, arrived in 1948, full of adventurous Caribbeans bent on making good in Britain. There was no shortage of work, quite the reverse; so much in war-torn Europe needed building up again. So it was that Jamaicans came to Nottingham.

The first contact which they had with the Glory folk was on Mansfield Market. A Jamaican called Tom was greatly blessed through the testimonies of Hilda and Olive. He told his wife Linnette about it; she in turn was thrilled at the prospect of coming along. The next week it so happened that Henri and Connie held a meeting in the Nottingham Ice Stadium and followed it by a large gathering in the open air.

During the open-air meeting Henri was led by the Spirit to call Linnette onto the van to testify. The Spirit fell on her in a very wonderful way and for the first time in her life she danced in the Spirit right off the van, singing, 'Get the Glory! Sing and shout and testify,' dancing for sheer joy. [1] No one was more surprised than Linnette, for she had been brought up in a denomination which was calm.

When many Jamaicans came to England they found it hard to find a spiritual home. Their expansive extrovert personalities felt bottled up, damped down. When those who had come to Nottingham heard that there was a good Pentecostal gathering in Newark, they swarmed over, like bees to a honeypot. One of these, young Tommy Smith, wrote,

It was a happy day when a Jamaican friend told me that he had found a Pentecostal church at Newark that was different, for I went over there at my first opportunity and ... I met a man who through the grace of God is distributing the hidden treasures of salvation. [2]

Lindo Hall said that when he came to a Glory meeting 'it was like stumbling upon a goldfield, it was so precious.' [3]

Una Royes said that when she arrived in England she was disappointed in all the churches she attended, 'for I had been used to red-hot Pentecostal meetings.' But when her husband told her about Henri's meetings she could not believe it was true. [4] Dorrell Williams even moved from Nottingham to Newark to be close to the Glory folk. He said,

No longer do I miss the fellowship in Jamaica, for I have found just the same liberty and blessing in Henri's glory meetings ... There is a real spiritual lighthouse at Newark, and you will get some of this 'glory light' in your soul ... The fellowship here is so sweet I just cannot live without it. [5]

So the West Indians came and they brought their choruses with them. It was a great enrichment. The Glory folk were already singing choruses of the old Pentecostal and evangelical heritage, such as 'Victory! Victory! Blessed blood-bought victory!' and 'Give me oil in my lamp, keep me burning!' The Jamaicans now added, 'Cry out and shout! Praise the Lord!' and 'I shall have a new name in that land,' and many more. They were very rhythmic, having a distinctive Caribbean lilt, derived from their ancestral Africa, the continent of rhythm. Henri and Connie welcomed them and their music with open arms. The Jamaicans brought their tambourines and they swayed as they sang. It was hard to know who were more glad: the Glory folk to find that they were not alone in their particular enthusiasm, or the Jamaicans to find that there were people of a like spirit in Britain.

It was about the moment the Jamaicans came that the Glory folk started dancing in the Spirit. It was a question of the chicken and the egg. Connie remembers,

We'd never seen anybody dancing then, moving – like – with the rhythm. Then the Jamaicans came. One Sunday they were there. There was a great big Jamaican lady. She was about this size! (She indicated with her hands.) I'll never forget it. We were singing and she'd got both hands up and she gets into the middle of the aisle and she danced down the middle of that aisle on her heels. Her weight! And she danced and she danced right round the place, and others joined her. Then we started this marching round, the Glory march. It was fantastic. The Spirit of God was so wonderful. The Jamaicans had never ever danced in the Spirit before they came. They said, 'Well, the American missionaries came to us. They were all right, but this is different.' And, before you knew where they were, they were off dancing. They were falling down on the floor, weeping and laughing. They couldn't understand it. They were singing, they were getting right with God, they were being saved and getting filled with the Spirit. We all started to dance after that. We couldn't help it. It just got a hold of you. You know how it is. Very unusual. It had never been heard or seen. Other people thought we were crackers, naturally.

Altogether, the meetings flowed in a wonderful way. Unmistakably they were anointed. They were packed out with people. Musicians came: pianists, guitar players, banjo, accordion, drums. It was a touch of God. It just drew people. There was a family from Barnsley, the Races, who brought their young son Gerald. Mrs Race used to say, 'Do you know, as soon as we get within half a mile of the meeting place, we have to run to get here. There's something draws us like that!'

Two Songsters

'Not only did God anoint us,' Connie explained, 'He brought the tools and He brought the gifts, and it was different. Actually, we didn't understand what was happening to us.' True revival nearly always brings with it a burst of new Christian music. So it was with the Glory Way.

Sally Bills

Two Londoners, Eric and Sally Bills, happily married and full of fun and go, moved up to a village, Stanton-under-Bardon, just outside Leicester. Sally said,

It seemed so dead after city life, so I determined to wake it up with my idea of life. It was not long before I was a noted character in the village and was known as the life of the party. One night in April 1955, however, instead of the usual piano-playing in the local pub, I stayed at home. With a packet of cigarettes by my side and curled up on the settee, I anticipated a night's entertainment on the TV. Instead of the usual shows there was a relay of Billy Graham's Glasgow Crusade and, having read so much about this man in the press, I made up my mind to listen to what he had to say. As he spoke about sin and man's need of a Saviour, the realisation suddenly dawned on me that I was a sinner. I'd never given it a thought before ... I thought I was all right and on my way to heaven. As I realised my lost condition, I found myself weeping. I had never worshipped anything other than myself and what money could buy.

Sally explained how the Lord was working on her heart and directed her steps to the local chapel,

where, for the first time in my life, I heard folk praying from their hearts instead of a prayer book ... There, like a weary, beaten and lonely soul, I walked in, knowing that I needed Christ more than anything else in the world.

The understanding pastor led her to the Lord, and she was saved and knew it. Back home she tried to explain to Eric about God and what had happened to her, but her husband did not want to know. A very unhappy year followed, in which Sally was in danger of neglecting Eric in her zeal to go to meetings. She became church-minded. Then about this time she happened to read a copy of the *Glory News* and this drew her like a magnet to Newark. Amongst the Glory folk the joy of her salvation was restored. Home again she still could not get through to Eric. This led to a crisis and a real test of her faith. He asked her to leave him. She left, but after four days she received a letter asking her to return. She did, and now Eric was willing to listen to her, and 'accepted Jesus in to his heart there and then.' Sally exclaimed,

Oh, the joy that flooded my soul ... We are united in Jesus and our home is a real love home, and we are enjoying this full and free salvation, and we are led by the Spirit of God. [6]

Before long, Sally was invited by Henri to join the musicians as everyone praised the Lord. It was a wonderful experience for her to find herself surrounded by tambourine-playing, dancing Glory people. How rhythmically the Jamaicans moved as they sang. What a joyful shout of praise together. Sally's fingers flew up and down the keyboard of the piano. No longer was she now playing to the clink of beer mugs but to the glory of God. Good practice in the pub had now led to performance in paradise. Now the joy of the Lord was her strength and her expertise.

Then, to her surprise, words and melodies of her own came to her and she was enriching the Glory meetings with her own compositions. She began with,

> *Some folk may ask me, some folk may say,*
> *Who is this Jesus you talk about every day?*
> *...He is my everything, He is my all...*

This was followed by,

> *Blessed Holy Spirit searching me through,*
> *Let the fire burn in me.*

Most memorable was the way she took the Apostle Paul's affirmation in Galatians 2:20 and turned it into,

> *It is no longer I that liveth,*
> *But Christ that liveth in me.*

In this, as in a Schubert song, the words and melody flow beautifully together.

Roy Turner

In the late 1950s there was a young journalist working in Mansfield called Roy Turner. He was born in nearby Sutton-in-Ashfield and came from a very musical family. He had a cousin who was a child prodigy on the piano, and another cousin who was a professional singer. Roy sang in his school choir and always felt that he had some music within himself that was bursting for expression. In a Methodist church he received the Lord Jesus Christ as his Saviour, and was baptised in the Holy Spirit in a Pentecostal church.

One of the senior reporters with the newspaper Roy worked on at Mansfield was a Baptist. He was sent to report on a Glory Rally at the Co-op Hall in Mansfield. He came back and threw a couple of *Glory News* on Roy's desk, saying, 'You've had an

HE IS MY EVERYTHING

Composed by SALLY BILLS

Arranged by CONNIE WINGFIELD

Some folk may ask me some folk may say . . . . Who is this Je - sus . . . you talk about ev - 'ry day? He is my Sav-iour, . . . He set me free, . . . So listen while I tell you . . . what He means to me, . . . He is my ev - 'rything . . He is my all . . . . . He is my ev-'rything . . both great and small, ... He makes my life complete, . . makes ev'rything new, . . . He is my ev-'rything, . . . but how about you ? . . . . . .

N.B.—All single notes in bass to be played as octaves.

Copyright 1960

experience. These might suit you.' For Roy, the effect was electrifying. He said:

> I took them home and read them from cover to cover. I can't describe the sensation but it was almost like coming home to me. There was a Spirit about it that wrapped itself around you. I wanted to know more.

Roy sent off for some reel-to-reel tapes. Henri himself sent some, with this note, 'Praise the Lord, lad! Glory Hallelujah! Hope these tapes bless you and you'll get the Glory!' Roy said,

> I'd never heard anything quite like this and I can actually cast my mind back to the room at home when I put these tapes on the reel-to-reel recorder. It was a Mansfield open-air meeting in the Market Place and I remember the effect the singing and the music had on me. Immediately I heard it, I felt something inside. I can't find words to express it. Unless you have been in a Glory meeting and felt the Spirit of the Glory, you cannot actually tell people. It was the Love, it was the Joy, it was the blessing, it was God's presence, it was something wholesome and powerful. I can never explain what came over me when I first put that tape on. I wanted to be in it. I wanted to be part of it, I wanted to know more about it!

Roy told the senior reporter that he'd listened to the tapes. He replied, 'Oh it's marvellous; there are huge crowds there every weekend!' And he described how Connie's singing stopped in their tracks people walking down the street. Soon Roy and other young people from their fellowship went to a Glory meeting in Newark:

> They were clapping and dancing and I just felt, 'I've come home!' This was wonderful, marvellous, and I found myself dancing and shouting and praising God. It was right! It was what I wanted! It released what I had inside.

In that very first meeting they came to, Henri invited two or three of them up onto the platform and allowed Roy to teach everyone a chorus (not one of his own) and he was thrilled to see how folk were blessed. After this, Roy started coming regularly.

It is surprising that with his strong musical urge he could not play the piano. He would watch Hilda playing with great admiration. However, he soon swung into accordion playing. He was having a holiday in Portsmouth in fellowship with a Baptist church. There were open-air meetings at Southsea, at which they sang all the Glory choruses. One day somebody who was playing an accordion didn't turn up. The instrument was sitting there with no one to play it. On an impulse, Roy picked it up, felt the keys for about five minutes, found a few chords on the left hand and was well away. He never looked back. He took to the instrument like a duck to water. Back in Newark he would sit with Hilda and get the beat of the music and gradually became quite proficient on the piano also.

It was a short step from this to composition. He had always loved words and was an able writer. He set to and wrote, 'Take your harp down off that willow,' and it was printed on the back of a *Glory News*, the first one of a whole succession. As he said, 'It expressed perfectly what the Glory was all about.' He found that it blessed people, and he wanted to compose more.

> People draw it from you. It wasn't just a question of sitting down and writing choruses, though I was full of the Spirit and I wanted to communicate the blessing in some way. God was leading me in my life. I wanted to spread the Gospel and the Glory.
>
> I went to Ireland with David and Glyn Greenow, ministering and sharing, and I found God had given me the gift of communicating His blessing through music and singing. I didn't sit down and actually write choruses; I found it began to be spontaneous with the outpouring of the Spirit and my own experience. Gradually I began to realise that music could be something spontaneous, for the moment. There would be a message or a testimony in the meeting and suddenly there was a song born there and then to express the experience, the experience of God working in reality in our lives. As every convention came along, for the few months before, I used to find these choruses coming through. By the time we got to the convention there were about half a dozen new choruses waiting to bless the folk.

Roy went on to explain that they made a simple recording of six of them on three inch reel-to-reel tapes which they advertised in the *Christian Herald* with enormous response. Things were beginning to snowball, and at this stage Roy's contact with the Cameron family from Peterhead in Scotland broadened his horizons greatly. We shall see later in our narrative of the Glory movement how the Camerons come into the picture. Here was a friendship in the Lord which enriched all concerned. Roy explains,

> The Cameron family were greatly blessed by coming down from Peterhead, Scotland, to Newark. The Apostolic Church turned on its head. Because of the singing and the dancing, they were on the television in Scotland on several occasions. When Henri went to Peterhead, Charlie Stephen, one of the Camerons' nephews, composed the chorus, 'He set me free, my lovely Jesus set me free,' and others started writing choruses, including Aunty Janet, another member of the family. I went up to Peterhead and in the car I was singing a few of my choruses and Simon Cameron said, 'Are these your choruses?' After that they couldn't get enough of them. Every time I went to Peterhead they used to sit there with a tape recorder and get me to sing the latest choruses. [7]

As can be well seen, Roy Turner became an extremely useful member of Henri's and Connie's Glory team. He travelled with them all over Britain, and then on further extensive tours with Glyn Greenow to Scandinavia and with the Camerons to the United States. Like Caedmon, the seventh-century bard of Whitby, compositions poured from his fertile heart and brain. Here are a few:

> 'I've found reality, glorious liberty'
> 'All over the world'
> 'Let me sing of the glory in my heart'
> 'Mighty, mighty is His name, precious bleeding Lamb'
> 'Praise the Lord, my burden rolled away'
> 'I've taken my harp down off the willow tree'
> 'It's the latter rain, the latter rain'
> 'Hallelujah! I want to sing all about it!'

Roy explained how, when he was in the United States, Simon Cameron was preaching about the way the Glory of God would spread everywhere. He said, 'The chorus *All over the world the Spirit is moving* came to me. I got up and sang it, having instantly tuned into something that was real in the Spirit.' [8]

ALL OVER THE WORLD

Composed by
ROY TURNER

Arranged by
WALTER EDEN

Moderato

All o – ver the world the spi – rit is mov-ing All o – ver the world as the pro-phet said it would be All o – ver the world there's a migh – ty rev – e – la – tion of the glo –ry of the Lord as the waters cov-er the sea.

3

Then again one is reminded of Sankey's remarkable tour de force in composing the five whole verses of 'There were ninety and nine that safely lay' in the middle of one of Moody's evangelistic meetings. But Roy's 'The Dancing Heart' is barely less extraordinary. He was being given a lift to Tulsa, Oklahoma by Georgia Simmonds, who had been recently widowed. In the car she said how the singing of Roy and the Camerons had lifted her spirit and had changed her life. 'God has blessed me in a way I can't describe,' she laughed. 'All I can say is, I've got a dancing heart.'

> As she said it, something struck me. 'That's it!' I exclaimed. 'Got a paper and pencil?' And as we drove along *The Dancing Heart* song came just like that, eight verses and a chorus. When we got to Tulsa we knew one or two of the students at the University, and they wanted us to have a meeting, so they hired a hall down in Tulsa. The Glory meeting was in full swing there, when somebody mentioned dancing and I was prompted there and then by the Spirit to introduce *The Dancing Heart*. I had no tune, just the words. I stood up and just started to sing and really by the end of the six months we were in America I had sung it thousands of times. It went on and on in the meetings once it started, and set the people dancing. Really, if anything sums up my experience of the Glory, that song is it. [9]

There is a rather extraordinary sequel to this as recounted by Simon Cameron. A woman accused his son Philip, 'You broke my finger!' She was sitting on a settee watching television. Philip started to sing: 'The Holy Ghost will set your feet a-dancing.' She sprang up from her settee and banged right into something, breaking her finger!

Roy himself told me of another quirky moment when he was driven to mental exhaustion. Once in the middle of a meeting, having sung *The Dancing Heart* umpteen times, he totally dried up. His mind went a complete blank. Certainly Roy needed courage to keep going, and it threw him greatly into dependence on the Lord. A good number of times he had the experience of composing a chorus in the middle of a meeting. He has described to me how it certainly took faith to do just this. All right, it was lovely to find the words and music coming spontaneously to his mind. But then the snag came, the second time round, in trying to remember with any precision what he had just composed.

OH WHAT BOUNDLESS LOVE

Composed by
ROY TURNER

Arranged by
WALTER EDEN

THE DANCING HEART

Composed by
ROY TURNER

1. Da - vid danced be - fore the Lord, he danced with all his
2. Da - vid danced be - fore the Lord to mag - ni - fy His
3. Out of E - gypt long a - go the Is - rael - ites were
4. There was a cel - e - bra - tion up - on the Red Sea
5. The prod - i - gal was far a - way, wan-d'ring out in
6. The fa - ther's house with mu - sic rang, to wel - come home his
7. Now man - y saints are cold and bound by un - be - lief to-
8. In the Bi - ble we can read that in the lat - ter

might, His heart was filled with ho - ly joy, his spir - it
name, In God's Al - might - y Pres - ence, he felt no
led, By a might - y mir - a - cle they were all
shore, Tim - brels rang, and des - ert sand be - came a
sin, But he came back to fa - ther's house, and fa - ther
son, Wine was flow - ing full and free, all mis - er -
day, They want the bless - ing of the Lord, but wor - ry
days Men would leave their first love and turn to

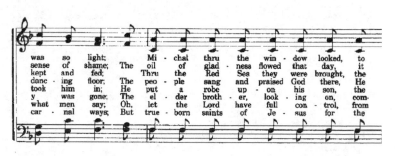

was so light; The Mi - chal thru the win - dow looked, to
sense of shame; The oil of glad - ness flowed that day, it
kept and fed; Thru the Red Sea they were brought, the
danc - ing floor; The peo - ple sang and praised God there, He
took him in; He put a robe up - on his son, the
y was gone; The el - der broth - er, look - ing on, com-
what men say; Oh, let the Lord have full con - trol, from
car - nal ways; But true - born saints of Je - sus for the

crit - i - cize did start, She did - n't know that Da - danc - ing
quick - ened ev - 'ry part, He had - n't on - ly danc - ing
wa - ters stood a - part, And God gave sis - ter Mir - i-
made the gloom de - part, And put a dance of love and
mer - ri - ment did start, The prod - i - gal got danc - ing
plained it was - n't fair, He had - n't got a danc - ing
dead tra - di - tions part, And He will set you free with-
Bride - groom set a - part, Are wait - ing for His com

"A merry heart doeth good like a medicine . . . . ."

Proverbs 17:22

"He that is of a merry heart hath a continual feast."

Proverbs 15:15

Telephone Testimony

Henri used to say that music is our secret weapon. Music touches a deep chord in our subconscious. This is why the singing of Christian music has played such a key role in times of revival. Music can wing the truth anywhere. It steals upon the ear and draws out the heart.

As the Glory meetings progressed the telephone in Henri's flat became red hot. When the Glory office opened, the telephone there was ringing all the time, with all kinds of contacts. And amongst other things people wanted to hear the Glory choruses. They would say, 'Sing for us over the telephone, sing!' In the middle of the day's work someone answering the phone would call out, 'Come on, Connie, come on, Henri, bring your accordion. So and so wants to hear a certain chorus.' In this way they used to sing and play over the telephone. And, as Connie said, 'We didn't know this for ages, but as we sang God anointed that singing.' One of the people they knew in Newark happened to work at the telephone exchange. She said, 'Do you know what's happening? When they hear that you two are on the telephone it's going all over Britain, from telephone exchange to exchange! The country's tuned into it. We can't resist it!'

Chapter 7

Behind the Scenes

Henri's Shops

Certainly Henri was a born businessman, a born salesman. His work for the Lord grew out of his business. He applied his business sense to the organisation of what he was doing for God. And in his business contacts he had a ready-made parish. As he told the Assemblies of God tribunal, 'I'm going out on the streets, I'm going to my customers ... I have a job to do.' To which they replied, 'Very commendable, brother.'

With an echo of John Bunyan, Henri called his string of shops in Appleton Gate *The House of Progress*. That was characteristic of him. He was always pushing forward. Business was an adventure, just as evangelisation and Glory meetings were an adventure.

It was second nature that he should honour God in his business. Pearl Dryhurst describes how every morning Henri would come in and all the staff would drop on their knees, whether they were saved or not. Henri would seek the Lord's blessing on the day's work, imploring God's power and mercy.

They had some wonderful answers to prayer. There was the remarkable case of Eddy Johnson, who was badly disabled with arthritis in a wheelchair and had to be carried about. Eric Staples used to carry him upstairs to the Glory meetings in the Glory Room, and then one day he took him to an evangelistic healing meeting of the American preacher A.C. Valdez. Joyce Walter, who knew Eddy well, describes how in this meeting God touched him and a marked improvement took place. It was an initial experience of a gradual process. From that moment Eddy came regularly to Henri's meetings instead of going to the pub! 'God wonderfully saved him and set him free in his spirit.' Furthermore, he no longer needed his wheelchair and Henri sold him a

bicycle! Although he still had some pain and swellings occasionally, he was now so happy, riding his bike everywhere, visiting
Glory folk and shopping in the market for bargains. Then
through Henri and Connie he was introduced to a certain Hilda
Clark and before long they were married, in July 1959, and they
had a daughter called Velma. 'It was all so amazing and wonderful,' said Joyce. Eddy also went to work in the factory of
Worthington Simpson, always wrapping himself up well to keep
himself warm. He had a saying, 'Whom the Son has made free is
free and easy!' which went down well. Hilda's mother, Elizabeth
Clark, came to live in one of the cottages in Jallands Row.

Peter Cowling came to work for Henri in 1958 as a TV repairer
and was employed by him for years. He points out that Henri was
respected by everyone who worked for him, in spite of using
Christian names. This was unheard of in business at that time. He
just had the right touch, friendly and warm, straight and honest.
He was quick to sum up a situation and trusted his own judgment
to make a snap decision. Peter says,

> One day someone came into the shop and asked Henri if his
> tape recorder was ready after six months. Henri went to find
> out in the service department what had happened to it. He
> asked Jack, the service manager, about it and was told that
> while they were waiting for a part another tape recorder
> came in which needed a part, so they took it off that one;
> then a second one came in which needed yet another part
> and they took it off that one too. So now it needed three
> parts. 'That's not the way to go on, Jack, is it?' said Henri.
> 'Well, if you're not happy with me, I can leave,' said Jack.
> 'Oh, all right then,' replied Henri, and walked round to the
> back of the shop and asked someone else if they would like
> to be the service manager, starting on Monday. Henri
> couldn't be threatened like that.

Yes, Henri could be tough. On the other hand, he was very
natural and friendly, with an eye to giving employment to able
workers. One day he felt prompted by God to ask Peter Cowling if
he would work for him. Peter says,

> I was living in Mansfield and Henri came over on a Saturday
> morning in his Rover, and made the proposal. He said,
> 'Come back with me to Newark and I will bring you home
> again, and see what you think about it.' When I went into

the shop there was a parson there with a white collar and he was talking to Henri and saying, 'These TVs are no good, these are what's taking the people away from God.' Henri put his arm round him and said, 'He'll be all right when he gets saved, won't he, Peter?' Henri could get away with doing things like that.

Peter's wife, Violet, remembers the weekend when she went to stay with Henri and Connie. She went into the shop and Henri shouted out,

'Come on, Violet, someone here wants praying for.' Henri stood behind the counter and as I went in I could see this policeman's hat standing there and he had got the policeman on his knees waiting to be prayed for. The thing was that I didn't feel embarrassed because Henri could do it, and it made me feel I could do anything too.

Dynamic Flywheel

Certainly Henri had drive. This was his nature, his temperament. Not a scholar or teacher, not a visionary dreamer or poet, but an entrepreneur, and opportunist who was quick to seize a moment of practical advantage, a man of energy immediately harnessing the abilities and gifts and willingness of those within his orbit as they strove together towards a burning common aim. Henri was of uncommon mint and there were two sides to the coin. Jean Guiteri, the Bristol teenager who subsequently became closely involved with the Glory folk, put it like this:

People talk about the compassionate Henri, pouring out the loving kindness of the Lord in the meetings. This was only one side of Henri. He also had such authority. You simply did as you were told. He did not ask you how you were or whether you had time. He didn't spare himself, and he didn't spare anyone else either. He told people to do things, and he expected to be obeyed! In no other way could he have built up a movement from just a handful of people to a very considerable number of folk going flat out, with influence in many towns in Britain and places abroad. Henri would say, 'We've got a big meeting coming up. Everybody fast next week.' And we did. It was so important; and the power would fall.

In no uncertain terms, this was a practical outworking of GMT, 'good missionary training,' and in its spontaneous discipline and discipleship was exemplary Christian behaviour, the very thing that many Christian communities put an awful lot of effort into aiming at.

Henri lived on his nerves. Two or three times he suffered from some kind of breakdown. He used to get really nasty ulcers in his mouth. This would bring him to a standstill. He was torn between the running of meetings and his business and the only way he could get clear again was to clear off. They had a caravan which became a real haven for them. Once he and Connie went down to Cornwall in it for three months for him to get built up again. He found it hard to go to sleep. Often the answer to this was to put the radio on to lull him to slumber. He would sleep in their caravan like this. Understandably, Connie became very protective of him.

As the years ticked by, the strain of keeping the two things going, the shops and the Glory work, did not ease off in any way at all. On the contrary, the tension increased; the demands were sometimes overwhelming. A mere glance in a few pages' time at the steady expansion of activities will clearly show why. So Henri at the age of 54, and Connie at 51, found themselves at a crossroads. Henri decided to wind up his business. He wrote in the magazine:

> I shall always remember this last year, for during 1962 I had to make a very important decision in my own life. The Glory work had so developed that it constantly demanded more of my time and so I was faced with the choice for the rest of my life in the work of the gospel, or to put all my efforts into my business. This was not an easy matter to decide, as all my working life I have been a businessman and for the last twenty years I have been in business on my own account. But Jesus said that where our treasure is there will be our hearts also, and I thank God for His grace and power that enabled me to decide to go all out in the work of the Lord. It had to be one thing or the other. [1]

Actually once Henri had made this decision, God allowed him to continue in business for several years before he sold it to Wigfall's.

In later years Henri started to lose his hearing. It came on gradually after 1985. Obviously, this made the leading of meetings difficult. Sometimes he couldn't hear himself playing or hear what people were saying. But if or when he misunderstood folk on the platform, even that could be turned to good account and become a ploy to set people free. In fact, it was amazing to see how God enabled him to keep his touch, and one would forget his disability. Those of us who remember his last swansong of effectiveness, the six months autumn to spring of 1988–89 at Fiskerton, recall the anointing of joy in the Holy Spirit that rested on him and the words of wisdom and compassion that flowed from his lips. The old Methodist chapel in the village near their home was packed Saturday by Saturday with gypsies and travellers who were drawn irresistibly to the meetings.

Firm Base of Operations

It was a great help to Henri when, in 1956, Bob and Hilda Nicholls moved to Newark and Bob started working full-time in a room below Henri and Connie's flat in Appleton Gate. It was next to shop No. 5. They called this the Glory Office. Bob was a born organiser. Joyce Walter describes him as 'a very upright Christian man full of grace and truth.' And Laurie James says of him,

> Bob was completely the opposite to Henri, and whilst Henri would be forever enthusing about the latest blessings, Bob would be trying to get on with the increasing administration.

There were a good number of things to keep tabs on: bookings for meetings around the country, the recording of meetings on reel-to-reel tapes and sending these out on a regular basis, and the writing and the editing of the *Glory News*. (Henri kept his finger firmly on this with the printer Arthur Hampshire.) This periodical was very necessary, a real lifeline to people scattered all over the country and also abroad.

From the very first, Henri and Connie had made an effort to keep folk in contact with one another. They used to reproduce Glory letters and send them out with Oral Roberts's magazines. When young Jean Guiteri was still living at home in Bristol, Henri gave her about fifty names and addresses to write to. These became real pen friends; in this way she got to know folk in Newark and Mansfield extremely well before ever she moved there. Joyce Walter said,

One of the things Henri got us to do when he first knew us all was to write letters to one another all over the country to encourage one another, and he always had us read John 17 two or three times until it sank in. The glory makes you one.

As we have seen, it was through letter writing that Joyce was first put in touch with Laughing Les, down in Worthing; a friendship which blossomed into happy marriage. In this way, a lively network of pen-friendship built up over the early 1950s. Bursts of enthusiasm over the blessing of God on the meetings, surprise even that such free meetings should exist at all, the sharing of experience in awareness of the working of the Holy Spirit in people's lives, fresh light on the Word of God; so much was shared, and increasingly a magazine was needed to pull all the threads together. Bob was the man of the moment for this. Evidently he had not had any journalistic training, and at the beginning admitted to being rather intimidated by the challenge of the task. But he trusted the Lord to show him how to put it together, and in the event, he clearly had a very real ability for the job. The editorial of the First Issue in 1956 began like this:

Hello Friends, here we are at last with Britain's first glory magazine ... This magazine is entirely undenominational and we pray that all who read it will be knit together in the wonderful love and glory of God. The Lord bless you all. Bob Nicholls.

Some time later he wrote:

Twelve months have now rolled by since we issued our first magazine, and what a wonderful twelve months they have been. Praise the Lord. God has indeed confirmed His work with signs and wonders. Hallelujah. By means of the written word, the recorded tapes and our revival meetings here in Newark, we have seen a threefold ministry going out to the people of the British Isles and overseas, that is anointed of God to bring deliverance to the captives in our day and generation, spreading the glad tidings of joy and liberty in the Holy Ghost. [2]

Bob went on to edit forty-nine editions of the *Glory News* and he was Henri's right-hand man for twenty-two years, 1956 to

1978. They had a succession of faithful secretaries, their right-hand women. The first to come was Pearl Dryhurst from Birmingham, she who had so longed with an intense hunger for the reality of Spirit-filled fellowship. Pearl was a trained secretary and so had the skills needed, and was thrilled to bits to be involved. She worked there for about two years at the end of the fifties. She remembers how in the Glory Office she used to have some real good laughs with Henri and Connie, and how sometimes in their meetings here and there they invited her to share the platform. 'Oh, what a privilege,' she thought.

Pearl was quick to fly to Henri's defence. Once someone began running him down in her hearing. She turned round and asked, 'Have you ever met him? Have you ever heard him speak?'

'No.'

'Well,' Pearl replied, 'I've been on his team, taking meetings all round the country. Before we start the day Henri has us all down on our knees, imploring the Lord's power and mercy.'

And so she went on. The critic was absolutely amazed and could say nothing more.

Pearl finished working in the Glory Office in 1960 and Margaret James, recently married to Laurie, took over; she also was trained as a secretary, and worked there for a year until she left to have her first child.

Margaret was followed for a year by a young woman, Sylvia Nicols, and then Joyce Walter for about six years. Joyce, in her turn, was so glad to be involved because of the friendship between Bob and her husband Les, and between Hilda, Bob's wife and herself; all four of them influenced one another for good towards spiritual freedom in worshipping and serving the Lord.

After Joyce came Olive Parsons, Bob's sister-in-law, who helped him for about ten years, the end of the sixties and most of the seventies. It was during her time that the Glory Office moved from Henri and Connie's flat in Appleton Gate to a room below Beacon Hill Chapel. The office was extremely busy. Earlier, in the 1960s, Roy Turner, the journalist and gifted chorus writer, was always popping into the Glory Office to help out, aided by Jean Berry (née Guiteri). Eventually, Henri and Bob invited him to join the Glory staff permanently. In 1972 Roy masterminded a new format of the *Glory News*. Bob handed on the editorship to him and Roy brought out a newspaper publication. It ran for sixteen issues during three years or more. Moreover, Roy was now Bob and Hilda's son-in-law. He had married their daughter Anne in 1969 at Christchurch in Newark, the wedding being attended by Glory folk from all over the British Isles.

In the mid-seventies, two other secretaries came in to help, Joan Ellis and Elaine Powell. Joan was the wife of Robert Ellis, who was very active in bringing the gospel to prisons: she worked in the office for about a year. While Elaine, a young person who with her sister Enid had grown up in the Glory fellowship, had about three years there. Elaine's parents, Ivor and Beattie Johns, were typical of those who seemed drawn to the Glory Way as though by a magnet. They had been members of a Pentecostal assembly in Lincoln, had seen an advertisement about a revival meeting in Newark, went to it, and before long they joined the fellowship. As Elaine typed and filed papers alongside Olive Parsons she came to have the highest regard for her as an elder sister in God's family. Olive had unusual qualities: 'a remarkable person,' Elaine said. Altogether, the Glory Office were a closeknit band, a hive of activity, at home with one another.

From 1956 to 1978 Bob Nicholls provided that firm anchor hold which the Glory Way needed. As Henri was continually branching out in all directions, following up every lead like quicksilver, Bob plodded away at the headquarters. They were so different and yet so very essential. Bob led the meetings in Henri's absence. His particular gift was teaching the Word of God. 'This was much needed,' said Elaine. 'Henri was used by God in revival, in conversion. But then folk must not stay babies. They need to grow. Bob gave them that nurture.'

Bob's sudden death in 1978 was a terrible shock: to Hilda and his family and to the whole Glory fellowship. Roy, his son-in-law, tells how on Saturday morning 7th October Bob had finished his usual morning work in the Glory Office and gone to minister to one of the fellowship who was having marriage difficulties. On returning to his home he decided to go back into town to purchase some bacon for his Sunday morning breakfast and pick up some sweets for his two grandchildren, Susanna and Sarah. Because it was such a short journey he had decided to take his moped instead of the car.

He was nearly home again, just outside his house; he stopped to make a right turn, feet on the road, when his rear wheel was hit by a motorbike, driven by a young man, which came from nowhere along the empty street. Bob was flung into the air. At the same moment, his wife Hilda, who was playing the organ and singing Glory choruses to Susie and Sarah, heard the crash, dashed to the window and saw Bob lying in the road. She hurried out and knelt beside him but there was nothing anyone could do but await the arrival of the ambulance. Bob was placed on a life-support machine and died in hospital the following Wednesday. He was with Jesus Whom he loved and served. *'Blessed are the dead which die in the Lord ... and their works do follow them'* (Revelation 14:13). Henri added:

> In our sadness there is joy in knowing he is with the Lord. His loss is greatly felt by all of us, making us more determined to press on to share more of the power of this Glory in our lives with others while we can. [3]

Before moving on, one must mention two other dear folk who went to be with their Lord about this time, both in 1972. These were Henri's mother, Gran Staples and his brother Eric.

His mother, who died at 84, had played such an essential part in supporting Henri and Connie in everything they did. Her continually open home in Jallands Row showed how much she loved people as she lived for the Lord.

Eric caught the vision of outreach in those early days in Mansfield Market. As a driver of vehicles, carrying people about, and as indefatigable recorder of meetings he was one of those sheet anchor folk, a behind-the-scenes character, who could always be relied on. Though his health was failing, his home call in middle age through a stroke was a sudden shock. It happened in this way. Eric used to pray and intercede for the world in the early mornings. One day his wife called up the stairs for him to have breakfast. He came down and was just about to start eating when she spoke to him and he gave no answer. Eric was immobile. He was taken straight away to Newark Hospital. Dorcas, David Willows's wife, remembers visiting him there. He lingered in hospital for about ten days and then peacefully passed into the presence of his Lord.

Chapter 8

Dramatic Expansion

D own the years, people have often said, 'If Henri had been born in the USA, God would have used him to spark off a world-wide revival.' Or this? 'If only Henri had been born thirty years later he could have filled Wembley Stadium at the drop of a hat. His video messages would have filled the shops and spread out across the world.' So what? If he had been born over a millennium ago he might have paddled down the coast from Lindisfarne in a coracle and been the first to evangelise his beloved Midlands! God has His own master plan, which He unfolds at His leisure.

However, the fact that folk are liable to say things like this shows the degree of Holy Spirit power which they recognised in the wiry Newark salesman. 'How Henri's eye flashed during the meetings,' Pearl Dryhurst recalled. 'He had such fire. No doubter or unbeliever could stand up against him.'

An accordion, a van and a microphone on Sunday evenings in the market place of a mining town; encounters with customers over the counters of his shops in Newark. Henri and his Connie struck a match, kindling fire which spread across the country and beyond. Yet for all that, Henri's name is barely a household word. God has used him to have very great influence for good. It has been an influence which has by now permeated the mainstream churches and assemblies, an unseen leaven or yeast.

Whether leaven or fire, the message of true freedom enjoyed through the Holy Spirit darted from place to place. No high-powered publicity was needed; nothing more than the announcement of meetings in local papers and the circulation of a magazine. Satisfied customers are the best publicity. Folk gossiped the Glory gospel. The telephone of the Glory office would be ringing. Meetings were booked: in assemblies, in mission halls, in little village halls, in big town halls and chapels in valleys. The movement was spontaneous, Spirit led. Opportunities were seized as they came up, with a conviction that God was opening doors and that they should simply go through them.

Anyone looking at a map of Britain and Ireland will be greatly impressed by the large areas affected by the Glory Way. Over a period of forty years or more – and particularly during the 1960s and 1970s – the Glory bush fire spread from a broad swathe of the Midlands to London, to Kent and Essex, to the Central South Coast, to South Wales, to East Anglia, to Yorkshire and Lancashire, to County Durham and Northumberland to eastern Scotland and to Northern Ireland.

The Midlands

It was natural that towns and villages on the doorstep of Mansfield and Newark should hear of the Glory meetings and ask for a team to visit them. Henri and Connie and their friends went to Grantham, Lincoln and Scunthorpe and then to the flower town of Spalding in the Fens. To their immediate south and west were Loughborough, Burton-on-Trent, Stoke-on-Trent, Derby, Uttoxeter and Stafford. In and near the Derbyshire Peak District they had meetings in Matlock and Chesterfield. In the Birmingham areas they went to Darlaston, Hockley, Digbeth and Selly Oak. Further south in the picturesque stone belt of Northamptonshire and the Cotswolds the Glory folk got repeated invitations from Wellingborough and Irchester, Evesham and Banbury, Cheltenham and Gloucester, Oxford and Bristol.

London

The great capital city inevitably drew them. There were scattered meetings in Croydon, Westminster, Walthamstow, Ealing, Acton and Fulham. It was particularly in Lambeth Town Hall and Willesden Revival Centre that a really effective impact was made; also, from 1967 onwards, in Hammersmith and the Spencer Hall at Wimbledon.

Although today we do not have much of an account of the regular rallies at Wimbledon, Cecil and Grace Pywell of the Surrey Group have very vivid memories of wonderful times there, when the power of the Holy Spirit was so present.

In 1958 a Glory meeting was held in Lambeth Town Hall (which is actually situated in Brixton). In this area there is an extraordinary mixture of races, of Asians, West Indians, Africans. A pastor from Walthamstow, Bill Newman, coming to Lambeth Town Hall said,

> Prior to this meeting, I didn't know what worship in the Spirit meant ... that night I went home from the meeting, weeping for joy. I shouted, danced, clapped my hands, jumped and laughed around my room for hours. I rejoiced and worshipped God in the Spirit, singing and making melody unto His Name. [1]

By this time, Laurie and Margaret James had moved south from Newark to settle in the London area and Laurie persuaded a lay pastor cum successful garage owner Archie Friday, from Paddock Wood in central Kent, to come to one of these rallies. He in turn became so enthused that, in 1960, he and some Glory folk in London arranged four or five rallies at fortnightly intervals. This was a trial run which then became extended. He brought along a support group from Paddock Wood, and folk came from all over London. He wrote,

> When Henri came to London to hold a Glory meeting in Lambeth Town Hall ... it became apparent that there were many folk in the Metropolis who were hungry for liberty, blessing and power, but where could they go to get it? When they sought to praise the Lord and encourage others to do the same in their assemblies, they were discouraged and in some cases shunned and regarded as fanatics.

When Brother Friday arranged the fortnightly rallies, he was amazed at the response:

> Praise, worship, singing, clapping, hands upraised, pent-up energy being let loose to uplift Jesus, people pouring out to the front in consecration; and judging from the look on the faces of these precious brethren and sisters, one would say that they live for these meetings and shall they be denied them? A thousand times no! [2]

Laurie and Margaret James became very involved with these Lambeth-Brixton rallies, which were usually held on a Friday evening, spilling over into two more meetings on Saturday. Laurie says,

There were very good numbers attending. Sometimes Henri would come down for a meeting on Saturday afternoon and evening, and it was on one of these occasions that I remember the biggest crowd ever at a Glory event. The town hall was packed. I have no idea of numbers, but there could have been a thousand plus; certainly more than the usual numbers. One instance we recall at this meeting. Margaret and I were sat with the platform party. Everywhere was crowded, including the platform. A chap from the London area was there playing his trumpet for all he was worth during mighty times of praise. The backdrop to the platform was a curtain and during one rousing song the trumpet player disappeared from our side through the curtains. We were alarmed and looked through the curtains to see him lying amongst stage debris about eight feet below us, still playing his trumpet! I am not sure if he knew he had fallen; certainly most of the people were unaware he had, and he eventually rejoined the platform party none the worse for wear.

Frank Preudhomme, a church officer in the large Peniel Chapel in Kensington, worked in the City and he was asked by Phyllis, who had a job at the Head Office of Barclays Bank Dominion, Colonial and Overseas, if he would be willing to help start a lunch time prayer fellowship. This got well off the ground and before long became a branch of the Full Gospel Business-men's Fellowship. Frank heard about Henri's meetings and in July 1959 drove over with some friends to a Glory meeting in Reading. He said,

> During the afternoon we felt our way, just watching and wondering and feeling something wonderful in the atmo-sphere. [3]

About this time Frank's invalid wife Elsie went to be with Jesus. She had suffered with multiple sclerosis for sixteen years and Frank had nursed and cared for her all that time. He was very distressed and broken in spirit. Then someone invited him to one of the Lambeth Town Hall Glory meetings; he went and was quickened and blessed. One day he phoned up Phyllis to tell her about it. Together they really entered into the spirit of the meeting. Thinking back on this Phyllis said,

We were both used to body ministry and liberty. I was used to dancing in the Spirit and we had always loved to 'let go and let God'. There was however with the Glory meeting a realisation that God had given a special ministry of liberation to Henri and people came from dead and dry churches far and wide to get a touch from God and to dance and rejoice in His presence.

In time Frank and Phyllis became engaged and linked up with Archie and Minnie Friday, and also with Fred and Mary Johnson of Stanford le Hope (near Basildon, Essex) to hold meetings every alternate Friday evening in Lambeth Court House. On the other Fridays they used an old church building in Hammersmith. They were joined enthusiastically by Gib Rudkin and the Surrey Group (more of them anon).

Then, just before Frank and Phyllis were married, Frank was asked to expand a house fellowship group at Willesden, two miles from Wembley Stadium. In October 1960 they met in the Boy Scouts Headquarters there. Straight away they experienced real joy and liberty in the Holy Spirit; as Frank expressed it:

> No longer does the pastor act as almost a self-contained unit; the body of His saints functions again as God has ordained in His precious Word, each joint supplying a portion and the church, His body, is built up in her most holy faith. [4]

After a time they needed a place of their own. Phyllis amusingly tells how she saw an old worn stone step protruding from underneath very high advertising hoardings on a corner in the High Road. On hands and knees, peering underneath, they found an old derelict grey stone building with slates off the roof and broken boarded up windows. It turned out to belong to the council and was destined for demolition. They negotiated for it. Then four months of blistering hard work pulled the old building round and in February 1964 a resplendent new Revival Centre was opened amid great rejoicing. Ron Wray came down from Yorkshire to ably lead the meeting, Bob Nicholls and Henri travelled from Newark, the Fridays came from Kent and members of the Cameron family from far northern Peterhead joined with the Londoners to sing on the street outside and then pour into the building. Phyllis Preudhomme wrote,

He set His seal upon us. Here we want no bondage, no ideas of man, no tradition or broadened phylacteries; but that having the mind of Christ, we might have His ears to hear the cry of the sick and needy and go to their rescue, His wisdom to win them, His love to draw them, and his eyes filled with the VISION to save men from perishing. Amen! [5]

In February 1966 the Preudhommes organised two memorable Glory rallies in Hammersmith Town Hall, which certainly proved to be a true rallying point for people from a considerable distance. There was a bus-load from Norwich; others journeyed from Portsmouth, Basildon, the Isle of Wight, Oxford, Wimborne, Brighton and many parts of London. The place was packed to capacity, with some people standing in the corridors. Roy Turner said,

Henri was in fine form ... there was much rejoicing, but there was great heart-searching too, as the Holy Ghost worked upon each one challenging us to enter into a closer fellowship with God. [6]

In time a difference of opinion arose, revealing a vulnerable facet of the Glory work. Archie Friday, Fred Johnson and Frank Preudhomme tried to set up a structured oversight for the meetings in the southern half of England. Henri was not very happy about this. He was uneasy with the whole question of church oversight: pastor, elders and deacons. And anyway this was not a question of the organisation of an individual church but of control over different fellowships. (In a different guise, it was the old knotty problem of Presbyterians versus Congregationalists.) Alan Churchill recalls,

Henri and many of us in the south of England were very upset because there was a bid by these people to structure our local meetings under their umbrella. None of us agreed. We wanted to stay independent. This all happened during the years when Henri was poorly and unable to take any meetings.

Henri was a free spirit and would not be tied down to anything which he felt was connected with dead religion. He always said his calling was not to build churches but to liberate and bless the people! He challenged the others to stay a hundred per cent with the Glory Way. Phyllis Preudhomme said,

> We loved Henri and his people and I'm sure they loved us, but we felt we could only be 100% Jesus, and that was that. All ministries in the body are not only profitable but necessary.

Just to prove that brotherly love did continue, Archie Friday ten years later apologised to Henri for putting his case too strongly. He came back to Henri's meetings and admitted he had been wrong to have caused division. Henri encouraged him and Archie in his turn produced a series of tapes for Henri in the mid-seventies called *Archie's Fireside Chats*. And quite some years later Phyllis was suddenly surprised by Henri when he sought her out at the end of a big Maurice Cerullo meeting in Leicester and gave her a warm Glory hug. And yet again, Henri and Chris Wingfield visited her flat in Potters Bar.

In the mid sixties Frank got involved in helping the evangelist Maurice Cerullo, acting as his director, arranging his meetings. However, after two or three years, he died suddenly. He had suffered with chronic asthma from childhood. The pressures of overwork and an attack of acute bronchitis made him very poorly. Two days after Christmas 1970 he inhaled black smoke when some oil burned in the kitchen; he was taken to hospital and died a few hours later. It was a terrible shock to his family. But Phyllis took over, both as Cerullo's director for some years and as pastor of the Willesden Revival Fellowship up until 1989.

The Lord gave the Willesden folk a concern for the needs of the wider world, in that they supported two Costa Rican brothers through the T.L. Osborne organisation; they also sent out to Taiwan their missionary secretary, Myrtle Taylor, who had the call of God to work amongst the Chinese.

In 1989 a new pastor, Paul Sinclair, came to the Revival Centre. The name was changed to *The Church on the High Road*, and they became an Elim church. Recently a surprising thing happened; a betting shop next door were willing to sell their premises for less than half price! They are now running this as a flourishing children's and youth centre.

Essex and Kent

Downstream from London at the mouth of the Thames, on both banks, the Glory Way took root. In Billericay, Laindon, Stanford

BOSCOMBE GROUP

CECIL AND EVELYN STEWART

ED AND FAITH BREWER

BOSCOMBE BOAT TRIP

BEE, DOUG, ROSE, CONNIE AND ARTHUR WARREN

PEARL, ROY AND MIRIAM

TOM AND ANN SPURR

PETERHEAD GLORY BOYS

TOM AND LINNETTE

MIRIAM BURT AND HENRI

HIS BANNER OVER US IS LOVE

SOME OF THE MUSICIANS

DAVID GREENOW

THE HARPERS FROM RINGWOOD

BETTY MICKLEWRIGHT,
JAN VAN GINKEL, PETER
COWLING AND BOB NICHOLLS

VIOLET COWLING

SIDNEY FROM THE SURREY GROUP

THE JOHNS FAMILY ISLE OF WIGHT

HENRI AND LIL MARSHALL
CONNIE'S SISTER

BETHEL GOSPEL HALL
ASSEMBLIES OF GOD
SERVICES

SANDOWN ISLE OF WIGHT

ISLE OF WIGHT MEETING

STAN AND GILL HECKFORD

SEDLEY PIMLOTT

SHIRLEY, STEVE AND ALAN CHURCHILL

THE SANSONS

FRED AND MARY JOHNSON

MOLLY AND FRED PERRY WITH HENRI

ROY TURNER

RON WRAY

AUG CONVENTION 1957

AUG CONVENTION 1957

HENRI EXHORTS

GLORY BAPTISM IN THE TRENT AT NEWARK

BURSLEM MIRACLE TESTIMONY

BURSLEM WHITSUN 1958

BURSLEM WHITSUN 1958

BURSLEM WHITSUN 1958

CONNIE EXHORTS

HENRI AND PETER HAWKE

HENRI AND PAT BUCKINGHAM

THE PLATFORM IN HOLLAND

OPEN AIR IN THE HAGUE

JAN VAN GINKEL

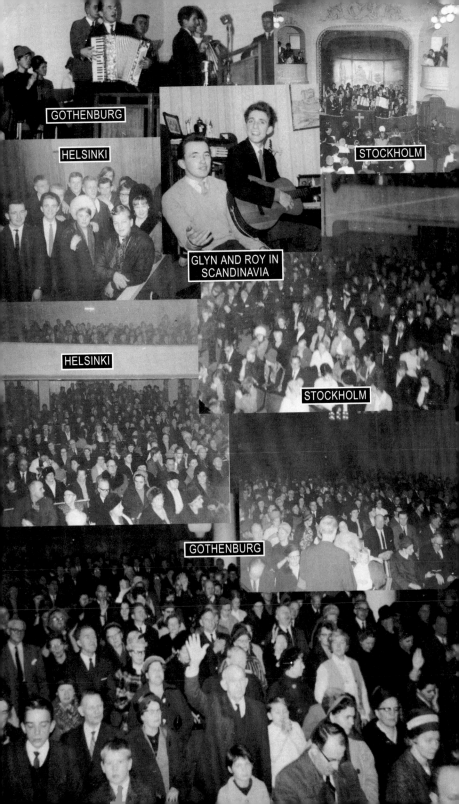

GOTHENBURG

HELSINKI

STOCKHOLM

GLYN AND ROY IN SCANDINAVIA

HELSINKI

STOCKHOLM

GOTHENBURG

le Hope, Basildon and Southend-on-Sea were many meetings, which were to bear particular fruit in the future because a permanent Glory centre was established by Alan and Shirley Churchill at the strategic Central Hall in Wash Road, Basildon (now known as Noak Bridge Christian Centre). They are the initiators of this book, and at this moment of writing the hall is in the middle of modernisation and considerable extension in sympathy with the mushroom building of a new estate around it. You can read about more of the ways in which God has blessed the Glory movement in Essex in Alan Churchill's testimony in Chapter 13.

On the other side of the Thames, in Kent, is Northfleet, visited by the Glory team many times in the early sixties, with meetings also in Gillingham, Ashford and Folkestone. Above all, near Tonbridge there was Paddock Wood, home of Archie Friday, Arthur Burt and their families, who had very distinctive ministries of their own, as will be seen later on in this book. In fact, Paddock Wood was pivotal. Archie Friday was a businessman, a garage owner and dealer in vehicles who nevertheless regarded his secular work as 'tent-making' while he got on with the more serious business of preaching the gospel and nurturing the Lord's work wherever he found it. God used him as an evangelist with the Assemblies of God to plant church fellowships in Lincoln, Corby, Stanford le Hope (near Basildon) and Dagenham, where he led an evangelistic campaign in a large tent. When Archie encountered Henri and Connie and the Glory people this, without a doubt, renewed his vision and revitalised him.

The Central South Coast

Moving round the country, we come to the Central South Coast, the Isle of Wight and the New Forest, everywhere between Weymouth and Portsmouth. In 1959 and the early 1960s the spark of Glory revival flared up first in one place and then another: Gosport, Sandown, Shanklin, Ryde, Southampton, Christchurch, Wimborne and then further inland in Dorset at Chard, Crewkerne and Haselbury Plucknett. The list reads invitingly like a travel brochure.

The Isle of Wight was an ideal place for the Glory Way to pioneer their seaside holidays. Freda Johns today reminisces how her parents, in 1957, went to a Glory meeting in Newark. She said, 'Their enthusiasm was immediately obvious and infectious, and over the years numerous trips were made from the Isle of

Wight by them, and by my sister Mavis and me and other friends. Fired then by the encouragement of Henri and Connie, we arranged a number of Glory Holidays here.'

The contact was spontaneous. Gladys and Cyril Dimmer of the Assembly of God in Sandown described what happened:

> Could this be of God or was it of man? We had heard of Henri's Revivals and then Henri and his team came to Shanklin and we went to see for ourselves, knowing the Holy Spirit would witness if this was of God. Those two nights left us in no doubt, for we were left with the assurance of the power of God and a hunger for more of His glory in our hearts. On our return home we prayed to God that if the glory was for us in Sandown then God would send Henri and Connie right into our hall. We remembered at this time that the Lord had told us through the gift of prophecy several times that He would baptise us in glory.
>
> One eventful Sunday evening, just as we had started our meeting, the door opened and in came Connie accompanied by friends from Shanklin, closely followed by Henri. We had no idea they were coming. The Lord had answered prayer and sent them. Glory! Hallelujah! We on the platform looked at each other and said, 'This is it.' We gave Henri a free hand in the meeting and, as he told us of recent blessings and healings, our hearts burned within us and we rejoiced in this new way of deliverance as the fire came down upon us. As we sang the glory choruses, liberty and freedom in the Lord came and the glory of God filled our hearts. [7]

So before long the Glory holidays got under way. Freda Johns describes how folk would gather together during the day from where they were staying for coach trips or beach parties and then again each evening for a Glory meeting. At first these were held in halls but demand soon meant that a large marquee was needed. Writing in the *Glory News* one year, Freda stirred up interest:

> Maybe you are feeling in need of a change or a rest, well, here is a ready remedy – take positive action and write straight away to book accommodation ... You know, God's desire is that we enjoy LIFE in all its fullness and beauty and He knows that we need times of refreshing and times to recharge our souls and spirits with His almighty power. [8]

A comment in the *Glory News* in 1963 ran:

> Each night and all day on Sunday about 120 folk gathered together at the Vectis Hall, Ryde, in the presence of God and experienced mighty blessings. His love was certainly shed abroad in our hearts more and more, everyone experiencing a closer walk with God. Hallelujah, souls were saved and many were the prayers answered. Each night after the meetings we continued with tea and snacks and the Glory folk were so happy it was difficult to get anyone to leave the hall![9]

We move on to the New Forest town of Ringwood which is very close to the area where the animals roam free and unfettered across the heath and woodland. Don and Elsie Harper, who led the Pentecostal Mission there, had been longing for unfettered spiritual freedom and power in their lives. They said,

> The beginning of 1959 found us nearly ready to give up. We had sought, together with the loyal little band of saints here at the Pentecostal Mission, to maintain what liberty we had, but it was such a struggle and we didn't seem to be getting anywhere. Then I read an account of blessing at the opening of the new Evangelical Church at Paddock Wood...[10]

They invited Archie Friday to come over to the New Forest. Immediately they recognised the spiritual reality they were looking for. 'The Paddock Wood Revival Party in action,' Don Harper explained, 'decided me to go right in for the Glory Way.' In turn they travelled up to the first Lambeth-Brixton rally; then Henri visited them and folk came in from all around. It was truly wonderful when they considered how near to giving up they were.

This Pentecostal Mission became a true Glory Centre, affecting the whole area. Meetings also started in Boscombe on the outskirts of Bournemouth. They were in a rather cramped hall and things were not going very well. Then the Ringwood Glory Band tackled the problem. They found a much better meeting place, the Freemantle Hall. It was a dream come true! Elsie Harper wrote:

> About six months before we launched out in Boscombe I had a dream. I was in a fair-sized hall which I had never seen before. The place was nearly full and the blessing was wonderful.

Came the day when they were having their first meeting in the Freemantle Hall and they were singing the chorus, *It's the Blood that sets me free,*

> Imagine how thrilled I was as my dream came vividly back to me. This was the very place: the same size, the same coloured walls, everything. Praise the Lord! [11]

Six years later there is the touching instance of Fred Jordan who passed the door of the Freemantle Hall on his bicycle. He was a true believer, longing for greater reality in his life. He said,

> Sometimes I would pray, O Lord, lead me to people who live and worship Thee and do as the New Testament Christians did. Then I would think, But there can't be any for they would be famous and I would have heard of them.

As he passed this Pentecostal mission hall he was arrested by the singing; he stopped to listen, leaned his bike against the wall and out of curiosity cautiously pushed the door.

> Someone inside seeing the door move, pulled it wide open, grasped my hand, saying, 'Come in, brother,' and drew me inside. There was no churchy decorum, people looked round to see who had entered, saw me a stranger and beamed the love of Christ to me, someone they didn't even know, and I felt it! I had come home. These were the kind of people I had longed to be with, Praise the Lord! [12]

Before moving on further, it is worth noting that the Harpers and their friends in Ringwood and Boscombe expressed practical concern for needs abroad. As they put it, the Lord was making them *'a fruitful bough by a well; whose branches run over the wall'* (Genesis 49:22). They supported a T.L. Osborne native evangelist in India who established a church there about 1967; and they supported another native worker in Nigeria.

South Wales

We now come to South Wales. It would have been very surprising if the Glory Way had had no welcome here, the land of the great revival of 1904–5. The first Glory meeting was held in

Llwynhendy, about ten miles west of Swansea, in 1958. A year before, Gwylfa Richards had read a copy of the *Glory News* and he said, 'I felt my heart beginning to burn within me.'[13] Then he had listened to a couple of Glory tapes. When Henri and his team arrived in their assembly, they made a deep impression on him. Before long Gwylfa went to Newark. Then he took his wife there, and together they experienced liberation of spirit, as did their two daughters Bethan and Eirian. However, their assembly could not accept the Glory Way, neither could the Richards family look back. So they constructed a wooden building at the back of their garden which became a veritable Glory haven.

In 1960 and 1961 Henri and Connie and their team came to Llanelli, and again to Llwynhendy and neighbouring Ammanford. It was in fact in nearby Loughor, in Moriah Chapel, under young Evan Roberts, that the Welsh revival had broken out. One meeting led to another, right across the whole mining area of 'the valleys'. Starting with the cities of Newport and Cardiff in 1962, there was in the following year a veritable blaze of Glory rallies which took place in Treorchy, Ystradmynach, Pontypridd, Aberkenfig, Maesteg (the home town of the Jeffreys brothers), Crumlin, Cwmbran, Pontnewydd, and in English sounding Bridgend, Blackwood, Cross Keys, Rogerstone and Chepstow; most of them communities which know only too well the back-breaking lung-threatening work of coal mining, towns perched steeply on the rugged hillsides, distinctive with their patterns of solid lines of stone terrace houses and steep twisty roads. It was in this same area and only three years later, in October 1966, that disaster struck the village of Aberfan in the Taff valley south of Merthyr Tydfil, when a waterlogged colliery tip slid down a hillside, smothering a school and several houses, killing 144 people, most of them children. It so happened that the very Saturday after this disaster Henri held a Glory Rally in Treorchy in the Rhondda Valley, eight miles to the west of Aberfan. The Spirit flowed in a special way that evening and many needs were met among the devastated local people. The Glory folk returned the next year and it is encouraging to read words like these of Mrs F. Hughes of Llwynhendy:

> It is so very wonderful to have the love of God real in our hearts, also to have Henri and team with us again recently. I could see the Lord filling them and using them in the power of the Holy Ghost; their faces were lit up with the joy of the Lord and radiated with His fullness. [14]

East Anglia

In Puritan times East Anglia (the counties of Norfolk, Suffolk and Essex) was known as the Galilee of England, so much was the pure Word of God preached in its villages and market towns with their timber-framed or flint-walled houses. From here many godly families emigrated to New England in the wake of the *Mayflower*. We find the Newark Glory team taking meetings in Chelmsford, Braintree, Stowmarket, Thetford and Norwich. For instance, in October 1965 Zion Chapel fellowship run by Sedley Pimlott and family invited them for a whole weekend of meetings. They were joined by the Cameron family, coming all the way from Peterhead in Aberdeenshire. Roy Turner wrote,

> In the afternoon Connie was greatly anointed as she ministered on the need for a real heart-hunger after God and the wonders of this latter-rain outpouring. There was a wonderful flowing together in the love of God as the meetings progressed and the barriers were broken down under the anointing of the Spirit. Praise the Lord! ... There is certainly a wind of change blowing in the Church of Jesus Christ in these momentous days. The evening meeting was a glorious climax when the power of God fell on many of the young people and swept them into a new experience with God! [15]

Yorkshire and Lancashire

In the late fifties and early sixties the Glory fire flickered hither and thither amongst the northern cloth manufacturing towns of Yorkshire and Lancashire. Henri, Connie and their team had meetings in '58 and '59 in Bradford, fast filling up with immigrants, and in Barnsley (the birthplace more than a century before of the great missionary to China, Hudson Taylor). These were followed in 1960 with the large manufacturing centres Manchester, Leeds, Sheffield and the historic port of Hull. At Leeds, Henri hired a reception chamber in the monumental Town Hall, and one man was caught unawares:

> On 6th June I was in Leeds wondering whether to go to a dance and I met some friends outside the Town Hall. They told me about Henri's meetings so I thought I would go for a laugh, but, praise the Lord, I got saved instead. Now I'm enjoying life and praising the Lord. [16]

A Scottish lass, Jane Stephen from Peterhead, was on holiday in Huddersfield and went to this rally in Leeds:

> The first thing that I noticed was the shine on everybody's face and brother Henri's face was beaming. I knew the first time I saw him he was a genuine man of God. [17]

Some years later, after another Glory rally in Leeds, someone signed Miss E.M. wrote in to say:

> I feel I must write or burst! I went to my first Glory meeting last Saturday and, praise the Lord, I've not been the same dull girl since. I was told to go with an open mind, which I did, and had delayed action! I came home from the rally, went to bed, but found myself praising the Lord, I just couldn't stay in bed. I was dancing round my flat at midnight and I think it was about 2 am when I finally managed to get to bed again. Hallelujah! He gave me the liberty I have never felt before. [18]

There were personal links with certain places like Bradford, who always gave the Glory team a warm welcome. Throughout the sixties they were continually invited back there, as they were to a much smaller town like Thorpe Hesley (between Sheffield and Barnsley). Jack and Claris Witham of Thorpe Hesley were a couple in whose hearts revival fire was burning. As they met Henri and Connie the flame leaped higher. Claris was outstanding in her ministry. She was a great exhorter, and would roll up her sleeves and stamp her feet, she got that excited.

On the other side of the Pennines, invitations for Glory meetings came from Stockport, Manchester, Colne, Nelson, Blackburn, Oldham, Lancaster, Preston (always a Pentecostal centre) and on the Irish Sea coast there were meetings at Barrow-in-Furness, Knott End-on-Sea, Blackpool, Cleveleys and Fleetwood.

Lancaster is a good case in point, showing how the individual streams of the Holy Spirit's power flow together. Leslie Richardson of the Lancaster Revival Centre had been a Pentecostal pastor for some twenty years when at Easter 1960 he himself had a new visitation from God; 'the Glory came in,' as he said, 'setting me free in spirit, soul and body.' This brought a quickening to his assembly. Straight away they filled up a coach to go to Henri's Easter convention, where God touched their lives.

At last my assembly had been set on fire by a divine visitation. Glory to God. What a change took place. The Glory that came to the Assembly brought with it a new fellowship of love, and, as one of the members said, we are too busy talking about Jesus to talk about other people now ... the anointing came down from heaven, people were falling prostrate under the mighty power of God, six and seven at a time were being baptised in the Holy Ghost without the laying on of hands, sinners were sobbing their way to Calvary even before any preaching started. Many times we were unable to minister because of the mighty anointing of the Spirit on the meetings. [19]

Throughout the sixties, Henri and his team took a number of meetings in Manchester, in the Octagon Church and also in Alma Road Methodist Church. Betty Micklewright has vivid memories of those meetings and also of others in Bolton. She remembers so well Roy Turner leading choruses, dancing before the Lord and running down through the church. 'It was quite extraordinary,' she said,

it was as though there was a golden glory mist in the building, or something like glory dew on the grass, fresh and sparkling. And we felt as though we were lifted up as the power of God came down.

As to the rallies in Bolton: in 1966, for instance,

the Bridge Street Methodist Church, with its great pipe-organ and formal pews, rang with the Hallelujahs of the Glory folk. Henri told how thrilled he was to minister in a place where revival fires had once burned. [20]

In Calvary Christian Mission at Bolton, led by Pastor W. Barnes, as in Lancaster, they found a completely independent Glory work with a lively group of young people, who were only too happy to link up with them. Another assembly in Bolton spontaneously joined up with the Glory Way after one of their members, Douglas Hallam, lost his map while setting out on holiday on his moped. He had fully intended going south from Bolton, but he found himself going south eastwards instead, and it dawned on him that the Lord was leading him a different way. He got off his moped and looking up said, 'Please show me the way. Tell me when to turn or to go straight on.' In this way he arrived in Newark.

> I wondered why I was here but I remembered meeting a brother down in Devon who told me about a man who preached in Newark and when this man talked to you he would put his arms round you. I had never heard of anything like this before in my life. No one could tell me where I could find this man. [21]

Well, through his enquiries the Lord led him to Eric Staples and to his mother Gran Staples and Henri himself!

County Durham and Northumberland

Moving another stretch further north the Glory way took root in County Durham and Northumberland. In West Auckland in the foothills of the northern Pennines, Pastor Nan Logan told how she had been serving the Lord in Pentecost for years, but she felt she was sadly lacking in joy. Then God started to renew the assembly:

> There came a something amongst us I knew nothing about. First of all there came a holy clapping, then there came a holy laughter and this was followed by a holy glory, but none of us knew quite what it was at that time. It was because of this that somebody said to me, 'Have you read Henri's magazine?' 'Who's Henri?' I asked...

When Pastor Nan found out, she and her fellowship decided to invite Henri and Connie there and then, and she also contacted a good number of assemblies in the area.

> They were all very agreeable to come along but the moment they knew that it was Henri of Newark that was coming, it was just like giving them a dose of poison. They almost gave me to think that I had committed the unpardonable sin. Some said that whatever I did, I was to get them packed off to Newark as quickly as possible.

But Pastor Nan stuck to her guns. She said to the pastors of these assemblies, 'Having booked Henri to come, upon principle we must have them and if they are all you say they are they'll not reign two days.' In the event Henri and Connie came for two weekends.

> It was two weekends of the humbling of my nature; two weekends of brokenness of heart did God give me. He revolutionised our assembly at West Auckland and doubled our congregation.God has set us wonderfully free and made us to be the Glory family of West Auckland. Hallelujah. [22]

There were also Glory groups in Newton Aycliffe, Stockton-on-Tees and Bedlington, about ten miles north of Newcastle which had a thriving group of Christian young people. There were also meetings at nearby Newbiggin-by-the-Sea and Blyth; also in Newcastle and Sunderland (which knew the first Pentecostal blessing in the country in 1907).

In Bedlington Revival Centre were many who had a personal tale to tell of the grace of God.

> When they hear people saying that God is dead and that miracles don't really happen these days, Robert and Gladys Lloyd of Blyth, Northumberland, just smile knowingly to themselves. For the sceptics and modernists have come just a little bit too late to persuade them that Jesus Christ is just a 'figment of man's imagination' or merely an historical figure.

Bob was an epileptic, needing a strong dose of phenobarbitone every day, but at the age of sixteen, as he was led to believe God's promises, he was completely healed. However later, when he was in the Army, he turned away from God and was put on trial for theft at the Old Bailey. This brought him to his senses, and the Lord had mercy on him and restored him. Mercy followed on mercy, for when he was married his wife Gladys, for a long time childless, at last had a baby boy. It was a wonderful answer to prayer, an absolute miracle, it seemed.

Stuart McGregor told how as a teenager he led a gang. 'Together we would go out and break the law in a very wild fashion.' Then he suffered from shame and guilt. He said,

> Sin was a reality to me. I was under great conviction. My mind was in confusion and I became so self-conscious and shy that I couldn't face people. I would walk down the back lanes ... I just couldn't face life at all.

Then a man on a bus invited him to a gospel meeting where he heard that Jesus Christ could give him relief from his tormented mind. He repented, surrendered and was saved. Now he could say, 'Instead of walking down the back streets of life I am walking with Jesus in the King's Highway!'

Stuart invited his family to meetings at the Revival Centre. His sister Christine thought them really strange. 'I saw people clapping their hands in church and playing tambourines.' It was certainly different from church services which had bored her stiff. Her mother and sister and then she went forward to be saved.

Michael Lavelle was a young Methodist preacher, who as yet did not know the Lord as his Saviour. But then he came to a turning point when he heard an open-air preacher in a fairground in Newcastle. Robert Foster enjoyed playing the guitar, in a church on Sundays and then in dance halls and discos midweek. But then he realised he could not serve two masters and gave his heart to the Lord. His sister Jean suffered from great depression and fear, until she learned to go God's way. She said, 'The devil used to be like a giant in my experience but, praise God, I now know that he is under my feet ... through Christ Jesus!'[23] John Reay was depressed and confused, with deeprooted mental problems stemming from his disturbed home background. A kind Christian brother came alongside him to point out the way of truth and God delivered him and broke every chain.

Eastern Scotland

As for Scotland, Henri and his Newark Glory team linked up with folk in Paisley and Edinburgh, in Methil on the Fifeshire coast, in Dundee and particularly with Mount Zion Tabernacle in Peterhead.

The Central Gospel Mission in Methil had been a faithful witness in the town for many a year. But times had been discouraging and they were struggling. Then one year David Brunton and his wife and family went on holiday to London. David and his son-in-law were buying a fish supper in Tooting when they heard hearty and joyful singing in a shop, which had been made into a hall. Immensely attracted by this, they were drawn in. David said, 'although it all seemed so strange and unorthodox, we realised that this was the true fashion in which to glorify God.' In fact they had found themselves amongst the

Surrey group and they listened to Gib Rudkin preaching. Back in Methil the Lord filled them with a joy and power in their lives previously unknown. They invited the Surrey group up there and then Henri and Connie, who festooned their rather dull hall in its industrial environment with their bright banners and placards. 'First convert the chapel, then you'll convert the people,' Henri would say. It was as though burdens were lifted and light and life flooded in. Said Elizabeth Keddie, 'The small assembly here was lifted from its drab routine into a great supernatural wave of the Spirit of God. I was blessed beyond measure.'[24]

When God transforms a situation He is often fulfilling the hidden heartbeat and yearnings of His people. Jim and Elizabeth Keddie, for instance, were a couple who had always had the joybells of salvation ringing inside them. Jim was very conscious of the wonderful way God had saved him, when he walked into a Seaman's Mission:

> He turned me upside down, He took me into his surgery and gave me a new heart and from that day fifty odd years ago the Lord said, 'Your life's going to be transformed into a life of holiness.'

Elizabeth had been brought up in a Christian home who knew what it was truly to rejoice in the Lord. When she was thirteen she was filled with the Holy Spirit in a lady's home.

> As she got on a tram to go home she was shouting, and there was an old gentleman; he said, 'My, you're looking happy. What's happened to you? Have you been to the cinema?' I said, 'No, I've been to the prayer meeting.' He says, 'What!' He said to the conductor, 'Look at her face! It's lit up!' ... What a wonderful life we had in our family. We had prayer meetings in the parlour, people were saved and filled with the Spirit in our house.'[25]

Concerning Peterhead, John Betjeman describes his surprise at having to travel so far north to Aberdeen:

> Could there be such a thing as a great city with tramcars, electric lights, hotels, and cathedrals so far away among empty fields, so near the North Pole as we were going?[26]

And the fishing port of Peterhead is yet thirty miles further up the coast. Yet this distance never deterred any getting together. When the weatherbeaten fisherman Lewy Cardno caused surprise by venturing 400 or 500 miles south for fellowship, he would reply with great feeling, 'My Saviour travelled all the way from the glories of heaven down to this sin-sick earth to save me. Is it too far for me to come to you?'

Simon Cameron describes how his family and the assembly were greatly quickened when coming into contact with Henri. It was just at the right moment. They had left their Pentecostal denomination, the Apostolic, and were seeking the Lord for the next step. They first heard of Henri through their sister Chrissie in Huddersfield when they were staying with her on holiday. Simon was booked to preach somewhere in the town, when his brother John said, 'Why not go to Henri's? There's a meeting at Leeds.' Why not? Simon phoned the pastor of the church where he was going to preach and managed to cancel this and fix up another date. However, at the mention of Henri's name the pastor drew in his breath and said, 'Watch yourself!' But to Newark they went. 'Oh, we were so straight-laced,' said Simon. Before long, in the meeting, a young man came and grabbed Simon's hand; he in turn grabbed Wendy his wife's, and she Chrissie's, and off they all skipped and joined in a great Glory march.

When they drove back to Huddersfield, John suddenly pulled into a lay-by on the side of the road and Simon pulled in behind him. John jumped out of his car and began to sing his own composition:

> *This Glory Way, this Glory Way*
> *Has been revealed. It's for today.*
> *So enter in, whate'er men say,*
> *And praise the Lord, this Glory Way.*

The brothers fell about laughing through the sheer surprise of it all. Then spontaneously they all had a really great Glory meeting in Chrissie's house in Huddersfield. They were staying there in caravans, and John came bouncing round from his caravan to Simon's, exclaiming, 'I've got it!' 'Got what?' 'I've got the Glory!'

They drove up to Nan Logan's fellowship at West Auckland, where hearts were kindled. From there they returned home, and began to sing and dance in their Peterhead assembly. Dad Cameron exclaimed, 'You're a bunch of deadheads!' Whenever

they praised and danced there was a rumpus, and they lost a lot
of folk. In fact they were down to about a dozen people. But
when they were together, they spoke out as though there were
five hundred there. Anyhow, some gave their hearts to the Lord,
some came in, folk were quickened, and altogether their lives
were revolutionised. Simon said, concerning the Glory: 'One
moment I hadn't it; the next moment I had it!' As often happens,
those who opposed the Glory most were the ones most in need
of it.

This exuberance spilled over into the streets of their fishing
port. The Cameron brothers organised open-air meetings to
preach the gospel in Broad Street and then in the Market Square.
They were meetings full of dancing and praise, and drew as many
as 1500 people. One can imagine the impact on the town. They
also went to the fishing village of Cairnbulg near Fraserburgh,
where they were always given a very warm welcome. As time
went on Chrissie (the sister then in Huddersfield) proved to be
outstanding in the support she gave to itinerant evangelistic
trips.

Northern Ireland

Henri and his team crossed the Irish Sea in July 1963 to bring joy
to the little town of Portglenone about ten miles north of Lough
Neagh. The Christian Fellowship there organised a fortnight's
camp and the Glory folk came for the last three days. It was
memorable. Young Jean Andrews wrote,

> Thank God for sending Brother Henri to Ireland. He really
> brought something with him from God. Since then I have
> received a new release and a deeper experience in my
> Christian life and the love of God has become so real.
> Hallelujah! [27]

The visit of Henri's team had one practical result. The
Christian Fellowship launched out in open-air work and started
holding monthly Glory rallies.

The next year, 1964, the Glory folk visited Belfast, the nearby
town of Lisburn, and on to seaside Bangor where they competed
with Orangemen's celebrations. The place was packed and the
town clerk allowed them to use the Sunken Gardens. The Irish
were really stirred up by these meetings. Shirley Morgan of
Saintfield near Belfast wrote,

Ireland has been set on fire and you know there isn't enough water in the whole world to put it out. There's nothing like it. I'm spoiled for everything else. I will never, never, never be the same again. [28]

And Victor Stewart of Belfast said,

I thank God for ever sending Brother Henri and his team to Ireland, for, as a result of his visit, hundreds of lives have been changed and bound spirits set free. I believe that only eternity itself will tell of the miracles that have been wrought in the lives of some of the Irish folk ... A flame has been kindled in the hearts of us Irish, that all the devils in the world can never put out. Hallelujah! [29]

In August 1965 Cecil Stewart, Victor's brother, organised a tent campaign at Monaghan in Eire, just over the border from County Down. Roy Turner and Simon Cameron came for the first week, and the brothers David and Glyn Greenow for most of the remaining fortnight. There was opposition; many people got mad and told them to get back to Northern Ireland, as they had never been invited. But lives were changed, were saved, received the baptism in the Holy Spirit. Sick folk said that they had been healed. Greatly encouraged by this, Cecil Stewart said, 'Let us go all out in 1966 to do more for God than ever. Time is short and undoubtedly it is *revival time* now!' [30]

Since those days the Lord has prospered Cecil Stewart, for in 1968 he formed the Sandown Group which grew to be the largest privately owned nursing home group in the United Kingdom, employing about 2000 people. For this he gained the OBE from Prince Charles for the company's contribution to the economy.

With this divine sense of urgency did Cecil have a premonition of what lay only three years in the future: the outbreak of the Irish troubles in 1969 with all the violence and hatred that was unleashed then? It is telling to think that God sent Henri and the Glory team to bring joy and light to the Emerald Isle just before these terrible things broke loose. Also it is a simple and wonderful fact that the grace of God is not stifled by wicked events and many Irish people have been saved during these difficult times. Who knows but that the very dangers have made people flee to God? And who knows how much people at large had been moved by the Glory Way's demonstration of the love of the Lord Jesus Christ?

Conclusion

Let's stand back a moment and try to see the sovereignty of God in all this. For a start, Mansfield and Newark are pretty close to the centre of England; just a little north of centre, in fact, which means that Scotland is that little bit closer. Henri and Connie did not choose to be born or brought up there, but these towns were in the right place. When it comes to travelling all over Britain, then Newark is wonderfully strategic, far and away better than London. (Though our metropolis is strategic for Europe.) Major communications north and south, London to Edinburgh, run through or past it: an express railway line and a junction with another, and then there's the ancient Great North Road, the A1. From the late fifties onwards – just at the time that the Glory Way dramatically expanded – the road system of Britain was revolutionised. Many major trunk roads became dual carriageway and, starting with the M1 in 1959, the motorway system was built. Newark was easy to get to, and from Newark it was easy to reach anywhere else. How cheerfully along these roads the Glory buses flew, driven by Norman Parsons and Eric Staples. Many a hired coach from Stoke-on-Trent, West Auckland or Ringwood tipped out their happy singing passengers at Newark for a bank holiday convention, or at one of the seaside holidays at the Isle of Wight, Blackpool, Scarborough or Southend-on-Sea.

It is painfully obvious that there has been a moral decline in the Western world during the twentieth century. Many things have contributed to it, some on the face of it quite harmless, such as the colossal advance in technology and communication. The Bible says that in the end time *'many shall run to and fro and knowledge shall be increased'* (Daniel 12:4); but it also shows that a positive nose-dive towards evil would take place, *'that in the last days perilous times shall come. For men shall be lovers of their own selves'* (2 Timothy 3:1–2), resulting in treacherous, violent behaviour. In a sense this has not happened overnight; the roots of this go back five hundred years or more. In this century our chapels and churches well nigh emptied as a result of liberal theology, or disbelief in or even antagonism to the plain truths of the Bible, and so moral poison has been passed down the ethical food chain of society.

Since the beginning of the sixties this has been particularly alarming: permissive legislation by governments, startling assassinations, a new strident sound in music and the media which brutally disturbed our peace and quiet, student revolt and flower power. At the time the whole thing felt like a great tidal wave engulfing us.

Well, when you think about it, wasn't the Lord's timing with the Glory Way really rather remarkable? The moment when Henri and Connie moved out from their open-air witness in Mansfield Market to other towns and an altogether wider sphere was in the last two years of the fifties. By 1960 invitations were coming into the Glory Office thick and fast, the phone was ringing continuously and the Glory buses with their teams were shooting away from Newark in every direction. The Glory Way was right there, 'Blazing a trail for a mighty Holy Ghost Revival,' as Henri put it. With a shout of joyful praise, they were holding up to the world the eternal gospel of Jesus Christ saving the world by His precious shed blood, at the moment when we most needed to hear it.

Of course, the Glory Way has only been just a part of the whole great spiritual scene. Billy Graham's gospel preaching in stadiums followed by other big-scale evangelists, world-wide Christian radio, a healthy movement in the churches back to the dynamic truths of Scripture, and the rise of the charismatic movement with a new awareness of the work of the Holy Spirit: these have all been on the Godward side of things against sin, evil and decline. But I am saying that, when the chips are down, we see that Henri and Connie and their Glory folk with their distinctive witness were bang on, right there, in the right place and at the right moment.

Chapter 9

Glory Friends

Naturally, the Glory Way made many friends over the years. It is very interesting to see what a number of them did as God directed their lives.

Arthur and Marjorie Burt

Born in 1912 at Whitley Bay, near Newcastle-on-Tyne, Arthur Burt was just four years younger than Henri. He had a difficult upbringing; his father was a doctor from Southampton who had committed some malpractice and moved north to escape his reputation and start a new life.

Young Arthur had no Christian background, but he heard the gospel from a Baptist preacher and was saved, as were both his parents some time later. About this time an unusual thing happened. Arthur went to hear Stephen Jeffreys at Wakefield, Doncaster and another Yorkshire town, all meetings with thousands of people, and on each occasion the great man singled Arthur out from the large mass of people, pointing straight at him and calling out: 'Young man, God wants you.' The message was unmistakable. Arthur obeyed, though not without a struggle, for he had ambitions to be a journalist and writer.

Anyone who has met and heard Arthur Burt will recognise the fact that God has given him a striking gift of ready speech, unhesitating, incisive and dogmatic, with a delicious touch of humour. He has also had a long life, so that he has been preaching continuously for about seventy years. His is the kind of voice that might well have filled an evangelistic stadium. But the Lord has chosen to map out for him a life of roving pilgrimage, led by the Holy Spirit, to make decisions and go to places which have been a surprise to himself.

It was in the early 1930s, when travelling through the Midlands with another young evangelist, that he first met Henri. He said,

> We were in Newark holding meetings and I was preaching in the open air. We had a big Chevrolet caravan; the back let down, making a platform, and we would preach from that. Across the road was a shop called Public Benefit; so I picked on the title of the shop to speak on it. I was speaking of the Public Benefit, who of course was Jesus, and I noticed this little man down by the side of it, smoking his cigarettes and smiling and beaming. I didn't know who he was. Then he started jumping up and down, waving his arms and crying, 'Go on! Go on! Bye, that's right! Go on!' So when the meeting was over he came across the road and asked, 'Would you like to stop at our house?' (We lived in the caravan.) So I said, 'Thank you,' and we went to stop with this Henri fellow and his wife Connie. We also met his brother Eric who had a bicycle repair shop.
>
> Well, we got to know them quite well and I remember this little man playing the piano. He played the chorus:
>
> *I am ever so glad that He sought me,*
> *He sought me, He sought me,*
> *I am ever so glad that He found me,*
> *To make me His very own.*
> *From the glory of heaven He willingly came,*
> *Thinking not of Himself, but my sinning and shame.*
> *I am ever so glad that He found me,*
> *And made me His very own.*
>
> That's my first memory of Henri, bubbling, shouting, playing the piano, and on fire.

As a young man Arthur Burt did extensive tent evangelism, exhausting work, particularly when a storm blows your tent to shreds. He had pastorates in north London, Nottinghamshire and Kent. Much of the time he laboured at secular jobs, as a salesman, market gardener and so on. In all his vicissitudes he has had a wonderful camp follower in his wife Marjorie, born in China of missionary parents.

When a young man he spent time with a character he greatly honoured, Smith Wigglesworth. Arthur writes,

It is amazing how people put men on pedestals. Many people, especially Americans, think very highly of Wigglesworth. They often ask me if I had known him, and sometimes mischievously I will answer, 'Oh yes, I knew Wigglesworth, slept in the same bedroom with him, ate with him, carried his bags for him.' I knew and esteemed Wigglesworth, but I didn't worship him. I didn't even think he was wonderful, but I knew he had a wonderful God. He had a God-given faith, and he believed, like a child, that God said what He meant and meant what He said. [1]

After the War Arthur was compelled to take a secular job in order to qualify for family benefit. He took to selling pressure cookers, blankets and other things in the Mansfield area. He built up quite a clientele and made a real success of it, winning the trust of many people and gaining many opportunities to witness for the Lord. It is very interesting that he should experience this kind of thing roughly in the same area as Henri and the two men were thrown together when Arthur found that he had to resign from his pastorate. As a result, in 1958 he linked up with various Christians in Mansfield and with Henri and Connie in Newark. He had this to say:

Henri was a go-getter. He was also a non-conformist and never did what I thought he ought to do. With his piano accordion around his neck, Henri was unpredictable ... Like the rescuer administers artificial respiration, Henri would exhort people who, half-drowned in tradition, unbelief or pride, failed to respond to the prompting of the Spirit.

Many a time in the meetings he would call out, 'That sister over there – no, don't look behind you – it's you with the green hat. Come on. If you don't come, I will fetch you.' And he would do it. The poor woman would come trembling to the front, and there would be eager, loving hands to lift her onto the platform. 'Oh, I do like your hat. It matches your coat,' he would smile. 'Come on, folks. Give her a clap.' I used to complain silently, 'What is all this, a crowd of people clapping because a woman's hat matches her coat? What have I got myself into?' I considered Henri's meeting shallow, empty, irreverent, and unspiritual, especially whenever all the people would link arms as if at a party ... I used to criticise everything in Henri's meetings, and my attitude produced an iceberg of pride deep inside my being. One night while they were having a Jericho march round the hall, God corrected me, 'Stop judging, start marching, and your icy heart will melt.'[2]

Arthur obeyed – a hard lesson for him – and before long he found himself in genuine heart-felt fellowship with the Glory folk. This began a long association with Henri; he contributed some dynamic articles to the *Glory News*, and from time to time he would preach a good word, particularly at the summer holiday conventions.

In 1960 Henri linked Arthur and his family up with Archie Friday and his break-away assembly in Paddock Wood in Kent. They were co-pastors there together. Twenty years after that the Lord led Arthur and Marj to buy a large house, Bron Wendon, at Penmaenmawr on the North Welsh coast which they have run as a centre for Christian fellowship and conventions. They have around them members of their family and younger couples who have become a marvellous team.

Also, in the late 1970s, Arthur began to cross the Atlantic. The initial contact was most unusual and un-called-for. But it has led Arthur out into a most fruitful world-wide ministry to the United States in particular, but also to Central and South America, Israel, Australia and Hong Kong.

The Surrey Group

In about 1958 Gibson and Joyce Rudkin and some friends were driving through Mansfield in their Bedford Dormobile van. They stopped in the road and another car drew up alongside them. It was Henri. He called out cheerily, 'You're the Surrey Group!' And Gib Rudkin greeted him, 'And you're the Henri Crowd!' Henri had been alerted about this band of Pentecostal Christians from north Surrey. So they met and theirs was an instant bond of friendship. The group came from Ashtead, Epsom, Sutton and Croydon. Gib, a builder, was tall, with a commanding bearing and a very able speaker. Then there were Cecil and Grace Pywell and Grace's brother Jack and sister-in-law Felicia from Grenada in the Caribbean, and others.

They never had a church building because they made a point of keeping themselves free at the weekends to travel in what we could call a ministry of encouragement. From about 1955 to 1959 they were a great support to the evangelist Peter Scothern. In turn, through him, they were introduced to Henri and the

Glory Way. It was just at the time of expansion, with meetings in many parts of the country. The Surrey Group would faithfully come along to Stockton, Darlington, Doncaster, Leeds Town Hall, Barrow-in-Furness, then to London, to Willesden with the Preudhommes and the big rallies at Lambeth Town Hall. Once going north they broke a fan belt, but they tied the pulley wheels round with a woman's stocking and made it all right.

The group also went on their own up to Scotland, to Methil and St Andrews in Fife, and finally to Peterhead. How well they remember one of those open-air meetings in the middle of the town, with the Cameron brothers preaching from an open lorry and the main street absolutely crowded.

Cecil and Grace express real appreciation of the tremendous welcome that the Glory Way always gave them. They always made the Surrey Group feel wonderfully at home. 'A great chap, Henri!' enthuses Cecil. He recalls how Henri's ministry was one of pure encouragement. He was always emphasising basic doctrines and making salvation so personal. 'It's in you, brother! It's in you, sister!' And then he would call out, 'This is a deliverance meeting.' He would always talk about the joy of salvation and how this leads to glory! Cecil reminisces how excitable and outgoing Henri always was, and how he loved to pray for people there on the spot. Connie was a great help to Henri in the Glory meetings as she would bring the Word of God very powerfully as the Holy Spirit anointed her. Grace especially remembers her speaking on 'The camels are coming', when Isaac was in the field meditating and his bride arrived.

There was also the enormous hard work that went into every meeting; there was so much that went into getting a hall prepared beforehand and clearing it up afterwards, quite apart from the expenditure of energy in the meeting itself.

Back on their home territory the Surrey Group for a time hired a Salvation Army hall for mid-week meetings. In particular they had an ongoing visiting ministry in Brookwood Hospital for the mentally ill and depressed. They have been greatly used by the Lord to bring encouragement and hope to these people.

Outstanding were the monthly Glory rallies which were organised by Gib and David Willows, held in Wimbledon, also occasionally at Lambeth Town Hall. With Joyce Rudkin on the piano and a team of musicians they had wonderful times of praise and true liberty in the Lord, the presence and power of the Holy Spirit so evident.

In 1994 Gib Rudkin experienced a remarkable healing. In fact it was a return to life from a state of death. He described it most graphically at the Glory summer holiday that year. During a period of five months he became very weak, lost nearly three stone and then contracted jaundice, which turned him yellow and then green. A friend phoned him up saying, 'Gib, whatever you do, don't go green.' And she added, 'When you go green, it's terminal.' So he knew where he was. One day he felt as though all his physical functions had packed up and two hands scooped what was left of him out of his body. All went black, then brilliantly light. He was lovingly placed on a beautiful mattress covered in soft down, and was given the extraordinary choice of entering heaven or returning to earth. He thought of family and friends praying for him and he saw the Lord Christ kneeling in Gethsemane. This broke him and he consciously decided (like Janie Marshall in her vision) to return to earth. The pair of hands brought him back into his body. He came in with a convulsive jerk and rattled the bed. He was completely whole and healthy. In this way the Lord gave Gib six more years of useful service. He went to be with his Saviour in September 2000.

West Auckland and Newton Aycliffe

As referred to in the last chapter, it all began with Nan Logan, who for years led a Baptist mission for drunks and down-and-outs in the docks of Sunderland in County Durham. One day she was invited to hold an evangelistic campaign at a Methodist church in West Auckland, on the other side of the county. In this she was supported by a group of praying women from an Assemblies of God fellowship in Bishop Auckland, and through them experienced the baptism in the Holy Spirit. She moved from Sunderland to West Auckland, and in time became pastor of the West Auckland Assemblies of God.

Jack and Pansy Dickenson and their two daughters Pamela and Jeanette were members of her church fellowship, as was Lily Bainbridge their niece, who was particularly close to them. Lily has a strong memory of the West Auckland Assembly building, which was constructed rather like a lecture theatre on a slope with pews rising up one behind another.

One Sunday, in the autumn of 1959, Archie Friday from Paddock Wood in Kent (who had recently been greatly challenged and blessed by Henri) was preaching at an assembly in the area and, as a result, Nan Logan invited Henri and Connie to come a week later to West Auckland. Nan described the impact that they made:

> Since stepping into this Glory Way, I feel twenty years younger. I possess a reality that cannot be moved and I am convinced that God in these last days has charged us with something new for this world. I've been in Pentecost for years and have gone forth here and there declaring the mysteries of God, but I was sadly lacking in joy and you know, friends, the joy of the Lord is our strength. [3]

Certainly Henri and Connie brought nothing less than a spiritual revolution to West Auckland, and it was natural that a strong link-up with Newark should follow. They travelled to each others' meetings in their buses. The West Auckland folk even came to Henri's for Christmas and loved going to Glory rallies, like the large gatherings in Leeds Town Hall. Nan Logan also explained that, along with their new found liberty, they found their vision enlarged. She in her thorough-going way founded an independent Revival Centre in West Auckland. She said, 'Wherever there is an open door we are going in. We are claiming Durham and Northumberland for God.' [4] There was a cost to this too; they found that old friends cold-shouldered them.

Mention must be made of yet another group, that of Jim and Cynthia Wilkinson at Hollybush Farm, near Thirsk in North Yorkshire. Jim Wilkinson is a farmer, feet firmly planted on the ground, with his spiritual roots in Methodism. First Cynthia and then he came into the experience of the baptism of the Holy Spirit. Round them grew up a close knit band of hard working, rejoicing Christians who have known what it is to see and expect real miracles of healing and deliverance (as vividly recounted in the book *Miracle Valley*). Contact in the early seventies with Nan Logan, and then with Chris Wingfield, Mick Copeman and Doug Aistrup, followed by Roy Turner, the Camerons and others brought an added joy, liberty and refreshment to a fellowship already active in serving the Lord. Henri himself took a meeting there in the 1980s.

To return to West Auckland, Nan Logan and the Revival Centre were often visited by George and Gladys Breckon and their young son Rodney, who later married Jeanette Dickenson. For many years George and Gladys pastored the flourishing New Life Baptist Church at Northallerton and had many links in North Yorkshire and the Dales, including the Hollybush fellowship. George used to say, ' I'm a Pentecostal Methodist on the Glory road.' In time Rodney and Jeanette took over the leadership of the Northallerton church. When Rodney as a youngster was first taken to a Glory meeting he remarked about the music, saying he could not believe that you can be Christian and have such wonderful times singing such happy songs. He has now proved to be a gifted musician and has been used in a tremendous way with music and song.

Speaking again of the Dickenson family, Jack was a miner, a deputy at the mine where he worked in County Durham. He and Pansy married and it was not until he was forty that he was saved. Pansy had had three hard years praying for him. Jack now had to face the issue of working in the mine on a Sunday. He said no to it, and so was put on stone work for a while. He then managed to get a factory job in nearby Newton Aycliffe (which was a new town that had sprung up after the War). Jack only had the work of a labourer, but he was conscious that it was a miracle that he had the job at all. He did not mind; he saw it as the will of God for him at that moment, and he delighted to quote the text, *'godliness with contentment is great gain'* (1 Timothy 6:6).

Naturally they continued to support Nan Logan's assembly in West Auckland. But one Sunday evening they stood at the bus stop for an hour; the bus never came. As Jack walked back into their house, he heard, as it were, the Lord telling him to start a meeting in their own home. They had with them an uncle of Pansy's, Sid Palmley. He was a retired Pentecostal pastor, and widowed. He had started life as a Methodist and he knew all the hymns. Jack and Pansy's younger daughter Jeanette could play the piano well. Their uncle said, 'Let's praise the Lord,' and so they did. There was such a sense of the presence of God in their living room. It was as though Jesus was standing there.

From that moment things began to happen. Pansy said, 'We didn't want to be pastors and we didn't want to be a church.' But people from roundabout started to come. One week they were joined by David Greenow from Hereford and his younger brother Glyn. Jack asked them to preach. Later they hired a hall for meetings, and also organised a campaign in a tent on a green near them, with the evangelist Cecil Stewart from Ireland. They made quite a stir in the community around them. Folk were saved, including their mayoress. New people kept coming. They would phone up for prayer. A number of people were healed of their illnesses, and were delivered from oppressive spirits. God answered prayer in wonderful ways.

God has blessed the work and in 1987 a new building was erected which became known as Christian Life Centre, in Wood-ham Village, Newton Aycliffe. Many people are drawn from around the North East, coming to be blessed and receive the anointing in a truly vibrant way. Further expansion has recently taken place with the purchase of additional buildings, enabling the gospel to be taken to a wider audience.

Glyn Greenow was now married to Pamela Dickenson. Glyn became co-pastor of the fellowship under Jack in 1978. And when Jack retired through ill health, Glyn took over and is pastor there today with his son John. Pamela's cousin, Lily Bainbridge, in turn married Douglas Aistrup, who had been wonderfully delivered from alcoholism. His story is told in Chapter 13.

Pansy Dickenson is emphatic that their Newton Aycliffe fellowship was born directly out of the Glory Way and Glyn Greenow had this to say in appreciation:

> Henri had no time for labels, no inhibitions. He just wanted to bless. The Glory folk had an impact on thousands of lives. Only heaven will reveal the influence that Henri and Connie had.

Mention must be made of the Foster family with Mark, Lena and their children, Ann, Jean and Robert. They came in contact with the Glory people when Henri and team used to visit Bebside and Bedlington Station near Blyth, Northumberland, where they attended Bob and Betty Lloyd's church, eventually moving further south to the Christian Life Centre at Woodham. Jean and Robert are gifted musicians and the Lord has greatly used them in the meetings over the years. Jean has travelled to America with Bob Lloyd and is now very useful in the adminis-tration of the church at Woodham. Robert assists Doug Aistrup in the Glory meetings in the North East as does Ann's husband Alan Gilmore who is a gifted singer.

International Gospel Outreach

The Glory Way had a formative influence on another young couple, Bob and Ann Searle, who eventually moved from the south coast via Chorley Wood to Newton Aycliffe and, after 21 years there, again on to North Wales. Here is Bob's own story:

One afternoon in the late 1950s, along with a number of friends from my Air Force base in Cambridge, travelling in an old Austin Seven car, we visited the Glory Room above Henri's shop in Newark. We were immediately hit by what can only be described as 'a wave of liquid love'. For a bunch of young airmen, seeking more of God, this was revolutionary and *very* welcome. Our lives were impacted in a mighty way, a move of God broke out at our base, and for me, at any rate, the rest of my life was completely changed. Some months later, after demob, my new wife Ann and I, along with a few interested friends, pioneered a fellowship in Portsmouth and later also in Gosport, called 'Portsmouth and Gosport Glory Group'. This was greatly blessed of God and visited on occasions by Henri and the Glory Team. The Group travelled many miles together to be at Glory meetings around the country, and in August 1961 Ann and I were attending the Glory Convention at the Technical College, Newark with around 600 others from all over Britain. During that time, David Greenow was ministering and Ann took Cathy, our three-month-old daughter, up to be dedicated to the Lord. As David prayed, Ann was mightily baptised in the Holy Spirit, Cathy went flying and a lovely black lady on the platform caught her!

In the years that followed, a number of those who ministered at Glory conventions would get together annually for tent outreaches on Southsea sea front and a strong bond was formed between these evangelists. Eventually they joined together to form a Charitable Trust, which in 1967 became known as *International Gospel Outreach*. David Greenow became President and was a wonderful blessing for thirty years. At the end of that period David handed over the Presidency to Kingsley Armstrong, the husband of the baby he dedicated in Newark in 1961! IGO, by nature non-denominational, has grown and developed over the years and now has members in many nations around the world and it links together pastors, evangelists, Christian workers of all kinds, missionaries and so on, for mutual support and encouragement in prayer and fellowship. Apart from one brother, Jack Dickenson, who went to be with the Lord some years ago, the other 'originals' are still 'together' and serving the Lord all over Britain and around the world. [5]

In 1994, the headquarters of IGO moved from Newton Aycliffe to Dwygyfylchi in North Wales and in 1996 moved into a former hotel, which has now been totally restored from derelict and has become the Oasis Christian Centre. This is near to Penmaenmawr, where Arthur Burt and family have their base at Bron Wendon. Arthur's sons Steve and Joe, with their building team Willy, Gary and Mike, were a great help with some of the restoration work at the Oasis in the early days and since the restoration Arthur has used the Oasis, an ideal Centre with its beautiful views, for his Conventions. Willy Moffat and Eileen in fact live in Peterhead and regularly drive a Faith Acres relief lorry to Romania. Willy has spearheaded the distribution of tracts and New Testaments in North West China. It is fascinating to see such cross currents in the Lord's work.

Leah and Levi Ben-Israel

The Glory Way has been like a fire with sparks flying out in all directions. Hearts and souls have caught fire spontaneously. To change the metaphor, vision and activity were brought to birth in Glory meetings. Once born, they had a life of their own. There was no knowing where they would lead to. The wind of the Holy Spirit blows where it wants to. The experiences of Leah and Levi Ben-Israel bore this out. They first went to a Glory meeting in 1960; this was in Newark. Leah described it like this:

> When I went to my first Glory meeting I was baptised in the Holy Ghost, but was shy and full of inhibitions. But God set me *free* in the Holy Spirit as He gave me a baptism of *love* beyond any *love* I had ever known before, as I basked in His eternal light, glory and compassion.
>
> We ran to the doors and, as we heard the singing and music, we burst open the doors and the glory hit us as we entered. The glory came first to the instrumentalists at the front and rolled down in waves of glory from the front; and as the glory hit people, some would shout and sing for joy and glory, others would crumple with weeping. Some would dance, some who could not enter in would sit, hardened in heart, feeling exposed and alone in the midst of a praising people...
>
> I remember one meeting; all the chairs pushed back, and two brothers in the Spirit came from opposite ends, NW and SE, and met in the centre in an intricate dance step, to

whirl around as they linked arms; a kind of Slavic or Swiss dance, in power and identical movements. I've never forgotten it.

I remember being doubled up as a spirit of laughter swept over us, as the floor was cleared, and one brother swirled around in a clownish way and we could not stop laughing. Asked about it afterwards, he said it was a tremendous discipline to yield to the Holy Ghost to become a laughing spectacle before all the people; and it taught him obedience and discipline in the Holy Ghost. It relaxed all tension and inhibitions in us as the spirit of laughter took hold of us in uncontrollable paroxysms of the Spirit, setting one another off till tears rolled down our cheeks and our stomachs ached. All tension fled and we were set gloriously free and true to ourselves and our God.

Meetings like this are certainly very unusual. Leah's descriptions may be criticised as far-fetched, exaggerated and therefore totally unnecessary side-tracking from the real issue. But we answer, If the Holy Spirit so chooses in sovereign grace to visit folk in this way, who are we to quarrel? Leah has a further memory,

I remember being taken out to the front to Henri and Connie and they pulled me between them and we three danced in triplicate, steps and movements all in the Holy Ghost. I was completely liberated as we all three danced in complete unity and rhythm in the Holy Ghost in front of all the people, and let God take over.

I received a revelation and vision of the heavenly view of Calvary, looking down from heaven to earth, to Jesus on the cross, and I rested in eternal peace in the *finished completeness* of the redemption available to the whole world. 'It is done,' as God said in the scripture. 'Joy unspeakable and full of glory' beyond anything I had ever received on earth was mine as I basked in the eternal realities in heaven.

The reaction of Levi and Leah to all this was to take it to a needy place. God quietly spoke to them to 'take the Glory to bleak, dark, post-war, post-holocaust Germany.' They found a church 'generally in mourning, a land *in ashes*, a darkness hanging like a pall over the land wherever we went.' Their mission was to bring 'a measure of healing'. In the event it was really amazing the way that the Lord used them.

As they were preparing to leave England they were joined by another sister who also felt clearly called of God to visit Germany and who also spoke the language fluently. With six-month-old Miriam in a carrycot, they had their fares to Harwich, and their fares on the ferry across to Holland and no more. Ahead of them lay three-and-a-half months of travelling in four countries. They ventured by faith and their needs were met each step of the way. They had been given a beautiful prophecy:

> God said He would take us out and bring us safely back to these shores. That He would go before and touch the hearts of the people to receive us. That he would take us to a place and there we were to stay and preach His Word until He moved us on to a new place, and He would not provide too little lest we did not go far enough, and He would not provide too much lest we go too far...

They did not have an itinerary, but were totally free to move just when and where the Holy Spirit led them: north to Denmark, then south to Hamburg and up the Rhine Valley and into Bavaria to Nurtingen, near Stuttgart. Then east to Salzburg and Austria; once more back to Bavaria and so home. There were many crushed lives, many hungry hearts. Some folk immediately received them with joy. On the other hand they found that so many of the meetings were heavy, oppressive and the people oppressed. Levi and Leah cried to the Lord that He would use them to bring the very glory of heaven to these people. Time after time God opened the way and they brought refreshment of soul and burdens were lifted. A good number of people were healed. There was one outstanding case, that of an eighteen-year-old lad Dieter, who had been brought home from a blind school with an egg-size tumour on his brain. He had been given two weeks to live. The Lord Jesus gave Levi a vision of his deliverance. Several folk fasted and prayed for Dieter and laid hands on him. Within a short time he was totally healed and his sight restored.

> Faith then was high in the village of Grossbettlingen and many came for healing. Several touched the hem of His garment and were made whole from deafness, demon power and stomach trouble.

Levi went on to add, 'One sister, a school teacher, was mightily filled with the Holy Ghost and fire.' In this way Levi and Leah carried a breath of heaven and healing balm to a Europe still stricken and torn by a terrible war.

In 1964 God called them out again, initially to Ireland. With them now were Miriam aged three and Caleb aged two. They sauntered around a park in Belfast, praying for guidance. A young woman reading a Bible on a park bench told them of Glory meetings in Ballymena, led by a brother called David Gaston. This was the door to a remarkable experience, for David said that for some time God had been calling him to North America, and invited them to come with him, all expenses paid. They landed up in the Canadian Rockies, where David bought Pinegate Lodge, 160 acres of unspoiled wilderness, 4000 feet above sea level, the home of caribou, moose and rainbow trout. They had seven cabins built of huge logs. It was literally heaven on earth. For four years they ran it as a Christian retreat, and people flocked to them from a very wide area, to experience the love of Jesus in their midst. They were a big Glory family. There was great joy and wonder and much spontaneous praise. Leah said,

> I remember coming up the driveway after dark one evening, and a shimmering cross lit up the heavy log door, and Jesus spoke, 'It is the way of the cross for you.' I remember the silence of the pine forests around the lake, moose coming down to drink, the call of the loon on the lake, the times I rowed out into the lake alone to hear the Lord speak to me.

However, the peace of this golden moment was shattered when the government divided the lakeside into lots and sold them off. Construction machines, motor boats with oil fouling the water, blaring music, water skiing took over. The wild creatures came no more to drink, the water fowl were scared away. And so the retreat was sold. But the Lord said,

> Don't grieve. This is not the end, but the beginning. You will yet thank Me for taking this place from you when you see the greater thing I will do in the future.

Zion Fellowship in Peterhead

Certainly, the Glory Way link between Newark and Peterhead has always been very strong. How did it all begin? You could say, in a negative way, that it started with the terrible Battle of the Somme in 1916 when a staggering 420,000 British soldiers lost their lives. Mr Cameron from Peterhead survived this. His son Simon writes:

> Out of the thousands of young men who were sent overseas from the Highlands of Scotland, only a mere handful returned. What weeping and anguish there must have been all over Scotland when word was received of the terrible carnage. Whilst he was in the trenches in France, my father was given whisky and rum, along with the other Scottish soldiers, to enable him to withstand the terrible sights he saw. He was wounded in the head and in the shoulder, and came home a hopeless alcoholic! He was that way for forty long agonising years. He just couldn't help himself. He would sell everything he had to buy liquor. Many a time my mother would say sadly to me: 'Simon, your father is drunk again. Go and see if you can find him.'[6]

In the family there were four sons, Michael, John, Alex and Simon, and three daughters, Chrissie, Annie and Jessie. The eldest son, Michael, during World War II was stationed on the island of Stroma, between John o'Groats and the Orkneys, where great convoys of allied ships passed through every night, vulnerable to German attack. Michael's job was to save as much material as possible from badly damaged ships beached on the island. Michael was also known for his drunken habits, but one day, up there in the north, God spoke to him. For some time life to him had seemed empty and pointless and death a fearful threat. When passing through John o'Groats, he stopped at a tea shop and read some tracts scattered on the table in front of him. He found Christ as his Saviour and his life was changed and revolutionised. It was as though a light 'brighter than the light of the noonday sun' shone round about him.

When he went back home and witnessed about his new found faith, to his surprise and grief none of the family wanted to know. However, in a little Pentecostal meeting, Michael received through the Holy Spirit a direct word:

> To my young servant do I speak at this time. If you remain faithful, I will bring in your whole family.

A few years later two young evangelists, Donald Walker and Herbert Harrison, came to Peterhead to hold a six-week campaign.

It was a reaping time for God. Ninety people were brought to the foot of the cross and were saved, including about sixty Camerons! And what a joy it was, a little later, when alcoholic dad, intending to go to the cinema, turned into a chapel where his son Michael was preaching and was wonderfully saved and delivered from drink, in just a moment of time!

Simon and Wendy Cameron were married young; Wendy was overjoyed at the birth of her first child, a boy, but was absolutely devastated, three days later, when she held him dead in her arms. For a time she turned her back on God. Meanwhile Simon was called up to do his army service and was stationed in Italy. Wendy then heard a young man preach on *'What profiteth a man if he gain the whole world and lose his own soul?'* She turned to the Lord, and was saved. Joy flooded in. But she had to wait seven whole years for Simon to follow suit, during which time they had four children. He was absolutely mad with Wendy. He said, 'I was determined that my way of life would never be changed by this Christ.' But at last the breaking point came. Under great conviction of sin he turned to God for forgiveness and new life.

> It was indeed a miracle! Simon never stopped weeping for three days and three nights. Jesus cleansed him in His own way. Yes, Simon was really changed! As forceful as he had been in the world, just as forceful was he now for the kingdom of God. [7]

In fact, it was wonderful the way the whole Cameron family were saved: the brothers Michael, John, Alex and Simon and their wives and children. They were members in Peterhead of an Apostolic Church (a Pentecostal denomination). Then they came in contact with the Glory Way and they founded their own fellowship called Zion Fellowship with Simon as pastor. With them the gospel veritably burst out upon the community around them. I have already mentioned their open-air meetings. They were really quite something. It was Mansfield Market all over again. Simon Cameron mentions how they made a conscious decision to bring their joy and liberty out into the open street. He recounted,

> It was a cold night and we had not announced or advertised the meeting and as we started singing there wasn't a soul in sight. There were about thirty to forty of us rejoicing in the Lord and we hadn't been going long when a car came down

the street. There was a sudden squeal of brakes and out
jumped the occupants to see what was going on. Other cars
followed suit, doors were flung open, folks seemed to come
from nowhere and within a few minutes we had a big crowd
gathered round. There was a great interest created as the
people had never seen it on this wise before ...

My! What a crowd was there waiting for us the next
Sunday. I never saw such a crowd in my life. We preached
the Word, rejoiced in the Lord and testified of His goodness
and the folks were blessed. On the third Sunday night there
was so much traffic with people coming to the open-air
meeting, that it was necessary to redirect the vehicles and
three policemen to come and control. Hallelujah!

The Police put pressure on the Camerons to move to the
Market Place, which they gladly did. They now brought a lorry
which they used as a platform, with a piano mounted on it. There
were other instrumentalists, and Roy Turner, when he was
present, would bring his accordion. The team would sing, dance,
preach and give their testimonies. They certainly created an
impact. Simon, who earned the nickname of 'The Pied Piper of
Peterhead', said,

> The next week the local paper took the story up and we had
> in the region of fifteen hundred people at the very next
> meeting as a result, and what a grand time we had. Praise
> the Lord! It was really wonderful. Every day during the week
> I was continually being stopped in the street by people
> saying how they were blessed and healed, and they agreed
> that the Christian life should be a joyful life. It was the
> common people who heard us gladly. They know reality;
> they know when people have the goods but, as you may
> expect, we have had opposition from some of the religious
> leaders. But it is well worth it, to see deliverance that is
> coming to the other folk. [8]

In the next chapter the story of the Camerons in the United
States in the sixties will be told. Since that time the Camerons'
work for the Lord in Peterhead has forged ahead. In 1974 Simon
bought another property in Peterhead which they called Faith
Acres. They bought this to open a Bible school. Wendy Cameron
said of her husband,

Simon felt the need to reproduce this wonderful experience with others and started a Bible school which flourished, sending quickened people across the world. The students from Faith Acres have blessed many.

This Bible school certainly gives a good grounding in the Christian faith. They have a particular link with Teen Challenge which deals with drug addicts, bringing them help and deliverance. Faith Acres then feeds them with the Word of God. Wendy continues,

Simon, myself and our children work full-time in the gospel. Our grandchildren are also totally interested in sharing the excitement of the gospel. The Glory Way has left its seeds to grow in the next generation.

The church fellowship at Faith Acres is called New Hope Assembly. The pastor of this is Neil, the son of Simon and Wendy, who is doing a tremendous job. Their assembly is well attended. On Friday nights they have a Powerhouse Kids Club with 150 children. Two double-decker buses go round the town and pick them up. On Sunday evenings, in their secondary hall, they have Night Base with 70 to 80 teenagers. They come in from the Salvation Army and the Methodists and fill the place. The opportunity to influence the town for good does not end there because New Hope has a full licence with the Scripture Union and regularly leads school assemblies in Peterhead Academy.

Over at Zion Tabernacle there are two joint pastors, James Smith and John Cameron Junior, son of Michael Cameron. Simon and Wendy's daughter, also called Wendy, is the wife of James Smith and, because of her father's age, she plays a crucial part in running Faith Acres. She of course is the cousin of John Cameron Junior and the sister of Neil, so it can be seen how closely the two parts of their work for the Lord at Peterhead run together. And for any big meetings they combine. Zion also have their youth work, about fifty strong, which they call New Radical Church, led by John the son of John Cameron Junior. Every autumn they have a Youth Convention, with a Praise Band and groups from the United States, Scotland and England.

The north-east of Scotland is a morally needy corner of Britain. Drug addiction is a particular scourge. In nearby Fraserburgh alone there are five hundred heroin addicts, many of them wealthy fisher boys. It is not without reason that God has placed the Cameron family there to serve Him. Michael Cameron, who fought in the terrible Battle of the Somme, was blessed with thirty-eight grandchildren, many of whom love the Lord and work for Him – and their children too – in northern Scotland and in the United States. (John Cameron Senior founded Norcross Praise Fellowship in Atlanta, Georgia in 1980.)

You may ask, in the long run, has this recounting of events in Peterhead any great relevance to the Glory Way story? The answer is Yes, very much so. For a good number of years, Henri and Connie travelled north to conventions and rallies there. The Camerons were always eager to come south to link up with the Glory people. So that Wendy Cameron Smith said to me with very real feeling,

> Without any doubt the Cameron family in Peterhead owe a terrific debt to Henri and Connie Staples. Their impact, under God, left its mark on all of us!

In 1972 Simon Cameron wrote *Keys of Revival* which was published in America. In it he reflected,

> God spoke to me one day and I was meditating on His goodness to the Cameron family. As I thought about the way He has lifted us from such utter poverty, ignorance, degradation and sin, He gave me a motto and here it is. Why not make it yours also? 'We who are the objects of His mercy should be the trumpets of His praise.' Hallelujah!
>
> As the Cameron family ministers year after year, many people wonder how we keep the anointing of God in our lives. This is the secret: those who are forgiven much, love much! When God calls men and women it is often from the scrapheaps of humanity. He lifts the weak, the base and the foolish, from the mud and mire of sin, and transforms them into flaming evangels of His amazing grace! [9]

Mount Zion Fellowship in Norwich

'A fine city Norwich!' with its unique heritage of Christian witness, whether it be Juliana from the middle ages, the martyr Thomas Bilney or Puritan immigrants to North America.

Sedley and Mildred Pimlott, with their farm just north of the city, had with their family been members of the Assemblies of

God fellowship for a good number of years. Sedley himself was a deacon there. But they and a number of friends began to hunger for more of God and Sedley and Mildred opened their home for cottage meetings and, as Murray Norman recounts, 'The hunger for God grew more intense and the desire keener to know the blessing of the Lord.' They then had wind of a meeting to be run on Glory lines at Ipswich (with one of Henri's friends as a speaker) and they went along. Norman continues,

> Sedley still testifies that when he listened to the Word being preached that night he realised what had been missing in the churches and also in his own life, the Joy of the Lord. The small party who had travelled from Norwich to Ipswich came back intoxicated with joy, so much so that they had to pull up in a lay-by and then they were lost in praising and worshipping the Lord. The beginning of a new Spirit-filled work had begun.
>
> The next major step forward was a trip to Southend in December 1963, to one of Henri's meetings and exactly the same thing happened. Those who came were simply lost in worship and praise.

The following New Year, or Hogmanay, they all went up to Peterhead. Again they were bowled over by the freedom, love and joy in the Holy Spirit which they experienced. It turned their lives around. In October 1965 Henri and Connie with a team from Newark came to Norwich for a weekend. They were joined by the Camerons and others down from Peterhead. Roy Turner described how there was 'a wonderful flowing together in the love of God ... and the barriers were broken down under the anointing of the Spirit.' After Sunday morning's Breaking of Bread service they had a Glory banquet in a nearby hotel, followed by testimonies of folk who said how their lives had been changed. Roy continued,

> The evening meeting was a glorious climax when the power of God fell on many of the young people and swept them into a new experience with God. Many were so filled with the glory of the Lord that they could not speak in the English tongue at all. They magnified God in other tongues as the Spirit gave them utterance; several for the first time in their lives. The waves of blessing rolled over our souls and filled us with joy unspeakable! Hallelujah! [10]

Cecil Stewart from Northern Ireland remembers going over a number of times in the mid-sixties to the Pimlotts' group in Norwich. He recalls a particular Sunday evening in August, having fellowship at their home, Beulah Farm. There was such a visitation of power and anointing on the whole company that, at about eleven o'clock under the night sky, there were about fifty people flat out lying on the lawn, 'slain in the Holy Spirit'.

Thinking back on these moments today Sedley says, 'Pimlotts took to the Glory Way like ducks to water.' They felt, like so many others, they would 'never be the same again.' Moreover, Sedley says again, 'It revolutionised our family life,' and there they were with their three fine boys and three fine girls.

They endeavoured to bring this new breath of life and freedom to their assembly in Norwich. They began to dance as they rejoiced. This brought tension, so they started their own meetings in a little chapel which they renovated on Ketts Hill. Everyone whom I've met who went to those meetings, including my wife Margaret, says there was something very special about them. There was such a reality of the presence of the Holy Spirit, such praise and rejoicing, such burning love.

Jill Everett reminisces that it was the most powerful time in her life. She experienced real quickening and the baptism in the Holy Spirit. There were times when they became really drunk in the Spirit; on one occasion praising the Lord in the garden till one or two in the morning. Everyone had what can only be described as 'Holy Ghost health'! Jill says how the Bible really came to life for her, and how there was such a sense of commitment and discipleship. She goes so far as to say that as a young Christian there was a depth and substance at Ketts Hill that she did not find in other Glory meetings. Moreover the folk there just longed and loved to be together. The young people would stay with one another, even though they might only live down the road. And they never wanted to go away on holiday on their own, in case they missed something! Sedley Pimlott said,

> I do praise God for dear brother Henri who, in spite of all the devices of Satan, has pioneered this Glory Way ... This gospel really works and many lives are being changed here in Norwich. It works seven days a week and even in the night there are songs. Never have I been so physically fit and enjoyed life so much. [11]

His wife Mildred wrote, 'This way certainly sets you free in body and spirit. It makes you feel better within, clean and pure.' Their son Trevor (who now pastors the present fellowship) said, 'So many people persecute us, but I am absolutely sure that this way is scriptural and it's God's way.' His brother Melvyn, after he started working in the world, felt dragged down and discouraged; he was not standing for the Lord as he should have been. Then in October 1965 the Glory folk arrived for that remarkable weekend, and Melvyn got back on track and baptised in the Holy Spirit. The youngest brother Alan said that since coming into 'this glorious way' God had given him a deeper love for others, a real desire to help folk, to read the Bible and to witness for the Lord. The eldest daughter Hilary expressed how meeting with the Glory Way meant that the Lord had altogether become more real to her.

As the years have gone by, Mount Zion Fellowship have made their mark in Norwich. On Sunday afternoons they held open-air evangelistic meetings in the Market Place. In time they moved out of their increasingly cramped chapel on Ketts Hill into a larger building in Nelson Street. Then in the nineties they have constructed their purpose-built Family Life Centre on Norwich's northern ring road.

William and Audrey Leadbeater

The Leadbeaters came into the Glory Way when Audrey was very wonderfully healed of a terminal condition in the Glory holiday at Margate in 1973. She was brought back from the very jaws of death, as will be told in Chapter 14.

Tall robust William Leadbeater served in the Coldstream Guards for nine years and was one of those rescued from the beach at Dunkirk in 1940. Eventually he retired from running a residential home for the elderly and mental after-care, believing that God had yet something for him and Audrey to do. Together they had a horror of simply ticking over as Christians. William said, 'I decided long ago, I wasn't going to heaven in a rocking chair.' [12] The way God used them was unusual. They had bold texts written in large letters and fixed in their front garden and downstairs windows of their house in Margate: 'Believe on the Lord Jesus Christ and thou shalt be saved.' 'Jesus said, I am the Way, the Truth, and the Life.' 'Be sure your sin will find you out.' 'Christ is your only hope.' There was no doubting this message to all passers by. One might think that these texts would shoo people away; but in fact William and Audrey found that people needing care and understanding were recommended to them by the social services.

They also had a van with equally bold placards: 'Where will you spend eternity?' 'Jesus! a living Saviour of a dying world.' 'Believe on the Lord Jesus Christ and you will be saved.' 'No Christ no hope.' They drove this van slowly through the congested traffic of every city from Land's End to John o'Groats. As they did this they could read people's reactions like a book: surprise and unconcern, mouths open and shoulders shrugged, sudden joyful recognition and downright anger and rudeness, cheerful waves and clenched fists. They made extensive tours through the country, across the Midlands, into Wales, up to Scotland, following up various personal contacts or breaking new ground. In particular they stayed on nearly every military camp in England and were allowed to talk to the soldiers in the mess. They were always treated with great respect.

Always game for any kind of outreach, they would stand in a street with a placard text and a handful of tracts. When at home they used to take a regular stance in the pedestrian High Street at Canterbury amongst the shoppers, students and a stream of tourists from all nations.

In the late 1980s the Lord directed their steps to eastern Europe. They took the van into Yugoslavia, Hungary, Romania, and once to the Ukraine, taking much needed food, medical supplies, good quality clothing, toiletries, toys, sweets, electrical items such as radio-cassette players, electric razors and cameras. For the orphanages in Romania they took about one thousand complete sets of underwear and outer clothing, with a complete van load of medical supplies with antiseptics and disinfectant. They brought hundreds of brand new dolls, teddies, footballs, toy cars and so on; also bin bags full of assorted socks and tights.

Besides these things they took masses of Bibles, John's Gospels, children's illustrated Bibles and thousands of tracts in Hungarian, Romanian, Russian and Polish. In the last years of the Communist regimes these were hidden behind false cupboard backs and under a false floor. It would take them three days to load the van safely and securely. Thanks to the generosity of so many Christian friends, they were always able to take large sums of money to share out; sometimes to various individuals, but mostly to the pastors and group leaders who knew where the needs were. As they brought all these goods with the love of Jesus to these people, they were rewarded by expressions of love in return, with fidelity, endurance and joy in the Lord.

Getting through customs at border crossings was always a challenge to faith and an answer to prayer. On one extraordinary occasion William and Audrey had their backs to the wall. The customs men were grimly going through everything, taking advantage of the language barrier, letting nothing pass, when rosy-cheeked Audrey, on a sudden whim, picked up a cuddly teddy bear and, laughing and giggling in pent-up desperation, pushed it in the face of one dour man. It broke the ice. He roared with laughter; so did the other customs men, and they were let through the barrier.

One contact which meant a lot to them happened in a curious way. In spring 1990 they were returning through Hungary towards the Austrian border when they stopped at a very lonely crossroads. Two very young children, aged about two and five, in ragged clothes, asked them for chocolate. William and Audrey were gripped by a sudden fear that they were decoys of gypsies intent on attacking and robbing them, and they accelerated away. On crossing the Austrian border their consciences worked overtime. Audrey said how miserable she felt. It would have been so easy to give them some chocolate. They prayed then and there that they would try to trace them and help them if they could. In May they were out there again and stopped at the lonely cross-roads. Some distance away was a derelict building. Audrey went over there. She could see children's washing on a line and then found a little old lady on a makeshift bed in a tumbledown room. As she walked in the elderly lady held out her arms to her. Audrey went over and sat on the bed and gathered her in her arms and nursed her. She was so thin and said she was sick in her head and in her stomach. She laid her back on the pillow and asked where the children were. The old lady replied that they were with their mother while she worked in a field. Audrey looked around the room at the terrible state they were living in and said she would pray for her. The lady said to her that she had been praying that morning for help. As Audrey held her hand and prayed she felt the Holy Spirit in great power in that room and they both rejoiced in the Lord.

Audrey gave her the chocolates they had brought for the children. She rejoined William and they drove away. After they had gone about eight miles once again they were prompted to turn round and go back, and they left what little they had, some bread rolls and some money. What was better, they rejoiced with the lovely old lady and praised the Lord together. Audrey said, 'Even though it's a foreign language you can always tell when someone is praising the Lord.' Asked if she was a Roman Catholic the lady replied, 'nem Maria,' no Mary. Pointing upward she said, 'Jezus Krisztus,' so they had confirmation that she was a real born again Christian. Later in the year, in August, William and Audrey called in on this home yet again and were able to leave enough food and money to last them through the winter. [13]

Certainly they felt a great sense of urgency to help these eastern Europeans during the period when Communism fell and a new freer epoch dawned uneasily. Quite apart from the mountains of stuff they brought, they had the joy of seeing the director of one orphanage giving his heart to Jesus and the surprised gratitude of various contacts; an under-nourished Romanian lorry driver, on receiving soap, money and tracts wept at such kindness from strangers. How conscious they were of God's protection; of willing help when they burst a tyre, and of William's alertness on a dark road when he narrowly missed an unlit abandoned vehicle. Not least, on lonely stretches of their journeys, was the encouragement of playing Glory cassettes and singing along with Glory choruses.

Going out to eastern Europe they would travel through France, Belgium, Germany and Austria. They had texts on the van in English, French and German, which were painted on removable boards which slid into runners. As they approached border posts they would turn them round to plain sides on the back. Coming back to Britain they would meander for two or three weeks in Switzerland, Holland, Belgium and France distributing tracts in villages and markets.

William could feel his days were numbered. Ill-health of a very painful and trying kind overtook him, blinding him in one eye. Audrey nursed him throughout 1993, and he went to the reward of his Lord in January 1994. Two years later Audrey married Edward Forster and together they have had an extensive trip to India, helping missionaries and experiencing God's provision and care in unusual ways.

Chapter 10

Glory World

Through the magazine, through tapes and cassettes, by correspondence and by word of mouth, the influence of the Glory Way spread to other lands. In 1963, at the time when Henri retired from his business so that he could concentrate full time on the Glory meetings, he wrote,

> Beginning with Con and myself I have seen the Glory work grow, until it has reached the uttermost parts of the world, and yet I believe there are greater things in store for us all. The day is not far off when we shall see the biggest auditoriums in this land, and in fact in the world over, filled with men and women praising God and enjoying real liberty in Christ Jesus. As Simon Cameron says, 'We are in a big thing. Praise the Lord, it is as big as God is.' Over the past six years we have sent thousands of tapes all over the British Isles and to many parts of the world and 220,000 magazines have been circulated and still the work goes on growing and developing all the time. [1]

This was Henri's vision, to let the light shine out. There is no limit to where it can reach.

Jerusalem

What better place in which to begin than in Jerusalem, where the gospel originated? Ancient maps, like the one in Hereford cathedral, made Jerusalem the centre of the world. I have seen Henri in a meeting at Fiskerton open an envelope with a particular sparkle in his eye, exclaiming, 'Here is a letter from a brother in Jerusalem!'

Whether it was this man or another, Henri and Connie had some American friends who went to Jerusalem to set up a printing press for Bibles. They had no contacts, but went because they felt such an urge. They found a big barn and a house right on a border between Arab and Jewish settlements. It was there, just waiting for them, as it were. They set to work, and before long they had a demand for Bibles in many languages. Then they set up some orphanages. Henri and Connie had a keen interest in them and supported them with profits from their shops.

Scandinavia

We British have much in common racially with Scandinavia ever since fierce Vikings invaded our shores and over time mingled with our native peoples. And certainly Pentecostal links between Scandinavia and Britain have always been close. It was a Norwegian Methodist minister T.B. Barratt (of English descent) who was invited to Sunderland in 1907 to share his experience of the baptism of the Holy Spirit. Events flowed on from there. In the 1920s in Stockholm the Pentecostal pastor Lewi Pethrus had a congregation of 5,000. He befriended both Smith Wigglesworth and Stephen Jeffreys and had them preach there.

In 1961 the Glory office in Newark received a letter from a young woman from Copenhagen, Lone Herluf-Pedersen:

> Henri, I want to ask you to pray much for us over here as the Lord is going to do a new thing. We are a few who really with all our hearts want to start some new meetings outside the churches. We know that the Glory Way is the only way. The churches are completely dead and dry and the Lord cannot work in them. The people are starving and backslidden. Why? The church has lost the vision and the glory! Jesus is coming after a glorious praising people. Hallelujah! [2]

Sweeping generalisations, maybe? But here was a soul panting after God like a hart after the water brooks. Lone Herluf-Pedersen and three other young friends went ahead and arranged two weeks of meetings with Bob Shiels, an Irish deliverance evangelist (who was fluent in Danish), as the main speaker.

She wrote again to Henri, thanking him for a letter and his prayers:

Well, Brother Henri, I just don't know where to start. I could jump in the air for joy, for God is moving by His Spirit in Denmark and we praise God that we ever stepped out in faith ... Many came just out of curiosity, many were shocked; they are not used to lively meetings, you know. We have translated your Glory choruses into Danish; oh, they are so wonderful. We have an accordion, trombone, guitars, piano and violin ... Bob Shiels ... really has a dynamic, faith-building, inspiring message to bring ... People are saying to us that they have never experienced such wonderful meetings since Pentecost first came to Denmark. Hallelujah![3]

A woman with a broken arm was healed. There was spirit deliverance. One lady said 'how she actually saw a demon leaving a young fellow' they prayed for. People were clapping and dancing. Lone continued,

The other night all the churches had a great conference about us and our meetings. All over Copenhagen people are talking about it, for and against. We don't care. We know that God is with us.

About three years later Roy Turner and another young man Glyn Greenow made a fifteen-week tour of Scandinavia. They found the people of these lands just the same as the British; they were hungry for reality. Everywhere they went with this Glory

VIERAITA ENGLANNISTA

Helmikuun 1—3 päivinä vieraili Siion-seurakunnassa englantilaiset veljet Glyn Greenow ja Roy Turner, jotka iloisuudellaan ja palavuudellaan saivat kuulijat haltioihinsa. Heidän julistuksessaan tuli esille Kristus pelastajana ja todellisen ilon antajana. Pahoittelemme, etteivät veljet tällä kertaa voineet viipyä kauemmin keskuudessamme, mutta lupasivat syksyllä palata takaisin.

Glyn Greenow

Roy Turner

Roy Turner and Glyn Greenow

blessing, folk entered into a new experience, being filled with love, joy and peace in the Holy Ghost. When they left the shores of England bound for Sweden, they only knew two people over there and they could never have imagined the mighty way in which God was going to lead them. From the very start of the meetings, God just poured out upon the people His wonderful love and many were melted and broken by the Spirit. It was the same testimony everywhere they went. In Sweden, Norway, Finland and Denmark people were saying, 'This is what we have been longing for.'

In the four countries they held one hundred meetings, travelled 6,500 miles and ministered to over 200,000 people. In many places the halls were packed to capacity and, unfortunately, hungry folk had to be turned away. One Sunday in Stockholm they had to have two meetings on the same evening, six hundred each time. (The second lot had been waiting for hours in the driving snow.) Roy and Glyn felt, 'Truly it is revival time!'

> At every place they begged us to stay longer and to return as soon as possible. We are quite sure now of the truth of Henri's words, 'Britain will yet be a blessing to the world.' God has started this wonderful Glory Way in our land and we believe it is what men and women everywhere need. This love of God is the greatest power in the whole universe. Brothers and sisters, let it flow through us all and then we shall help spread this blessing to everybody, everywhere. [4]

Roy and Glyn were truly grateful to the Lord for what they saw He was doing in Scandinavia and, they said, 'for the link that He has forged in the Spirit between our countries.'

It is very moving to learn how these northern people were affected by this Glory tour. For one thing there was evidently no language problem; the interpreters must have been very able. Besides which English is widely taught in Scandinavia and a surprising number of people are fluent. The interpreter in Norway was Gyda Eikeland, a really liberated Spirit-filled sister who embraced the Glory Way wholeheartedly!

A young woman, Vivi Mehlum, listening to Roy, Glyn and Gyda in the town of Skien, to the south west of Oslo, found the shackles of her life broken and her heart melted:

> I was saved but I would look at my faults and it grieved me, and the more I saw my own faults the more I began to see

the faults in others. This gradually built up an ice-cold wall between us.

Then she went to hear Roy and Glyn:

Praise the Lord! There was a wonderful spirit of love in the midst and it melted my heart. I received such a wonderful love as Roy and Glyn ministered, that I wanted immediately to beg all my friends forgiveness. Oh Jesus, Jesus, Jesus!

In Sweden they had an evangelist Roland Eriksson as interpreter. He had this to say:

My heart is overflowing with thanksgiving for what God is doing in the world ... The fire of God is burning all over and I believe this coming revival will be the last one before our Saviour comes again. Praise His lovely Name! ... You know, brothers and sisters, in the past many spiritual realities have been lost in dead churches ... Our dear English brothers Roy and Glyn, from the Glory Revival, have been a great blessing to us in Sweden. I have felt in a mighty way, that the will of God has been to show us a wonderful new and living way, the way of love, joy and liberty, in the Holy Ghost. This He has done in many parts of our land, through our two brothers.

Eighteen-year-old Ann-Charlott Ljung from Falköping, inland from Gothenburg, wrote in the *Glory News*,

I would like to mention especially one Sunday meeting when the Lord revealed Himself to us in a mighty way. Hallelujah! Souls were renewed as heaven was opened over us, and a sweet spirit rested upon the congregation. One young sister received a wonderful blessing from the Lord and God filled her whole being. She got a song in the Spirit and our dear brother Roy got the music. Oh how wonderful! [5]

Another teenager Barbro Lundgren said,

I myself have experienced God in such a mighty way I could never explain it in words. I had for a time been lukewarm, but in the first meeting I came through into a wonderful victory ... These meetings have been of great importance to me. I felt so small in the presence of the Lord, but it was really wonderful. Praise His Name! O that He will help me to keep in His will. My longing is to be a soulwinner and lead souls to Calvary. [6]

In Gothenburg Sister Vivian Martensson said, 'I realised that this was the thing I had been longing for.' And Maranatha leader Enoch Carlson declared, 'It is wonderful when the Lord sends His servants along with the right food at just the right time.' [7]

Another young Swedish girl, Inga Jaktlund, wrote,

For a time I had been dried up, but Jesus met me again in a wonderful way in the meetings at Falköping, where Roy and Glyn ministered. Praise the Lord! I can't explain in words how mighty the meetings were. I got really renewed ... I have tried all the things in this world, but when I received salvation through the precious blood of Jesus, He set me free from all its empty meaningless ways. Praise the Lord! I am now a happy girl and want to live whole-heartedly for Jesus.

A Danish young woman Henny Jorgensen seemed swept along in a kind of rhapsody as she wrote,

For a long time I have had a deep longing in my heart for a closer walk with Jesus and I prayed earnestly to the Lord, that He would meet with me in a new way ... Then Brother Roy and Brother Glyn from England came along to have meetings in our country, with their interpreter Sister Gyda. At the first meeting we felt an heavenly atmosphere while they were singing and playing and we could see the love of God shining through them. There was one cry in my heart: 'This must never stop.' At a meeting a few days later ... my mouth was filled with laughter and my body was shaking under the power of His love, while our brothers were singing and testifying. Yea, the very music seemed to reveal the love of God to me. I was filled with Christ's compassion for souls and I shall never be the same again.

I give thanks to God first of all, and then to His young servants, for their message in Denmark, which really worked. The Glory of the Lord filled the house while we were together. Revival is here, and my prayer is that the people of God will awaken, so that it can sweep over all the earth. [8]

Finally, a word from the two young men from Sandnes, near Stavanger, in the southern fjord region of Norway. Helge Anderson said,

> I was lost in this dark world with all its emptiness, when God suddenly called on me and I said 'Yes' to Jesus ... at our last meeting in Stavanger God blessed me in a wonderful way such as I have never experienced before. Hallelujah! Afterwards I was able to embrace everybody and glorify God. [9]

Lars Stokka quite simply expressed this: 'I believe that this love which comes from the Lord will overcome all evil and make all the darkness to flee, for God is love.' [10]

The accumulation of these Scandinavian testimonies brings its own overwhelming impression, that the Lord used Roy Turner and Glyn Greenow to bring with them a very breath from heaven. It seems that there were many longing hearts who were waiting to be touched, awakened, renewed and refreshed. One gets a glimpse of this in a letter which Roy Turner wrote to Albert and Janie Marshall from a house in Gothenberg in January 1964. Speaking of a meeting in that city,

> ... about 200 folk were in the Jericho march we had round the hall and all the young folk and the leader's wife (who had been a bit stiff and rather against this way) were quickened in a wonderful way and all put their arms round each other and danced on the platform! ... Oh we can't praise God enough for what He is doing here! They want us to stay for months in each place but we are following the Spirit's leading and giving them all a taste of this new and living way! Glory! Hallelujah! The folk are being set free and their lives are being changed! They say they have never been in such meetings!

Speaking of a visit to Falköping about 120 km away, Roy continued,

> I could never describe what God did. The whole meeting was ablaze with God's love and power! Souls saved! Saints revived and blessed! Glory! I'm full of His blessing now! I just praise God for the Spirit's moving! How I love the Holy Ghost way! The Glory way of Love, Joy, Peace. It was wonderful to hear Henri, Connie and you all on the tape!

The two-way flow between these northern countries and Britain continued. Already, in 1964, Karin Melin had left Sweden to come to work in a hospital in Eastbourne. She went on the Glory holiday that summer in the Isle of Wight. She followed it up with another Glory week at Southend-on-Sea and finally she changed her job and went to work in Newark. Longing for a real outpouring of the Holy Spirit in her life and getting desperate, 'It was not long,' she said, 'before I found myself praising the Lord in other tongues and suddenly the Lord flooded my soul with blessing that eclipsed everything I had ever had before.' [11] When in Newark she lodged with Bob and Hilda and helped out in the Glory Office from time to time.

By the early seventies there had been several visits of Glory teams to Scandinavia and these northern people in turn came to Britain. Jan-Olaf from near Stockholm stayed some time in England and said how he was 'thrilled with this wonderful Glory revival.' Another Swede, Brigitta Strombeck, said,

> I am so happy for this Glory revival ... In the Glory meetings, I have experienced things that I had never experienced before. When dancing in Peterhead last New Year convention, I felt like I was in heaven, rejoicing with the saints who have gone before us to the heavenly world. They rejoiced with me and I with them before the throne of God, in the presence of our lovely Jesus. It was a wonderful foretaste of heaven on earth. [12]

The Zion fellowship in Peterhead rejoiced to 'see-in' the New Year of 1973 with a good number of folk from overseas: from the United States, Sweden and Finland. A photo in the *Glory News* shows a Finnish evangelist who 'thrilled the folk with his Spirit filled witness and skilful accordion playing'. [13] Certainly the Glory ties between Britain and Scandinavia have been precious ones.

The Netherlands

A certain Dutch woman, Mrs Overduyn, from the town of Meppel, east of the Zuider Zee, had for quite some time been receiving the *Glory News* and Glory tapes. She persuaded a certain Brother Kranenburg to invite Henri and Connie over for meetings, starting at the Hague, in the German Church there. This was in September 1959. They rose to the occasion and brought with them quite a little team: Bob and Hilda Nicholls, Tom Spurr, who had a gift for speaking, the young couple Laurie and Margaret James and Violet Lowe (shortly to be married to Peter Cowling). They were joined by a certain H. Leijger from the Hague who was their interpreter. Over their ten day tour they went on to visit the old historic towns of Dordrecht and Utrecht and the great port of Rotterdam. Henri explained,

> It was the first time that we had gone forth to a foreign land to preach the gospel and, although none of us knew a word of the Dutch language, we were confident of this one thing, that God was with us and that there was a language that all could understand regardless of their mother tongue and that was the language of love. Praise God for His divine currency. It never fails. The love of God will open up the hardest of hearts and liberate the most reserved of natures. Hallelujah! ... What grand folk these Dutch people are. Everywhere we went a warm welcome awaited us and although the Glory Way with its wonderful liberty was strange to them, they opened their hearts wide to receive it and God truly blessed them ... We experienced many difficulties, obstacles and restrictions, but what joy filled our hearts as we saw our Dutch brethren being set free. Many tears were shed as the Holy Spirit worked on their hearts, the young people in particular entering right in to their purchased possessions. [14]

Violet looking back thirty years or more could not restrain a laugh. This tour with Henri's Glory team was full of the unexpected:

> The visit to Holland was uproariously funny. Until Henri had an interpreter, he couldn't cope with it. He'd say a few words, then he would ask Connie to have a go and then one or other of us. It caused a great deal of mirth. But once the interpreter came he was all right, except that he couldn't say the next thing fast enough, because of having to wait for the previous sentence to be interpreted. He had great success in the open-airs there. They were the most fantastic meetings. The roads were packed with people and it was easier to get away with things outside. Henri did have some opposition in one of the churches. He had his accordion and he went up to the front of a particular church where

there was a low platform with a wooden surround. We all went round to get on this platform, but Henri was told we couldn't stand on it. We could stand in front of it but not on it because it was 'holy ground'. 'Well duck,' he said, 'the ground might be holy, but I'm standing on it because I'm a holy man!' This seemed to break the barriers down, because when the Spirit got moving in the meeting, the stern faced Dutchmen had to go along with it.

The tour gathered momentum, and many people blessed in the Hague followed the team round to the other towns. One particular moment to remember was an open-air meeting in the centre of Rotterdam where the crowds flocked together to hear the good news put over in the inimitable Glory Way manner. Henri continued,

> Throughout the campaign souls were saved, bodies healed and many filled with the Holy Ghost and set gloriously free, and it is with hearts full of gratitude to God that we look back upon these ten days and see how He set His seal upon all that was done. To God be the glory.

Brother Kranenburg put a great deal of effort, thought and care in supporting Henri and Connie, as did another couple from the Hague, Ben and Wilhemene, who amongst other things kept the accounts. Many of these Dutch Christians from the various towns had not met one another before, said Henri,

> but a bond of fellowship was soon forged and they all united to put their shoulder to the wheel to bring about a very successful ten days campaign. [15]

Those on the receiving end of these meetings had some moving things to say. A young woman Elle Koller wrote in the *Glory News*,

> Formerly I used to live my life without a thought of God. I hated attending church on Sundays when everybody seemed so good and virtuous, yet looked so grave-faced and totally lacking in joy. This form of religion held no attraction for me. Even when we came into contact with the Pentecostal movement and when with my parents I attended their services, I remained unchanged and was always glad when

the service was over. Early in September I received a hand-bill advertising the visit of Henri and his Revival Team to the German Church at Den Haag and I was surprised to find that I had a strong desire to go to those meetings ... I was busy helping my mother with the washing up when I suddenly remembered the little man with his accordion and I said, 'Mum shall we go to the meeting in the German Church?' ... When we entered the building the thing that struck me with amazement was the glad look on the face of every member of Henri's team. They just glowed with joy and happiness. [16]

Elle entered into the meeting wholeheartedly, and those that followed. She could not stay away and pursued the Glory team to Dordrecht. God changed her life. She became a happy young Christian. Marga Visser, also of The Hague, spoke for herself and her young man Frans Jackson:

My parents always went to church every Sunday and I used to accompany them simply to please them and I became educated in the things of Christianity, but in August 1959 I took Jesus as my own personal Saviour. Among my acquaintances were a boy and girl who were always talking about Jesus and for this reason my boy-friend and I would have nothing to do with them. To think about Jesus Christ was good but to talk about Him did not meet with our approval. After Frans and I were converted we saw that these two young people were so joyful and we wanted to be joyful too. It is so wonderful to have the joy springing up from your heart. We talked with this boy and girl and discovered that they had something we had not, for they were filled with the Holy Spirit. We both began to seek God for this blessing and, praise God, three weeks after our conversion I was filled with the Spirit. Oh I was so glad. I felt the power of God, Hallelujah.

A few days after this joyful experience I went along to the first meeting held by Henri and his team in Den Haag. Oh it made us so happy. All the people were so glad ... we sang and sang and a great gladness filled our souls. Praise the Lord. After the meeting we both went along to some friends where Tom and Tony (two brothers in the revival team) were staying, and my boy-friend Frans asked Tom if he would pray for him next day to be filled with the Holy

Spirit. 'Tomorrow?' said Tom, 'Why not now? Now is the time. God's time is always now.' So we all prayed and Frans was wonderfully baptised with the Holy Ghost and fire. Oh Hallelujah. Praise the Lord.

Marga and Frans followed the Glory team round to the other towns and Frans was frequently asked to be interpreter.

The final meetings were in Rotterdam and there we saw the Lord move in mighty power. Many people were healed and filled with this heavenly joy. Glory to God. [17]

The story of Jan Van Ginkel of Utrecht is an unusual one. God met very wonderfully with him in his hour of need and led him on from one point to another. He was saved as a boy of ten in a Salvation Army children's meeting in Utrecht. In his youth he had ill-health, and at the age of twenty was afflicted with a form of nervous rheumatism which only got worse as the years passed. He found breathing difficult and at times he could not move his arms and legs. By October 1957, when he was forty-eight, death was near; so violent were his aches and pains he used to pray to the Lord to take him home. Then in August 1958 T.L. Osborne had nine days of remarkable meetings in The Hague and Jan went along and was completely healed. It was amazing.

A year later, at the door of a Pentecostal church he was attending, Jan saw two boys giving out leaflets; they were invitations to Henri's Glory campaign. The leader of the assembly, as he shook hands with Jan, strongly objected to the boys and told them to go away. But Jan felt prompted by the Lord to contact Brother Kranenburg, and he took on the responsibility of spreading the leaflets. He said,

I spoke to several leaders about the meetings but they had no good word for the Henri team, so my son and I got busy giving out the invitations in the street. The devil got mad and tried to persecute us but we were pleased to suffer for the name of Jesus. I visited one of Henri's Glory meetings in The Hague and experienced the power of God in the midst and I went home to give myself to prayer and fasting for the meetings to be held in Utrecht.

That prayer was answered. As the Glory team came to their city it was so evident that God was with them.

The next day Brother Henri and his wife were our guests in the afternoon and I took care that an interpreter was present so that we could converse with one another, and we had a great time of fellowship. We laughed and we cried and were of one mind in Christ Jesus, and my wife experienced the real love of our brother and sister ... My wife had been most wonderful to me throughout my years of illness and I could never compensate her for her faithfulness. I just wanted to see her back on fire for God. [18]

And his wife Cobie was certainly blessed. She wrote later to Connie and Henri to say,

I wept a lot after you left Holland, not because you went, but because it seemed that all the Spirit of those wonderful meetings had gone with you ... If only I had the money I would come over to England to be there with you ... Every Sunday afternoon I say to my husband, 'They are having their usual gathering now and it makes us feel that we want to be there, but then we quickly put a tape on and it brings to us the same Spirit of love and glory.' [19]

In fact Jan himself kept in close contact with the Glory Way right up to the year of his death in 1996. His son Govert would bring him over, frail in health, to Louth in Lincolnshire to stay with his close friends Frank and May Gostlow, who would take him over to the meetings in Fiskerton chapel. So those brief ten days in 1959 bore fruit for eternity. Brother Kranenburg continued to hold Glory meetings in Rotterdam and young people in The Hague banded together to hold open-air meetings each Saturday to win others to Christ. Many Glory tapes and copies of the *Glory News* were sent out from Newark to Dutch homes, as Henri said, 'bringing untold blessing to hungry hearts'. God had obviously given the team a great love for the Dutch people and they were sad to say good-bye as their boat slipped away from the Hook of Holland.

We give the last word from a certain Brother H. Krul. Holland is a country of bikes, solid ones with large wheels, and he was a happy cyclist:

Well, it seems that you have broken my heart in two pieces. One piece of it is in The Hague and the other piece in Newark. Sometimes I whistle on my bicycle the songs, 'If you only knew the blessing that salvation brings,' 'It's coming down, down, down,' and 'Oh river of God flow down on me,' and yet I've only seen you at The Hague and Rotterdam. I am the person who asked you to sing, 'He is my sunshine,' because my son was blessed by it. On the same day the girl with the guitar passed me like an angel from heaven with the words, 'God bless you brother'. Afterwards I realised that Jesus had passed me in that girl. [20]

Elsewhere in Europe

What follows here are the testimonies of four other Europeans. Admittedly, it was in England that they had contact with the Glory Way and not in their own countries. However, their foreign backgrounds give their encounter with spiritual realities a decidedly different slant.

Dankfried Spindler came from Eckernfoerde on the Baltic coast of Germany near the Danish border. In 1960 he wrote in the *Glory News*,

> A few months before my visit to England I found myself longing to go to the Glory meetings in Newark. A copy of the *Glory News* had found its way into our office in Eckernfoerde and had really stirred my soul. I got such a blessing through some of the testimonies that I decided to attend as many Glory meetings as possible and with great expectation I looked forward to the day of my arrival in Newark.
>
> It is now eight years ago since I accepted Jesus into my heart and during that time I have attended many different churches in various countries, but nowhere have I seen such liberty of the Holy Spirit, such joyful praise, such deep divine love as I have found at the Glory meetings at Newark. I came as a stranger to England, but amongst the Glory folk I felt at home from the first. The blessed Spirit of God is the same throughout the whole wide world and wherever men and women are baptised by Him they are truly one.
>
> I shall never forget my first Glory meeting; it was a wonderful experience. The shouting and the dancing was absolutely strange to me, but it took only a few minutes for me to realise that such meetings are really the best preparation for life in eternity and in heaven. Hallelujah! God's

people need to be prepared for the rapture of the saints and for the wonderful atmosphere that we shall find in the realms of heaven where praise is ascending unto God both day and night. Never have I sung so many choruses in one single meeting, but the more I sang the more blessing filled my soul. I cannot express how much this strengthened me and brought me nearer to Jesus. He became very real. Glory be to God.

Dankfried was greatly impressed by the love fellowship he found at Newark and he said that, if he had his way, he would like to attend a Glory meeting every day of his life until that day when he will meet Jesus face to face in Glory. It rejoiced his heart to see in Newark, and then later in Leeds, so many young people in these gatherings. He said,

> They looked so happy in the enjoyment of their salvation. Europe urgently needs young people on fire for God, who are not bound by religious traditions but who are alive in the Spirit and burning for Jesus Christ our wonderful and blessed Redeemer. [21]

At the time of writing Dankfried was a missionary candidate in a home for refugee children and sent greetings to Newark from the Karlsruhe Revival Centre.

Heinz Thoma was a young man in Zurich in Switzerland, who paid a visit to England in April 1959. He said,

> I was longing for love, for peace and for happiness. In the big city of London I was feeling very lonely but on my third week, while changing my bus at Hyde Park, I saw a crowd of people and went to see what was going on. It happened to be a Pentecostal open-air meeting and I stood there for over three hours thinking the people were very funny, singing and dancing as they did.
>
> As I was moving away a young man came up to me and asked if I was a Christian. I said 'Yes', not knowing what it meant to be a Christian. We talked together, when suddenly he asked me if I would like to give my heart to Jesus. I was quite puzzled for I did not know what he meant but, praise the Lord, I said, 'Yes'. We went back to the park and the young man prayed for me and then invited me to pray too. This made me feel very uncomfortable but I said some very

helpless words and, Oh! wonder, I felt that God heard those few words and He saved me in a very wonderful way. I did not realise what had happened but I felt somehow very happy in my heart. That evening was the start of a new found life and it is really wonderful what the Lord has done for me since that evening. I have received blessing upon blessing and God has changed me all over. Praise Him.

Some weeks later I received a *Glory News* and was greatly impressed with all the testimonies. Praise the Lord, it is no secret what God can do. Soon after, I attended my first Glory meeting. What a happy crowd; but I felt so sad for I could not believe that such joy and liberty could ever be mine. I was kept so much by religious feelings but, praise God, only a few days after, the Lord baptised me in the Holy Ghost and two days later I was in another Glory meeting at Paddock Wood. What a change. Oh, glory to God. I felt the fire burning in my heart and I started to dance and shout too. What a blessing I got from Jesus.

August bank holiday I was privileged to go to the convention at Newark and I shall never forget what the Lord did for me there. He set me completely free. Free to love, brothers and sisters. Free to testify. Free to enjoy the liberty of the sons of God. Now that I have returned home to Switzerland I am still conscious of God's presence with me and I know that He will use me to spread the blessing over here. Praise His wonderful name. [22]

Stephanie Cooke was a Yugoslavian. She was happily married to an Englishman and they lived in Exeter. In 1971 she wrote in the *Glory News*,

It is now five years ago since I got saved, when I was taken to a meeting by a lady who was working for my sister. I couldn't understand English very well at that time and I didn't know what sort of a church I had come to, but the people seemed very happy ... Because of the language I wasn't able to follow the speaker very well, but at the close of his message he invited people to stand to their feet, lift up their hands and take Jesus as their Saviour.

My companion whispered softly to me, asking if I would like to accept the Lord Jesus into my heart. I had never heard of such a thing before and always thought I was a Christian. The word 'accept' was foreign to me and I didn't understand it, but my friend whispered again, asking if I would like to receive Jesus, and from this I understood it was something to be taken in, but what for, I didn't know. My parents had taught me that Jesus was the Son of God, but I didn't have faith to believe that; yet in the moment of the preacher's appeal the Holy Spirit moved on my heart and revealed to me that Jesus was the Son of God, and I said to myself, 'Even if you don't understand, the Son of God will not hurt you. If you take Him in, He will do you a lot of good. So why not receive Him?'

I stood to my feet and raised my hand saying, 'I want that Jesus. I believe He will do me good.' I was the last person to stand and the preacher did not notice me, so I sat down disappointed. I felt my need of God and somebody to pray and help me. I turned to my companion and said, 'He didn't see me,' but she replied, 'Don't worry. Jesus has seen.' Immediately I was filled with peace and assurance. The work was done and I've never been the same since that day. I love God.

I went to my first Glory convention at Boscombe this year and I did enjoy it. I had heard many Glory tapes and have been greatly blessed by them, but it was far better to see and feel the glory than just to hear it. I thank the Lord for opening the way for me to get to the meetings with my husband and daughter. It thrilled me to see the people of God, joyful, happy and filled with the Glory of the Lord. I have never seen anything like it in my life; my heart was longing to see and feel God's love flowing through His people towards one another. I was hungry for that and now the Lord has fed me well. The Lord blessed me so much. I was overwhelmed and could not sleep for thinking of the meetings and the blessing of God. I believe the Glory Way is God's Way, because I felt such harmony in the Spirit. [23]

Don Odon had been an officer in the Hungarian tank corps during the war and afterwards God met with him and put a dance of joy in his heart. He was on a course at Goettingen University and in a philosophical debate a colleague said to him, 'After all, Christianity boils down to this one principle: love thy neighbour as thyself.'

On that night, as I was walking through the poverty-stricken streets of Goettingen in the hungry post-war Germany, it suddenly flashed into my mind: this love-law would solve all the problems of the world. 'Why, this Jesus must have been a genius of a philosopher,' I thought. 'What is wrong with our scholars that they have overlooked this fact?'

That week he put this into operation, giving some American cigarettes to a starving German soldier who had just returned from a prison camp in Russia. 'You may sell them in the black market and get some food,' he said and the soldier was so surprised and grateful. Then a battle started to rage in Don's heart:

'You must decide now,' said a voice in my conscience, 'You have risked your life for your country, you have pulled out the wounded from the firing line, you are proud because you have been a professional officer. Will you now risk your life for the truth?'

On that memorable night in my study room I felt I had to decide. I shut my English grammar book and sat on the bed. It was a difficult thing to make up my mind. How can I be a true disciple of Jesus? I shall not be able to keep it up. In a desperate effort I called out aloud: 'God, You promised to help everyone who calls for help. Help me now. I want You!' I do not know why I said this in the way I did. I must have remembered something of what I had learnt of God in my infancy.

Then it happened! I saw the wings of God; shadowy, feathery wings arising from the left and covering me slowly. A swelling inexpressible joy burst out upon me. I jumped up. Tears were streaming down on my face. 'Jesus!' I've got Him! I am on the other side, at last! On the joy side! Who can be against me now once God has covered me with His wings? I felt something like standing once more in the tower of my tank and riding against the enemy with a cavalcade of tank regiments behind me and silver trumpets blowing the signal of full-scale advance. I felt I had conquered the whole of the Northern Army, the whole world, in fact. What a security, what a peace, what an intoxicating thrill! My feet began to move fast. It was the Hungarian 'Chardash' I found myself dancing, and what a dancing it was!

Oh, dear reader, call upon God from the depths of your soul and come and dance with me. Life is not worth it without Jesus in your heart. He brings down Heaven's glory, He makes this miserable world look ridiculously puny, He changes the law of gravitation and causes you to walk on air, to float in joy, and lie down on the glory-carpet. I would be happy to meet you, clasp your hand and embrace you. Only call upon the Name of the Lord! Come and meet at Brother Henri's. The Lord Jesus richly bless you.[24]

North America

In the early seventeenth century, while Shakespeare was writing his last plays, a group of born-again believers left the Lincoln-shire coast for the Netherlands. As it happens they came from a cluster of villages only about twenty-five miles north of Newark. Then after a few years, in 1620, they banded together with other Puritans to sail in the *Mayflower* to the Massachusetts coast. A gospel acorn was planted then which has become the great flourishing oak tree of American Bible Christianity. So it would indeed be strange if there had been no spiritual friendship between the Glory Way and North America.

In 1962 a young English evangelist Ted Seymour wrote to Henri from California, from Hollywood in fact. There is his photo looking out from the pages of the *Glory News*, clean shaven, trim hair cut, white collar and tie, just as the crest of the wave of the pop revolution, student revolution and long-haired flower power was about to break over California and all our Western countries. He explains how he had come to Newark some time before and how vividly it had stuck in his mind because, he said, 'you opened a door of contact with the Spirit of God ... I learned from you all that *there is nothing better than the anointing of the Spirit upon one's life and ministry.'* [25]

A year later in 1963 Ted Seymour wrote again, a much longer article, in which he gave a blow-by-blow account of the impact of the charismatic movement on the Methodist College where he was studying for a BA degree. He was doing this while also working as Staff Evangelist for Teen World International. When you think of it, it's important to notice that the charismatic renewal with its spontaneous seeking after more of God and the baptism and infilling of the Holy Spirit took place at the same time as, or even slightly ahead of, the flower power pop revolution. So that this sudden bursting out of the spirit of the world and its sub-culture was more than matched by a godly resistance to it. Ted made an extremely interesting general statement, in which he quoted but did not name a prominent Christian leader. He wrote,

> I frankly would not have believed possible the things that I have recently seen come to pass, if somebody told me a few years ago that such things would happen ... Many great men are stating that they need to feel a power in their lives and in their churches. One such man, to whom we owe so much, said these words at a ministerial breakfast in Sacramento, California, last year: 'In the main denominations we have looked a bit askance at our brethren from the Pentecostal churches because of their emphasis on the doctrine of the Holy Spirit, but I believe the time has come to give the Holy Spirit His rightful place in our churches. We need to learn once again what it means to be baptised in the Holy Spirit. I know that we can rationalise and immediately ten thousand theological questions arise and we try to figure it out, but I want to tell you that we need to accept, we need to get something. Give it any terminology you want, but we do not have the same dynamic and the same power the early church had. They had the filling of the Spirit.'
>
> This is the cry from many a minister, preacher, priest, layman and woman in the churches today. Some could not care less, but to those who are hungry and thirsty, God, in His divine order of things, is giving an almighty outpouring of the Holy Spirit. [26]

In Ted Seymour's Methodist College, the Professor of Science found that all his academic training 'could not fill the empty void within his spirit.' He sought the Lord and was filled with the Holy Spirit and spoke with other tongues. Soon the young Student Body President, the Director of Religion and his friend the Missions Leader all sought out the professor and all received the Holy Spirit baptism. 'My, oh my! The key people in the college! From then on it was just the Lord working through each person, telling of the blessing of the Lord.' Then in downtown Los Angeles, Episcopalians held a week's meetings on the Holy Spirit and the walls between the denominations came tumbling down as Episcopalians, Lutherans, Methodists, Baptists and others sought the power of God together. A Spirit-filled Episcopalian bishop laid his hands on a badly crippled young woman who was just about to have both legs amputated and she was wonderfully healed. This sent out shock waves, and more and more sought baptism by the Holy Spirit. Violent opposition sprang up but then 'The ones who fought the hardest are now the ones who contend for God the best.' Pentecostals were thrilled with the various testimonies and the media caught on too. Altogether, it is extremely interesting to read in a back number of the *Glory News* from the pen of this young Englishman the first fresh gracious outpouring of the Holy Spirit in Los Angeles in what we have come to know as the charismatic renewal.

Henri and Connie never set foot in the United States (although they were invited several times), but the Cameron family from Peterhead travelled extensively across and round that great country and with their own Scottish lilt and kilt brought the Glory Way to very many places. There were four brothers, Michael, John, Alex, and Simon; of these John and his family eventually settled over there, and started a church in Atlanta, called Norcross Praise Fellowship.

Simon and his wife Wendy first went to the States in 1966 and for the next twenty years they made continuous tours there. On the first few of these Roy Turner accompanied them. Travelling about in a campervan, they eventually went to just about every state. One thing led to another and the invitations snowballed. At one point they went to a Full Gospel Businessmen's convention which in its turn led to many bookings. Also, when they started a tour they would be given the chance to appear on National Christian Television. In this way they became known and then, wherever they went, there were sell-out crowds. The amount of time they spent in the country was extensive; they had, on one occasion, as much as ten months on the trot, with a meeting every night and twice on Sundays.

At the beginning they did not realise the perfectly enormous distances involved. A church fellowship would contact them and they would say 'Yes' to the booking without looking at the map, and then find to their dismay that they had let themselves in for a marathon of driving. After a time they got canny to it. When invited somewhere Simon would reply, 'We'll certainly, willingly come on condition that you can fix up some other meetings nearby. Is that possible?'

On one occasion the whole praising team were nearly wiped out. It was a miracle of catastrophe averted, of God's unseen hand. In the spring of 1967 Michael drove their station wagon containing Roy Turner and six other Camerons from California to the East Coast. The drive had been exhausting. It was early morning and they were making their way over the Blue Ridge Mountains of Virginia at a height of 4,000 feet. It had been raining heavily and gravel on the hillsides had slidden down onto the twisting road, making it very treacherous. Coming round a bend, the tired driver put his foot on the accelerator instead of the brake and the vehicle went into a crazy spin, coming to rest on its side, poised over the edge of a thousand foot precipice. Hardly daring to breathe, they all managed to crawl to safety. When the breakdown van arrived and hauled the wagon upright, nothing could be seen underneath which could have prevented the plunge to death. [27]

Roy Turner recalls the time when he and the Camerons travelled the 3,000 miles from New York to Los Angeles in three days. They were heading for the Full Gospel Businessmen's Convention journeying across country through the states of Pennsylvania, Ohio, Indiana, Illinois, Iowa, Nebraska, Wyoming, Utah and Nevada, arriving in Las Vegas at four in the morning. After a couple of hours' sleep they continued through the Mojave desert and on to LA. 'There was no time to check into the motel properly or unpack,' remembers Roy,

> just time for a quick wash and brush-up and for the Camerons to don their kilts and accompanying Scottish attire, and it was straight to the Convention Hall. As soon as we walked in we were called up to the platform to sing and minister to the several thousand people who had gathered. Naturally we were all tired in body but, as always, we carried the Glory anointing in our hearts ('the anointing you have received abideth...') and when we opened our mouths the Holy Spirit took over and many were set free and blessed. The congregation would not let us go but wanted more and more! Many testified afterwards that they had received something new from God, and had seen something they had never witnessed before.
>
> Afterwards we received many invitations to take the blessing to fellowships and churches around the area, culminating in a few days' ministry at a Tent Revival, where the Glory of the Lord filled the tabernacle; spontaneous praise and dancing broke out until the whole place was in a state of 'Holy Ghost disarray'! This was repeated wherever we went across the States. It is no exaggeration to report that the lives of thousands were transformed through the Glory ministry there.

'The Cameron family changed the form of worship in America.' Simon Cameron makes this simple statement without any false modesty. Allowing certainly for the traditionally lively worship of black congregations in the deep south there was, before the Cameron tours, very little praising and dancing before the Lord in the United States. So they created something of a riot. Wendy was the first woman to dance in praise on National Christian Television. After it was over the phone rang continuously. It was red hot. Folk went wild.

The point I believe is this, that when Henri in Newark, in 1948, fell off his piano stool, pushed as by an unseen Hand, and rolled across the dour prayer meeting floor speaking loudly in tongues, ripples of spiritual liberation were set off across the world. In this case, when taken up by ebullient Highlanders in kilt, sporran and criss-cross gartered legs, with generations of deer-stalking heather-scrambling energy behind them, this joyous expression of Christian discipleship hit a new high. Praise God. The Americans were perfectly shocked and delighted.

The Camerons were in the van of a new move of the Holy Spirit, bringing a new-found and surprising freedom to praise and worship, breaking down many barriers between denominations, classes and races. *'If the Son therefore shall make you free ye shall be free indeed'* (John 8:36). The fresh individual Scottish Glory novelty which they brought took the lead and then merged with the upsurge of the Jesus movement and the charismatic movement. Yet it always retained a very distinct character of its own.

Leaders of the Glory Way are used to the perennial criticism, 'Oh, it's all froth and bubble!' The scripture that immediately leaps to Simon Cameron's mind are the words of Jesus when praying to the Father, *'those that Thou gavest Me I have kept, and none of them is lost'* (John 17:12). The Cameron brothers can stand their ground and point to their children and grandchildren: they are not only saved but, as they should be, wholeheartedly serving the Lord and on fire for Him. Exuberant expressions of praise are not simply a passing firework display of religious emotion, but a joyful outworking of love to the Lord, showing forth a settled, even defiant, conviction and commitment to God. It is a nailing of colours to the mast. The Apostle Paul said, *'stand fast in the faith, quit you like men, be strong'* (1 Corinthians 16:13).

One gets a taste again of what it was like to be in the thick of all this as one looks over the shoulder of young Roy Turner pouring out his heart in an airmail letter to Janie Marshall. He was staying in Brooklyn, New York in 1967.

> Well we had a most marvellous meeting, a real red-hot Glory meeting. The pastor broke down and wept as he told the people how he had received something new from the Lord. Scores of folk came out to seek the Lord, weeping, speaking in tongues, laughing and praising the Lord! It was a sight to behold. They will never be the same again. I'm so glad that God is leading us by His Spirit. We may plan, but praise the Lord, He plans ahead of us. It was hard to get the folk to go home. The next morning it was the talk of the place. Hallelujah! When Jesus comes in we don't need to advertise – the hungry, the seeking, the sinner, the saint come unto Him for rest and blessing. Hallelujah! On Tuesday night at our final meeting there were many real testimonies of changed lives. One woman said she had got a new husband, another said her eye had been changed – she could hardly tell it for the tears that rolled down her cheeks. Bless her! And more and more it will go on because Jesus is alive today and pouring out the latter rain. We will be in meetings in Harrisburg on Friday, Pittsburg on Saturday, Baltimore next week and so on as the Lord leads. Keep praying. God bless you, Janie, I do love you and all at No. 22. Love to Henri and Connie also. I miss you all but praise God to be in this part of the field for Him!

In the 1960s the spiritual situation in many places became suddenly fluid and Simon Cameron had invitations to lead meetings in Roman Catholic churches. This was a result of the genial liberalising influence of Pope John 23rd and the general impact of the charismatic movement. Simon seized the opportunity because he saw it as a chance to get alongside these people. Because of what he was doing, leading praise meetings, he did not see it as a question of doctrinal compromise. As an heir of the land of John Knox's radical Reformation, Simon was fully aware of the fact that he was sharing an activity not simply with another big denomination, but with a body which regards itself as the only true apostolic church. This immediately creates a dilemma because an Evangelical Pentecostal Protestant must say that such a body, the Roman Catholic Church, is an absolutely massive usurper. The doctrines of this church as defined by the Council of Trent and upheld by the supposed infallible authority of the papacy are simply not the same as the doctrines of the Bible alone. These differences are often acute. The position and claims of the papacy, the role of the priesthood and its celibacy, the mass, purgatory and the spiritual exaltation of Mary are blatantly unbiblical. There is no point in papering over the cracks. However, all this should not prevent people from meeting and seeing how far any activities can be shared.

When the Camerons were in New Orleans, Simon was invited to lead praise meetings in the Church of Our Lady of Prompt Succour and the Church of Edward the Confessor. They were packed to the doors; in the meeting of the first there were 1,200 present with a good number of nuns. In both churches the meetings went like a bomb. The parishioners entered into the full spirit of free praise. The nuns took off in their dancing, as did most other folk. They loved this new way of praising God, it seemed to them so natural and spontaneous. Each church had social halls, where the Camerons laid out tapes of their music. The Catholics took every one; they were clamouring for them, hungry for them. Simon and Wendy had to look in their baggage for any spare ones; they were cleaned right out. What a contrast with certain Pentecostal churches they went to, where people would walk right past their wares; they had everything, so they thought.

Simon also went to a huge Roman Catholic church in Chicago where, alongside a priest, he laid hands on people at the front for the baptism of the Holy Spirit and for healing. In time, two years later, they returned to new Orleans, to those two churches, only to find that they were closed to them. The Camerons were not surprised. A window of opportunity had opened and then closed again. The Roman Catholic hierarchy had caught on to the fact that the charismatic movement was boosting the numbers and influence of their churches. However, they wanted to claim the kudos, the renown, for themselves. Praising Pentecostals were no longer to have a look-in.

It is truly amazing how far the Glory influence permeated the Catholic Church as is illustrated by the following account from Roy Turner. He writes,

In 1982, Pope John Paul visited Great Britain and over the period of a week he ministered at huge rallies in the major cities. On 1st June, I was sitting at home and decided to switch on the television to watch coverage of one of these gatherings at Bellahouston Park, in Glasgow, Scotland. Imagine my surprise and amazement at the sight which met my eyes. There on the screen was a very large choir of Scottish young people dressed in the vivid colours of the various tartans. As the camera panned across this sea of radiant faces framed by technicolour scarves and hats, I realised they were singing the Glory chorus I had received from the Spirit almost twenty years before, in America, *All over the world the Spirit is moving*. What's more, they were really getting lost in liberty and praise! It was just like a Glory meeting!

On and on they sang, over and over again, joined by the massive throng who had gathered in the Park. When they finally stopped singing, David Dimbleby, the TV announcer, said, 'And yet again we hear one of these uplifting songs which the Catholic Church seems to have made their own during this visit of the Pope'. Following the Pope's address, when he was being driven in his 'Pope-mobile' amongst the vast crowds (estimated to be about 300,000 people) the strains of *All over the world* were taken up again and again, the great truth of the Spirit's worldwide influence breaking through every man-made barrier! No wonder Henri's clarion call was always ... THE GLORY MAKES US ONE!

Since then I have received letters from various Catholic Churches in Australia about that chorus, been told of Christians sailing the sea of Galilee with the same chorus upon their lips, heard it on several television broadcasts of *Songs of Praise*, including the last night of the Edinburgh Festival, and found it printed and used by folk of all denominations. Surely this shows the deep hunger, known or as yet unrealised, in the hearts of men and women everywhere regardless of nationality, creed or religion.

Early on in their tours, somewhere at a convention, Simon and Wendy Cameron met Bob Doorn, the pastor of Pleasant Plain Gospel Church at Cameron, Wisconsin, a town about a hundred miles south of Lake Superior. He invited them over, and this was the first of many regular visits. A warm friendship grew up between them; in fact, Pleasant Plain Church quickly regarded themselves as a Glory centre with regular Glory meetings. The coincidence of the name caused some amusement and added to the bond of fellowship between them. And it was a proud moment when the Cameron family stirred themselves in true Highland clan fashion to bring no less than forty-two blood relatives over to Cameron at one moment. They shouted and praised and had a whale of a meeting together. They must have been a formidable sight in their kilts and Highland dress, a little foretaste of the moment when every kindred will stand before the Throne and before the Lamb (Revelation 7:9).

It is very interesting to get a first-hand account of the impact of the Cameron ministry on various people. Young Rick Nelson came from a fine Canadian Christian family. He said, 'The Lord made Himself real to me when I was very young; it happened in a small town ... called Kitimat in northern British Columbia.' The family then moved to Vancouver,

> And although I still professed to be living a Christian life at home, my whole outlook had changed ... through the study of sciences I was taught to rely only on my own mind and ability. I majored in physics and, though I believed there must be a Supreme Being, I wasn't going to believe in anything that I couldn't understand with my mind. I thought that everything could be proved by research and scientific methods and that God and Jesus were just crutches that people needed because of their fear of the unknown and death. At that time, as far as I was concerned, when you were dead that was the end, so you had better make the best of life while you could.
>
> Besides, Christians seemed so negative; they were always known by what they didn't do, rather than what they did, and most of them seemed to have long miserable faces and to be living joyless lives. [28]

This terrible misconception was blown sky high when he met Roy Turner and the Camerons. Several months later, when working on an Indian Reservation, he came to a cross-roads in his life and surrendered to Christ.

In the mid 1960s Billy Van Zandt, a Southern Baptist pastor in Midland, Texas, disillusioned, disturbed and depressed in himself and the unreality he saw amongst church people, sought the Lord for fresh experience. He was wonderfully baptised in the Holy Spirit and found, through this, not a snap answer to his problems, but 'the beginning of the way to real peace and glory in Jesus'. He explained,

> It was almost a year before I began to walk in real victory, but the Holy Spirit made it gloriously possible for me to find the power to do so.

Then in 1969 they had a visit from Roy Turner and the Cameron family. He dryly remarked that, until they came,

> we were as free as we knew how to be, but since their visit we have come into the Glory experience of real worship, praise, joy, peace and victory. We are learning to desire and walk in the will of God totally and now life is a wonderful adventure. Hallelujah!

Roy encouraged Billy to get a piano accordion. Within three months he was playing it well enough to lead church meetings in praise, and then he formed a church musical group which travelled from coast to coast in America, 'setting the captives free and ministering in the liberty and joy of the Spirit'. They came up against opposition to their lively meetings. Billy said, 'Isn't it strange that not everyone wants the real thing!' [29]

In 1972 the Cruthirds family came over from the United States to a Glory convention in Peterhead where it was a real joy for them to meet all the Cameron family, Brother Henri, Roy Turner and so many more. Each of the Cruthirds was very conscious of how good the Lord had been to them in their lives. Mildred, the mother, explained how after four years of marriage she had been told by specialist after specialist that she would never be able to have children. This led her to a point of desperation, but through this experience the Lord truly saved her. What is more, she went on to have seven children! Her husband Les was brought up a Methodist in small sawmill towns. His parents were very strict and Les thought he was a Christian. He also said,

> In each town we lived in there was always a group of Pentecostal people. They were considered odd and folk thought they had gone overboard as far as religion was concerned. Many would go to their revivals to sit in cars and watch the show. The way they acted always seemed strange to me, but for some reason it scared me when people were in real worship to the Lord. When they were speaking in tongues and verbally praising God, I felt like I was in the wrong place. I was very ill at ease. In spite of this I couldn't say anything against these people. I knew them and was in daily contact with them in school and at work. They were good living folk! [30]

Les went through the War as an airman in the US Air Force and read his Bible. But in fact he did not give his heart to the Lord until 1949 when he attended a Pentecostal assembly with Mildred. Certainly at that point his life changed, and since then he had a great awareness of God caring for their family life. On this trip to Peterhead three of their children were with them, Leslie Junior (who had just come through a time of rebellion), Marsha and Richard. Each of them was walking with the Lord and it was a great encouragement to them to be with such joyful Glory believers.

That same year, 1972, two more young American Christians, Kathy Ireland and Randy Fish, were touring through England and shared in a Glory meeting in Newark. They rejoiced in the freedom of the fellowship they found there. Randy, who was a licensed Southern Baptist preacher, had experienced the baptism of the Holy Spirit in his life. He knew he had found reality. Kathy too was rejoicing in the Spirit. A highlight of the trip to Europe that summer was a visit to the Munich Olympic Games. They had talked to the athletes in the Olympic Village and gave away Bibles in about fifteen languages. Kathy said,

> Some of the expressions on the faces of the Russian athletes when we gave them the Word of God were indescribable; just like giving someone a million dollars. They registered unbelief and then just shock! One of the boys with us gave a Russian a Bible and he told us afterwards that the athlete thanked him in every language he could think of! [31]

Africa

It was simply through the distribution of the *Glory News* magazine and Glory tapes and cassettes that contact was made with Africa. The feedback from letters was always stimulating. For instance, in 1958, a *Glory News*, popped into a parcel of books sent to Siriba Government Training College in Kenya, sparked off an enthusiastic reply from Cuthbert Dawkins and his family. He was an Anglican missionary in charge of religious instruction of what was the largest African training college in Kenya. He explained how two years earlier God brought them into the light of the Full Gospel, his wife being miraculously healed through the prayer and laying on of hands of a Pentecostal missionary. Cuthbert continued,

Since then the Lord has continued to bless our whole family (we have six children) and has started to use us in a new way amongst the African people. Some of us have received the Pentecostal experience and others are seeking it, but we are all waiting on Him for still greater blessing. We need the fullness of joy and power which you folk obviously have got.

One of their children, Christine, aged twelve, added this letter:

Dear Brother Henri, I would like to tell you how much we enjoyed your Glory tapes. The other day we were listening to them and when you prayed for one or two sick people in the meeting I prayed with you. I felt something come over me and from then on I have been healed of a small trouble I had. I enjoy reading the *Glory News* that we get and we always remember you in our family prayers ... I am trying hard to witness for our precious Saviour and He has helped me to win other girls for Him. Every Wednesday I have a meeting for them and once in a while one gets saved. To Jesus be all the glory. With love to all the glory friends, Christine Dawkins. [32]

Five years later the Dawkins family, on leave in England, turned up at an Isle of Wight Glory holiday. Henri and Connie were thrilled. Altogether it was a memorable time:

Never in all its long history has the ancient Carisbrooke Castle experienced anything like it did, when two coach loads of Glory folk marched round its keep, singing praises to God with tambourines and accordions. Other folk certainly stood amazed ... Each night after the meetings we continued with tea and snacks and the Glory folk were so happy it was difficult to get anyone to leave the hall! [33]

To turn to Zambia, two pastors wrote to the *Glory News* in appreciation of the Glory tape ministry. One said that he simply had to write. He explained,

Some of the prayer meetings we have had were a little 'cold' so one night I played the Glory tape recorded at Leeds and we had real Pentecost for a blessed change. God bless you.

We usually think of African brethren warming us northerners up with their bright smiles and free gestures. But on this occasion the blessing flowed the other way. Then a second pastor wrote,

> Dear brother in Christ, I have listened to one of the tapes from one of the meetings in Leeds; it was such a blessing to my soul. As I sat and listened to the service I didn't know what to do. I tell you, brother, I was not sure whether to cry, laugh or dance, so I did all to the Glory of God. [34]

Then an evangelist in the Cameroons wrote in with these words:

> A copy of the *Glory News* you sent to me has revived me. I have read many testimonies of my fellow folks in Christ and they have brought me nearer to my God. I gave it to a friend to read and it has done a great work in my friend's life. [35]

Ruth Elton, working with the World Christian Crusade in Nigeria, was the daughter of Pentecostal missionary parents. Whilst in Britain for some time as a young person she was seeking for more of God with all her heart. She wanted reality. And the Lord led her into so much more. So then, back in Nigeria she witnessed wonderful healings, as in Bible times, of the lame walking, the blind seeing and the dumb speaking. And the Glory Way? In 1955 and 1958 Ruth went to Newark and there instinctively and immediately she felt one with them. It was for her a great encouragement and refreshment. And she took this blessing and fullness of the Holy Spirit with her as the way opened up for her to travel into northern Nigeria, into predominantly Moslem country.

Moving to the south, the Glory tapes and magazines brought encouragement to Christians in Cape Town. An evangelist, L.G. Dullaert, wrote,

> I was on my way to my office before 8 o'clock in the morning and whilst sitting in the bus, I took out the latest *Glory News*, No. 16, to read and as I opened it the Holy Spirit fell upon me and I began to sing softly in the Spirit. My eyes were full of tears but my heart was full of Glory. After getting off the bus the Holy Spirit continued to rest upon me and fill me with unspeakable longing for more of Him. I had read the Editor's Notes and a few other testimonies and

I believe that the Notes sparked off a revelation to me from God the Holy Ghost. [36]

Another reader from Cape Town, Mr C.F.B., said,

We read your magazine with joy and only wish that it came out more frequently. Also the tapes we listened to ... The last one ... with Brother Cecil Morris is an excellent one and his message is a real knock-out for the can-do-it. That is what we need more of, this positive, can-do-it Gospel. It makes folks want to act on it, as that is just the line that is missing in the lives of people today. They won't act and I don't wonder when they are told all the while that they are miserable sinners and only failing human beings. Bah! [37]

From the middle of these apartheid times Fred Beverley wrote to the Glory Office from Cape Town to talk about an outreach particularly to non-whites. Fred was leading a band of four musicians who called themselves *The Word of Faith Ministry* (one of them John, an ex-gaolbird), to bring the gospel to those who are 'underprivileged in the things of God'. They held Glory meetings, and said that they saw hundreds filled with the Holy Spirit and with joy in their hearts. Fred wrote,

Then we teach them the wonderful faith-building truths about the Holy Ghost. His ministry; His work in us; how we can be a blessing; how we can be *indigenous*, that is, have *our* faith in God. Instead of always going to the pastor and saying, 'O brother, pray for me, I'm so weak', we come to the place where we are strong in the Lord and we say, 'Pastor, I want to help you in being a blessing to others.' [38]

Contact with the Glory Way seemed to bring with it a certain surprise element. One can sense this in a letter from Regina Killa of Cape Town, in 1971:

About six months ago the founder leader of our Evangelistic Association handed me a copy of Henri's *Glory News* ... Oh brother! I felt something I'm unable to explain run through my body as I read through the magazine. So much was explained in a moment. I just had to praise the Lord. I started writing the letter to you, but could not finish it. The very next evening as we were having a faith healing service,

I was suddenly blessed with the baptism of the Holy Ghost. Hallelujah Lord Jesus! ... Oh, those testimonies! Even now I'm writing with the copy just in front of me. I just can't wait to finish all my housework so that I can read it again ... Some of the clergy still believe in witchcraft and so on. What they are doing is trying to serve the Lord and Satan both at the same time, but now Christ has started revealing Himself and the ordinary churches can't stop the true faith from spreading. We are definitely fighting a winning battle with Christ right in front ... I speak, hear and walk with Christ. At times, sitting in trains or buses or just walking, I suddenly find myself smiling. Oh the happiness He gives me when He speaks to reassure me. Praise Him. [39]

Australia and New Zealand

These countries could not be further away from Britain, yet in ties of family affinity they could not be closer. Very many British have 'down-under' relatives. Spiritual links and understanding are close too.

The Glory Office in 1964 received a letter from Henry Gallus of Moss Vale, seventy miles inland from Sydney, full of pastoral wisdom. He emphasised the importance of the feast of Tabernacles, which was at the time of the fullness of the harvest ingathering, a moment of great rejoicing. It was at this feast that Solomon's temple was dedicated, and Glory filled the house. This feast was in the seventh month. He went on,

> Seven is the number of *divine rest*, and points to the rest of faith in Hebrews chapter four and you Glory folk are proving that *His rest is glorious*. I do not envisage that which has started in England is on a great scale yet, but it is a beginning.

Against all set-backs and problems of false brethren Henry Gallus could foresee a day when 'the Glory Cloud of perfect love will come down over all' and the church will be 'a Bride without spot or wrinkle'. He was so glad to read these *Glory News* with photos of happy and honest faces. He ended,

> Yes Henri, it did me good and I say, may God help you in the immense and difficult task that lies ahead of presenting every man perfect and complete in Christ. [40]

In 1972 Peter and Dorothy Schelcher from Brisbane wrote in the *Glory News*. Hungering for more of God they both received the baptism in the Holy Spirit. Peter was the pastor of a Pentecostal church. Dorothy had fallen painfully ill with a spinal disease and had been completely and wonderfully healed. Not long afterwards someone gave them copies of the *Glory News*. 'As they read it, they witnessed that here was reality.' So they continued to receive the magazine and the Glory tapes. Many of their friends were blessed and strengthened through them. Dorothy said,

> What impresses me most is the *love* that is manifested in the Glory meetings and can be felt coming from the recordings we receive. [41]

A Scots couple, Bob and Cathy Owens, went out to Western Australia in 1961. Cathy was saved after suffering intense depression after the birth of their first child. Three years later this same child, Catherine, warned her daddy at breakfast to be very careful as he worked on a construction site. Two weeks later, after rejecting the Saviour in gospel meetings, Bob had a very dangerous fall; he landed on a metal bracket which saved him from terrible injury, as underneath were hard concrete, wiring and building materials. Next Sunday he gave his heart to the Lord. Both Bob and Cathy received the fullness of the Holy Spirit and found much joy in witnessing. The Lord led them into open-air work on beaches and on the streets of Perth. They ran a youth group in Balga Christian Revival Centre and saw miracles happening, 'Blind eyes have been opened, crossed eyes straightened, the paralysed walking from their chairs, and the prisoners liberated!' In 1974 they came to Britain on a tour, preaching and singing the gospel, and enjoyed a Glory weekend at Newark, where they thrilled everyone with their experiences they shared. [42]

Moving to New Zealand, the *Glory News* reported that in May 1972 there was a march for Jesus in Auckland:

> Singing hymns, chanting 'Jesus' and holding Bibles above their heads, about 10,000 people, most of them young, marched for Jesus. As the marchers prepared to begin their procession down Queen Street a group of people appeared on the other side of the street carrying placards which read, 'God is dead' and 'Jesus Never Rose'. A radiant expression

on her face, one young Jesus marcher called out to them: 'We love you, brothers.' [43]

A year later the Glory Office in Newark received this unusual story from the same city, Auckland. Gordon Rickard was the child of a broken home and from the age of one was brought up by grandparents in the village of Havelock North, half-way down the east side of the North Island, New Zealand. In 1939 he married Australian Evelyn; they had two sons and a daughter. At this moment they went to church, but were not Christians. They made a wrong move when they left a good job and home and went to Sydney. Gordon said that from the day they arrived there began seven years of trouble until death almost overtook him. They were living in an old caravan and makeshift hut, awaiting a Housing Commission home, and one day in August 1952, as he went to work, Gordon picked up the morning paper to read that two circus trapeze artists, on their way to Melbourne, had kipped down by a railway line, and had been killed by an express train, *The Spirit of Progress*. Little did he realise that almost the same fate was about to happen to him. He wrote later,

> As I rode over the railway line at Bandiana, I was distracted by a noise behind, turned to look, and knew no more. I was struck by the first train to be in that area for 15 months. Bus passengers found me sixty yards down beside the line with my boots torn off and feet bleeding. I had ten fractures and many other injuries. Police picked up my wife Evelyn, who was shocked. I was given only two hours to live. She called on Christians to pray. They did! For four days I was in the death ward, unconscious with 100,000 units of penicillin administered. At 4 pm the fourth day I regained consciousness, to be astounded that I had nearly died!
>
> I admitted then that I was like a sheep who had gone astray. I had turned to my own way. I was lost. And yet there was One who had come to seek and to save, the Lord Jesus Christ. He had laid upon Himself the sin and iniquity that was in my heart. *I accepted Him* into my life and within ten weeks was out of hospital, witnessing and testifying to His power and grace! [44]

To begin with Gordon could not work and had a disablement pension. Then, some time later, on hearing a radio sermon, God gave him the faith for complete healing, and he was restored to health and strength. He and Evelyn moved to Auckland, where he became the caretaker for the New Zealand Sunday School Union.

In contrast to her husband's experience, Evelyn was converted to Christ very simply, but no less truly. She said that before she came to know Jesus as her Saviour she was a very self-righteous sort of person, going to church, reading the Bible, paying her tithes, saying her prayers, but never born again of the Holy Spirit. She said,

> It wasn't until He convicted me of my sins and made me see straight that I began to go the right way in life ... It was the great love of God that drew me to Him! Jesus just showed me how very much He *loved* me, even though I was a sinner. [45]

Coming back from a cottage one night, she was under such conviction that she yielded herself to the claims of Christ. She found that 'the Lord is nigh unto all them that call upon Him' and He became a glorious reality to her from that moment. Some time after, they were sent a *Glory News*, and before long were listening to Glory tapes too. Gordon said,

> The messages on the tapes have done much to increase our faith, especially during times of sickness. There is such *liberty* in the Spirit. It makes us laugh, it makes us cry. We are never the same again, Hallelujah!

India and the Far East

It is wonderful to think of that moment in the future when a great multitude, which no man can number, from every nation, kindred, people and tongue will stand before the throne and before the Lamb (Revelation 7:9). It is enriching when believers cross cultural barriers. Indeed, we must say that it is very necessary for some to do so, otherwise the gospel would never reach the uttermost parts of the earth.

The Glory Way had some extremely interesting contacts amongst the enormously varied cultures and peoples on the great continent of Asia. In 1961 a Glory meeting in Stockport near Manchester had a visit from a Siberian believer, Mrs Sophia Popova; she greatly enjoyed it. Then in the *Glory News* we are told about Brother and Sister Morgan, faithful missionaries in

Formosa (Taiwan), who loved to receive copies of the magazine. Likewise Mr and Mrs T.C.W. from Ceylon (Sri Lanka), who passed the *Glory News* round to other eager readers. [46] From Singapore came this enthusiastic letter from seventeen-year-old Olga Bodestyne:

> The Glory Way is really wonderful, bless the Lord, for only Christ is seen. Hallelujah! I love this Glory Way, for we are free from bondage and chains. We are free to worship the Lord in the fullness of His Spirit, and oh, what blessings we receive here in this humble home which the Lord has provided. Yes, it's a home not a church, for *we* are the church. It's no use going to church miles away when we can worship the Lord right where we are ... Since our beloved brother, Tom, and sister, Eva Fox left us last March the Lord has brought many more souls to join us. God is ever so faithful to keep that which He has promised ... At present we have also a Sunday School, in which the Lord is using and drawing the little children unto Himself. [47]

In 1960 another young woman, Rosy Esther Cheng, wrote in from Selengor in Malaya (Western Malaysia):

> Dear Brother Henri, I felt led by the Lord to write to you this letter of thanks to you for the *Glory News* which blessed me so much. Praise and thank the Lord for a brother in Christ who sent me a few copies. Glory to God! The Spirit stirs me up greatly as I read those inspiring messages. Hallelujah, the Lord is so real to me and I love Him and, even though I hardly know who you are, yet thank God for the Spirit of Love flowing in my heart for you all. And be assured that I shall be praying for you ... I was brought up in a Buddhist family of eleven and for many years my heart was yearning for the true God. I was living in sin for years, until the Lord led a brother in Christ and he induced me to attend the Assembly of God Youth Camp held on the 20th April 1959. Well, praise God, the next day the Spirit convicted me deeply of my sins and I wrestled with Him for three solid hours and when I got up it seemed like only a few minutes. That night my soul found divine joy and peace. Hallelujah!
> On the 22nd April the dear Lord wonderfully baptised me in His sweet Spirit and I spoke in several different tongues as the Spirit gave me utterance and I've been

speaking in unknown tongues and praising God freely ever since. God called me into the Bible School on 4th January 1960, so I resigned my job and stepped out in faith in obedience to His divine call. I am standing on the faithfulness of God to see me through the three-year course. Please pray for me. I praise God that I have Pentecost in my soul and I thank God for His great deliverances in my life. My heart is yearning to present the Gospel to my people here, thousands upon thousands in spiritual darkness and my desire is for the reality of God's power with signs and wonders to be manifested to these never dying souls.

The Lord spoke to me through the *Glory News* that He will see me through this commission and I just want to thank you for this wonderful magazine. I would greatly appreciate some more copies and inspiring books from you. My heart is hungry for more spiritual truth and I thirst for a deeper walk with Christ, that I may know Him well enough to present Him to all lost sinners. Please pray and help me, dear Brother Henri. [48]

From the large island of Sumatra, in Indonesia, Paul Pohan, the Deputy General Superintendent of Batak Christian Church wrote in 1974 to say:

From Sumatra I bring you greetings in Jesus' Name! A few weeks ago, someone sent me a copy of *Glory News*. It was a back issue, but I really saw that everything you had in it is simply the plain truth of God's word which, of course, will never get obsolete or out-of-date. I am so thrilled to see a paper like *Glory News* being so brave and knowing no compromise with the world... [49]

We learn of a group of Glory folk in Singapore. A young RAF airman Graham Potts was invited by a New Zealand brother to listen to a Glory tape. Back on leave with his wife Olga in England, they both met Henri and his team in Banbury. Full of enthusiasm for the Lord, as they returned to Singapore, they linked up with another Glory couple, Brother and Sister Fox. Graham wrote,

I believe the work out there is going to spread into all South East Asia as the Lord showed a dear brother in a vision. Glory to God! [50]

Ten years or so after this we hear of two other young airmen in the RAF in Singapore. There was Ron Street (from Yarm, in Yorkshire) who was there for two-and-a-half years. He had been saved just a few months, and he cried to God to lead him to a church fellowship where he would feel really at home. The Lord sent him a young Christian from Malaya, David Ratcliffe. They were both thirsty for more of God, and they were led to an experienced Indian brother in his fifties who took them to a house meeting in a village. Ron said,

> Hallelujah! On arrival we found it to be a Glory meeting. The atmosphere in that small, hot living room, less than ten feet square, was charged with the presence of God! There was no air-conditioning and no chairs to speak of. We sat on cushions on a bare floor, mosquitoes and chit-chats (small lizards) were everywhere, but the blessing and presence of God overcame all discomfort. I was so hungry to know more of Jesus in those days. More than anything else I wanted to be filled with the Holy Spirit and eventually God filled me to overflowing in a Bible Study when we were closing in prayer. How wonderful are His ways; so different from ours!
>
> For a good while after being baptised so wonderfully in the Spirit, I spoke in other tongues and a group of Malayan folk gathered around outside the small flat to listen. They were there because a curious thing was happening! An Englishman who had no knowledge of their language was speaking, by the Holy Spirit, fluent high-class Malayan! Yes, speaking words of praise and worship to God our Heavenly Father! Oh friends, how I cherish the fact that I am not limited to my own language and wisdom to worship and speak to God. I can just leave it to the Holy Spirit and He intercedes for that which is necessary, worshipping and praising the Lord in far more glorious words than I could ever use.
>
> Out in Singapore we would eagerly listen to the Glory tapes from Newark, drinking in all that we could and learning the new choruses and songs of praise ... Since those days I have always worshipped according to the light that I received in similar free meetings. [51]

Ron's wife Anne said that her Christian experience had not been a smooth one, by any means, but, she said, 'What are a few upsets and persecutions compared with the Crown of Life which awaits us?' She too had been baptised in the Holy Spirit; this was at a meeting in Stockton-on-Tees some years before. Then together, in 1973, they joined the Glory holiday convention in Margate and revelled in the fellowship they enjoyed there.

The Peterhead New Year Convention of 1974 had a visit of a choir of fourteen Filipinos, led by Clyde Shields and two other missionaries, Mrs Janice McKinney and Deanna Wright. They were called the Choir of Miracles, and the fact is that the singers were sons and daughters of head-hunters.

> The capacity crowds that filled Zion Tabernacle each evening were thrilled and stirred by the Spirit-filled witness of these young folk who were, until recently, still in heathen darkness and superstition, dressed in native costumes and living in abject poverty.
>
> It was a moving sight to see them worshipping and praising God, singing the songs of the redeemed and testifying of the changing power of Jesus Christ **today**! The realisation came afresh that God has got no favourites, is no respecter of persons, and is at work in every nation of the world. Hallelujah! ... One of the special features of the Choir's witness for Christ was the Dance of the Head-Hunters in which several of the group dressed in their native costumes to vividly demonstrate the background from which Christ has lifted them. With their battle-shields, spears and ancient brass gongs, they presented authentic tribal dancing.
>
> It was truly wonderful to see them later, dancing for joy in the presence of the Lord, expressing the blessing of their salvation together with the rest of the Glory Folk. Faces aglow, hearts bubbling over with thanksgiving to God who has delivered them and given them a new song, even a song of praise! [52]

They also brought us a chorus which has continued to bless people: 'Why don't you lift up your hands and praise the Lord?'

Some time later they went to Northern Ireland where Herbie Stewart of Lisburn fixed up twelve meetings for them. In their first evening, at Keady in County Armagh, 'the congregation sobbed and laughed aloud, clapped and praised God as these humble children of head-hunters exalted Jesus and His transforming grace.' They moved round to Belfast, Kells, Dundonald,

Bangor, Lisburn and Dungannon, the numbers increasing all the time. They were a breath of fresh air and a joy in the middle of the province's desperate on-going experience of tension and violence.

'You prayed for missions,' were the grateful words of the Filipinos, 'and God heard your cry and tonight you see the answers to *your* prayers!' How wonderful is the free flow of the Holy Spirit in the lives of those who love the Lord. The final meeting in Dungannon was packed. 'Young people offered their lives for service on the mission field and others professed a new-found faith in Christ.' [53]

As we have already seen, the Willesden Revival Centre, founded by Frank and Phyllis Preudhomme, sent out and supported a young missionary, Myrtle Taylor. It happened in this way. In the 1950s Phyllis had been working closely with Myrtle at the Head Office of Barclays Bank, Dominion, Colonial and Overseas. Phyllis witnessed to her and led her to the Lord. Now, Phyllis was dealing with Far Eastern finance and began to have a real burden for the Chinese. Then she met Frank and they were married and so she was immediately involved with her husband's very demanding work for the Lord. The missionary burden for the Chinese, as it were, fell on Myrtle. But she was a quiet young woman, who had always lived comfortably at her parents' home and had not knocked around much. She describes how the call of God came to her in a very insistent way:

> I remember, even before I was saved, when the Lord was drawing me to Himself, I used to feel uncomfortable when-ever the scripture, *'Go ye into all the world and preach the gospel'* was mentioned. I was fearful that if I gave my heart to Jesus, He would want me to be a missionary, but bless His Name, He gave me grace to yield myself to Him.
>
> Nearly a year after I was saved, I went to Bonsall for my first holiday as a Christian. It is the practice there to have a time of waiting upon the Lord, on a Thursday morning and many young people have been baptised in the Spirit in those meetings. There were many of us seeking the Lord, the morning that I was there. His presence became very real and it was then He spoke into my heart and gave me the scripture that is found in Ezekiel chapter 3, verse 4, *'Go and speak with My words unto them.'*
>
> I didn't know where I was to go, or when, but I never forgot those words and I often asked the Lord about them.

Time passed and eventually the Lord led me to Willesden and began drawing me into this wonderful blessing and liberty in the Holy Ghost.

One Friday evening Brother Henri and Sister Connie came to Lambeth and I shall never forget Sister Connie's words as she was preaching. She said, 'God is looking for men and women who will serve Him. He will take your life if you are willing and pour it out, that others might be blessed; but what does that matter? He took the life of Jesus and poured it out for you.'

As I stood with many others and yielded my life afresh to God, something happened to me and it is true, I have never been the same since. I can't explain it, but we call it being set free, don't we? Praise His Name! As I went home that night the words were ringing in my heart over and over, *'Go and speak My words unto them.'*[54]

A little later she read in a missionary magazine of the island of Taiwan, with a population of eleven-and-a-half million of whom only two per cent were Christian. She knew straight away that this was where the Lord wanted her to go. Certainly the need on that island was great. Half the population was under 21, and the overwhelming majority of these young people had no knowledge of Jesus. Myrtle saw that they were bound by the evils of Buddhism and Taoism: and by disease and sickness and the fear of death. A year at the Pentecostal Bible college IBTI near Burgess Hill in Sussex toughened her up, as she would say. She had the chore of washing piles of missionary students' socks. Meantime she was fast learning the language on audio-tape. Then in 1967 off she flew to Taiwan.

Frank and Phyllis Preudhomme knew a Swedish missionary in Taiwan, Ruth Helgerson, who arranged to meet Myrtle and help her to settle in. Ruth in turn linked her up with five American sisters at a church in the city of Taipei and then returned to the other end of the island where she was working. Through these American missionaries God led Myrtle to an Old Covenanters Church in a village some way outside Taipei called Shen Keng (The Deep Pit!). This church was just about to close down, but she brought to it a breath of Pentecostal life. The fellowship revived and has never looked back. She kept in contact with the five American missionary women and they all worked together in running summer camps and various other activities.

If a true missionary is a person who crosses cultural and language barriers with the gospel of Jesus, then Myrtle is one of them. She has become so wedded to her life in Taiwan that, now her elderly mother has died, she has no wish to return to Britain. Speaking Chinese all the time, she finds it difficult to speak English! The other missionaries have died, or retired to the USA. Myrtle is the only Westerner left in her fellowship. She is fondly known as 'Mother'!

In 1974 the Glory Office were in contact with another missionary hearted woman, Ruth Zingers. She came from a Christian home, and about the time she left school the Spirit of God moved on her heart, convincing her of her need of Christ. After about a year of seeking she was brought to the experience of really heartfelt salvation. She became conscious that the Lord was calling her to work abroad. After medical training she worked for nine months in Birmingham Children's Hospital where she met Ernests Zingers from Latvia, who was on his way to North India. They were drawn to one another and were soon engaged. In September 1939, just at the outbreak of the War, Ernests went to India and Ruth followed him out there the following March.

She worked as assistant to a lady doctor in a hospital in the hill station of Landour, 7,000 feet above sea level. In July 1940 they were married. She continued,

> During the next few years we continued to serve the Lord together, doing medical and evangelistic work in the villages in the Himalayan mountains and helping in a mission hospital. I was very happy with the work which was so varied and interesting. In 1941 Ernests and I trekked along the Hindustan-Tibet road, 200 miles there and 200 miles back, ultimately passing over a 15,000 foot-high mountain pass into Tibet, preaching the gospel, distributing Scripture portions and doing medical work where needed. It was a truly wonderful experience ... some of the medical cases I will never forget! Rabies, lockjaw, the woman who had been mauled by a bear and the man attacked by a tiger. Others who had been bitten by snakes. Sometimes we could do nothing but *pray*, and I began to realise that the Lord was able to heal without my help!
>
> At other times we worked very hard using the means we had and the Lord used the medicines and operations, *but He was always the Healer*. Praise His Name. How I thank God for my dear husband and the help he gave in taking me out in

the hills in the Land Rover, through the jungles to the villages. Sometimes the vehicle would get stuck in the mud and he would push or pull it out by many ingenious means. He would extract teeth, give injections and dress wounds and sores. He often says, 'My wife practises and I preach!' But he also practised and I in turn had opportunities to speak to the folk about Jesus. [55]

Their daughter Rachel was born and a year later they came back to England just after the end of the War. Ernests obtained British nationality and did much missionary work amongst the thousands of Latvians who had fled to England from the Communists. They followed this with another stint of several years in India. During this time Ruth experienced 'a tremendous hunger for more of God's fullness in my life' she said. 'I began to seek out Spirit-filled friends, having long talks and prayer with them. I realised that I needed to be baptised in the Holy Spirit.' Finally she and Ernests settled back in England, and she worked as an assistant in general practice at Walsall, in Staffordshire. A missionary colleague came to stay; she had been baptised in the Holy Spirit, and through her Ruth also entered into this experience. She said,

> I was filled with tremendous joy and love for Jesus and everybody. Hallelujah! That night I just couldn't sleep. I was praising the Lord and praying for all my dear ones, relations and friends ... Yes, in this conflict with the powers of darkness I am able to praise the Lord and sing in the Spirit in the new language He has given me. [56]

In Walsall the Zingers still had a foreign mission field around them, for about a quarter of their patients were Hindus, Sikhs and Muslims. After she was baptised in the Holy Spirit she found that God was healing patients in the practice who were only expected to live a few months or a year: they were still well after ten or fifteen years. They held monthly meetings for Asians in her waiting room, distributing much literature in their languages. They also gave a warm welcome to meetings in their own home. So the life of God flowed out to needy people around them.

Chapter 11

Glory Reality

U p until now we have been following a story. The Glory Way starts in Mansfield and Newark with the blessing of God on a young married couple. It blossoms out to touch the lives of many people in the Midlands, across Britain, in Europe and the United States and then various folk scattered across the world. This narrative has now finished, and we stand back to look more closely at the nature of what happened. Was there, in fact, something particularly special about the Glory Way?

The Lord Jesus Christ is building His church. The gates of hell shall not prevail against it (Matthew 16:18). God so loved the world and the remotest regions must hear the glad message of redemption. Spearheading missions are always necessary. There is no such thing as the status quo, or satisfaction with things as they are. There is always much land to be possessed. The Lord of heaven and earth, the Almighty God, the Holy Spirit is continually creating new initiatives. And, as Jesus said to Nicodemus, the wind of the Holy Spirit blows where it will!

It is not always easy, perhaps, for believers to recognise what God the Holy Spirit is doing, and certainly we are told to *'Test all things; hold fast what is good'* (1 Thessalonians 5:21 NKJ). The Apostle Paul told the Colossians that when he prayed for them he desired that they *'might be filled with the knowledge of His will in all wisdom and spiritual understanding'* (Colossians 1:9). This is no light prayer. Certainly this knowing the will of God – and not being deceived – must apply to the big decisions of life: what training and what job to have, who to marry or not, where to live and so on. But knowing the will of God will also have a direct bearing on a person's understanding of the Scriptures and their various important teachings and how these can be lived out in a practical way. 'Oh, I feel so confused,' may be a believer's heart-cry. 'Yes, I really want to trust the Lord (in this or that situation) but what is He saying to me?' 'What is the right thing to do?' Our wisdom and spiritual understanding are vital in deciding what assembly, church fellowship or mission to belong to. In particular, when you walk into a meeting which is unfamiliar, you need to have spiritual understanding as to what is going on. I remember when I first went to a Glory meeting, more than a little apprehensive as to what to expect, I found that I did not know much of the music being sung and the dancing, the tambourine playing and the free speaking in tongues was pretty unusual and daunting. I had been following the Lord for thirty years, but there was an awful lot to absorb all at once. This has been the experience of very many people.

With the general panorama of churches throughout the world in mind, Dr J.I. Packer has written,

> Now it is hard to deny that we inherit today a situation in which the Spirit of God has been quenched. Unnatural as it may be, the Spirit's power is absent from the majority of our churches ... Only styles and structures that serve the Spirit should stand. Everything bogging us down in lifeless routines or restraining the fruitful use of spiritual gifts or encouraging people in the pews to become passengers should be changed, no matter how sacrosanct we previously took it to be. The Holy Spirit is not a sentimentalist as too many of us are; He is a change agent, and He comes to change human structures as well as human hearts. [1]

Well said! This is exactly what newcomers to a Glory meeting experience. It has been in the very nature of the Glory Way to be a surprise, to shock, to jolt Christian people out of the patterns of behaviour that we have been used to in order to widen our vision.

They're nuts! It's not for me!

It is almost amusing to record the spontaneous reaction of distaste or dismay of various people as they have come up against the unfamiliar in a Glory meeting for the first time:

'I went there out of curiosity and I thought everybody had gone mad. I said, "They're just fanatics."' [2] 'I must confess I was rather dubious about attending. I didn't want to have anything to do with religious fanaticism.' [3] 'It was something of a shock to see them dancing and shouting and acting as if they were mad.'[4] 'In that first meeting I thought everybody was mad.'[5] 'I had never heard of the Glory meetings until recently. I thought, by what I heard, that the people concerned were as mad as hatters.'[6] '...some folk told me not to go as they did "crazy things" there.'[7] 'My first impression of the Glory meeting was that the folk were all quite crazy and that would be my first – and last – visit there!'[8] 'When I first heard of the Glory meetings a few months ago, I thought these people were crackers...'[9] 'To tell you the truth, I thought the folks were rather queer.'[10] 'I felt a bit dubious about what I had let myself in for ... As the meeting got underway I thought it was a very queer sort of service, for I was a Church of England girl.'[11] '...we were not very keen to go as we had heard such things about these peculiar people – things that caused us to doubt that it was God's way.'[12] 'It all seemed very bewildering to me for I had never been used to such carrying on ... Both my wife and I felt like fish out of water and ... we vowed that we would never go to another Glory meeting...'[13]

Remarks like these are enough to make one want to run a mile. That is not all, for others talked about irreverence, noisiness, emotionalism and superficiality:

'My first impression of Glory meetings was that they were far from reverent...'[14] 'I had heard about them and must admit I thought it was all very superficial and emotional. I did not agree with all this dancing and clapping and from what I heard I thought this way of praising the Lord was irreverent...'[15] 'I must confess that I found the noise – playing of tambourines, clapping of hands, folks praising God – somewhat overpowering! It did not seem *reverent* to me!'[16] 'What a noisy lot,' I thought, as I listened to the tambourines playing, the hand clapping and the hearty chorus singing.'[17] 'At first I was horrified and only stayed in the meeting for an hour...'[18] '...I hardly knew anything about the Glory folk, except, that is, that they were only sensation seekers. I had been told that there was no spiritual depth to their meetings and that fantastic emotion displays were common. Being brought up and converted in the Brethren meetings, the latter was enough to make me ill...'[19] 'I felt surely this was going too far, and I drew myself up inside, determined to resist this business, as I had no desire to be like them.'[20]

Happy U-Turns

In every case the dismayed people who uttered these remarks ate their words and went on their way rejoicing. They stuck with the Glory Way – they hung in there – long enough to let God do something new and fresh in their lives.

'However, at a cottage meeting ... Simon spoke on "Blessed are the pure in heart, for they shall see God" and my spiritual eyes were opened; I realised this was what I had been seeking for all this time.' [21] 'What's more, they seemed to like me, which was most peculiar as I had gone to church for years and nobody had ever said "I love you" or shown any interest in my being there.' [22] 'Praise the Lord! I am so glad that now I, too, am mad like that and I would much rather be a fool for Jesus than a fool for the devil like I used to be.' [23] 'It says in the Scriptures in Psalm 149 *Let them praise His Name in the dance: let them sing praises unto Him with the timbrel and harp.* I've experienced it for myself and I have seen people delivered and set free by the power of God. Praise His Name!' [24] 'I thank Him for the precious Holy Ghost I received during the campaign. I have never felt the same since ... "He set me free, my lovely Jesus set me free".' [25] 'I knew these folk had something I needed. I went back the following night and got filled with joy unspeakable and full of glory.' [26] 'I knew I must decide which way I was going to take in life, my own way or *God's way.* I do praise the Lord that He gave me grace to yield to Him ...' [27] 'I'm so thankful to God for sending Brother Henri and his team to Ireland. I have been to the meetings in Bangor and my life is completely changed.' [28] 'Well, praise the Lord, it did not take me long to fall into the Glory Way and Hallelujah, I am in it, dancing, laughing and shouting to the glory of God and it doesn't seem strange any more.' [29] 'However, the Lord was there and He worked on my heart and set me gloriously free from all my bondage.' [30] 'We came to understand that what God had done for so many others, *He could do for us! He has got no favourites!*' [31] 'To cut a long story short, we did go again and again and the more we went the more blessing we got until we found ourselves so united with the Glory Folk we sold our business in Corby and came to live here in Newark...' [32] '...but God showed me that the Holy Ghost had to make the meetings with men, not men make them with the Holy Ghost as many try to do.' [33] 'As soon as I entered the meeting I felt the moving of the Spirit bringing complete liberty and joy. I did not have to strive to enter in; the Holy Spirit just took over.' [34] 'I had not read the Psalms which exhort us to praise God with the timbrel, upon the cymbals and in the dance (Psalms 149, 150). One thing I could not deny, however, was the evident *joy* of the people as they worshipped God with all their being...'[35] 'Then as we sang the chorus, "Yes God is good," I realised with such an inner conviction that God *is* good, that it has revolutionised my whole attitude to life.'[36] 'We do thank God that Connie and Henri have gone forth to set the captives free.'[37] '...my feelings changed. There was power in your meetings that I had never experienced before. There was joy, peace and above all there was love.'[38] '...on the last night of my holiday He swept all doubts and fears away and I was able to enter into the fullness of this new thing that God had been trying to show me for so long.'[39]

Dire Warnings

It is not surprising also to find people who warned others off the Glory Way and the Glory meetings. For instance, when Henri and his team were about to go to Lambeth Town Hall in 1967, the pastor of an Elim church in Epsom 'made a special announcement, stating that his members were not to go to the Glory meetings, but,' said Violet Easton, 'I went and I thank God that I did, as I was greatly blessed.'[40] Julie Jeffries of Hackney in London said,

> From out of the blue a *Glory News* came into my hands. A dried old Pentecostal friend was in my kitchen at the time and said, 'Don't go there, that's not what you are seeking.' I replied, 'It seems to be the very thing. I'm going to try it for myself and prove whether it's of God.'[41]

Others themselves, on their own admission, were bearers of gloomy tidings. Eileen Cardno of Fraserburgh wrote,

> Until two years ago I was one of those Christians who tried to get along on a dried up experience and was firmly opposed to this New and Living Way ... I had been made to believe that the Glory Way was wrong...

However, Eileen quickly added,

> but I could not understand how a wrong way of life could make people love Jesus and one another more and more.

How grateful I am that God was so patient with me and did
such a wonderful work in my heart. After my first Glory
meeting I was never the same again. [42]

A young Assemblies of God pastor, Kevon Dickins, explained
how he came into contact with the Glory meetings and
admitted,

Attending one in a spirit of criticism, I went out wholeheartedly to condemn them. All Christians I met warned
against the 'glory', and I believed that it was of the flesh.
Surely God was only pleased to work in those who were
theologically trained? Yet I knew I was not in blessing.

In time Kevon came to a turning point. Henri was leading a
Glory campaign in Northamptonshire.

In the evening I went along again, desperate for the Lord to
bless me, and praise God, when we are open with Him, then
He does bless us. Praise God, what an evening! I felt the
power of the Lord and it broke me down. All my religion
went and as I was under the Spirit's power I saw a wonderful
vision of heaven. [43]

So many of the opponents got turned right around. God did a
radical work in them. Yet, depressingly, baleful criticism carried
on; the most mindless was second hand: 'I had heard so much
both for and against the meetings, but the people who criticised
had never been...' [44] or 'So many folk criticise this move of God,
without even going to a meeting.' [45] So Hazel Hall of Rushden
urged people to get a first hand experience:

There are so many who are in doubt about this Glory Way
but have never been to a Glory meeting to see for themselves. I want to urge you not to let pride, criticism and
prejudice stand in your way but go and enter in... [46]

In 1959 Henri wrote a passionate article, *The Church of God is
Moving*, touching on a good number of issues. This extract speaks
for itself:

When God is moving in such a wonderful way as He is
today, I cannot understand why anybody should hold back,

or stand afar off, as if the blessing of God is something to be afraid of. Of course many are turned against us because of the false rumours that the enemy of our souls has so skilfully engineered. They have never met us, but are quite content to let hearsay deprive them of the wonderful heritage that belongs to all the children of God.

The religious people accused Jesus of all manner of things that were not true, simply because He preached the truth and would not respect their vain traditions. Likewise the early disciples were evilly spoken against, as they sought to bring blessing to precious souls and it has always been the same all down the ages. Whenever men and women have sought to do exploits for God they have had to face the same malicious lies and accusations, but like the Apostle Paul I can say, *'None of these things move me.'* . . .

Remember, the Apostle Paul said that we should prove **all things**, so don't be put off by old wives tales and lying rumours but come and meet us and get a first-hand experience of these things and God will bless your soul. The proof of the pudding is in the eating.

Whatever else happens I am set for the defence of the gospel and I will ever seek to spread this love, joy, peace and blessing till all the world shall be filled with the glory of God as the waters cover the sea. The Lord bless you all. [47]

Froth and Bubble?

It is so easy for critics of Pentecostal experience to write the whole thing off as mere froth and bubble. At Épernay near Reims there are an unbelievable one hundred kilometres of champagne cellars. A panel on the autoroute nearby advertises this amazing statistic. Now, you may prefer non-fizzy drink, but I ask you, would you respect the wine-makers, with their carefully accumulated skill over several centuries, if all those millions of bottles were totally flat? Jesus Himself had no hesitation in using a wine illustration: *'And no one puts new wine into old wineskins; or else the new wine bursts the wineskins . . . '* (Mark 2:22 NKJ).

Froth and bubble seem so lightweight; they blow away on the wind and disappear. So outwardly are high spirits in a meeting; an emotion that afterwards dies down and disappears too. It is only too easy to use them as a metaphor. It is easy to say that certain Christian meetings are lightweight and of no account. Agnes Lowry from Northern Ireland turned this around: 'Some folk try to say that this Glory Way is too light, but we have found it to be very deep.' [48] And John Richardson, who was in the Navy during the War and who came to know the Lord as his Saviour in 1943, made this strong point:

> I have heard some folk say that this way is empty and has no depth, but let me tell you this, I have come through many experiences, in all kinds of places and I have found that real depth is not how much you know in your head about doctrine, or how long you have been saved, or whether you are a teacher of the Word, but how much love you have in your heart. For without love everything else is as sounding brass and a tinkling cymbal ... there is only one ocean of God's love and it is the deepest thing I know. [49]

To cap this, Pearl Cameron from Peterhead once said to me with great emphasis and feeling, on a Glory holiday in Bridlington, 'Henri is deep, och yes, Henri is deep. And I mean that.'

Fred Watson from Birmingham, in 1962 described how he was invited one day to a Glory meeting, where the presence of the Lord was real and he went away rejoicing,

> but there was a small voice saying, 'You cannot live on Glory, it's all bubble and fluff.' Even the overseer of our church told us to keep away as there was no Word of God taught or preached at Henri's.

Then, Fred managed to get to another Glory meeting quite close to his home:

> As soon as I entered into the assembly, God met me in the faces of His people who were filled with love, joy and peace; a people who wanted to know me and encouraged me and talked about Jesus. Here the Gospel was being preached, the Word being taught under the anointing of the Holy Spirit. Souls were being saved, bodies being healed and men and women who thirsted after God were being filled. This is what I needed, a baptism of love and glory. This is what young people, old people, in fact, everybody needs, for love conquers all things. It is the greatest power on earth and is everlasting. [50]

In a *Glory News* editorial, Bob Nicholls had further Bible thoughts about froth and bubble. He really tore into the subject.

He remembered how as a lad he used to help his father gardening and how when they were hot and thirsty they used to drink his father's patent home-made dandelion and nettle pop. He said,

> and I can tell you that if that pop was up to standard, when we pulled the cork out of the bottle, there was a lot of froth and bubble and it was a delightful drink. If, however, on drawing the cork there was no froth and bubble, then it was termed 'flat' and no matter how much we drank it would never quench our thirsts.
>
> I find that meetings can be very much like those bottles of pop. We know what it is to be in a thirst-quenching meeting and we also know what it is to be in a meeting that is 'flat'. Oh dear, how glad we are to get away from it. It is lifeless and such a bore. Thank God, when the Spirit is moving there is plenty of life and joy and blessing. The folks just delight themselves in the Lord and the praise flows out in volumes. Souls get saved, bodies healed, believers baptised in the Holy Ghost, the captives are set free and saints are revived and there is great rejoicing, for the very atmosphere is charged with the love and power of God. The outward manifestation of all this is what the critics say is all froth and bubble.

Bob Nicholls went on to point out that the dynamic element which went to make this sparkle in his dad's dandelion pop was yeast or leaven, and it is an ingredient so important that it is like the kingdom of heaven! For Jesus said, *'The kingdom of heaven is like unto leaven, which a woman took, and hid in three measures of meal, till the whole was leavened'* (Matthew 13:33). The yeast or leaven makes a loaf of bread rise and makes a drink fizz and have life in it. The word *leaven* is derived from the Latin *levare*, to raise, to lift up, to elevate, to make lighter, to lighten. Our English word *lever* also comes from *levare*. What a link with the resurrection of Jesus, with His rising or being raised from the dead, and with the apostle Paul's thought that the same mighty power of God which raised Christ from the dead is at work in every believer! This exceedingly great power raised up the Son of God and seated Him at the Father's right hand in the heavenly places and also *'raised us up together, and made us sit together in the heavenly places in Christ Jesus'* (Ephesians 1:19–20, 2:6, NKJ). Bob finished by saying,

Are we going to throw overboard a gospel that *works* simply because a few prejudiced people term it froth and bubble? ... Jesus said that the woman put the leaven into the meal until the whole was leavened and the Bible says that a little leaven leaveneth the whole lump. Well, I feel that this glory, this little bit of heaven that has come into our souls, is just as Jesus said it was, like leaven and it is spreading fast and it is spreading everywhere. I believe it will affect the whole of Christendom and, in fact, the whole wide world, for God Himself has declared in Numbers 14:21 these great words, *'But as truly as I live, all the earth shall be filled with the glory of the Lord'.*[51]

So much for froth and bubble!

Divisive?

Martin Luther was accused of splitting in two the church of his day, of dividing the seamless robe of Christ. A good number of spiritual leaders down the years have been blamed in this way. It is a very serious criticism. The Christian Church must be separate from, divided from the world; but to split the ranks of God's army, militant here on earth, when so much is at stake, is inexcusable.

Pastor Archie Friday brought up this thorny question in an article written in 1961. He quoted Romans 16:17, *'Now I beseech you, brethren, mark them which cause divisions and offences contrary to the doctrine which ye have learned; and avoid them.'* He went on to say,

one of the leading charges levelled against the Glory Folk is that we are causing divisions among assemblies throughout the country or wherever we go ... and to be truthful, we are in some quarters avoided like the plague! That the impact of this remarkable moving among so many of God's people is being felt cannot be denied. That many long-established meetings have lost their appeal and fail to satisfy the spiritual appetite of those who have visited Glory meetings is readily agreed ... the great work of liberation by the Spirit of God is going on apace.

Archie Friday then made the point that this, in and of itself, brought division:

SOUTHEND ON SEA OPEN-AIR
IN THE 1960s

SOUTHEND ON SEA SUMMER
CONVENTION IN THE 1960s

BANGOR NORTHERN IRELAND

SOME FACES FROM THE EARLY MEETINGS

THE GOSPEL AT CHRISTMAS

HUNGER FOR MORE

DOWN BY THE RIVERSIDE AT NEWARK IN 1956

THE TECHNICAL COLLEGE CONVENTION IN THE 1950s

PETERHEAD FOLK AT FISKERTON

FISKERTON YOUNG PEOPLE

CONNIE, HENRI AND FRED BREWER

KINGS ROAD GLORY FOLK

BEACON HILL REVIVAL CENTRE

CLEETHORPES 1966

SOUTHEND CONVENTION

YOU WILL FEEL BETTER FOR COMING HERE!

YOUNG PEOPLE'S NIGHT CLEETHORPES

LAMBETH TOWN HALL JULY 1959

CLEETHORPES 1966

KINGS ROAD

LAMBETH TOWN HALL JULY 1959

ISLE OF WIGHT TENT 1966

SELLYOAK 1958

JOE SMITH 90 SOUTHEND 1967

SEDLEY PIMLOTT AND GLORY GROUP

ROY AND ANN TURNER AND HENRI

LILY AISTRUP AND HENRY STRATFORD

GORDON DAVIES

YOUNG PEOPLE'S NIGHT

RINGWOOD REVIVAL CENTRE

A dividing is taking place. Everywhere the few saints of God, whose souls have been set free by the Holy Ghost in Glory meetings, seek by meekness and submission to support the assembly they belong to, but all too often the issue is forced by those in authority and they are ostracised or held up to ridicule, leaving one obvious path to tread, 'outside the camp', a pathway of reproach.

In all fairness let it be acknowledged with regret that some over-zealous groups who have been stirred up and blessed at Glory meetings return to their assembly and inadvisedly think they can revolutionise everything; but can a great and indisputable visitation of God be rejected on those grounds? A thousand times No. [52]

In John 7:43 we read, *'So there was a division among the people because of Him,'* because of the Lord Jesus Christ, the very Prince of Peace, because of things which He had provocatively said. So in certain circumstances division is unavoidable. It just happens and there is no point in trying to paper over cracks.

By complete contrast to this, Henri often delighted in opening up the truths of John's Gospel chapter seventeen, the great high priestly prayer to the Father, in which Jesus emphasised unity, *'that they may be one, as we are ... That they all may be one; as Thou, Father, art in Me, and I in thee, that they also may be one in us.'* Henri's clinching linchpin was that the thing which does the uniting is the glory. *'And the glory which Thou gavest me I have given them: that they may be one, even as we are one: I in them, and thou in me, that they may be made perfect in one ... '* (verses 11, 21–23).

If you dwell in the radiance of God's glory then you cannot be accused of causing division. If Jesus Himself was divisive, then He was not to be blamed for it, because He shared the Father's glory. The fault of the division was a human one; the fault was with those who disagreed with Jesus. So if believers are truly enjoying the presence of God and are acting in obedience to Him and His truth, then they are free from the accusation of causing division. King David sang,

> *Behold, how good and how pleasant it is for brethren to dwell together in unity! ... for there the Lord commanded the blessing, even life for evermore.* (Psalm 133:1, 3)

Brother W.J. Gill drove 250 miles from Newquay in Cornwall to go to one of the Glory meetings in Lambeth. He wrote,

The thing that struck me so forcibly was the wonderful feeling of unity that pervaded these meetings and Henri can very truthfully say that they are love meetings. Only God can unite people together like this. [53]

The Jamaican brother Tom, reluctantly returning with his wife Linnette to their homeland in 1972, said, 'We do thank God from the depths of our heart for this uniting spirit we have felt among you all in the Glory Way.' [54] So the true glory does not divide. It unites.

Another Denomination?

It is with a heavy heart one has to admit that new denominations have been formed. In 1662 nearly two thousand Anglican clergymen (who were puritans) were forced out of their livings by the hard-line Clarendon Code; most of them became Congregationalists. In this century many of the first Pentecostals were ostracised, so they became grouped into the Assemblies of God, the Elim churches and others. On the whole, in more modern times, the tide has been running against denominational barriers. Many missions, agencies, movements have openly declared themselves as undenominational or inter-denominational. This has been a healthy trend.

Certainly the last thing which Henri wanted to do was to form a new denomination. He clearly stated:

> We are pressing on from victory to victory, not forming a new denomination, not establishing new churches, but reviving the hearts of God's people everywhere; looking forward to the time when all chapels and churches of our land will be full of men and women praising the Lord in Spirit and in truth. [55]

Again, Henri was at pains to spell out his position very clearly,

> I ask no man to join us, for our work is not to establish a fat and flourishing assembly either here in Newark, or in any other place; neither do I seek to start a fresh denomination. But my heart's desire is to give to others what God has given me. Freely I have received and freely I give, knowing that all who really taste of this ministry will never be the same again. [56]

Ron Wray recalls how Henri was always stressing: 'Go back to your assemblies and churches with this Glory.'

In the very first issue of the *Glory News* in 1956, the editor Bob Nicholls simply stated: 'This magazine is entirely undenominational...'[57] And two years later he explained more fully:

> We are not out to start a new denomination or to establish new churches, but God has anointed us to go and set the captives free and our one desire is to see men and women filled with the Holy Ghost and on fire for God, dispensing love, joy, peace and blessing wherever they go ... Ordinary men and women are rising up in the power of the Spirit, and are claiming their inheritance in Christ Jesus. A new race of Christians are being born.[58]

Mrs H.S. from Maghera in County Derry, Northern Ireland echoed these strong statements of Bob Nicholls and Henri and many modern Christians when she said, 'We are Presbyterians, but I don't think it matters what church we belong to as long as on Calvary's side we stand. We are all one in Christ.'[59]

This is of God

In any endeavour in the Lord's work the stamp of authority comes from two sources, the Holy Spirit and the Scriptures. Jesus said to the Sadducees, *'You are mistaken, not knowing the Scriptures nor the power of God'* (Matthew 22:29 NKJ). The two of course are very closely related, because the Word is Holy Spirit breathed. Authority comes directly from heaven. There is no room for and no need for the approval of man or any human rubber stamp in any shape or form. This is why the approbation of a church hierarchy is completely beside the point. It is simply up to man to recognise and acknowledge the authority that God gives any of His servants.

It is therefore helpful and necessary to ask whether the Glory Way had this heavenly stamp. Or was the Glory Way simply the fruit of enthusiasm, force of character, a strong conviction, even human ambition? All who heard Henri in the Glory meetings will remember that he explained how, in the early stages, he had had strong doubts and questionings about his Glory mission. He would recount how he asked a trusted friend, 'Am I on the right lines? Am I deceived?' He had a fear of being presumptuous, of leading folk up the garden path. This was healthy. Anyhow, he evidently was greatly relieved when his friend reassured him that all was all right. To anyone who was looking on, he said that God was clearly with Henri. This friend could see the authority of God on Henri's life. And as one can imagine, this was a great encouragement to him.

Moreover, this conviction was amply borne out by those who came to the Glory meetings. As they saw Henri and Connie in action, they simply knew that their ministry was of God. Michael Lewis, for instance, from Newport in South Wales, wrote,

> A lot of people say that this Glory is not real; they say it is just emotionalism, a breakaway group from the established church denominations. Whatever others say, I *know* that this move is of *God* and is very *real*. [60]

Doris Anderson from London described how she did not want to be drawn into anything that was not of God. Like others that we have seen, she was suspicious. However, she started coming to Glory meetings in Newark, and although she found she could not enter into the spirit of the gatherings straight away, because of a barrier she had built round herself, God was working in her heart. She then said,

> the Holy Spirit opened my eyes to the truth, and then I knew without any shadow of doubt that this love and glory was real. Hallelujah. I came away from Newark a different person, for I had seen Jesus. [61]

Florence Neale, from Malvern, went to her first Glory meeting at the age of 73. She said,

> When I saw the folk dancing, I thought to myself, 'This is it'. I didn't need anybody to tell me whether it was of God. Of course it was of God. I could feel His presence there. I didn't need anybody to tell me whether it was right or wrong. I knew in my own heart it was right. So I went out and danced along with ... all the others. [62]

Jack Denton went to Newark convention in 1962 and in his enthusiasm wrote with great expression:

> How we thank God that we visited Newark to see God's move for ourselves. This is IT. We are one hundred per cent

behind this move of God. The proof that it is of God is that *Jesus is magnified*. Nothing can stop it. He will draw all men unto Himself. We see the beautiful Body Ministry in operation. There are no 'chief ones'. Jesus is the leader and the Holy Spirit can have His way. Thank God *'the anointing breaks the yoke.'*[63]

The wholehearted allegiance of other enthusiasts was irrepressible. They had no hesitations: 'I saw the love in the faces of Henri and his team and I knew God was with them.'[64] 'I received a mighty anointing of the Holy Spirit and had a vision that this was God's way ...'[65] 'I saw such a reality in them and I knew that they had something wonderful from God.'[66] 'I am in entire agreement with the Glory Way and I am sure Henri is led of God as he conducts these meetings. I am one hundred per cent with Henri ...'[67] 'My wife and I are one hundred per cent for this love and glory way.'[68] 'I am fully persuaded by the witness of the Holy Spirit that this Glory Way is one hundred per cent pure and true and will meet the needs of everybody whether spiritual or physical.'[69] 'I am one hundred per cent for the Glory and can say, from the bottom of my heart, there is nothing like it.'[70] '... as soon as I heard the revival singing I said to myself, "This is it!"'[71] And then quite simply, 'I knew it was all from God.'[72]

In the face of grass roots testimony like this the Glory Way surely has been vindicated. So many were convinced, 'This is of God!'

The Holy Spirit

The Other Strengthener, Helper, Comforter, to whom the Lord Jesus referred, is God Himself. The Holy Spirit was the agent of creation, and when the earth was made *'the Spirit of God moved upon the face of the waters'* (Genesis 1:2). God the Holy Spirit was sent by the Father and the Son into the world to be present with mankind. He can be quenched and grieved. 'He searches, speaks, testifies, commands, reveals, strives, creates, makes intercession, raises the dead ...'[73] So He is just as much a Person as the Father and the Son. When as believers we talk about the Presence of God we must mean the Presence of the Holy Spirit. He comes alongside men and women to convict them of sin, righteousness and judgement, to bring them spiritually to birth, to indwell them, to baptise them, to empower them. He is known as the Spirit of Truth.

It would be surprising if people in the Glory Way had no desire for the baptism of the Holy Spirit. John the Baptist said that the Lord Jesus Christ would come and baptise people with the Holy Spirit and with fire (Luke 3:16). Cecil Hill, for instance, of Craigavon in Northern Ireland, told how he was saved after he was married and that his wife was attending some Pentecostal meetings. He said,

> I had a longing in my soul to receive the baptism in the Holy Spirit which was promised in the Scriptures. I felt the need of power in my life; thank God the Bible says: *'Ye shall receive power after that the Holy Ghost is come upon you.'* I hadn't very long to wait, for the Lord filled me one night in my own home. Oh, what a night. I'll never forget it. [74]

Nellie Cooper, of Leeds, told how she had been baptised in water and that some time after that she knelt on her hearth rug in prayer, and God filled her with His Holy Spirit. She said, 'I had never heard of the baptism of the Holy Ghost and knew nothing at all about it, but I praise God for the wonderful experience I had.' [75]

Ann Scarbrow explained that after she was saved, when young, in a Baptist church in Purley, Surrey, she was very happy there; but, she said,

> as time went on I had a desire to know God in a greater way. I was brought into contact with some young people who told me about the baptism of the Holy Spirit and I realised that this was what I needed.

She then began going to Glory meetings.

> It was in the second one I attended that I was baptised in the Spirit. It was a wonderful baptism! God just melted my heart and poured in His love and peace. I just wept and wept, kneeling at the altar rail, and when I got up I was absolutely drunk in the Spirit! I couldn't walk straight for the life of me and I just had a love for everybody that I had never had before. The Bible became a living book to me. It was no longer the letter on the printed page but had become sharp and powerful, the sword of the Spirit of Life! [76]

Some Christians speak of being filled with the Holy Spirit rather than being baptised spiritually. It would appear to be a different expression for the same experience. Lily Worthington, of Culleybackey in County Antrim, explains how she was saved when she was sixteen, and how the Lord Jesus completely changed her life. But she continued,

> He revealed to me that there was a deeper experience with Himself, such as the early church had and I was determined to have it. I believed God meant what he said in Acts 1:8, *'Ye shall receive power, after that the Holy Ghost is come upon you,'* and I started to seek for this very thing. The Lord did not disappoint me, but He filled me with His Spirit and I spoke in a wonderful language that I had never learned; it was the Spirit of God taking full control in me by His mighty power.
>
> Some people don't understand us when we speak in tongues and question the purpose of it, but we who have been filled can say with Peter, *'This is that which was spoken by the prophet Joel'* (Acts 2:16), and if the preacher doesn't preach it, sure it's right anyhow.
>
> Ever since I got filled with the Spirit, the Lord has been very real to me and the desire fills my soul to go on to know Him, in the power of His resurrection, for the power of God is unlimited to those who will take God at His Word and dare to believe Him. [77]

Cynthia Powell of Hereford went to a Glory meeting at Evesham led by Henri. She found it very strange and unusual, but she realised Henri and the Glory folk had something that she hadn't got, and that she wanted it and needed it. She said,

> On the Wednesday following our visit to Evesham brother David Greenow came to our home with his tape recorder and played some of Henri's Glory tapes. We had a wonderful time and when they were finished David pointed to me, saying that God would baptise me with the Holy Ghost. He laid his hands on me and I felt the power of God go right through me and I fell to the floor under the power of God ... I began to speak in other tongues as the Spirit gave me utterance and, when I came to myself, I was full of the power insomuch I couldn't stand on my feet and I was two hours glorifying God in the Spirit. Hallelujah! [78]

David Barnes of Bolton, in Lancashire, described with some humour how he began to seek the Lord to be filled with the Holy Spirit. He said,

> I went to many waiting meetings, where they tried every method to get me filled; they tried to shake it into me, rub it into me, squeeze it into me, all to no avail. After one meeting I went to, I was told that I had received the Spirit, but when I told them that I hadn't spoken in tongues, they said that I had lost the gift. Sometime later I went along to Henri's Glory rally at Stockport ... and during the evening meeting I went to the front for prayer and, praise the Lord, Henri just put his hands on my head, the power of God took me over and I spoke in other tongues. [79]

We now move on to consider the anointing, the unction, the sealing of the Holy Spirit. Just as refined oil is poured on a monarch at his coronation to commission him to rule and give him authority and ability, so by a metaphor the Holy Spirit is poured on a believer in an anointing or a sealing. Cecil Morris of Bradford wrote an article in the eighth *Glory News* on The Anointing of the Spirit. He described it in this way:

> It is a mysterious power that comes immediately from the Lord. It is that indefinable indescribable something which makes the Word quick and powerful, and gives the speaker words that are pointed, sharp and powerful. It pervades the atmosphere, convicts the conscience and breaks the heart. It is the energy of God. Oh what a difference there is when God puts Himself into His own Word and upon the preacher? A flow of inspiration clarifies the intellect, gives insight and grasp and projecting power; and tenderness, purity and conviction flow from the heart of it. The anointing makes the ministry of the Word sharp to those who need sharpness, distils as the dew to those who need refreshment. It makes alive, spreads, softens, percolates, cuts and soothes. It carries the Word like dynamite, like salt, like sugar. It is the Divine in preaching. [80]

And also one might add, in the whole conducting of the Lord's work, in the leading of a meeting, in prayer, in music and song, in administration and arrangements, in getting alongside people in a personal way. Anointing shows itself in many ways;

in a spirit of freedom and joy, for instance. John Tweedie of Crawcrook, near Newcastle-upon-Tyne, told of Henri's inviting a group from their church to a Glory rally in Bradford. He said,

> The meeting was turned upside down because all on the platform were helpless, overcome with the Holy Ghost and with laughter for some considerable time. The heavens were opened up on us, praise the Lord. [81]

Winifred Thomas, of Bridgend in South Wales, gives a sidelight on what the anointing is. She was longing for more of God in her life and yet was more and more dissatisfied. Then one day, she said,

> I heard that the Glory folk were coming down to Llanelli for meetings in the Market Hall there. We decided to hire a coach and take the members of our church along. Praise the Lord! The meetings were so different from what I'd been used to. Everybody was so free and full of love and joy. When I got home I asked the Lord about it and He showed me in a dream that this was the anointing of His Spirit. Oh bless His Name! [82]

Joyce Price originally of Basildon, in Essex, describing the Glory Way, said that it fits the Christian life. She spoke of coming into a Glory meeting and letting 'the very depths of your soul open up to Jesus'. Concerning the Glory Way she said,

> It will fit you and every word of Scripture that was ever written because it is the reality of God. I've found it is all I've ever hoped for as a Christian; the power I always knew was available to the saints of God but never seemed to discover. [83]

Is not the secret of this 'fitting' the anointing of the Holy Spirit?

Frances May Connerton, a young Christian from Coventry, was taken to a Glory meeting in Birmingham. She commented,

> At first when the meeting was in progress, I asked myself, was it in the flesh or the Spirit? I soon found out that it was in the Spirit. My friend and I both started speaking in tongues and laughing in the Spirit. It was wonderful. I had

not danced in the Spirit before, but there was nothing to hold me back and it says in the Scriptures, *'Quench not the Spirit'*. [84]

Other believers speak directly of the Holy Spirit's power. Michael Lavelle, from Bedlington in Northumberland, said,

I attended a Glory meeting and was asked to give a testimony of what God was doing for me. As I went forward to do so, I felt the mighty power of the Holy Spirit strongly upon me, and instead of speaking I found myself jumping with joy. [85]

Sister Evans, of Bournemouth, spoke of the electricity of the Holy Spirit. She wrote in the *Glory News*,

This dynamic Holy Ghost power which envelops me causes me to do things I never knew before. It is just marvellous ... When Pastor Friday came to Ringwood first, the gathering all stood to sing and hold hands. I thought it was nothing but flesh and no flesh should glory in His presence, therefore I decided to remain seated. However, the two sisters on each side of me held out their hands to me and I couldn't refuse. Within minutes it seemed as though electricity came into my hands and spread throughout my whole being. [86]

The Holy Spirit works in the conscience, in the human heart in an intimate and mysterious way. Sometimes He sows a seed and it lies dormant for a spell and later springs to life. Sometimes it is after a meeting, in the quietness of the home, that the Glory of the Lord through the influence of the Holy Spirit will burst upon a person. Wendy Cameron from Peterhead, after going to Newark, had this to say:

At first I was a little apprehensive after hearing so many stories from people (whom I have since discovered have never been to a Glory meeting). However, I enjoyed the meetings, and as I thought over all I had seen and heard, I had to admit there was something very real and sincere in it.
    Well, the next day the time bomb went off! And such a flood of joy filled my whole being, I could hardly contain it. Now I know the full meaning of *'life more abundant'*, *'the joy*

of the Lord is your strength', and I feel so much better in health as well. [87]

Grace and Leslie Dacre, having read a *Glory News* and listened to a Glory tape, decided to go to Newark. (Grace was Archie Friday's daughter.) She said,

> That first meeting to us seemed so strange, some crying, some rejoicing and others dancing, but the joy was written so plainly I couldn't gainsay it. Although on leaving I said we would not go again, by the time our fifty mile home-ward journey was over, we had made plans to return the following Sunday ... By the following morning it was obvious something had happened, for I was filled with joy, and a change took place in my life. Instead of bitterness, love came in, and reunion with estranged Christians took place, denominational barriers disappeared, and Jesus became real to me. Love and joy came into our home, and I found myself praising God in a new way. [88]

Glory

It goes without saying that Glory is a really wonderful word. It means resplendent majesty and beauty, a burst of sunlight, radiant brightness, heavenly bliss and splendour, exalted and triumphant honour.

Admittedly the expression The Glory Way was a kind of tongue-in-cheek nickname, spontaneously applied to Henri and Connie and their friends. But what an honour! This Glory could be shared immediately with anyone God brought to them. For instance, life had been really miserable for Mrs G.M. Newton of Allington, near Grantham. She used to smoke 50 to 60 cigarettes a day and spent most of her time in public houses. Then, in February 1953, she was 'powerfully converted to God'. A few years later she said,

> Although I attended a Pentecostal church, my soul was always crying out for something more from God and, praise the Lord, my need was met the day I came to Henri's Glory meetings. My! did I get filled with this wonderful glory! It was just as if the heavens opened and Jesus reached down and put His hand on my shoulder. I was filled to over-flowing, Glory to God. [89]

A certain Mr R.W. wrote in to the Glory Office from Blackpool:

> Dear Brother Henri, for years I have been seeking for a
> deeper experience with my Saviour. It is very true, after you
> have been to the meetings, you can never be the same
> again. Praise God, He is changing us from Glory to Glory by
> the power of the Holy Ghost. [90]

This thought was echoed by Don and Elsie Harper, who led
the meetings at Ringwood, near the New Forest, who said,

> I see that J.B. Phillips renders the words 'changed from glory
> to glory' like this, 'ever increasing splendour.' I rather like
> that, for we haven't just got the glory; we are getting it in
> ever increasing splendour. [91]

Glory can take you by surprise. Margaret Urch was a young
Christian from West Auckland in County Durham:

> Last December I was invited to travel up to Newark with the
> West Auckland Glory Band, and Hallelujah, what a day of
> rejoicing that proved to be. When we were about three
> miles from Newark the Glory of the Lord filled the van in
> which we were travelling and the Lord met me in a very
> marked way, breaking me down so that all I could do was
> weep before Him. [92]

John Hall, from Sheffield, in his mind's eye saw glory radiating out from Henri and Connie's meetings.

> I am certainly praising God for the transmitting station that
> has been erected in Newark by the Holy Ghost. Through
> this transmitter the world is getting to know about this
> Glory and it is fast becoming a world-wide word. [93]

Bob and Louie Eastwood, from Thornton Heath in south
London, heard about the Glory meetings and decided to travel
150 miles to Newark:

> This time we were to see with our own eyes and to
> experience the mighty power of God being demonstrated
> by the Holy Ghost through the glory and praise of His
> people. We saw the sick healed, believers being set free and

filled with the Holy Ghost, and folks going forward to confess their sins against one another, and to surrender their lives afresh to Jesus. We have seen many movings of the Holy Spirit, but never have we seen it in this fashion. We laughed, we cried, we prayed and we danced, and then laughed again as wave after wave of *glory* filled and thrilled our souls.

Surely this was an experience comparable with that which we read of in 2 Chronicles 5:13–14, when Solomon had completed the temple, for we read, *'It came to pass, as the trumpeters and singers were as one, to make one sound to be heard in praising and thanking the Lord, and when they lifted up their voice with the trumpets and cymbals and instruments of music and praised the Lord, saying: For He is good; for His mercy endureth for ever, that then the house was filled with a cloud, even the house of the Lord, so that the priests could not stand to minister by reason of the cloud; for the Glory of the Lord had filled the house of God.'*[94]

My wife Margaret has the last word here: 'What struck me, when I first went to Glory meetings was that people's faces really *did* shine!'

Praise

Praise is the very activity and occupation of heaven. When we praise the Lord on earth we are simply having a heavenly rehearsal, getting ready for what we shall be doing for eternity. When someone is saved, there is a spontaneous urge within him to praise God. Quite simply, we are saved to praise.

Praise has many facets. Every detail of creation can be included; every atom, molecule, far-flung star; which no doubt is why the whole of eternity will be taken up with praising the Lord and speaking of all His wondrous works. In fact we can say that any kind of testimony or heartfelt explanation of God's love and greatness is also praise: an awareness of His protecting hand, His uplifting of the downcast, His spring of joy to the troubled heart. This form of praise has always been encouraged at Glory meetings.

Or again, think of someone you love, someone in the family. You can say, 'Michael, I really admire you for taking on that dreadful responsibility. Your shoulders are broad enough.' Or Michael can say to a friend, 'Sheila is the most amazing person.

How she can cope with everything every day is quite fantastic.' If we can genuinely admire and praise one another like this, how much more, times a million billion, can we praise the character of our wonderful God.

Praise involves the whole person. Praise is certainly opening your mouth and singing but it is much more. It is also musical movement, it is using one's arms and legs, it is gesture, dancing, clapping and the playing of musical instruments. The Greek orator Demosthenes said that public speaking is action, action, action! How much more should praising our Lord, Saviour and eternal King be action. Praise involves the heart and mind, too: *'sing ye praises with understanding'* (Psalm 47:7), and this is the very psalm which begins *'O clap your hands, all ye people; shout unto God with the voice of triumph.'* Spontaneous praise is liberating. Pauline Kyle of Bournemouth expressed it in this way:

> I have found such liberty in worship since presenting my body a living sacrifice unto Him. He causes me to sing and praise Him in the dance and so worship in body, soul and spirit. Bless Him! [95]

Mrs B.B. from Thornaby went to a Glory meeting at Newton Aycliffe in County Durham, and said,

> There was such a freedom to worship and praise the Lord, I felt as if I was at the Throne of the Lamb! [96]

Percy Anderson from London echoed this truth,

> It is just as Henri says, the more praise we send up, the more glory He sends down and I praise God that I have found this to be true in my experience. Since my visit to Newark I've never been the same ... All the religious starch has gone out of me and (I feel) free to sing and shout, laugh and cry, dance and rejoice to the glory of God. [97]

Laurie and Margaret James invited Henri down to Redhill in Surrey, where they had exuberant meetings:

> In the evening meeting the Glory came down in such a mighty way that no one could minister. We sang and praised the Lord together as the waves of the Glory rolled over our souls ... all the chairs were put to the side of the

hall and the floor was filled with folk dancing for the
very joy of the Lord. It was really strange and many must
have wondered what was happening but the Lord was in
control and gave us something new. Bless His Name! It is all
part of His great plan in restoring to the church the
abundance of *joy* and *praise* which rightly belong to His
people ... the prison doors are being opened and the
captives set free. [98]

Roy Turner comes into the picture with some telling
comments; for instance, after Henri and Connie took meetings
for the fellowship of the Pimlott family in Norwich, he said,

I wouldn't like to be at the great marriage supper of the
Lamb without my dancing shoes. In Ephesians we read of
the spiritual armour God has given, and we certainly need it
here, but it won't always be the battlefield. There will be a
great ballroom in heaven! Hallelujah! The knights of old
went out and won their brides through victory in combat
and then returned to the Banqueting House and celebrated
the victory! [99]

In the New Year of 1965 in Peterhead, Roy spoke of Hogmanay
with a difference:

It was not just a series of convention meetings, however,
but in the homes and in the street, in the cars and in the
vans, over the dinner, tea or supper table the fellowship
continued and the songs of Zion could be heard. We
laughed together, wept together, sang together, danced
together. It was a *togetherness* none but true-born Glory
saints can understand. There were days (and nights, for we
hardly saw our beds in the four days of the convention) of
heaven on earth. Hallelujah! [100]

The next year, after an Easter convention at Laindon in Essex
and Northfleet in Kent, Roy wrote,

Oh what a deluge of blessing! A Brethren sister testified how
God has blessed her. She laughed and shook under the
power of the Holy Spirit and folk in the congregation were
loosed in their seats, jumping and dancing with all their
might like David of old. [101]

We have a sidelight on Roy Turner himself from the pen of Reg Lyon of Gosport, who was searching for a deeper spiritual satisfaction in his life, and was brought by a friend to Newark:

> On entering the Glory Room what a sight met my astonished eyes. Most of the folk were sitting around the room singing with joyful rhythm and one young man, whom I later found to be Roy Turner, was dancing round and round the room. This was something so new and so different from anything I'd seen before, I began to question in my heart 'Can this be from God?' Later that night ... my friend and I found ourselves sharing a room at Gran's with Roy and he opened up to us the Scriptures, showing us it was right to glorify God in the dance and to make a joyful noise unto the Lord. It did not take me long to realise that this young man's experience was not light and on the surface as I had at first thought, but that he had a deep joy in his soul that made him give expression to his delight in the Lord. [102]

Harold Taylor from Bradford went to Newark in 1960:

> I had been to all kinds of revival meetings, but never to one like this. Here men and women actually laughed and in church too; they praised and praised and when people began to dance I felt stuck to my seat, but not for long. The joy that suddenly filled my soul was wonderful. [103]

Henri and the revival team came to Cliffe Bridge in South Yorkshire in 1958:

> It would have blessed the hearts of the old Methodists who used to worship at Cliffe Bridge to see their chapel once again packed to capacity with men and women praising God. It was thrilling to see them sitting on window sills and pulpit steps and standing right out through the door. [104]

True praise to God takes us out of ourselves. It brings life and joy, stirring the heart. Is this surprising when God Himself is said to inhabit the praises of Israel? This is a remarkable statement when you find that it is from Psalm 22:3, the psalm which prophetically described in great detail the sufferings of Jesus on the cross. This intense joy and praise is only possible because of the bitter pangs and sufferings of the Lord Jesus, because of His life laid down to cancel our sins. Moreover, Jesus came from the tribe of Judah, and the meaning of the name Judah is *praise*!

Joy

One of the fruits of the Spirit, joy is an extraordinary quality, bubbling up from the depths of a believer's personality. There is the glint of battle about it. '[Jesus] ... *for the joy that was set before Him endured the cross, despising the shame...*' (Hebrews 12:2). Jesus wanted His disciples to catch something of this. '*These things have I spoken unto you that My joy might remain in you, and that your joy might be full*' (John 15:11). The Glory people delight to quote Nehemiah 8:10 '*for the joy of the Lord is your strength.*'

Our great Bible translator William Tyndale (c. 1494–1536) caught a glimpse of this:

> Evangelion (or what we call the gospel) is a Greek word, and signifies good, glad, and joyful tidings, that make a man's heart glad, and make him sing, dance, and leap for joy ... Now, the wretched man, that knows himself to be wrapped in sin, and in danger of death and hell, can hear nothing more joyous than such glad and comfortable tidings of Christ. So that he cannot but be glad and laugh from the bottom of his heart, if he believe that the tidings are true. [105]

An Irishman, Eddie McAnally said, 'I am enjoying the experience of Peter who declared, '*It is joy unspeakable and full of glory.*' It wasn't always like this for me.' [106]

Eirian Richards, a fifteen-year-old girl from Llwynhendy, went to Newark where she got right with God, and she found 'that the people at Newark were really enjoying their salvation, which I also am now doing.' [107]

Hilda Johnson, wife of Eddy Johnson, who was one of those who came to live in Jallands Row in Newark, spoke of the time when she first came into contact with the Glory Way:

> I continually sought God, but the heavens seemed like brass and nothing seemed to happen. Then one day we had a letter, inviting our family to a Glory meeting at Newark. I shall never forget the words that greeted us in that meeting,

'Come and enjoy Jesus.' It seemed silly to me and I found myself wondering how on earth could anybody enjoy Jesus? When I got into the room, I found a company of people who were truly enjoying something. I had never seen anything like it before. It felt just as though I was stepping into heaven and I can never forget the shine on the faces of the people; all I could do was gaze at them and I found that I longed to be like them. [108]

Mrs Hilda Scott expresses a similar kind of thought:

It gives me great joy when I take the Glory tapes into various homes, that others may enjoy Jesus. You may think that is a funny thing to say, 'Enjoy Jesus', but I tell you that when you are filled with the love of God and have joy unspeakable flooding your soul, you just want to sing and sing and sing. Yes, we can enjoy Jesus and taste and see that the Lord is good. Bless His Name. [109]

Guitar playing West Indian Neville Smart expressed himself with gusto:

It is a Christian Super BP blessing via Henri's Revival Meetings ... Once you have been to these Holy Ghost services you realise what barren land you have just passed through. The meetings are like refreshing springs. A real super filling station for Christians, a place where you feel free to express yourself in the true Spirit of the Lord ... Henri's Super BP Revival Meetings give more miles to the gallon and help the individual to keep in the front line of his Christian experience. [110]

An elderly saint, Mr Temple Debenham, from Bournemouth, came up with this pointed reflection:

I had attended a local Baptist chapel where the Scripture read on two successive Sundays was from Psalm 47, '*O clap your hands, all ye people; shout unto God with the voice of triumph.*' But no one responded to the challenge. However, when I arrived at Newark Revival meetings, that is exactly what they did. I never doubted the genuineness of the expressions of joy and triumph which I heard and I knew enough about the Bible to know that those were quite scriptural. [111]

Joy brings tears as well as laughter. Joy sees the rainbow through the rain. Gordon McKinlay went to a Glory rally at Bolton:

> I shall never forget when brother Henri asked everybody to give a hearty clap for Jesus; I felt like having a good weep. Glory meetings don't always make you want to dance and sing, but many times you feel the need to weep before the Lord. Praise His holy Name! [112]

Two teenage girls the same year (1960) came under the convicting power of the Holy Spirit. One was Miriam, a daughter of Arthur and Marjorie Burt. She said,

> I went along to Newark and during the service they began to sing the chorus, 'Born, born, born again, Thank God I'm born again.' The Spirit began to strive with me as they sang and Henri was led to come to me. The power was so great that I just burst into tears and wept on his shoulder, and then as I knelt in contrition before the Lord, He wonderfully restored my soul. The last few weeks have been the happiest of my life. The joy of the Lord has filled me and thrilled me. [113]

The other girl was Grace Goodwin, a younger sister of Hilda Nicholls and Olive Parsons. She was envious of the joy of the Lord which shone from her elder sisters and their husbands. She made her way to Newark:

> The meeting came to the point where Henri told us all to get on our knees and receive something from God. As I knelt down a feeling of warmth crept over my whole being and I started to cry until the tears poured down my face and formed a puddle on the seat of the chair. I asked Jesus to save my soul and possess my heart. Meanwhile Henri had been going around praying for folk and, as he came nearer to me, my heart burned hot within me. The moment had come when I was to pass from death unto life and, as Henri prayed for me, I took Jesus as my Saviour and became so happy that I cried for joy and couldn't stop it. [114]

Joy accompanies a sense of home coming and belonging, of contentment: 'As I walked into the meeting there was a response within me as a duck takes to the water. I was in my element. Waters to swim in.'[115] 'I took to the Glory meetings like a duck takes to water.'[116] '...after being there a short time, I began to feel at home and joined in the singing of those lovely choruses.'[117] 'I had no doubts that this was the place for me. It was just what I was looking for...'[118] 'It was all very strange to me and yet I felt quite at home. Jesus was there in a very real way...'[119]

Joy also brings with it liberty and intense longing and a sense of occasion, with remarks like these: 'My heart is so full I cannot put it into words. Old things have passed away and all things have become new. Bless you all for standing and contending for this liberty of the Spirit.'[120] 'Since moving down to Devon I have been pining for your Spirit-filled meetings. Oh to be liberated again!'[121] 'Whenever people want to celebrate some special occasion or make a protest of some kind they carry banners. Well, I'm so glad that we can rejoice under God's banner!'[122] And again: 'Many folk think I have gone mad, but like Billy Bray I'm not mad, I'm glad. Hallelujah!'[123] As a last word Phyllis Preudhomme gives us this bracing encouragement:

> 'Work, for the night is coming,' but, beloved, let us enjoy our work, let us do the will of God with a new song in our hearts, with clapping hands and dancing feet – and sound doctrine to keep us in the narrow way with joy unspeakable and full of glory.[124]

Love and Humility

'*God is love*' (1 John 4:8, 16). If we were in any doubt, what statement could be plainer? There are many things about love in the Bible. At the centre of the Universe, then, there is Personality, God Himself, and He has a great heart of love for everything He has created. Why should it be otherwise? No wonder Jesus said 'Fear not' so many times. This love of God is a deep, strong, burning love; love strong as death; love which many waters cannot quench (Song of Solomon 8:6–7).

Love is the first fruit of the Spirit; and this quality of burning love marked out Henri and Connie and permeated their Glory Way. It is all of grace; no one can earn it; but God delights to bestow it.

Henri was once being cross-questioned: 'What is the nature of this fire you talk about?' He paused thoughtfully, and then replied, 'It's *Love!*' Olga Hadley, the wife of a pastor in Birmingham, wrote reflectively,

> Henri said that we were all one Love Family, and then I began to think, God is Love, God is our Father, we are born into the Family of God; then we as His children ought to love one another, as it says in 1 John 4:7. Then I realised that this love Henri and Connie had was not a carnal love, but a Jesus love. [125]

Margaret Stobie, from Dunfermline in Fifeshire, who had travelled extensively round Britain, visiting places where God was moving by His Spirit, said this:

> I saw nothing new in your meetings ... What impressed me more than anything ... was not what I saw or heard. It was something I felt. Divine love. I felt love emanating from the hearts of the people. To me, that was what made the meetings. That is what makes the people come from miles around. As the Jamaicans stood on the platform singing, testifying and playing their tambourines, it was like a river of love flowing on and on. I was overcome. [126]

Walter Crawford wrote in to the Glory Office a brief letter which said much:

> Those Christians who are filled with the Glory are earmarked, not by their freedom or liberty, but by their Love! A love which cannot be manufactured or worked up but is 'shed abroad in the heart by the Holy Spirit.' A love which is manifested in deed and not just in word, the *'more excellent way'* of which the Apostle Paul speaks... [127]

A young man from Gloucester, Gordon Davies, was full of gratitude to God:

> Newark is the place where God met me and opened my blind eyes and unstopped my deaf ears to see and hear the wonders of His Word and to realise of a truth that Jesus is the same yesterday, today and forever ... the love of Jesus was there to deliver me. It flowed into my heart and set me free. I had been religious, but I needed Jesus... [128]

Many others wrote, said and testified to these things.

At the time when the Glory Way suddenly blossomed out and meetings were held in many parts of Britain, the love of God became a constant theme: 'Although there has been a lot of criticism about this Glory Way, I feel that it is the way of love.' [129] 'What impresses me most is the Love that is manifested in the Glory meetings and can be felt coming from the recordings we receive.' [130] 'My wife and I went to Newark ... and oh, what a manifestation of the Love of God we saw and experienced.' [131] 'The love of God just flowed from their hearts. It was wonderful. I returned home full of gratitude to the Lord for ever leading me into this glory way.' [132] 'It seemed as though torrents of liquid love were filling me and sweeping over me!' [133] 'In Glory meetings one sees the love of God in action, not in word only, but in deed and in truth.' [134]

The love of Christ brings reconciliation. This is something very precious. It is so important for believers to be in a right relationship with one another. When this breaks down and there is antagonism, this is a stumbling block and brings dishonour to the cause of Christ. In November 1963 Henri and Connie had a weekend of Glory meetings at Cleveleys, just north of Blackpool.

> The most precious moment of the whole weekend was when a brother and a sister, who had been bitter enemies, were brought together on the platform and were firmly united in the love of God. During the past six years many tears had been shed in bitterness and hate, but on Saturday November 2nd, 1963, tears of love, joy, relief, forgiveness and gratitude were shed, giving praise to God, that He had brought Marie Jowett and Joe Hall together in this Glory Way. Many witnessed that reunion of those two dear ones from Crawcrook, County Durham, and it overwhelmed many and gave many more food for thought.
>
> The whole weekend was a Glory meeting in its right dimensions, setting us free to Niagaras of blessing, that were more than could be contained. Love was manifest on every hand and many human dynamos were set into operation, generating this wonderful power to all around. [135]

There is a lurking suspicion in people's minds, perhaps, that Christians who enjoy going to really expressive, emotionally charged meetings, ones that 'go over the top', only live from one high to the next. (I use these words guardedly.) Such Christians, it is thought, are unbalanced or overbalanced, and not quite sane. It is thought, when it comes to the daily walk with Christ, in the practical details of life, they do not perform very well. But that simply is not so. The fact of the matter is that believers who glimpse heavenly realities in the joy, love and power of a good Glory meeting prove their worth in steadiness of character. They endure adversity with a lighter heart than they would otherwise. They have the fruit of the Spirit as well as the gifts.

I have already mentioned Kevon Dickins, a young Pentecostal pastor in Northamptonshire who, on his own admission, had a very critical and judgmental spirit. The turning point in his story came when his family was asked to have two girls from Surrey to stay for the weekend, while they went to a Glory rally locally. He was reluctant to have them. 'However, they came,' he said, 'and I watched them to see their queer points, but praise God, they radiated the love and power of Jesus. This made me thought-ful...' [136] And it led to a complete turn around in his life.

Mrs M.E.B. of Falmouth in Cornwall, writing in 1972, said how much she appreciated reading the wonderful testimonies in the *Glory News*. She said,

> My heart has been really warmed up, and my soul uplifted, as I read the accounts of the 'rich experience' in lives that have been yielded to the Saviour. As one reads and sees so much of evil, sin and vandalism in the world today, it fills me with deep emotion and thankfulness to know that (although still in the minority) there are noble souls such as you and your team of loyal workers. [137]

George Ponting of West Auckland wrote a telling article for the *Glory News* in 1964, in which he showed that the very lives of the Glory folk spoke for themselves:

> Perhaps it is the opposition of those who speak evil of 'this way' which is alerting hungry hearts to come and see for themselves the sincerity, the reality, the power, the blessing, the love, joy and peace, the enthusiasm and the purity of the lives and homes of those who have run the gauntlet of criticism and tradition, to worship God in spirit and in truth.
>
> No doubt there are many reasons for its growth, but I believe that first and foremost is the fact that 'God is moving in the Glory Way', therefore it is bound to increase. Further-more, the radical change in the attitude, demeanour and character of those who are really one hundred per cent Glory

Folk is so apparent, that others cannot help but see the reality and so it should be and must be all along the line. [138]

Love is linked with humility, which is basically not thinking of oneself more highly than one ought to think ... *'in honour preferring one another'* (Romans 12:3, 10). As love looks outwards to others, so does humility. Gwylfa Richards of Llwynhendy (the father of the teenage girl Eirian) said about the Glory Way, 'What impressed me at Newark was not only the love, but also the humility, and true love is humble, for Jesus humbled Himself.' [139] Looking from a different angle, Mrs Beardsley from South Kirkby near Doncaster, showed this very attitude when she wrote,

> Somebody said to me, 'You don't know what you are letting yourself in for, you know. You will be surprised when you get there.' But I wasn't. You know, if you are hungry, you will eat, won't you, and you won't be finicky and picking this and picking that, but you will eat what is set before you and you will be thankful. [140]

Myrtle Taylor, who soon went out as a missionary to the Far East from Willesden Revival Centre, put the whole thing in a nutshell, 'I found that there is no room for self in the Glory Way...' [141]

Henri and Connie Themselves

The personalities of the husband and wife who led the Glory Way are an essential ingredient of the Glory reality. They were simply themselves, the way God had made them and dealt with them. Connie said, 'You're born more natural than natural, if you like, into this kingdom.' They didn't attempt to put anything on or dream it up, but played their lives out, as Spurgeon would say, in the key of B Natural!

Ivor John (who in time with his wife Beatty became very much part of the Glory fellowship) told how they went to a gathering of people in a house in the village of Ingham, near Lincoln.

> My wife and I had never met Henri before this time, yet it was easy to single him out in the home to which I had been invited. There was a love and joy that emanated from him the moment he came into the room, such as I had never felt before. After he had gone out I was told it was Henri and

that he came from Newark. I felt that anyone who can have with him such a presence of the Lord as was manifested in that room was enough for me, and I decided to go to Newark and discover what it was all about. [142]

L.G. Venton of Maidstone, after thirty years of joyfully following the Lord, hit a moment of intense discouragement, so much so that he could feel himself beginning to backslide. Then he heard two Glory tapes and managed to get to a Glory meeting.

Brother Henri came to Paddock Wood, and when I saw the love and compassion he and his team had for others it reminded me of our Lord, how He loved us with an everlasting love, so great was His love for us that He was prepared to die for us. Praise His lovely Name! [143]

There is no doubt about it, that the love of God so clearly indwelt this Nottinghamshire salesman. Arthur Burt recently said to Margaret and me, that he did not know anybody who *enjoyed* Jesus more than Henri! Here are some other comments: 'the first thing that I noticed was the shine on everybody's face and brother Henri's face was beaming. I knew the first time I saw him he was a genuine man of God.' [144] 'Love simply flows out of his heart as he speaks, and it is love that can be felt by all.' [145] 'I knew when I first met Henri that here was a man with something real. The love of Jesus was just radiating from him and the other members of the love family . . . ' [146] 'I saw the mark of God on him in that very first rally. One has only to look at him to see that he is a *real* saint.' [147]

One cannot help mentioning Henri's irrepressible sense of humour. Arthur Burt, again, tells us how Henri laughingly would tell this story against himself. A woman was brought into one of his meetings and people said she was demon possessed. Henri came and stood in front of her and commanded, 'Come out! In the Name of Jesus!' And his dentures flew out of his mouth into her lap!

Anyone who listens to a vintage tape or cassette of meetings of the time I am describing will be struck by the clear impassioned ring of Connie's voice as she strode up and down the platform. One is reminded of Frances Ridley Havergal's words:

Lord, speak to me, that I may speak
In living echoes of Thy tone;

She heralded out her message; often she would speak of the new Jerusalem, of the heavenly Bride and Bridegroom and of being really ready to meet with the Lord. Tom Lowry of Rathcoole in Northern Ireland, as he listened to her, said this:

> I felt a change coming over my spirit, as Connie ministered under the anointing of the Spirit. How wonderful it is to be filled with God and that He should dwell in these temples of ours. [148]

Bill Kirkham reported on a Glory meeting in 1963 at Cleveleys, near Blackpool, and said,

> Connie ministered in the might and power of the Spirit and one could witness the same might and power being infused in the lives of others and many would never be the same again. [149]

Here were the couple that God chose to make a spiritual spearhead into the enemy's camp and positively rout the powers of darkness with a shout of praise and victory.

An Interesting Sidelight

Although that bold and gifted Chinese preacher and writer Watchman Nee, sufferer for the faith, will not have heard of the Glory Way, a penetrating paragraph from his pen lights up an important aspect of the whole character of the ministry of Henri and Connie and those who stood with them. He said,

> When I was younger I sought to attain to a perfect standard of presenting divine truth, determined to leave nothing that could possibly be misunderstood by the hearers. I took great care to run no risks in my preaching, but I must confess there was very little spiritual value in it. God, I soon discovered, uses the weak things as His messengers. He does not demand of us fool-proof explanations but uses fragments, a word here, a sentence there, to bring to men His flashes of light. He is not looking for perfect understanding or for faultless teaching; indeed our very desire for perfection in these matters may itself hinder Him if it stands in the way of His first object, which is to bring life to dead souls, heavenly manna to hungry hearts. *'The words that I have spoken unto you are spirit, and are life.'* [150]

Chapter 12

Glory Link

The seven churches in the Book of Revelation had been founded in apostolic times and yet after about forty years or so most of them badly needed the reviving power of God. Their apostolic privilege was no guarantee against cooling off. In the same way it was so easy for the Pentecostal movement in Britain to flag in the same way. The fact of the matter is that God raised up Henri and Connie Staples to fan the flame of dying embers. The Glory Way proved to be a link with Pentecostal beginnings. At the time of Henri's appearance before the Assemblies of God tribunal, one of the committee, with very real insight, is said to have warned the others: 'If you don't take this on board it will bypass you.' Certainly the mantle of the older Pentecostal blessing rested on the Glory folk. There was a dear old saint who came to a meeting of Henri's at Barrow-in-Furness in 1961.

> [She] testified to this new move being exactly the same kind of meeting that she enjoyed in the Sunderland Revival in 1907. What better testimony than that could you ask for? Straight from a dear sister ... that these Glory Meetings are sincere and genuine and are, in fact, a replica of what she enjoyed 54 years ago. [1]

William Ridsdale gave his life to the Lord in 1904 in Leeds. Soon afterwards he also went to Sunderland:

> I shall never forget the glorious meetings that we had there. The Spirit of the Lord fell upon us in mighty power and there was born within me a great desire to be filled with the Spirit. I sought for this baptism and, praise God, He did not

disappoint me. Ever since those days the Lord has kept the
fire burning in my soul. Today I am 78 years of age and as I
look back to those early days and compare it with the
Pentecostal Movement of today, I am forced to the sorrow-
ful conclusion that what we see today is a poor substitute
for Pentecost as it really is.

I am glad that I came in contact with the Glory
Meetings, because I have been richly blessed in them. I
have waited a great number of years for meetings like these.
The love and joy that is manifest in them I find to be very
contagious and I can truthfully say that I have not found
such blessing anywhere else in these last days and I thank
God for it. [2]

In 1959 William Raine, from Maidstone, came in contact with
the Glory Way. He wrote,

I had heard and read of the power and presence of the Holy
Spirit and of the life and liberty experienced in Pentecostal
gatherings in 'the old days' of former years. The *History of
the Pentecostal Outpouring* details scenes of joy and praise
and of powerful gatherings, often continuing until after
midnight. I had also heard older Pentecostal believers speak
of the joyful character of Pentecostal meetings, with the
power of God in evidence performing the miraculous by
confirming the Word with signs following ... You see it's so
easy to lapse into a formality that ends in a calamity and
that is happening today. We are getting formal and stereo-
typed with a set order of service, so that the Holy Spirit is
unable to move or work as He would like, and seeming
excess of liberty manifest by some is classified as licence by
others.

William Raine then went to one of Henri's Glory meetings
(held in Paddock Wood):

The presence of God was very real, the praise was tremendous, the singing was triumphant, the testimonies were
thrilling and the liberty was truly wonderful. Praise the
Lord! I lost all sense of time and at the end was amazed to
discover just how long the meeting had been in progress. It
needed an effort to close the gathering for the joy and
praises were flowing in a continuous stream ... After the

meeting I thought on this wise: 'If the phrase in Acts 2:16, THIS IS THAT, sets forth the truth and proof of the baptism of the Holy Ghost, then I am sure the thought that came to my mind, THIS IS WHAT WAS, refers to present day Glory meetings, for to me they reveal that the past has come into the present, the characteristics of the early day Pentecostal meetings are here again, for all that happened then is happening now.' [3]

These quotations from the *Glory News* speak for themselves. They are unsolicited testimonials; and there is more to come. In particular Archie Friday – car dealer and garage owner in Paddock Wood in Kent and pastor of the local Assemblies of God – heard of the Glory Way. He and his wife Minnie listened to some Glory tapes and then in November 1958 they journeyed to Newark, where his life was transformed by a wonderful anointing of the Holy Spirit. He wrote,

Some of us can certainly look back forty odd years ago and remember the glory of *the Former House*. We remember the mighty Holy Ghost preaching which brought conviction of sin, and was followed by signs and wonders, when men like dear old Smith Wigglesworth, Stephen Jeffreys and others moved under the hand of God, and Pentecostal meetings were power houses and furnaces of Divine Glory from which the people could not stay away ... Though it may be true that we older Pentecostal folk think and talk of the former glory and confess to the lack of present-day power and blessing, the younger generation wonder what we are concerned about, being largely content with the present tempo of ceremonial Pentecostalism. It is apparent to all that what we need is a present day revival of holy living, holy loving and a deluge of glory and, praise God, He says it shall be so.

Permit a personal word of testimony. The writer received the blessing of the baptism of the Holy Ghost forty-four years ago and experienced the fire and fervour of those early visitations, but – but – but – he confesses to having been for years a 'sophisticated dry hide' or in the words of the Bible, 'a dry bone'. But something has now happened to him. The glory that Jesus said He would give enveloped his soul and at sixty years of age he has begun to live again and to know afresh the surges of Holy Ghost revival, a passion for lost men and women, and a joy unspeakable and full of glory. [4]

Archie Friday's heart was full. Once he had caught fire again like this his enthusiasm was irrepressible. A little later he again wrote,

> It is now about 12 months since I first listened to a Glory tape and later attended a Glory meeting at *Henri's*, Newark. I give God much praise and Henri many thanks for what these contacts have meant to me and for the fearless presentation of Pentecostal fullness by Henri, Connie and the Revival Party.

He then explained how he had worked with his wife as evangelist and pastor in Essex, Northamptonshire and Scotland.

> Why am I telling you all this? ... I just want you to know that my testimony is given with a background of wide experience of Assembly life and, I may add, with experience of signal success in business life as an executive, and I marvel at the goodness of God in stirring my soul from a settled down condition, largely dried up as far as a vital anointing was concerned, especially at my age of over sixty years.
> Like so many other souls who are yearning for a new anointing, I prayed, 'Lord, show me Thy Glory,' and one positive answer to that prayer was that I came in touch with Henri's. I soon had the witness in my heart that here was Holy Ghost power in operation, and although the flesh with me resented the things that brought about the crucifixion of self, I said, 'Lord, whatever the price, I'll pay it,' and I find that the words of Jesus are being fulfilled in me, *'The disciple is not above his Master, nor the servant above his Lord.' 'If they have persecuted me, they will also persecute you;'* and he that would follow Him must deny himself and take up his cross daily and follow Him. I can testify that by fearlessly praising God, by clapping the hands (Psalm 47:1), by lifting up the holy hands and by a full surrender, the fear of man has gone, wrongs have been put right, the love of Christ burns in my heart toward Himself and everybody else too and Jesus is more real to me than ever I have known Him in all my life. But that is not all. Oh no! Hallelujah! Christ within

me the hope of Glory is operating in power in quickening those contacted, and ministered to. It is wonderful. Men and women are being set free from their bondage and fears, the Revival is on! God is moving by His Spirit, and furthermore, all those that receive this glorious liberty and anointing are themselves moving out in confidence against Satan and sickness, and when we go out from our Assembly at Paddock Wood as a Revival Party, everyone is ready to testify, sing or preach if necessary; and rivers of living water are flowing out ... Oh Pentecostal Movement! Where is the power and glory of former days? You have organisations, choirs, preachers, churches, houses, funds, but where is the Glory?[5]

The little assembly at Paddock Wood became another Glory centre. The power came down, numbers increased and immediately they had almost unbelievable ostracism and opposition. Archie Friday was not dismayed, pointing out that Jesus was blamed by the Pharisees for being a deceiver and His followers, they said, were deceived and cursed (John 7:47–49). Archie riposted:

Glory meetings! 'What are they?' many ask, and so often the warning comes, 'Oh, don't go near them. It's nothing but a manifestation of flesh, lightness, noise, familiarity, excesses, holding hands and, as someone said, pandemonium' ... The remarkable accomplishments of the ministry of Jesus in His life, death and resurrection silence for ever the roaring criticism of the religious leaders of His day, and we in this latter day revival, this Holy Ghost visitation, can afford to disregard all the criticism, the misrepresentations and the opposition because we have no personal axe to grind, no denomination to fight for, but are living in the enjoyment of a wonderful spiritual experience of love, joy and peace and to try to stop this is just trying to stop God and He is well able to defend Himself and His doing.

The fact is that you CANNOT STOP the blessing of the Lord. I cannot say why it is that God has chosen to visit His people with a seemingly rugged move of singing and dancing which sometimes sounds like Rock'n'Roll, but I know that teenagers and teddy boys are being won to God in these meetings which are literally charged with Holy Ghost power.[6]

Furthermore, Archie bent over backwards to explain that he was not sheep-stealing. In answer to a letter inquiring about holding Glory meetings, he said,

> You may take it as definite that we at Paddock Wood have no intention or desire to encroach upon another brother's territory in holding Glory meetings without an invitation by a local pastor, so to do and when we do it is with an earnest endeavour to set men and women free in the Spirit, so that they will be of great service to their pastor, their assembly and to the Lord ... I am aware that false statements are being made about us and my answer to those who make them is 'Come and see.' [7]

These words of Philip's invitation to Nathanael (John 1:46) to come and find out for himself are eternally true. There is no alternative to first-hand experience. Take for instance Archie's wife Minnie – how she loved the Glory meetings and how she was so at one with her husband in this. Their daughter Ruth Kemp today bears this out. Furthermore Ruth recalls how her father had a great affinity with Henri. Whenever they met they would disappear and talk for hours together.

It so happened that Ruth's sister Eunice married Donald Crook, the son of an Assemblies of God pastor in Margate, and they went out as missionaries to India and then to South Africa to work amongst Indians in Durban. Eunice down the years had always been rather prickly about the Glory Way. She has been a careful Bible student and recently she admitted to Ruth that, combing through the Scriptures and checking the Glory Way carefully against them, she could find nothing at all against Henri and Connie's ministry. Every little bit of evidence helps!

Now, Donald Crook's father, Pastor Hubert Crook, found his spiritual life (like Archie Friday's) completely revitalised by coming into contact with Henri. At a Glory meeting in Newark he gave an extremely interesting testimony, explaining how he had been in the Assemblies of God at the very beginning. He was a Welshman, and a number of pastors had met in Newport to form an Assemblies of God of South Wales and Monmouthshire. Mr Crook was made the secretary. And from this were founded the Assemblies of God of England, and finally of Great Britain. Then he had this to say:

So I am speaking as one who has been in the movement from the beginning and I want to tell you this afternoon and evening that what I have seen here is what we had at the beginning. I remember at the beginning when the power of God fell in a greater building than this, and everybody from the back of the platform, from the gallery to the pulpit, everywhere, they were dancing under the power of the Spirit of God and everything was so orderly, and so good, and so clean, nobody could object to it. It was wonderful. It was wonderful to see the mighty power of God moving in the bodies of men and women, without them being conscious of what was taking place.

We leave the last word with Hubert Crook as he continued:

In every church, in every denomination, in every organisation they are praying for revival. What, I ask, do they expect to get? You can only revive something that has existed before and, when asking God for a revival, He can only revive according to the pattern of Acts chapter two. Hallelujah! That is the only revival. Praise the Lord. God can only give the Church, the Body of Christ, a revival after the order of Pentecost, with signs following. This power has not deteriorated throughout the Church age. Hallelujah! It will not deteriorate where God has men and women who will yield themselves unto Him. [8]

Chapter 13

Glory Testimonies

I t is always fascinating to hear the personal stories of Christians, to discover how God has become real to them. Everyone is different and everyone's story is different. God is always the same, and the truths of the Bible are like a rock, unchangeable, but the way each individual person reacts to them is as variable as the enormous variety in the world of plants, trees and flowers or the different patterns of snowflakes, and as endlessly enthralling.

This book, altogether, is full of testimonies. They are popping up all the way through the narrative. We have already had a good number and I make no apologies at adding some more. For the Glory Way, by its very nature, is chock-full of human interest. Not only is it interwoven with the biographies of Henri and Connie, but also, scattered through the copies of the *Glory News* are a very great number of salvation stories, of grace abounding and spiritual adventure. In fact, quite honestly, there are so many that a whole separate book could be made up out of them. Here is a brief selection, with the addition of the lives of people playing a part in the Glory Way today. To begin with, there were elderly folk whose memories went back a long way.

Jack Sharp

The first is an old Newark character, born one year before Winston Churchill.

> I came into this world in the year 1873, and was born and bred to farm life in the vicinity of Newark. My father was a staunch Anglican and my ancestors built and supported the village church at Barnby just outside Newark and there are plaques on the walls of the church to this day in commem-

oration of the Sharp family who were classed among the gentry of that day.

The ritualistic services of the Anglican church never appealed to me and whenever I spied the opportunity, I used to slip away to the village chapel to enjoy something with a bit more life in it. When I returned home after one such occasion, my father who had been hindered from going to church that night, asked me from what text the vicar had preached and I replied, 'Behold, I was not there.' He never asked me again.

I left school when I was eight years old, and went to work on the farm. My father was a big horse dealer and it was not long before this business was taking me to various parts of the country. There was a great demand for horses in the wool mills of Yorkshire and I found myself a frequent visitor to that part.

It was in the town of Halifax, on Easter Monday, in the year 1890 that I got converted at an open-air meeting in the Market Place, and straight way I launched out into public speaking for the Lord. Those were the days of real revival, when men and women were not ashamed to fall on their knees in the open air and weep their way to God. Many were healed as we prayed for them and the people sang and danced in the streets, filled with the joy of the Lord.

In the year that I first began to preach, I had my first accident and have had an accident about every three or four years ever since. On one occasion the doctor discovered that I had a broken spine which was the result of a former calamity many years before when half-a-ton of steel fell across my back. He wanted me to go to hospital for treatment but I refused and God healed me in a prayer meeting in the chapel I used to attend. Looking back over my life it seems one long story of accidents and many times I have been brought to the brink of death, but praise the Lord, He has delivered and healed me every time in answer to prayer.

From the time of my conversion I have always had a great longing to visit the sick and pray for them and over the years my faith has grown strong in the power of God to heal.

When I was approaching my eighty-fourth birthday, I had a further accident that was worse than any that I had gone through before. I had already had eighteen during my lifetime and I should have thought that was enough for any man but apparently this was not so. On September 22nd 1957, I was cycling home to Danethorpe which is about five miles out of Newark. I had been talking to Henri about some revival services we were arranging in our chapel and district and he had promised to come over and give us a hand. As I journeyed homeward I was suddenly knocked off my bicycle and run over by a car.

I was rushed to hospital in a critical condition, in a state of unconsciousness, with every bone down my right side broken save one rib, one lung pierced and a fractured skull. The police said there was little hope of my surviving and one paper reported that I was killed, a patient in the hospital read me the account at a later date. Of course as far as man was concerned they were right, but they reckoned without God for if the Almighty is on your side you can pull through anything.

For six days I knew nothing and even when I regained consciousness I found that Christ had lifted me above all pain. Praise the Lord. On coming to myself I found myself in Harlow Wood hospital and I can truthfully say that it was like a corner of heaven to me. The sister told me that on the fourth day of my unconsciousness I sang, 'The Lord's my Shepherd I'll not want,' which proves that although men may break your bones they can never break your spirit. Glory to God.

Within three weeks God had raised me up and I was going around the wards in a wheelchair preaching the gospel and cheering folks up. The surgeons say I am a living miracle. They have never known a man of my age suffer the injuries that I had, and still survive, never mind getting better so quick. They told me that all they can do is set broken bones but only God in heaven can heal them. There is no doubt that without the power of the living God in me I would have been lost, but Jesus has promised never to leave us nor forsake us and it is in times like these that we prove Him to be true. My temperature dropped right down to 57 degrees through loss of blood and they tell me that you are supposed to die when it drops to 60 degrees. Of course Jesus is the resurrection and the life, so it's no wonder I'm still here.

When I was discharged from hospital, I made my way to Henri's Glory meetings just as soon as I could manage it. I had often been invited but I had always been too busy to go, but since going I've got this one regret and that is that I didn't go sooner. These meetings remind me of the wonderful times I had up in Halifax when I first got converted and if Harlow Wood hospital was like a corner of heaven then these meetings are more so. I think I've been transferred to the Glory Department for I've had nothing but love, joy, peace and new life since I've been going to them. I'm not waiting to go to heaven, I'm enjoying heaven down here, and I'm very happy indeed.

Since this last accident I suffered a lot with my head but one night I was sat in Henri's mother's home listening to a Glory Tape and the Lord healed me there and then. Praise God, what the doctors cannot do He can. That's the wonderful thing about this gospel, it meets everybody's need just where they are if they have faith in God. It is the same gospel that Jesus preached and the same power that raised Him from the dead.

Men said I was done for, but through the grace and power of God I am still here, a living testimony of what Christ can do and I feel that my mission in life is not yet finished and I am more on fire for God today than ever before. [1]

William Draycott

Then we have 'our old pal Bill,' William Draycott of Liverpool.

I was born in the year 1881 and sixty years of my life have been spent here in the city of Liverpool. My life as a boy was not a saintly one, as I was often in trouble and got into the hands of the police, but through my mother's prayers I escaped the jails. I soon learned to drink the devil's broth (beer) and learned all the tricks of the devil with bad language thrown in. My father gave me many a hiding being expert with his slipper and I always got it in the right place (you know where).

At the bottom of the street where I lived was a Mission Hall and an old Christian brother made it his business to try to get me to one of the meetings to hear the gospel, but Billy Draycott was not to be caught like that, so he tried giving me tracts and talking to me about my soul. This brother often caught me coming out of the pub and he used to say to me, 'Willie, drink leads to hell, give it up,' but Billy couldn't. Every time I met this missionary I came under deep conviction of sin and I got real burdened and miserable.

One Sunday while in this condition, a knock came on the door of my home and it was that old brother (the 'are you saved?' man). He was going to take a meeting some- where in Liverpool and he invited me to go along with him. I consented to go with him this time for I longed to get rid of this burden of sin on my soul. At the end of his address he asked if there was any poor sinner who would like to get right with God. I could stand no more of this fiery preach- ing, so I let out a yell that I would. Oh, that night in Murray Hall's vestry at the age of twenty-two, something came out of Willie Draycott and praise God, Jesus came in. Hallel- ujah. My burden rolled away, my heart was free and I felt like I was walking on air and all I wanted to do was talk about Jesus. Hallelujah.

All this happened in 1904 when Wales was enjoying a mighty revival. The Superintendent of the Liverpool City Mission together with others organised a day trip to a Welsh village called Rhos near Wrexham and I went along. When we arrived at Rhos station one of the party enquired where the revival was and a Welshman replied, 'In my heart.' The meeting was in a big Wesley Chapel and it was crowded with happy faces all singing to the Glory of God. It was a sight to do sore eyes good. My hair seemed to stand up on end, for I had never heard such singing in all my life. It was glory, glory, glory all the time.

I looked at the pulpit but it was empty, for the Revivalist Evan Roberts had not turned up but the Welsh people did not seem to be perturbed, they just carried on singing. It was singing, singing all the time and occasionally some- one would shout aloud, 'Praise the Lord.' It was very wonderful.

It was through your advert in the *Christian Herald* that I got in touch with you. I've read your Glory magazine and it's real glory that I get in the reading of it. What a lot of jolly faces in it too. Hallelujah. I must try and come down to Newark and get a chip of the glory to bring back to hard- hearted Liverpool. [2]

Elizabeth Williams

Next come two women from Wales, who were of the revival generation. The first, Miss Elizabeth Williams, came from the village of Aberkenfig near Bridgend, in South Wales, which were in the same valley downstream as Maesteg, the home of the famous Jeffreys brothers, who came to a knowledge of salvation at this same time. Like Stephen Jeffreys, Elizabeth Williams was a link between the great Welsh revival and the Glory way. She wrote,

I would like to tell you how God has blessed me all my life. I was born July 21st 1883 and was saved at Eastertime 1904 during the Welsh Revival. In my young days, times were hard and I started to work at an early age. I worked long hours for very little money, but looking back over my life, I can see how the Lord led me.

When I got converted, what a time that was, seeing folk filled with the Holy Spirit and the blessing was such, that we didn't mind if we stayed all night singing and praising the Lord. It was wonderful! Everybody seemed so happy and they all loved one another, just like the Glory Folks are doing today.

I had been working at a farm-house where I started at one shilling per week and my food. I had been there for years, but God had something better in store for me. A minister of a chapel wanted a maid; thirteen girls had been after the job and I was the fourteenth. They liked me the best so I got the job and went to live in and I was there twenty-seven years, until God called them home. Those were very happy years, for the minister and his wife lived to serve God and win the souls of men. God blessed that home and the church. Every meeting was packed and it was a glorious sight often to see forty or fifty people on their knees praying and seeking the Lord. In like manner the Glory Folk are on the right road. Praise the Lord!

After the passing of my master and mistress I returned home, but things were very different. I went along to a local chapel, but there was something missing. The folks didn't seem to have the love and joy that I had been used to and I missed the happy fellowship of bygone days.

One day I was invited to some special meetings at the Mission and as the minister preached and sang, the joy came back into my soul. I was pleased to join the happy band at the Mission and I have been happy there ever since. The folk have been wonderfully kind to me and I am now in my 84th year and still going on with the Lord. At the end of last year I fell ill with stomach trouble and was ill for three months. The folk at the Mission prayed for me and it pleased God to deliver me. Glory to His Name!

I have been to a good few Glory Meetings and I trust to be in many more. I praise God for claiming me when I was young, strong and free and for keeping me for over sixty years. God bless you all. [3]

Hilda Herold

Much further north, Miss Hilda Herold came from Arthog, at the bottom of the north-western slope of the beautiful mountain Cader Idris. She does not mention the revival, but makes some very telling points about living the Christian life:

It was Eastertime 1905 when God found me at the age of twenty-two, and turned my life from mere worldly pursuits and ambitions into a way where I was to follow and serve Him. I found peace for my soul, forgiveness of sin and an inner joy which has been with me ever since.

There have been several stages in this new life in Christ. It was three years after my conversion that I received an outpouring of the Holy Spirit, with joy unspeakable, setting me free from self-consciousness and my own efforts in serving God. I realised that I was just a channel for His love to pour through to other people.

My own family, some friends and relations who had previously been changed through seeing me a different person, also experienced this baptism of the Spirit and this experience made us one with an ever spreading movement in God's plan, at that time. I was wonderfully led in my personal circumstances too in the years following. Far beyond expectations, my long life has been blessed with happiness and contentment, in good days as well as in hard times. When God is a reality in our lives, our own feelings, or comfort, or success, are not of foremost importance, but take their proper place in God's plan for his kingdom, which ruleth over all.

A very marked new experience came to me in 1932, when I met a group of people in a private house in London, who seemed to have gone ahead of me, not only in changing the lives of others but in their own conduct too. They challenged me with a standard of living according to the Sermon on the Mount, which I had never faced up to quite so thoroughly before. This meant a new consecration for me and a willingness to let Christ into all departments of my life. There were several closed doors in my heart, behind which I had not cleared up the cobwebs and the rubbish and unpleasantness that had collected there.

The cleansing power of fresh air by the Holy Spirit swept through as I opened up these avenues of my being, and He made a good job of clearing it all out. The searchlight of absolute standards in honesty, unselfishness, purity and love, made me realise that I could not have done it myself. God's love is very gentle and tender to a repentant sinner, or a saint for that matter, if you consider yourself one. He forces no one, but if you yield yourself in a new surrender, you will find an ever closer fellowship with Jesus Christ and with those who will listen to God's commands and walk with Him, as Enoch did of old.

I have made a habit of spending the first hour of the day in communion with God, praying as well as listening to Him. He may have a special plan for even the ordinary things of my daily routine. Otherwise I am inclined to drift into undisciplined waste of time and energy. I also have a paper and pencil ready, to jot down any particular thought that comes to mind. I am over eighty years of age now and my memory is even weaker than it used to be and I do want to obey the Lord's will, so that I can still fight the Lord's battle, under His command and be part of His campaign to renew the world in these modern times. [4]

Ben Davies

We have yet another link between the Welsh revival and Henri and Connie in Ben Davies, from Ammanford in South Wales, on the western edge of the Black Mountains,

It was in the 1904–5 Welsh revival that I was saved, when I was just a lad. Glory to God. In 1920 God revealed to me by

His Spirit, through His word, the truth of the Baptism of the Holy Ghost with signs following in spite of my being among the spiritual 'Icebergs'. Praise God. He led me to a cottage meeting and there He filled me with His Spirit. Hallelujah. For weeks I could not restrain speaking in other tongues. It was wonderful.

For thirty-two years I have been a member of a Pentecostal assembly, where God spoke to us through the prophetical gift, declaring that He was going to send a New Anointing and a New Day. Praise the Lord. My wife and I said straight away that we wanted it, and we went all out for it, and glory to God He filled us with this New Anointing, but sad to say this wonderful blessing of God was not generally accepted by the people, and so after much prayer and weeping before the Lord, He wonderfully opened the way for us to have fellowship with those who preached and ministered Deliverance and Restoration. Hallelujah.

The last few years have been the most joyful in all my life. Praise God for this Glory Way. Oh it is wonderful. His word is true. I will restore to you the years that the locust hath eaten, and praise God, we are drinking in the Latter Rain. The rivers that flow from the Throne of God. Hallelujah.

My wife and I went to Newark for the August Convention and oh, what a manifestation of the Love of God we saw and experienced. Truly as Henri said, 'We shall never be the same again.' Praise the Lord. Thank God for the Glory. It has come even to our feet and causes us to dance to the Glory of God. Oh that men and women would come and taste and see that the Lord is good. We are enjoying the corn, oil and wine of Canaan land. 'If here it is so blessed, what will it be up there?' Heaven is better than this, Glory! Hallelujah! Blessed be the name of the Lord. It causes us to sing, dance, worship and adore, our blessed Saviour. Oh, that men would praise the Lord for His wonderful works toward the children of men. I just feel I want always to exalt the name of our Lord Jesus Christ, on seeing such a manifestation of His love and life flowing out from His people. It was a tonic to my soul to see the old and the young, coloured and white people, loving each other, in God's presence. May God multiply His blessings upon us all for His glory. Thank the Lord for 'something new.' [5]

Sally Marlow

The story of this true Messianic Jewess has its own fascination:

My father was a Greek Jew, and my mother was a Rumanian Jewess. Dad being a strict orthodox believer in the Jewish religion saw to it that we were brought up to observe and respect our father's faith. My two brothers used to attend the synagogue regularly with my dad, but mother and I only went on special occasions. It was our duty to stay at home and make certain preparations at the table in readiness for their return. This we did every Sabbath day and evening.

Dad always conducted the ceremony in the Hebrew language (of which we others had no understanding), and all present partook of the bread and the wine. Every atonement day we were obliged to fast, and we were given to understand that this was done to acknowledge our sin before God. For eight days we celebrated the Passover, eating only unleavened bread. At that time we were living in Egypt and dad always reminded us that during those eight days we were to purchase nothing from the Christians. He also told us the reason for keeping the Passover for eight days instead of seven was because we were not living in the Holy Land.

In spite of the fact that these and many other Jewish festivities were observed in our home, our religion brought us no joy and little understanding of God and, apart from these festive occasions, I gave little thought to our religion and, as I grew older, it became burdensome and tiring. It was only in an effort to please my father that I showed any interest at all.

I would like to mention also, that we lived in very poor circumstances. Our home consisted of a very damp basement in a most undesirable part of Alexandria. At that time I was about eighteen years of age. My brothers were both younger than I and were being educated at the Scotch Mission School for boys. About this time, the headmaster at the school decided to hold Christian meetings for the young boys and also meetings for the adults on Sunday evenings. My brothers used to attend these meetings and seemed to enjoy them very much.

The headmistress gave my mother an invitation to some women's meetings and she seemed very impressed by the love and kindness shown to her and spoke of the meetings with much feeling. All this aroused an interest in my own mind towards these things and I was glad when my mother invited me to accompany her to the meetings. I could not speak the English language at that time, so it was necessary for my mother to translate the service to me into my own tongue, which was Italian. It was all so very new to me, but I really enjoyed the service, especially the lantern service once a month.

By this time my brothers had gained permission from my dad to have Christian servicemen in our home. They very kindly bought me a New Testament printed in the French language.

We had always been taught never to mention the name of Christ in our home, so I knew quite well that my father would certainly not approve of me reading a New Testament. To overcome this difficulty I decided to read it in secret, which I often did by the aid of a torch light at night. To conceal the book from my father during the day, I made a small hole in my mattress and kept it hidden there from sight. As I read I grew more and more interested and one day when reading a portion from John's Gospel, I came across a word that I could not understand: it was the word 'Whosoever'.

I approached one of the Christian Servicemen and asked him if he would kindly explain the meaning of it. This he did and very wisely pointed out that the word whosoever also included me. That very night, alone in my bedroom I lifted my heart to Jesus Christ and accepted Him as my Saviour. I told nobody about this but kept it a secret. My dad had no suspicions of what had transpired for when I was in his presence I conducted myself as I had always done.

Unknown to my dad I began to attend meetings regularly but one afternoon all unknown to us he followed us to the meeting place. He was greatly annoyed and forbade me to attend any more Christian gatherings, but for once I disobeyed my dad and at one particular meeting I decided to make a public confession of Jesus Christ as my Messiah. By my continuing to attend the meetings, my dad became more and more infuriated. He often beat me and threatened to take my life. For days I went in fear of death and dared not undress at nights lest he attacked me. On one occasion, whilst preparing to go to the meeting, he attempted to stop me by jumping over my bed to thrash me with his strap and in doing so he fell and broke his toes. Many times he cursed me and even went to the extent of performing the Jewish funeral ceremony at the Synagogue on my behalf. As far as he was concerned I was dead, but in reality I was very much alive in my new found faith.

My one desire was to please my Lord, so I decided to be baptised in water and prove once and for all to my father my determination to press on in the Christian life. Needless to say, taking this step of faith in obedience to my Lord's command did not improve things at home. Mother too had become a Christian and remained strong in faith until the hour of her homecall. My father continued to look on us with bitter disapproval. At different times he would rise up in great indignation and do the most unusual things, often striking my mother, and at one time he offered me a considerable sum of money on condition that I renounced my faith in Christ. Of course, I told him that this could never be. Jesus my Saviour meant more to me than all the money in the world. I just asked the dear Lord to help me to manifest a true Christian spirit towards my dad and after three years of trial and testing the time came when I left home for England to be married to a Christian young man to whom I had been engaged. Before leaving, my father called me on one side and asked me to forgive him for all that had passed and I was glad to assure him that I really did.

Some time after I was baptised in water, I learnt that it was God's desire to fill me with the Holy Ghost and I sought the Lord along this line and one day in my bedroom the Holy Spirit came and filled me and I began to praise my God in other tongues. It was wonderful. For nearly sixteen years now I have proved the reality of Christ and He is my delight all the time. Hallelujah!

It was at the Easter Convention in 1957 that I first met Henri and the Glory People. There was such an atmosphere of love and joy in the Lord in the meeting that I was moved by the Spirit to give my testimony and tell what great things the Lord had done for me, and I am thankful to God for the happy fellowship that I have enjoyed from time to time at Newark. It has really been a blessing to feel the liberty of the Holy Ghost among the people there. [6]

W.A. Parsley

The focus now switches to Brother W.A. Parsley of Watford, who has a totally different kind of narrative:

My father was an avowed atheist, and also a professional gambler, owning several men's clubs in London. In the midst of this I was born and brought up. I was never sent to Sunday school or ever went to any place where the Name of Jesus was preached. I did not know anything about the Bible. At the age of seventeen I was a confirmed gambler. All the art of gambling was in me. Christless and vile was my condition, money was plentiful as far as I was concerned and I spent it in my wild condition and pursuits. My companions were men much older than myself and I was quick to learn from them much of their wickedness. That was my life.

However, one Sunday afternoon, I went to meet some companions but, owing to a mistake in the time of appointment, I arrived with twenty minutes to spare. Whilst I waited, a young man came to me with a tract and an invitation card to an Evangelical meeting which was being held in a tent just near where I was standing. I refused the tract, saying that it was not in my line and I was not interested. The man drew my attention to the tent saying that it was a fine tent. 'Yes it looks good,' was my reply. 'You ought to see the inside,' he remarked. He then went away.

Having still a few minutes to spare I walked over and looked inside. It was fairly full of men (it was a men's meeting). On the platform a man was reading the Scriptures, but I did not know they were the word of God. In a moment I forgot my friends whom I'd promised to meet and was, for the first time, listening to the story of Jesus; but I did not know who He was. An invitation was given to all who would follow Jesus to come out and seek His pardoning grace. I went out with a number of other men, for I wanted to find this wonderful Saviour. That afternoon I got to know Him as my Redeemer and went home walking on air (or so it seemed).

My father was at the table ready for tea. His first words were, 'Have you had a good time?' 'Yes,' I replied. His next question was, 'Where have you been?' (Very seldom did he ask me where I had been.) I told him that I had been to a Gospel Tent (that is what it was chalked on the board outside), and that I had decided to follow Jesus. My father looked at me. 'Do you mean that?' he asked. 'Yes, father,' I replied. 'Well I will give you until tomorrow to change your mind and if it is not changed then, outside this home you go!' he said. I did not want to wait until the following day as I had already made up my mind to follow Jesus so I was told to leave at once and not to return. Back to the tent I went and saw the brother who had pointed me to Jesus and told him what had happened. He took me to his home and gave me food and shelter for the night.

Next morning I went to find work. Walking along I came to a large factory where vans were being loaded. On a platform a man was opening goods and I asked him if there was a chance of a job. Looking at me, he told me to jump up. I followed him into his office and he asked me where I had been working. I told him I had never worked before and he wanted to know why I had asked for a job. I said, 'Because yesterday afternoon I decided to follow Jesus, in the tent which is near the factory, and if I am to follow Him I must find work.' Placing his hand on my shoulder he said, 'God bless you my boy. I wish I had done so when I was a lad.' He gave me a job and I started straight away. For three years I worked there and the devil told me I was a fool to leave home and companions and also work for a wage that I could get in a few hours without work.

I attached myself to a band of young men on fire for God. They called themselves *Daniel's Band* and witnessed at street corners and in public houses. Then I moved to another town and worked there for a number of years. I have seen many precious souls saved, healed and filled with the Holy Ghost.

Two years after my conversion, a friend of my father came to let me know that father had been to the races, won a lot of money and, in an argument which arose, had taken an oath asking to be struck dead and immediately fell to the floor – a corpse. At the inquest which followed, a verdict was given that he died as an act of God. No other cause could be found. Sad to say, he died as he lived, but I had the joy of leading my mother to Christ.

It has been my greatest joy in life to help men and women to know my wonderful Jesus, and since the Lord saved a wretched sinner like me, He is surely able to save from the uttermost all who come unto God by Him for He ever liveth to make intercession for us.[7]

Jim Partington

An article in a *Glory News* bears the quaint title, 'Brethren Brother gets baptised in the Spirit.' Jim Partington from Wigan had this story to tell:

'I wonder if I could ask you a question,' he said. 'Yes, go ahead,' I replied. 'Do you believe in the baptism of the Holy Ghost?' he inquired. 'No, I don't,' I was quick to let him know.

This little conversation took place on the night of Wednesday 9th October, 1963, between a visiting evangelist and myself, Jim Partington. When I woke up the following morning, these words flashed into my mind, 'Powerless disciples until Pentecost'. God impressed these words upon my heart all that day and after supper the evangelist, who had stayed the night with us, began to discuss with me once again the baptism of the Holy Ghost.

Very soon I reached my limit and began to get bad-tempered, for I adamantly refused any suggestion of a second blessing experience of any kind. However, he suggested we had a word of prayer and, in order to terminate our conversation and get to bed (it was nearly 2 am), I agreed. We knelt down and prayed, I in a formal manner, and he in reality.

We finished praying and to my amazement, before I could get up off my knees, he came and laid his hands on my head and told me to ask God to baptise me with His Holy Spirit. I thought, this is crazy, here's me, a grown man on my knees and he, a grown man, standing beside me with his hands on my head, telling me to ask God for something I did not believe in. However, I loved this brother, so I decided to wait there for a few minutes and then the thought came to me, that perhaps after all, God did want to bless me and baptise me with His Spirit and here was I, ridiculing and refusing it, so I prayed, 'Lord if you really do want to baptise me in your Holy Spirit, then I want it too, please do it now.'

Suddenly I felt very afraid, my lips seemed to pucker up. I was immersed in brilliant Holy Ghost light. The vision that Isaiah had became a reality in my heart. Just as the angel flew with a live coal from the altar and touched the prophet's lips, that he might speak forth, so I too suddenly found words, strange words and they just poured forth out of my mouth. I had no understanding of these words, but I know I was praising God, praising God as I had never praised Him before, for the Spirit gave me utterance.

I had never been to a Pentecostal meeting, nor had any experience of tongues, but I continued praising God in tongues for about two hours or so, telling Him how sorry I was for being so unfaithful and unworthy over the years even in times of highest endeavour, still only trifling with Him and playing at being a Christian.

Before very long I realised that God had a purpose in my life in giving me this experience. Pastor Grigg from the Assemblies of God gave me a brotherly warning, that whatever else I did about this experience in my life, I must not deny it or quench it for, if I did, in six months time I would never remember it. I was still worshipping with the Brethren at this time, but then God laid upon my heart a little Pentecostal Church that was closing down. There was no pastor and the congregation had dwindled. God guided my footsteps to care for this work.

A short time after being baptised with the Holy Spirit, I found myself almost by chance, as it were, at Henri's Glory Rally which was held at Cleveleys on the 2nd November 1963. I have just checked on this date in my diary and all it says is – Henri's. Wow! It was a good job that God had already baptised me in the Holy spirit, because I thought I should have walked out of the meeting upon my arrival there. I thought they had all gone mad. They sang a chorus, 'I'm going to the feast,' for twenty minutes after I had arrived and they had commenced it before I had got there. All the seats were filled except at the front and, sitting right there near the platform, I suddenly realised a woman was preaching. Connie, bless her. She spoke about the man who hadn't got a wedding garment on. I was bursting with indignation and with what I called a righteous wrath, at a woman daring to speak and teach in the presence of brethren.

I immediately turned to 1 Timothy 2:11 and 12 and if I could have scooped the words from the page and hurled them at her, I would have done so. I glared and glowered at her and dared her to defy me and go on preaching, which of course she did. After about half-an-hour, I realised that neither Connie nor anyone else was taking any notice of me. In fact they were all having a wonderful time. They started singing again, dancing too and clapping their hands and by this time I felt really left out, so I decided to relax a little and join in the singing and clap my hands. As soon as I did this, the Spirit started to fill me with love, joy and peace and I started to bubble over and really, for the first time ever, I enjoyed a meeting. I had always thought that one should be reverent and quiet in a meeting, but praise God, He has taught me that if I praise Him day by day and moment by moment, then I can always rejoice and be at ease in His presence.

God has given me the thrill and joy of this wonderful liberty, free from sin, free from bigotry and bias and He has laid upon my heart the desire to see the captives set free and brought into this wonderful blessing. How wonderful it is that we can share this love and joy with one another, as we receive it from Him, in good measure, pressed down, shaken together and running over.

I never really understood in the Word of God such things as *'out of his belly shall flow rivers of living water,'* but I now know this as a reality in my own life and this blessed experience can belong to every child of God, as they believe, accept and enter in. There are waters to swim in. Hallelujah! Praise His wonderful Name! [8]

Joseph Gallaher

The next article is an extract from a remarkable address given at a Lambeth Glory Rally by Joseph Gallaher. Jesus Himself said that it is the Scriptures which bear testimony to Him (John 5:39). They are the rule of faith; we must not add to them. And we say with tears that we must stick to this, and we believe we do not limit the grace and love of God by sticking to this. So I would say to any Roman Catholic who happens to read these words, please bear this in mind. Joseph Gallaher said,

The first indication of Glory Meetings I had was when I went to Canning Town Elim Church to preach, and a brother said, 'You remind me of Henri.' I asked 'Who on earth is Henri?' and they told me about Henri, but this is the first time that I have had the opportunity of seeing Brother Henri. I thought the Jamaicans were the only people God was pouring His Spirit upon, but this meeting has been a new revelation to me of how God is working in this 20th Century and how God is pouring out His Spirit upon all men and all flesh.

Friends, I was brought up a Roman Catholic, which means to say, I didn't believe that the work that Jesus did on Calvary was completed. I believed I must punish my body and that I must whip myself in order to get redemption from sin. I was brought up in the RC Church and I was religious. When I was out on the hillside shepherding the sheep I used to build an altar and perform the Catholic ceremony upon those altars. I was so religious, I went to church every day; I served the priest every day; I was religious like Nicodemus, but Jesus said, 'Nicodemus you must be born again.'

When I came of age I was sent off to college in Dublin in Eire and in New Jersey in the USA. I was in one of the most terrible organisations of the Church of Rome; we were chosen for our ability to preach to the people, to tear our hair out and make demonstration. Why, the Pope himself in Rome said that he feared us. We were the Jesuit priests. When I had completed my study I was ordained a priest of the Roman Catholic Church and I went out to my appointment but I wasn't able to fulfil it, for I say this, that God stepped into my life. Amen!

I went over to Ireland and received there a copy of the Scriptures for the first time in my own language, in a language I could understand, from a Bible colporteur. I took that Bible with me to my room and I began to read, and the first verse that my eyes lighted upon was 1 Timothy 2:5, *'There is one God, and one mediator between God and men, the man Christ Jesus.'* Friends, it says nothing in there about the Pope; it says nothing about Mary; it says nothing in there about scourging my body; it says nothing in there about working my own salvation; it says Jesus is the mediator between God and men. Glory to God! I'm thankful tonight that there is no Pope and no priest betwixt me and my Saviour.

It is true that *'Ye shall know the truth and the truth shall make you free.'* Well the light came to me, that there was one mediator between God and men, and that was the man Christ Jesus. There was no other mediator. There was nothing else to be done, and you know I went along to my chief priest and I said, 'Look; here is the word of God and it says, "There is one God, and one mediator between God and men, the man Christ Jesus".' Do you know, before I could stop him, he had that book away from me and into the fire. This is what the Church of Rome thinks about the Bible, because the Bible is a direct contradiction of all that the Church of Rome teaches. They won't have it, they burn it, but what God has put in my heart cannot be burned. If they burned all the Bibles in this world, they could still not take away this experience from my heart.

The priest said, 'If you must read the Bible then read the Catholic Bible.' So I took myself off to the Bible shop and I came back with a whole stack of Bibles – Knox's translation, Rheims version, Douay version, everything I could find, and I turned up that verse and what did it say? – Same thing – 'One God, one mediator between God and men, that man Christ Jesus.'

One thing that really opened my eyes to the light of the gospel was the account in Numbers 21 of Moses lifting up the serpent in the wilderness. The people in that day rebelled against God, they were sinners and they were afflicted, so much so that they died by being bitten by snakes, but God provided the remedy. He said, *'Set a serpent upon a pole, and it shall be that whoever looks upon that serpent shall live.'* Now He didn't say whoever dances around about it, or whoever confesses his sin to Moses will be healed and live, but 'Whoever looks at it'. It's wonderful how God reveals these things to our eyes, for I read in John 3:14, *'As Moses lifted up the serpent in the wilderness even so must the Son of Man be lifted up, that whosoever believeth in Him should not perish but have eternal life.'* This was the remedy – believe and you shall live.

Now you know, I realised I was smitten with a terrible disease that was incurable, for I was bitten by that old serpent the devil and the only thing that could cure that snake bite was the Cross of Calvary. I realised that I didn't have to scourge my body, I didn't have to work out my own salvation, all I had to do was to believe on the Lord Jesus Christ. I didn't have to dance around the cross or confess to the Pope, to the bishop or to the priest.

Here was the remedy – the Cross of Calvary; and the moment I realised that, I said, 'Lord Jesus, I'm not a mediator, I'm not a priest, I'm a sinner and need a Saviour,' and the moment I did that I was saved. I could sing with Charles Wesley, 'My chains fell off, My heart was free, I rose, went forth, and followed Thee.'

They tell me that they have given me the works in the Catholic Church, they've given me the bound book and candles, which means to say that they have closed the book and my life is at an end. They've extinguished the candle, which means to say that my life has gone out before God, but that small light that was kindled there on the hills of Donegal in Ireland has gone on and flamed until He led me into this new experience of the baptism of the Holy Ghost and fire. My name has been written out of the Catholic book, but I thank God there's a new name written down in Glory and it's mine, oh yes it's mine and tonight my name is in the Lamb's Book of Life and this is the most wonderful thing of all. Truly it is wonderful what God can do and I am so glad to be able to testify to this fact, that God can save Catholics even today. [9]

Henry Archer

Here we have the faithful pastor of a West Indian assembly in Derby. It was tragic when very early one morning, he was killed in a road accident between Uttoxeter and the Potteries. This was in March 1969 and he was only aged forty-two. There was always an extremely close link between his church and the Glory Way, and when Henri celebrated his Eightieth Birthday in 1988 it was this warm-hearted fellowship of West Indians who were the hosts. In this following testimony Henry Archer tells quite simply how he came to true saving faith in Christ:

It was not in a church but in my own home that God saved my soul. I had no man to instruct me in the way of salvation but I thank God for a real experience whereby I can say without any shadow of doubt that I know I am saved. Brought up in a Christian home, I was told the story of our Lord Jesus Christ and taught to believe in God, but did that change my life? No, not at all. As a young man I wanted to have a good time in the world and I sank deeper and deeper into sin.

Seeking for life I began to travel to other countries. I saw all the worldly life in the USA. I went back to Jamaica the same as I had left. Two or three Sundays each year I would attend church and think that I was OK.

In the year 1948 I left Jamaica for England still following a life of sinful pleasure. I wanted to hit the headlines and make some quick money, so I took up the boxing game and became a professional boxer. I remember fighting at Leicester and appeared on the same bill as Don Cockell and Johnny Williams and the next day I felt so good when I saw my photograph in the paper. I used to pray to God to help me win in the ring, but I was praying in vain and when I suffered a defeat I always wondered why God had not answered me; but now I know that I was not asking according to His will.

Seven years after coming to England, God began to work in my life. It began with a vision that I had of the Lord sitting on a cloud with a rod in his hand and He looked me straight in the eyes: it was not a pleasant look. Because I thought the vision was but a dream, the consequences of too much to eat the night before, I just carried on having what I thought was a good time. It is recorded in the second Psalm, verses 9 to 11, *'Thou shalt break them with a rod of iron; Thou shalt dash them in pieces like a potter's vessel. Be wise now therefore, O ye kings: be instructed, ye judges of the earth. Serve the LORD with fear, and rejoice with trembling.'* If I had known this I might have realised that the vision was no idle dream, but God speaking to my heart and trying to show me that I was on the wrong track.

The last Sunday night in October 1955, I was in a public house drinking and singing to the old piano that was banging away, when I heard a voice speak to my heart and it said to me, 'What will you tell Jesus if He should come and find you in here?' The next day being Monday I went to work as usual and there Jesus began to use the rod of iron on me. My head began to pain me, followed by pains in my stomach and my legs shook so much that I could hardly stand and one of my workmates said how pale I looked, and since you can see the colour of my skin you will perhaps realise how ill I felt. I began to think that my time had come and I was not ready to meet death. Being a hell-bound sinner and not knowing better I lifted my eyes to heaven and asked God why He was causing me to suffer? Thank God He did not come to call the righteous, but sinners to repentance, and He was merciful to me. Praise His holy name.

Again I opened my mouth unto the Lord and said these words, 'My Lord, if you will heal me this day, I will serve you and give you praise the rest of my life.' In a split second I was completely healed and made strong and I began walking up and down the workshop. A few minutes before I had vomited up all that I had eaten that morning and now I could hardly believe that I was healed in so short a time. So to prove to myself that I was well again I ate and drank my fill and felt none the worse for it. Glory to my Lord and my God.

When I arrived home that night I sat down and thought of what the Lord had done for me that day and I began to weep before Him. Remembering what I had said to God if He healed me, I sank to my knees and repented of all my sins and I asked the Lord Jesus to come into my heart and to write my name in the Book of Life. That night I knew that my sins were all forgiven and, a few months after that, I was in my home praying to God and I began to speak in a new language that I had never spoken before and I felt the presence of God so real.

I began to read my Bible to see if it would throw any light on this new experience and I came across the second chapter of Acts, and I found that what had happened to the disciples on the day of Pentecost had also happened to me. God had baptised me with the Holy Ghost. Hallelujah! My friends, it was like rays of liquid glory. Praise the Lord.

Now that I was a real child of God I began to consider going to church, but I could not make my mind up concerning which one I should go to, as there were so many different denominations all claiming to be right. I thought the best plan would be to look for a people who had got the same as I had got, so I went to a Pentecostal Church, but to my surprise I found the people were cold and not hot as Pentecostals should be.

I wondered where to go next, when a Glory magazine came into my hands, so I decided to make the trip to Newark and see if there was any fire in Brother Henri's meetings. Thank God this glory that Jesus gives according to St John 17:22 is real. My brother and sister, if you want to see the power of God and the Spirit of God and the love of God, then go to Newark. I pray that Jesus will open your eyes to see that this glory is real. Hallelujah! [10]

Bill Welsh

In 1951 a young Scotsman called Bill Welsh was stationed at Syerston RAF aerodrome, four miles south west of Newark. It was not long since he had become a Christian, and the pastor of his Assemblies of God church was Stephen Black, the husband of Gladys, who were near neighbours of Henri and Connie. Throughout his life Bill has been most grateful to the Blacks for the trouble they went to in befriending him, and building up his faith. He wrote,

> Pastor Black used to take me on a Sunday afternoon to Sherwood Forest and teach me the Word of God from his ever open Bible. Only eternity will reveal the extent that these wonderful people blessed me with in nurturing a new convert in Christ.

Stephen and Gladys Black worked for a farmer in the village of Long Bennington, and one day Henri came to the farm while Bill was there. He writes of the meeting,

> Like Zacchaeus of old he at first sight was to me little of stature. However I was about to be introduced to the inner anointing on this man's life at this time, for having been introduced to me by Gladys, he promptly proceeded to sit down at the piano and began to play. There were three ladies there that day, if I remember correctly, including Gladys. Henri went along those octaves as though each octave was a close friend and each single note were a relative of his, for he knew that keyboard like the front and back of his hands. While he played he began to sing the words of the choruses he was playing, being joined by the three ladies present.

Bill Welsh did not know the choruses, but something in his spirit responded deeply to Henri's fullness of joy and anointed playing. He was so busy watching Henri's hands that he did not notice the three women had keeled over on the floor. When he noticed them there he was startled. Forty-seven years later this still stuck vividly in his memory, adding that what always thrilled him about the Glory people 'was their insatiable capacity for joy'. Bill continued,

> My next meeting with brother Henri was one he arranged with me himself. He invited me down to his shop in

Appleton Gate in Newark. When I arrived he was dealing with a lady who was in tears. She had got badly behind in her hire purchase commitment and obviously was extremely depressed. I well remember Henri saying to her 'Come on, my love, don't you worry,' and speaking to her of Jesus coupled with the remark, 'Don't you worry any more. We will arrange to reduce your payments until you get back on your feet.' Don't we need more of this very practical aspect of the Gospel today? Jesus spoke of letting others see our good works which, He Himself declared, glorified His Father in heaven.

Bill Welsh has one more snapshot of the Glory people at this early date when he was invited to a prayer meeting in the flat above the shop. Here he experienced the great enthusiasm of those around him. Henri said, 'You need a bit of joy, brother!' After this another man 'intoxicated with joy' grasped Bill while he was on his knees, lifted him up and danced him around.

Bill returned to Edinburgh in 1953, and in time became a preacher of the gospel. Years passed by, in fact a complete lifetime of work. It was in the summer of 1997 that Roy and Betty Hollingworth were in the Isle of Skye on holiday and got into conversation with a man at the Kyle of Lochalsh. They were amazed to find that he knew Henri and Connie in the early days and that they had probably seen or met him at that time. He turned out to be none other than this very same Pastor Welsh.

David Greenow

David Greenow, with his younger brother Glyn, was born and brought up in Hereford. The Lord called him, when a young man, to be an itinerant evangelist. He has this to say:

During the mid-fifties we began to hear of times of spiritual refreshing being experienced somewhere in Nottingham-shire. Then we heard further that the services were called 'Glory meetings', and that the channels being used were a brother Henri along with his wife Connie. There was a lot of difficulty accepting the term 'Henri's Glory meetings' and the critics were quick to say that they did not want anything to do with 'Henri's Glory'. Henri would say that it is 'God's Glory' – Amen. However, the reports of blessing persisted and we discovered that the blessing location was a place called Newark. People visited Newark and came back with glowing testimonies. Some had difficulty in accepting the reports and all kinds of rumours were flying around.

But news of this refreshing continued and in 1958 I was in Wales for meetings at a place called Llwynhendy. We were praying and believing for revival and were busy with our own programme, when a brother who came to our meetings said that he and his wife had been to the Newark Glory meetings, and gave us great accounts of them. He talked so much about these Glory meetings that we were probably rather annoyed by this repeated news of blessing. What did these folk have that we didn't have? I had been tremendously affected by what was called 'the latter rain visitation' in 1951 in Wales. There was a great move of the Spirit that impacted many lives for good.

Then I arrived in Ireland in March 1952 and some of the blessing of the 1951 visitation was moving there. Many fasted and prayed and in 1954 the hand of God moved in a big way, so much so that multitudes found Jesus as Saviour, Healer, Baptiser and Miracle-worker. There was a tremendous sense of the presence and power of God in every gathering. What, then, had these Glory folk that we didn't have? The day came when Bob Nicholls and some of the Glory team came into South Wales for a holiday and the brother who was always on about the Glory Way asked if they could come where we were for some meetings and fellowship. This was the test, and I can remember discussing with the leading brother whether or not we should receive these Glory folk. We decided that we should and then we would see and be able to judge for ourselves what we thought of it all.

They came and there was much blessing in the first couple of services, and then we heard that Henri himself was on his way down from Newark to join the team. I remember preparing to meeting him – after all we had heard so much concerning him. He arrived and, throwing his arms around me said, 'I do love you, brother.' I was totally disarmed, and Henri and the team won our hearts completely and great blessing resulted. There seemed to be such a ring of reality about everything they did, and there was such a beautiful flow – nothing forced – in the testimony, ministry and song as they sang, *If ever a time we needed the Lord, we surely need Him now*, and other anointed songs. Henri said something that first night in 1958 that I have never forgotten and have often quoted since: 'If we love one another, everything else will work out all right.' I remember thinking, 'How true!' I had experienced much blessing and witnessed God's power in action, but here was an emphasis on and an experience of love that I had never encountered before. I remember going to embrace brother Henri after that first meeting and the anointing upon him was of love. I certainly felt it.

The next year was my first visit to the Newark Glory meetings, and what a blessing I received! It was August convention time and there was a glorious atmosphere of love, joy, peace and praise. I had been missioning in the south of Ireland and I felt discouraged and exhausted. Brother Henri called me out in the first meeting and seated me at the front. No one touched me as I sat and wept and the renewing love of God flowed into me through the brothers and sisters around me. I was revived, Hallelujah! There was a precious flowing together in love, joy and peace. I have never forgotten the end of the final evening when they cleared the floor of the seating and danced and sang:

Life is wonderful, oh, so wonderful,
Life is wonderful now to me.
I let Jesus in,
He changed everything.
Life is wonderful now.

I had never seen it on this wise before, but, as brother Henri used to tell us, 'If there were more happy Christians, there would be more Christians!'

It was my privilege to visit the Newark Glory meetings several times after that. I had the joy of taking part in many of the gatherings in Newark and in different parts of the country where the Glory team ministered. Emily and I along with thousands of others will ever be grateful that we came under the influence of the Glory ministry. I have since been in a fellowship team with other brothers, preaching and serving the Lord for well over thirty years, and found we could work together in an ongoing relationship. I am convinced that so much of this is due to the bonding of the love of Jesus we found in the Glory meetings. There was such heart warming reality about brother Henri's ministry and the whole church needs this 'mighty baptism of love' which he spoke of. Certainly, my life and thousands of others were impacted by the Glory move of God and I have never been the same again. Praise God!

In 1969 the troubles began in Ireland and by 1972 there was tremendous hate and hurt because of the situation. Henri was in Fleetwood, Lancashire, and I with friends made my way over. My heart was hurting with the Northern Ireland problems, but I had an unforgettable time in the meetings as the love of God flowed, and in one service I experienced what I have likened to standing under a waterfall, but this was a *lovefall*, for Jesus's love was pouring down all over me. Hallelujah! There was so much experienced in those meetings and through the Glory ministry that could never be forgotten by those who were there: the loving welcome and acceptance, the tears of repentance, joy and devotion as people felt the reality of Jesus and His love, the inspiring testimonies and uplifting ministry, relationships being restored or strengthened, hearts overflowing, faces shining, anointed and exuberant singing and dancing unto the Lord.

Henri would say, 'This gospel works. It's the love!' We had a foretaste of heaven. Family members and friends were changed and blessed by the heart reality that pervaded the atmosphere. Meetings often concluded with the singing of 'Hail Saviour, Prince of Peace,' or 'God be with you till we meet again.' Then we left to face whatever the future days might bring, lifted in heart and boosted in our faith, for brother Henri reminded us that, because of Jesus, 'Every day is a good day, but some days may be better than others.'

Only eternity will reveal how far-reaching the influence of the Glory ministry has been. I for one can gladly testify that my life has been touched and transformed and I am extremely thankful that this love, joy and peace ever reached me, ever came my way. Truly, these were times of refreshing from the presence of the Lord. Thank you, Jesus. Thank God for the Glory.

Douglas and Lily Aistrup

Born in Holbeach, Lincolnshire, in 1942, the third of four children, Douglas had a very happy childhood. His father was an ophthalmologist; his mother was a great organiser and was full of fun.

Doug had a terrible experience even as a teenager of being drawn into drinking and very quickly becoming a chronic alcoholic. But God had His hand on him. In his late teens, when he was fitfully following a course of study in Norwich, he lodged with a woman whose son had been saved in Malaya during World War II as a prisoner of war in a Japanese camp. A Malayan Christian woman would push food under the fence and witness to the prisoners, risking her own life. This man now witnessed to Doug about the Lord and took him to an Elim evangelistic meeting, where an eyeless man started to grow new eyes. This deeply impressed Doug as his father told him it was totally impossible. It was not until eight years later that he heard the gospel yet again, with much of that time spent in hospitals and the first addiction unit of its kind to be opened in this country at Nottingham. Although having held some responsible management posts, he ended up not being able to care for himself. After a period in hospital it was decided that he should stay weekdays in a hostel attached to what was then the Redbourn Iron Works in Scunthorpe, taking up the post of sweeping floors in the Instrument Department with his weekends spent in hospital in Lincoln. However, although the Chief Engineer knew his situation, as the company had a working relationship with the hospital, he was soon upgraded to manage and re-organise their works stores.

After a few months of continually falling off the wagon, he joined Alcoholics Anonymous who helped him stabilise. It was at about this time that he felt a deep spiritual longing within himself and decided to try a few different church meetings, which did not meet his need. Then one day he was walking by a building with the word Elim above the door. This rang a bell and the following Sunday he decided to try it. An evangelist from Canada, Bert Dearden, was preaching the gospel. Doug yielded his heart to the Lord, and was filled with such joy that he did not realise for a fortnight that he was not craving alcohol. At that time Doug was befriended by Roland and Josie Steeper, who spent hours with him, even into the late hours of the night, instructing and reading their Bibles with him.

One evening they put on a Glory tape with Roy Turner singing. This had such a profound effect upon him and they invited him to go to a Glory meeting in Thorpe Hesley, where, upon entering the meeting, Doug was swept off his feet and felt 'he had come home'. Thereafter, Doug followed round after the Glory folk, travelling with Henri, Connie and Roy Turner. Finally he married Lily Bainbridge from Cockfield and settled in Louth in Lincolnshire, where he met a pastor called Gordon Fovargue, who ran a meeting in the town. One free Sunday evening Doug decided to go to Gordon's church taking his tambourine with him. This he placed under his seat, as the meeting was very quiet and subdued. At the end of the meeting Gordon asked if anyone had a hymn and, suddenly prompted from within, Doug asked for *O for a thousand tongues to sing*. The Holy Spirit came upon that meeting. An elderly man tapped Doug on the shoulder, pointing to the tambourine saying, 'Play it'. Over and over again, waves of blessing swept through the place. He was asked, 'Who are you? Will you put on a meeting?' Doug invited Roy Turner over. There was much blessing, and from there he set up a mid-week meeting at the back of his business premises, later moving to a larger hall. Mention must be made of Frank and May Gostlow and their daughter Mandy, who came into the Glory Way through these meetings. They travelled with Doug to the early Fiskerton meetings, which they have now staunchly supported over many years, bringing with them many others into blessing.

Doug and Lily with their young son Matthew subsequently moved to the north of England. In March 1993 he received a tremendous anointing. This is his testimony,

> I was invited to speak at a Full Gospel Businessmen's meeting in the north of England. After giving my testimony, I felt strongly I should invite the people to come forward, hold hands and pray. A prompting came from within to pray for a particular lady as I laid my hand upon her. To my great surprise she burst out laughing and collapsed onto the floor. A gentleman next in line stood looking down at her with great consternation. I heard myself saying, 'Do you want the same?' The Holy Spirit came upon him in similar fashion. Turning around and walking toward another man, a word of knowledge came to me. 'You are depressed.' 'Yes! Yes!' was the reply, 'I have been suffering from depression for months.' I laid hands on him in the name of Jesus. Joy flowed out of that man as the Holy Spirit came upon him. 'Please pray for me,' another man said. 'I want what these people have.' Just a touch in the name of Jesus and the man fell to the floor with the most powerful and magnificent tongue pouring from him.
>
> Many others were prayed for but, to cut a long story short, at the close of the meeting, the leader addressed the

people, partly apologising for what the Holy Spirit was doing in our midst. He stopped in mid-sentence, pointed to a musician and asked if he had been prayed for. The musician responded, saying he wanted more of God, and the leader asked me to pray for him. I suggested that the first two people who had been released into such joy should pray for him. The musician moved into the centre aisle. I stood with my hands behind me and my back to the lectern, where the leader stood with his wife. The pair started to pray for the musician and it was just as if somebody had lit a fuse. Suddenly the people were falling about laughing and rolling on the floor. There was an almighty crash from behind me; the leader's wife had collapsed onto the floor, taking the lectern with her.

Well, I sat in my car before going home, to try and make sense of it all. What strange happenings, what joy. 'It really is You, Lord.' I knew that, because of the burning fire of joy deep within my being. The Holy Spirit impressed upon my heart to speak of Jesus and tell of His love, 'And suddenly I will surprise you and anoint you, that many may be touched in this land in these last days and I shall transfer My power from one to another, if you will obey My promptings within you.' Over the past few years, with great trepidation, heart searching, trials, tribulation and much joy, we have seen the Holy Spirit moving in tremendous power in meetings, up and down this country, where there have been hungry hearts as we have told of Jesus and His love. His precious Spirit has come among us in dynamic power, changing us and filling us with His unconditional love, so that we may be partakers of His heavenly kingdom here on earth bringing many souls with us to Glory. [11]

Since then Doug has held rallies in Darlington, Northallerton with Brompton village nearby and Hollybush Fellowship; then also in Skipton, Pontefract, Harrogate, Ripon and Lincoln. Many have travelled from all parts of the country to these meetings and have been tremendously quickened and filled with much joy, with the deliverance of alcoholics, drug addicts, depressives, healings and salvation and the testimony continues. Doug is also much involved with the Glory meetings countrywide, having a close working relationship with Alan and Shirley Churchill with whom he has maintained a close friendship over many years. In closing he recollects a particular incident:

Out of all the journeys we have made over the years, one of the funniest experiences was when Henri Staples, Ron Wray, Chris Wingfield, David Willows and myself were returning home in Chris's caravette after taking meetings in Peterhead. We left around midnight, stopping off at an all-night café in Stonehaven. On returning to the caravette it refused to move as the clutch was not working so, with David driving, the rest of us had to push the caravette to jump start it and then, one by one, jump in at the side door, falling on top of one another. There was much singing, banter, praying and sleeping.

At about 3 am we arrived at the Tay Bridge, Dundee. The engine stalled and the man in the tollbooth said we couldn't go over the bridge and that we had to push the caravette backward away from the entrance. This we proceeded to do, but it fouled a magic eye that set off a loud siren, which could be heard all over Dundee. It was like a cartoon with the way the tollbooth man was jumping up and down shouting, 'Push it forward, push it forward!' When we eventually managed to move it, the siren stopped and the tollbooth man said we had better go across. Can you imagine it? There we were, three of us, pushing the caravette, Ron, David and myself with Henri lying on the bed inside and Chris at the wheel. As the van started, all three of us chased it across the bridge. Ron leapt in, followed by me with David bringing up the rear. We all ended up in a heap on the bed, thankful that we had not been left behind.

Continuing our journey we arrived on the road leading up to the Forth Bridge, which is a toll bridge with a tollbooth at the far end. Chris was determined that this time he wasn't going to stop. Who could argue with Chris? So, much to the surprise of the man in the tollbooth, Chris, driving as slow as he dare so as not to stall the engine, threw the money into the booth shouting, 'I can't stop. Clutch gone!'

At about 4 am we arrived in Edinburgh with its many traffic lights. Wondering what we were going to do we started to pray that all the lights would be green and, would you believe it, they were! After leaving Edinburgh Chris noticed the caravette was running out of petrol and, travelling on the Jedburgh road, there were no petrol stations open.

HENRI AND HIS MUM GRAN STAPLES

CONNIE AND HENRI

JANIE AND ALBERT CONNIE'S PARENTS
ON HENRI'S ROOF GARDEN AT JALLANDS ROW

HENRI'S 80th BIRTHDAY

CONNIE

HENRI'S BOAT

BORN AGAIN

I MUST WORK THE WORKS OF HIM THAT SENT... WHILE IT IS... THE NIGHT CO... NO...

ERIC, WYN RICHARDS
CONNIE AND
ARTHUR BURT

CONNIE AND
VERA WRAY

CONNIE CHRISSIE CAMERON
AND ROY AT PETERHEAD

IDA MARTIN
BILLY BRAY'S CHAPEL

SALLY & ERIC BILLS, LENA
GREEN, DAVID PHILLIPS,
CONNIE AND ROY

ROY TURNER

FRANK PREUDHOMME AND
HENRI AT ISLE OF WIGHT

JOHN, ALEC, SIMON
MICHAEL AND DAD CAMERON

ROY, RON, JOY, CONNIE
AND CHRIS AT BASILDON

CONNIE AND TO THE
RIGHT WENDY AND
PHILIP CAMERON

GRAN STAPLES, JOAN
AND CONNIE

HENRI AND TO THE
RIGHT JOAN BETWEEN
MR AND MRS ADAMS

JOHN, ANN, ALEC, CHRISSIE, SIMON CAMERON AND ROY

GIB AND CHRIS

WALKING ADVERT IN OXFORD

CONNIE, SHIRLEY & LIZ CHURCHILL JOY WELLDON ALAN C. & JIM W.

THE BAINBRIDGES AND DOUG AISTRUP

HENRI AND ROSE HULL

ROLAND RON AND CHRIS AT FISKERTON

DAVE WILLOWS

GLADYS MAULSON

MARGARET AND BRUCE HYATT

BILL MAULSON

MICK AND SUE COPEMAN

ALAN AND SHIRLEY CHURCHILL

BILL AND MARGARET PRIGMORE

DOUG AISTRUP

BETTY AND ROY HOLLINGWORTH

NORMAN AND JOAN PARSONS

FRANK AND MAY GOSTLOW

DAVID AND MARGARET JARVIS

PETER & VIOLET COWLING

BRIDLINGTON AT CONVENTION TIME

FISKERTON AT CONVENTION TIME

Jerusalem Joy

FISKERTON NEW YEAR 1991

Jerusalem Joy

SMILE LOVE GLORY

BRIDLINGTON CONVENTION GROUP

At around 5 am, on entering a small village we stopped at a little petrol station with a house attached and woke up the occupant, begging him for petrol, which he kindly gave us, dressed in his pyjamas. He 'saved our bacon'. Again we had to push the caravette off, in like manner as before. When we reached Newcastle at about 7 am there was early morning traffic including slow milk floats. We prayed our way through every hindrance and red traffic lights, 'In the name of Jesus', without having to stop, finally arriving at the home of the uncle of Ron's wife in Harrogate, to be greeted with much love and care before continuing our journey for another three hours to Nottingham without mishap.

What joy, what fellowship even in the midst of adversity. How we have laughed many times since at this and other experiences.

Mick and Susan Copeman

Another young man – from Nottinghamshire – who began to tread the Glory Way was Mick Copeman. He has this to say:

As I look back I am sure my great grandad was saved. Sunday mornings found him weeping in worship as he joined in the morning service. He died when I was about ten but I will always remember my father taking me to see him just a couple of days before he died. He was a lovely chap. When I walked into the room to see him he grabbed my hand and hung on. His face was radiant; he could not say much but he just lay looking at me with intense eyes and a loving smile. I am sure that man prayed for me as he was laid, waiting for the Lord to take him. I am so glad he did. I was nineteen when the Lord came into my life. When my parents realised that I had become 'religious' life became very difficult at home. They just did not agree with 'it'. I had led quite a rebellious life up until then. A lot of what I had done they did not know about, but what they did know was bad enough and it had caused them considerable pain. This just seemed to cause them even more pain.

The likelihood of 'God' seemed remote to me. I looked at what was happening: wars, starvation, the horrendous crimes of humanity. How could there be a God if He would allow all of that to happen? – common theme. Of course, our perspective is not right and we fail to see the root cause for all of these things. There is one loose in this earth that has perverted and seeks to destroy the creation. He will use whatever and whoever he can to further his purpose. But Satan's days are numbered: sentence has already been passed upon him.

I was brought to the Lord through the faithful witness of the Wingfield family. Chris just would not leave me alone until I finally consented to attend one of his meetings; I only went to keep him quiet. It happened at Scunthorpe. I saw a man wonderfully healed. Apparently I was the only one of a large congregation to witness this act, but I was transfixed. An atheist suddenly saw the truth; I also felt the warmth and love that these people had one for another. Henri and Chris came and asked me if I wanted to give my heart to the Lord. I said yes. They prayed. I was not aware of anything happening.

Everyone else was really excited that I had got 'saved'. Perhaps I would feel different later. I left the meeting full of questions, full of self-doubt. Six weeks later there was another meeting. They got me up to tell everyone what had happened to me. I told them but I did not tell them how confused I felt. Henri prayed for me again. This time something wonderful happened. I just lay on the floor weeping and praising God. The experience was totally beyond my control and I knew it. I felt so different.

That sequence of events was the start of the greatest adventure. At that time He set me free from smoking. Since then I have never had nor wanted a cigarette to this day. He is a real friend and He has supplied all my needs and guided me through a great part of my life. He found me a lovely wife. The love between us has blossomed as we have grown together and we have a son Paul who has a wife and children of his own now.

In the early days I used to travel all over the UK with Henri and the Revival Team. We saw some mighty times as the Lord changed lives through this powerful deliverance ministry. I remember going to a meeting at Thorpe Hesley and meeting a young chap called Doug Aistrup who the Lord had delivered from chronic alcoholism. He has been like a brother to me. Truly God is no respecter of persons. I also travelled with David Willows and again the power of God was mighty. I especially remember the Wimbledon meetings and the Surrey Folk with great affection. The Lord continued to bless our family. For a short period I took the meetings at Fiskerton and then the Lord moved me on. During a period of great trial I found the Lord leading me into a richer, deeper experience with Him. The Lord constantly abides but there are times when He puts a specific landmark in our lives.

In 1993 the Lord started to deal with me in a way that would radically change my relationship with Him and the ministry He has used me in. I would drive home from the office praising and worshipping the Lord. Before long I would be weeping and seeking God; so much so that at times I had to stop the car. Such a hunger came upon me that I started to spend more and more time on my own just seeking the Lord. I was desperate for more of Him. This went on for some time. Then one weekend I went with Doug and Alan to a Rodney Howard-Brown meeting in Bradford. The Lord directed him to pick me out and pray for me. I was slain in the Spirit, and stayed there for the rest of the meeting, stuck to the floor. I could not move! I remember repeatedly saying to the Lord, 'Whatever you need to do just do it.'

I have never been the same since. The Lord did it, just as though a veil has been removed. He has opened my understanding. The Scripture has become alive. Revelation just flows and the Presence of God in my life is so real. I just marvel at what He has done. I really cannot believe how different my experience is now. He has always used me but I seem to have entered into a new dimension. Wonderful Jesus! From that time on I feel as though I have been in school. The Lord is preparing His people for His great end-time revival when many more will come to know Him.

Now we travel the country blazing this message of Love and the Lord is greatly blessing us. There is much more to follow. That feeling of great hunger has never left me and I constantly find myself seeking more of Him. If we want to operate in the power of the Holy Spirit we must have that vibrant, intimate relationship with the Lord. We need to realise the significance of recognising our place in the Vine and all that being a branch means, what we need to do to bear fruit and what happens when we do bear fruit. Start giving Him more time from today and realise your potential in the Spirit.

Sue and I regularly attend the Beacon Hill Revival Centre on Beacon Hill, Newark, where a warm welcome awaits you.

If you do not know the Lord Jesus Christ as a real friend and Saviour, you can. It's easy. All you need to do is invite Him into your life. Just get on your own and say these words with me now:

Lord Jesus, I ask You to come into my life right now. I acknowledge that through Your death on Calvary You have redeemed me and I am now a Child of God. Cover me in Your precious blood, Lord Jesus, and cleanse me from all impurity. Come into my heart and change me now. Teach me to walk with You and build a relationship with You. I want to know You Lord as a real Friend and Saviour. Thank You, Lord Jesus, for saving me.

Alan and Shirley Churchill

Alan was born and brought up in Basildon in Essex. On leaving school at fifteen he says that he had no particular ambition and aim in life and was very sceptical about God. He started working in an agricultural manufacturer's, Howard Rotovators Ltd, and it so happened that one of his first supervisors was David Tourle, who encouraged him to attend a Sunday afternoon Covenanter Bible class of which he was the leader. Through them, after a year or so, he was taken to a Tom Rees Rally held in the Royal Albert Hall. Faced with the clear challenge of the gospel, he went forward and made a full commitment to the Lord Jesus Christ that night. That was in 1952. Alan recollects,

I was very sceptical, but I found the gospel worked. The main effect it had on me at that time was to make me more certain of what I wanted from life. I started a five-year apprenticeship and college and Christ gave me the drive after five years to pass the Higher National Certificate and become a design engineer.

It was at the same Brethren-style Bible class that Alan met Shirley, and they were married in 1956. Alan then had to do his two years of National Service in the RAF. He says,

I found this period a severe testing time as regards to achieving anything. As far as I could see the whole business was a complete waste of time. It gave me a desire, though, to use my freedom to the full on my return to civvy street.

This he proved in no uncertain way on his return home in 1958 to Basildon. He and Shirley began having fellowship with a group of people, including Jim and Joy Welldon (Shirley's sister), from all denominations who were seeking more of God. During an all-night prayer meeting, where they were praying for revival, Alan was baptised and filled with the Holy Spirit; something, he says, which revolutionised his relationship with the Lord.

About this time they attended their first Glory meeting. This was at Northfleet in Kent, in 1959. They only stayed one hour and walked out totally disgusted. But a seed had been planted. Alan says that he did not realise then that God works not on the outside, but on the heart. The love they felt in just one hour had got through to them, and within a couple of weeks their prayer group contacted the office in Newark and through them they invited Eric and Sally Bills to take a meeting in Langdon Hills. This was the beginning of regular meetings there, with various people coming down from Newark and staying with them.

Alan and Shirley then met up with Fred and Mary Johnson, whom they had known for some years, for Fred preached regularly at the undenominational chapel where they had been saved. The Johnsons had experienced wonderful things through the power of the Holy Spirit earlier in their lives in the Sunderland revival. Fred arranged Henri's summer convention in Southend-on-Sea at the Palace Hotel, looking out over the pier. More than six hundred came to these meetings. Large contingents poured in from Peterhead, Newark, Paddock Wood, the Isle of Wight and, later on, from Norwich. Roy Turner and a group of young people led the singing, introducing many new choruses. You needed to get there early to get a seat. The meetings were mightily anointed, and many hearts were touched. For instance, George Hughes, a very stout man who used to do the rounds from pub to pub, could not walk past the hall door. He was drawn in and was marvellously saved, Fred Carter leading him to the Lord. His Salvationist wife Margaret had prayed for him for years. George never looked back. He replaced strong drink with the wine of the Spirit, and it often took six of them to carry him down the stairs to the car after the meeting!

After the Southend convention, Archie Friday offered Fred Johnson a mobile church. It was a converted bus which folded out into a space about fifteen feet square and which held about sixty people. It was one of a number used by Archie for church planting. Fred put it on a site in a car park at Stanford le Hope, between Basildon and Tilbury. It was packed from the very beginning. Fred regaled everyone with stories of revival in Sunderland and how he had been filled with the Holy Spirit then. Their hearts burned within them, and fire fell again and again. There was hardly any room to go down under the Spirit; but people were saved and healed. After the Southend convention Connie visited the mobile church and it was a riot. Shirley and Alan took it in turns to go to the weekly meetings, for there simply was not enough room for the children to move around; the little church was so jam-packed.

In 1962 God miraculously made it possible for Alan to start in the design office at Ford Tractor. To return to the mobile church, it certainly proved to be too small. So in 1965 a group of the Basildon folk started meetings in the Kingswood Community Centre in the town; it was a large upper room.

In a convention meeting in 1966 at Northfleet, on the Kent bank of the Thames, God met with Alan in a new way. He says,

> He set me really free. I came to see that I didn't have to prop God up any more, that He had done the work of redemption on Calvary and all I needed to do was to enter in and enjoy it! I found reality, something nobody can talk me out of. God gave me a positive spirit and made me to be myself instead a patchwork quilt of what other people had tried to make me. I do thank God for the denominations in that they were responsible for my coming to know Jesus as my Saviour, but they had bound me with their traditional teachings. I had taken other people's word for what God wanted me to experience, not realising that in Christ I could have a first-hand relationship with Him. The flesh had condemned me for being less than God demanded on all counts, but the Spirit encourages me to be what I am in accordance with the power He has given. I do praise God for His down-to-earth ministry! He has taught me not to expect more of others than of myself, therefore I am not running after 'big men' any more. [12]

At this point we should mention a few of the people from the Essex area, who were touched by God at this time and who are now serving Him overseas. There is Royce Franklin who is church planting in Australia and New Zealand. His next door neighbour in Stanford le Hope, Bert Neil, was saved through the mobile church ministry and now has his own church in New Zealand.

While Fred Carter, a Spirit-filled brother brought up in the Salvation Army, is the pastor of a church in Western Australia.

In 1971 the Kingswood Community Centre was no longer available to them, so Henri, who was very friendly with Mr Burnstein, the owner of the Palace Hotel, arranged for them to move their meetings to the White Room, a large hall in the hotel, where they were able to stay for the next six years. Mr Burnstein was so keen for them to meet there weekly that he let them have the hall free; which was quite a surprise. During this time they teamed up with David and Selena Masters, a Jewish Christian couple. David worked at Ford Motor Company with Alan and they regularly preached and sang in the open air on the seafront at Southend. During this period Henri visited Southend a number of times.

In 1977 the Palace Hotel was refurbished and they had to leave the White Room. So they moved back to Basildon and started meetings in their house and then in 1978 at the Central Hall in Wash Road, on the edge of the large Noak Bridge suburb of Basildon, where they are today. It was a very simple mission hall built at the beginning of the 20th century for the local villages, placed rather out on a limb, with broad fields stretching away under a wide sky to Billericay on the north, and a copse of willow trees and rough ground on the other side. Much has happened in just over twenty years. The willows have gone and the feeling of wildness, as pleasantly variegated and well-built houses of the Noak Bridge estate nestle closely round the hall, which in turn has expanded and extended out of all recognition, with all mod cons. Alan and Shirley have not been slow to forge ahead by faith, as the Lord has given them opportunity.

It was also in 1978, after Bob Nichols death, that Alan and Shirley were called by God to take the responsibility for the Glory Office, moving it from Newark to Basildon in their home.

Alan writes:

> We are so grateful to God for the blessing we have gained from just seeing an advert in the local paper for Revival Meetings at Northfleet 42 years ago. This Glory changed our lives. It was hunger for more of God that drew us on and still does so today. We're even more hungry than ever.
>
> Those days were blessed, but today the horizon for the Glory Way is much greater. Henri's vision was for all the world to see the Glory. Connie used to say, sometimes wearily from trying to keep up with him, 'Won't you settle

for half the world, Henri?' He would reply, 'No! God says, all the world Thy Glory see!'

In 1992, just before Henri went to Glory, Alan was able to retire seven years early from Ford, where he had spent his final five years as Computer Systems Manager. This has given him and Shirley the marvellous opportunity to go full-time for God, to outreach both from the Glory Office and also the church at Basildon.

More Glory Witnesses

In the Bible we have the names of many people who are mentioned in passing. When the Apostle Paul sat down to write his great letters – particularly the one to the Romans – brothers and sisters in the Lord that he knew flooded into his mind. He held them in affection and he named them.

Very many people have come to Glory meetings at one time or another and God has touched their lives. There are those who have particularly pulled their weight in the meetings and who, through being blessed, have brought their own personal breath of joy to any gathering.

For years Roland Steeper from Scunthorpe has given his time and support to Fiskerton Chapel, his genial face welcoming many at the door. He has put his building skill and effort behind extensive refurbishing of the building. He is brother-in-law to Chris Wingfield; his wife Josie and Connie Wingfield are sisters.

Billy and Gladys Maulson, the parents of Susie Copeman, were long-standing friends of Henri and Connie. Billy worked along-side Henri in reconstructing Riverside Cottage at Fiskerton. He recalls once how they found a hollow space under a concrete floor. This meant breaking the floor up and relaying it, which they did, adding an extra four inches to the level. At the next maverick flooding of the River Trent the bungalow badly needed these extra four inches! Billy worked on the maintenance of the Technical College in Newark and had many contacts for the Lord among the students. He was also a clever violin maker.

The retired sea captain Des Ashley-Emile and his wife Gwen always spoke with an authority which comes through tested experience. In a storm Des was once swept off the deck by a wave which in the returning swell miraculously brought him back on board again. Recently God spared either of them much bereavement as they entered heaven within the same week.

Ruth, the daughter of Archie and Minnie Friday, was only in her twenties when she was tragically widowed. Then she worked at the headquarters of the Assemblies of God. In due time she married Ken Kemp who, during World War II, had had a hush-hush security job. They are both now part of the fellowship at Basildon where David Tourle lived. He was the link in the chain which led Alan Churchill to the Lord in 1952 and has now married Jean (née Guiteri) and lives in Mansfield.

Betty Micklewright from Moss Side in Manchester was deeply moved in her spirit by visits of the Glory team in the sixties. Ever since then, when she has been quickened by the Holy Spirit, it has caused her to dance supernaturally before the Lord. At Stoke-on-Trent we now have another Glory fellowship with meetings arranged by Keith and Beverley Scrimshaw. Beverley has a clear singing voice and her parents and grandparents were in the early Glory meetings in the Potteries. Nimble Peter Kenworthy and his wife Grace encourage our meetings with a transparent spirit of joy. Peter's cheer is expressed too in his accordion playing. His mum and dad from Selby brought their family into the Glory meetings in the early days. They had close connections with the Thorpe Hesley meetings with Jack and Claris Witham. (Claris was a powerful Holy Ghost lady.) They in turn had close links with three women from Barnsley: Olive Sidebottom, Mabel Hurst and Olive Race. Olive's son, Gerry Race, used to play his banjo in clubs and pubs; when he turned to the Lord he sold his instrument, but then bought it back again when he realised God wanted to use his rhythmic flair for leading choruses. Gerry's wife Mary, a retired schoolteacher, is well remembered for her timely and persistent words and Doreen Robinson for her enthusiastic exhortation. Olive Race also had an impact in the lives of Paul and Julia Elliott, also from Barnsley. Julia is a great encouragement with her words of exhortation and her skill on piano and organ, both at Fiskerton and the Glory holidays.

We are very blessed with musical talent. George and Jan Wakefield from Warrington lead the praise and worship at many of our outreach meetings, including our summer conventions. George has a way of mixing the old choruses with the new as he plays his guitar. He learnt many of his choruses from Lewis Cardno from Fraserburgh. Lewis was known to many of us as the singing fisherman. He will be remembered by many at the summer conventions in the sixties where he used to play his mandolin and sing to us in his own special style. Andrew

Churchill who plays the accordion is a great asset to all of our outreach meetings. He grew up in Henri's meetings and so has a fine ear for all the Glory choruses. He is a great blessing with his wife Karen at his home church, the Noak Bridge Glory Fellowship Basildon. Another pianist accompanying our singing is Margaret Hyatt, both in Basildon and at the Glory holidays. She has been filling this role ever since she was about ten years old.

Harry Ramsden as a young man beat featherweight champion Jackie Turpin and gained his gold belt. He was saved through the preaching and witness of Ruth, whom he married, and as business people they have stood for the Lord in Skegness. They have been running a café, His Place, in Skegness today as a centre for evangelism. Although seldom at the Glory meetings, there has always been a warm bond of friendship between them and Henri and Connie and the Glory people. Another sportsman who has greatly valued Henri's ministry is Tommy Smailes from Featherstone near Pontefract, one-time captain of the English Rugby team.

There were groups in many towns spread all over the UK where many were touched in the early days. Stan and Phyllis Powell from Hereford and their son David and daughters Judith and Cynthia came into the meetings through David Greenow. (These were at Evesham.) Soon after a gathering was started in Gladys and Will Davies's house in Hereford. Eric and Cath Weaver also came along and God touched their lives. Bill and Margaret Prigmore from Irchester in Northamptonshire enjoyed many visits of the Glory team during the sixties, as did Joe and Ivy Osbourne from nearby Wellingborough. David and Margaret Jarvis from Banbury and their family found the Glory Way in 1959 through the *Glory News*. It was like a breath of fresh air for them. As they travelled by car to their first meeting one of the rear wheels started to wobble badly. Her husband said, 'We'll have to turn back.' But she insisted, ' No! It's wobbling for joy. We must go on.'

In Doug's testimony we read about the Louth meetings and Frank and May Gostlow and their daughter Mandy. May came to know the Lord through the witness of a faithful pastor, Gordon Fovargue, and exercises a gift of discernment and knowledge. Frank suffered from intense depression but, praise the Lord, God delivered and saved him out of it. He has a fine solo singing voice for which we are very grateful in our meetings. Marjorie Curwood from Nottingham (now from Mablethorpe) was serving behind a bar. She felt her life was in a mess and she was at wits-end-corner. In desperation, at her back door, she called, 'O God, if You're there, help me!' And the Lord heard her and saved her. Henri christened her 'Sparks', because when she testified sparks would fly in the meeting.

Alan mentioned in his testimony the mobile church at Stanford le Hope near Basildon. It was during these early meetings both there and at Southend that many were touched by the Holy Spirit. Peter Richards and his wife Eileen (now in Norwich) came in during this period. Peter, a Baptist, worked with Fred Carter at the Bata shoe factory nearby and was encouraged to come along at that time. They used to have regular meetings in the factory and soon after Peter was introduced to Eileen at one of the meetings. Also during this time Mary Barton, from the Southend area, came along to Garon's Banqueting Hall and was prayed for by Henri and has never been the same. She now has fellowship with us at Basildon.

Linking with these meetings in Essex were a couple of people from London, Julie Jeffreys and Rose Hull. Many will call them to mind in the meetings at that time. Julie will be remembered for her dancing and infectious laugh, Rose for her string of bells and a football rattle which she would use with gusto on occasions during the praise. Rose was very encouraging to Henri, writing to him weekly. She would go to the butcher's and ask for wrapping paper and write long large letters of encouragement. She had a vision for what God was doing at that time, which was second to none, and would illustrate her letters with graphic pictures of the Glory – sparks and all.

One of the hall marks of these days was that people would travel just to get under the anointing that was being poured out. To drive from London to Peterhead in those days was a time consuming business. The motorways were only beginning to be built: few towns were bypassed. But people just turned up unannounced and the Spirit flowed. There was such an all-consuming joy in all these meetings, it made people hungry for more. The growth of the numbers of people who received something positive from the Lord was phenomenal.

Obviously this book can contain only a sprinkling of people who have followed on from the first group in the Glory Way. The Holy Spirit of God touched the lives of so many folk. They are far too numerous to include. So many more could be mentioned. If you have been coming to Glory meetings and your name is not here, please excuse us. The task is impossible. A great number of people have come in since 1970 with dynamic testimonies, but because of space we chose this as the approximate cut off date for inclusion in the book. As the Psalmist has said, *'The Lord shall count, when he writeth up the people...'* (Psalm 87:6). And the Apostle Paul adds, *'The Lord knows them that are His'* (2 Timothy 2:19).

Chapter 14

Glory Word

'It is often said that our Glory meetings are not scriptural, yet everything we say and do is backed home by the Scriptures.'[1] With these words Henri was at pains to answer a criticism that got bandied about. In fact, from the beginning of this century Pentecostal gatherings have been vulnerable to this charge, for the simple reason that they have made a stand for free meetings, depending on the leading of the Holy Spirit, without a carefully worked out *order of service*. This being so, the reading of Scripture and preaching of Scripture can get squeezed out. Certainly this is a danger that has to be guarded against.

But I must say this, that in the Fiskerton meetings which Henri led towards the end of his life – meetings that stick in my mind so vividly – he would take one of his favourite passages of Scripture, such as Psalm 118 or Isaiah chapter 61, and plough right through it, carefully reading and expounding it and applying it with great verve as he went along. Bert Kelly described Henri at a meeting in Manchester, in 1965: 'It was grand to see Henri in full swing, as he delivered the Word under the anointing of the Spirit.'[2] Henri himself said,

> The apostle Paul writing to the Philippians declared in chapter 1 verse 17, '*I am set for the defence of the gospel,*' and that folks is just what I am doing. It is absolutely true, the Spirit of the Lord is upon me and I am set for the defence of the gospel. Let me emphasise, the gospel.

Of necessity, that is expressed in God's Word. Freedom in the Holy Spirit does not and must not supplant in any way the practical use of the Bible and one's attitude to it. In an early copy

of the *Glory News* Bob Nicholls, the editor, made a clear statement, putting his cards on the table,

> our fundamental beliefs are just the same as most Chris-
> tians. We stand upon the divine inspiration of the
> Scriptures, believing that God gave His only begotten Son
> to die on Calvary to pay the penalty of sin for us. [3]

How painfully needful it is to spell out basic Christian
truth and not to take anything for granted. Pastor Richard
Wurmbrand, who suffered under Communist hands, languishing
for fourteen years in a Romanian prison, gave a serious warning
of rank unbelief to be found amongst church leaders:

> Anti-Christian forces have invaded the church. *Capitol
> Voice*, 1st August 1974, published the results of a recent
> poll: 51% of the Methodist ministers in the USA do not
> believe in Jesus' resurrection; 60% don't believe in the
> virgin birth; 62% contest the existence of Satan; 89% of
> Episcopalian priests don't believe the Bible to be the Word
> of God. They believe there is no truth. [4]

But Glory folk, by their very nature, witness to this truth. I
remember so well, at the end of the Hunstanton Glory holiday in
1985, the rugged retired sea captain Des Ashley-Emile, stocky
in stature, getting up and saying that the blessing he had received
that week would send him hurrying and scurrying back to his
Bible. Elderly Mrs Shaw from Birmingham wrote,

> I want more and more ... Our weekly Bible study is
> wonderful, and we are all fed on the finest of the wheat.
> Glory! Glory! [5]

Joyce Price of Basildon showed how the Bible and her
experience of the Lord went together.

> When you come into a Glory meeting and let the very
> depths of your soul open up to Jesus, you will find it fits all
> right. It will fit you and every word of Scripture that was
> ever written because it is the reality of God. [6]

Ann Scarbrow, a young person who collapsed with a nervous
breakdown and who was completely healed after Henri had
prayed for her, said this,

The Bible became like a living book to me. It was no longer the letter on the printed page but had become sharp and powerful – the sword of the Spirit of Life! [7]

A fascinatingly youthful testimony comes from Eunice Travis, aged twelve:

One day one of our masters asked us what we thought of the theory suggested by scientists that we came from apes. I raised my hand and quoted the scripture from Genesis which says, *'God created man in his own image'*. At this the master stormed out of the classroom but later he returned and asked me about the Bible. [8]

Eddie McAnally of Bradford explained,

One day I went along to a certain church to give a little of what God had given me and one of the brethren, when he knew I was Pentecostal, asked if I had got any credentials. I said, 'Brother, the only credentials I have got is the Word of God.' [9]

Peter Warsop of Loughborough opened out these thoughts:

The most important thing in life to all the human race is the revelation of God to man. The means of this revelation is by the Word of God. A word is the vehicle by which we transmit our thoughts from our hearts and minds to each other, and God expresses Himself to us by His Word ... In time past, men and women spake as they were moved by the Holy Ghost. These were the prophets and prophetesses of the Old Testament days; men and women who were clean through and through. God had cleaned them up and they became the mouthpiece of God to the people of their day. If there is one thing that must be a mighty experience, it is to know that you have been made the mouthpiece of Almighty God. What a responsibility. What a high calling. [10]

These quotations alone will convince anyone that the Glory folk take the Bible seriously. If people want more proof they do not have to look far, for scattered through the copies of the *Glory News* you will regularly find articles based on a scriptural truth, often applying a Bible story or doctrine to present-day experience. In the first twenty years of the magazine one can count up about forty different authors who have written provocative and perceptive contributions. In the first issue, in 1956, Connie wrote a piece with the title *Get Down off the Camel*, based on the moment recorded in Genesis 24:64 when Rebecca dismounted from her camel to meet her bridegroom Isaac. Connie was making the point that for long enough a church, an assembly or a denomination may have been giving you a ride, and that it is now high time for you to get down and make your own way on your own two feet, for the Heavenly Bridegroom is coming to meet you! In No. 43 Connie and Henri pointed to Ecclesiastes 3:14 *'I know that whatsoever God doeth, it shall be forever,'* showing that God's Spirit does an everlasting work in our hearts.

Bob Nicholls, of course, gave a guiding hand to issue after issue, with many thought provoking comments. For instance, in an editorial note he took 1 Thessalonians 5:21 *'Prove all things; hold fast that which is good,'* with the comment,

> Not some things, but *all* things. Brother, sister, don't accept all that men try to put over and leave it at that. Test it, prove it and see if it works. If it doesn't, then throw it overboard. The real things of God always did work. Get hold of this reality and your actions will not be motivated so much by what you think, as by what you know. You become steadfast, unmovable in the things that matter most. An ounce of experience is worth a ton of theory every time. [11]

In another editorial he took the case of the widow whom Elisha helped to pay her debts. He went on to link it with a saying of Jesus,

> Here then is the answer to spiritual poverty and emptiness: just start to pour out. There is a spiritual law in Luke 6:38 that will start operating in your favour, *'Give, and it shall be given unto you; good measure, pressed down, and shaken together, and running over.'* As long as you hold to yourself what God has given you, then you will feel you have got nothing; pour it out on somebody else and you will feel that you've got more than you know what to do with. [12]

Arthur Burt has a gift of expression and imagination all of his own,

How often have we said those words, 'Thy will be done in earth'? Where is that earth? Within you, my brother, within you, my sister. Reclaimed earth. Jesus came to reclaim earth for heaven, that in you the fruit of the Spirit might spring forth. [13]

Talking of Ephesians 3:20, *'Now unto Him that is able...'* Arthur Burt challenged his readers with, 'Our God is so big that you have never considered in your wildest moments how much He can do.' [14] When considering the ministry of the Christian body in 1 Corinthians 12:12–27, have you ever heard a comment like this?

Now if I had arranged the members in my physical body, I tell you straight, I would not have arranged it like it is ... I would never dream of putting two eyes at the front and none at the back. I would put one at the front and one at the back, so that I could keep an eye on the fellow behind to see what he is up to. [15]

Tom Spurr wrote articles for the *Glory News* full of Scripture and telling phrases,

Our God who *is*, who sits upon the throne, who spake and it was done, who created the world by the breath of His mouth, parted the Red Sea, broke down the walls of Jericho, stopped the mouths of lions, quenched the violence of fire, sent forth His Son into the world to destroy the works of the devil. [16]

Any contribution to the magazine by David Greenow was similarly packed with scriptural thoughts,

God has also given us a sound mind, for we have been made partakers of the very mind of Christ (1 Corinthians 2:16). The world may think we are crazy, but we are never more sane than when fully yielded to Christ and rejoicing in the goodness of God, for in Him we live and move and have our being. God has not just saved our souls for the next world and left us inadequate to face this one, but faith in Christ means *abundant life now*, and He is made unto us *wisdom*, so that we may face life with divine understanding and spiritual sanity. [17]

Leslie Walter (nicknamed Laughing Les) in an article *Love and the gifts* gave a masterly exposition of the Love Chapter, 1 Corinthians 13, showing that we must not treat it on its own. We do so at our spiritual peril. He argues the point most convincingly:

> It seems to me now that we have been separating this chapter from the one before and the one after, putting it on a pedestal, calling it a real gem concerning love. We have gilded and embellished it with words trying to expound the thing called *love*. It has been read, and still is, far more than chapters 12 and 14. It has been endowed with a lustre that has grown brighter as time has passed and all the time we have been missing the real meaning ... What 1 Corinthians 13 is describing is not the 'more excellent way' of love, but the 'more excellent way' of the gifts of the Spirit with love. This is a vastly different thing! [18]

These articles are only a tip of the iceberg of the biblical way in which the Glory folk have expressed themselves. When a believer is moving in the fullness of the Holy Spirit he will also be full of the Word of God. This is normal Christianity, and is as it should be. For it is not a question of either/or: either being the people of the Spirit or the people of the Word. That is ridiculous. The two things are complementary. Jesus accused the Sadducees of being wrong on two counts: not knowing the Scriptures, nor the power of God (Mark 12:24). The Bible is in fact God-breathed (2 Timothy 3:16) and *'holy men of God spoke as they were moved by the Holy Spirit'* (2 Peter 1:21). For instance, Psalm 95 verse 7 is directly ascribed to the Holy Spirit in Hebrews 3:7–8, *'as the Holy Spirit says, Today, if you will hear His voice, do not harden your hearts...'* Also, if you compare parallel verses in Ephesians and Colossians that speak of 'psalms and hymns and spiritual songs,' you will notice that the apostle Paul encourages the Ephesians to be filled with the Spirit and the Colossians to let the word of Christ dwell in them richly in all wisdom (Ephesians 5:18–19 and Colossians 3:16).

In this chapter I have shown that Glory people at their best, and against all criticism, have been true to the Word of God. And I feel duty bound to press the point that we must keep it that way. The apostle Paul exhorted Timothy, *'Preach the word! Be ready in season and out of season. Convince, rebuke, exhort, with all longsuffering and teaching ... do the work of an evangelist...'*

(2 Timothy 4:2, 5 NKJV). This is absolutely basic. It is not an optional extra. All true Christian people of whatever culture and clime must not flag in presenting the truths of the eternal gospel to everyone. There are two things which militate against this, two pitfalls, two dangers, in the same way that we must have *'the armour of righteousness on the right hand and on the left'* (2 Corinthians 6:7).

On the one hand the truths of the Bible have been undermined by liberal or modernist theology. This has been going on for two centuries or more and the net result of it has been absolutely devastating. Bands of doubting and unbelieving scholars have questioned every jot and tittle of the Bible and in the process they have done away with the miraculous and divested the Lord Jesus Christ of His glorious deity, treating Him merely as a great spiritual figure, spiritual genius or superman. This has made a mockery of His atoning death and triumphant resurrection. This liberal theology no longer regarded the Word of God as *'quick and powerful and sharper than any two-edged sword'* (Hebrews 4:12); it shook the personal faith of many people and deprived many would-be preachers of any conviction, confidence and true spiritual effectiveness. This onslaught wrought havoc, emptying churches and watering down the saving testimony to Jesus Christ until it became totally wishy washy and useless.

On the other hand there is the danger of quietism. And here I am coming a little nearer home. There is a strange possibility – and this is very ironic – that a group of Christians standing squarely on the foundation of the apostles and prophets and the chief cornerstone of Jesus, can yet sink into inactivity, into a kind of spiritual vacuum. The awful thing is that dependence upon the Holy Spirit and upon His leading and empowering can be given a deceptive twist and people drift into laziness and into a low expectancy of God working in the midst. Momentum is lost and what I care to call osmosis witness and osmosis evangelism takes over. Osmosis is the way a liquid can seep through certain partitions or membranes and gently mix with another liquid on the other side. In the same way it can be thought that simply to get non-Christian people into a gathering with a particular atmosphere will, in some mysterious way, bring them to true saving faith in Jesus Christ. Nothing much is said. They are just vaguely influenced. That of course is all right and quite helpful as far as it goes. But very very much more is needed. Seeking souls must not be left high and dry, bewildered and befogged. They must be clearly told what to do: to repent, to seek God with all their hearts, to seek salvation and be sure of it, to put out the hand of faith, to give their heart to God, to close with God.

To come back to osmosis, it is not enough for a liquid somehow to seep and creep into a bowl; it must be poured in briskly from the gospel jug. The Lord's people must be up and doing, filled with the Holy Spirit, holding forth the Word of life, making the truth as it is in Jesus crystal clear.

Chapter 15

Glory Healings

I n the summer of 1973 William Leadbeater was looking after his wife Audrey at their home in Margate. She was extremely ill; at death's door. She had had months of acute pain and for this had been taken into hospital for a minor operation. Unfortunately things went very wrong; she developed a fatal disease of the blood and felt she just wanted to die. Audrey said,

Two weeks after the operation I had a severe heart attack in hospital and, as the doctors gave me medicine to help the heart attack, they accelerated the internal bleeding. After a period of weeks they said I had approximately three months to live and sent me home for William to look after. At that time I weighed less than six stone and William used to carry me about like a baby. I had over a hundred stitches in my wounds.

It was at that time that we heard about the Glory Holiday at our local school. William had heard a tape but we had never been to a meeting. We decided to go on Monday evening. The school was only five minutes away but it took us half an hour to get there. I couldn't bear to get in the car.

For two evenings they went, but were not at all impressed with the meetings. On Wednesday Audrey took a turn for the worse. William said he would go alone to the meeting and leave Audrey behind. But something made her plead with him to let her come too. They sat towards the back.

Henri and several others were playing and everyone was singing. Suddenly Henri put down his accordion and came

to the back where I was and said, 'The Lord has told me to
pray for you because you're sick.' He took my hands; so I
stood up and he wrapped his arms right round me and I
screwed myself up inside, expecting severe pain, because if
anyone touched me it left a bruise and it hurt. But I didn't
feel any pain whatsoever. He prayed that the Lord would
heal me and, as he prayed, he cried from right down within
his heart. He sobbed his petition to the Lord. I felt a heat
from the top of my head; I felt this burning go right
through my body from top to bottom. Henri went back to
playing his accordion and I sat down next to William and
said, 'The Lord has healed me!'

It so happened that she continued to feel really ill for the next
couple of days, yet she was convinced that she had been healed,
and when she went to the hospital she was given a complete
all clear. Soon after, the pain left her and she never looked
back. What is more, her diseased blood was, as the specialist said,
101 per cent healthy and it was of a different blood group. She
said,

They accepted then that a miracle had taken place and
since then they have used the white corpuscles out of my
blood for cancer patients. So, praise the Lord, God really
does heal and it lasts... [1]

This whole question of healing is certainly a very contentious
area of Christian discipleship and belief. In Exodus, soon after
the crossing of the Red Sea, God assured the Israelites, *'I am the
Lord that healeth thee'* (Exodus 15:26). As God created us and gave
us life, this is only reasonable. Clearly the ministry of Jesus was
chock full of healings, as He poured out compassion on those
around Him, and after the resurrection He gave a promise to
His disciples that they would have the power to heal people
(Mark 16:18).

Many people, needing healing, have been very disappointed
when, however hard they believed, nothing has happened when
they have been prayed for. Yet, it cannot be denied that, in our
own century and within our own living memories, there have
also been many very remarkable cases of complete healing. The
Lord has given some people an outstanding ability to heal. In the
United States and Britain, Smith Wigglesworth, Stephen Jeffreys
and Kathryn Kuhlman spring immediately to mind.

As for Henri Staples, along with the remarkable anointing and baptism of the Holy Spirit which God gave him in 1948, he also clearly received the gift of healing. To some extent, several of his friends and associates did so too. Recorded in the copies of the *Glory News* there are about forty instances of healing. Of these there are at least fifteen in which Henri was directly involved; very likely a good number more. Outstanding from them (besides Audrey Leadbeater) was the case of Mrs Mary Reeves, who during her life had been in hospital fourteen times and had had eleven operations. She felt an absolute physical wreck. Her sister somehow got her to a Glory meeting in Newark, and she told God to take her broken and diseased body and do as He pleased, as it was of no use to her. She said,

> I went forward for prayer and as Henri prayed for me God healed me in a miraculous way. There seemed to be renewing of all my internal organs and my bones grew strong again. Since that time I have had no heart attacks, no more growths, and no illness of any kind. I feel perfectly sound through and through. Praise the Lord. [2]

To recount a handful of other cases: Fred Pullam of Walthamstow, wearing a steel belt, was healed of a double rupture. Frances Daw was cured of a serious stomach complaint in Paddock Wood when she felt the Lord's power go right through her. In Leeds Town Hall Henri laid his hands on a little girl who was heading for total blindness and her sight was completely restored. Linnette Thomas, a West Indian, for years suffered from a terrible stomach complaint that reduced her to nothing but skin and bone. She was prayed for and started eating and regained complete health and strength. Edna Robinson, wife of a Newark businessman lay at death's door with an undiagnosed disease. Henri and Ron Wray prayed for her and after two weeks she was discharged from hospital perfectly healthy.

Going back to the Mansfield Market days, Margaret Pailing recalls this unusual incident,

> Once when Henri was telling the large crowds about this Glory Way, a man in the crowd started shouting and heckling. Henri rebuked him and the open-air meeting continued without incident. On the way home, however, a car pulled alongside Henri and Connie; it was the heckler who had followed them. He told Henri and Connie that he had broken

his arm and was suffering pain. As usual, Henri spotted his opportunity and said, 'I'm going to pray for you, lad!' So he prayed for him at the side of the road and this man, who only an hour before had been heckling the Glory people, was healed there and then! He went on his way rejoicing and every whit whole, just as the folks did in Bible Days!

Then there is the case of Susanna Eden, who had tuberculosis of the bones. She had to be carried everywhere. 'By the time she was two-and-a-half years old she had dislocated her left arm three times, broken her collar bone and her feet had stopped growing.' For three years her parents took her out for prayer at their local assembly, but to no avail. Then they went to a Glory meeting in Stockport, and Mary Eden remembers how she was urged by her mother-in-law to ask Henri to pray for Susanna and she replied, 'No, I'm sick to death of taking her out for prayer. Nothing ever happens.' Then she heard an audible voice – but not a human voice – say, 'Just once more.' So she took Susanna to Henri. He put his foot on a seat, sat her on his knee, 'and he prayed so beautifully for her. He was really childlike, not shaking and crying, You come out of her, devil!' Mary knew instantly that her daughter was healed. She put her on the floor, tapped her backside and said, 'Run to Daddy.' And she did. Her legs were strong. However, one minor defect remained; one foot was smaller than the other. Her parents thought of it as her little thorn in the flesh, to remind her of her amazing healing.

When they next went to church, folk were astonished to see Susanna walking normally. Mary explained how her daughter had been healed when Brother Henri prayed for her. One man exclaimed, 'Eh? Henri? He's of the devil!' (To say the least, this was very reminiscent of accusations of the Pharisees against Jesus.) Mary replied,

> 'All right, you say it's of the devil. But he prayed for her in the name of Jesus and she was healed. For three years I brought her out here and nothing's ever happened. So therefore I must give the devil the glory.' Oo, by gum, you should have heard him. He nearly went mad. 'Oh, no, no, no!' I said, 'Ah, yes! You say he's of the devil. So it must be the devil who healed her. I know it's not. It was Jesus who healed her.' And, I mean, she's never looked back and that is why Brother Henri has a very very special part in our heart. We love him so much.

Susanna grew up a strong, fine girl. In her teens she played the violin and the piano accordion in a family music ensemble. In time she married and had children.[3]

On a good number of occasions people were healed in a meeting simply because they were there; Henri did not pray over them, nor anyone else. One might say, 'the power of the Lord was present to heal them' (Luke 5:17). Singling out some of these: Mrs Handley was suffering with kidney trouble and a terrible pain in her back. She came to an Easter Convention at Newark.

> I thank God that Jesus can deliver and heal in less than three seconds. I had not been in the church very long before the Master touched me, as I sat in my seat. The pain vanished and I jumped to my feet praising and thanking Him for His goodness. Hallelujah. I danced for joy for I was completely healed.[4]

For four years Mrs M. Dowers had been suffering from disseminated sclerosis and she believed that, regardless of what men said, Jesus could heal her and make her perfectly whole. Henri and his team came to Paddock Wood assembly and she sat in the front row.

> I was in an attitude of prayer, while Henri was praying for other sick folk, when the healing power of God fell on me. Immediately I felt a different person and I jumped to my feet and danced for joy. Many sisters and brothers were shaken, when they saw me dancing and praising God. It was wonderful. He not only healed my body but set my soul on fire and I mean to continue praising God all the days of my life. Hallelujah![5]

Mrs Vera Soulsby of South Shields lost her sense of balance and could not walk alone. Her condition became worse, until she became a prisoner in her own home. Her son arranged for her to have a holiday with her sister three hundred miles away in Maidstone. Whilst there she went to two of Henri's meetings. In the second one she sat enjoying the singing,

> then I closed my eyes and said, 'Lord, do something for me tonight,' and immediately I felt a tingling all over me. I did not realise it was the power of God, until I felt the urge to stand up, a thing I had not done for a very long time, and

then I said to the girl in the next seat, 'How are you off for a march?' She said, 'All right,' so off we went marching round and I discovered God had healed me. [6]

Others in the fellowship of the Glory Way were used in healing. Gib Rudkin, leader of the Surrey Group, prayed at Ringwood for a certain Sister Evans, whose spine in the past had been fractured, preventing her from running and jumping. She said,

> After prayer he asked me to lift a heavy piano stool up above my head. Now at this time I could not carry a heavy shopping basket, but in the name of Jesus I lifted the stool, which felt as heavy as iron, up above my head. Praise God! Then as the Holy Spirit took hold of me I began jumping up and down, a thing that I could not do before, as I would have been in great pain. This to me was wonderful. The time had come for me to catch my bus home, so Pastor Rudkin opened the door and told me to run for it. In the excitement of it all I forgot that I had been unable to run, but the Lord had so delivered me that I ran without thinking. [7]

David Greenow prayed for a young person, Sue Maulson (later the wife of Mick Copeman), who had been struck down with glandular fever and had rheumatics in her knees. She said,

> for one at the age of nineteen who had been in the habit of rushing about in top gear, to be reduced to crawling along at a snail's pace, I did not take kindly to it and I felt very sorry for myself.

As David prayed for her, the power of God swept through her body. She got off her chair and started to dance. [8]

Richard Hardy, who earned his living as a postman in Newark, was the pastor of Collingham Baptist Church. He had received the baptism of the Holy Spirit and power to serve the Lord. One day he visited a young Canadian, Roderick Smith, in Riseholme Farm Institute in Lincolnshire. Roderick's back had been injured in a jeep accident. Richard Hardy felt the Lord direct him to pray for him,

> so in fear and trembling he went to the bedside. 'I must have said one of the shortest prayers ever,' related Richard,

'Father God, heal this dear brother in the lovely Name of Jesus, Amen.' Thank God it is not the length of our prayers that counts. Richard heard later that the moment he left the room Roderick ... swung his legs out of bed and began to walk without pain or any other after effects. Praise the Lord!

Some time later Richard also prayed for a neighbour's six-year-old boy, Gary, who was ill with leukaemia. He was instantly healed, and proved to be the toughest youngster on their housing estate. [9]

In the case of Anne Wardley it was a question of great care and sympathy shown to her. At the end of three years of ill health Anne was a nervous wreck, could not speak properly and was muddled with drugs. Betty Hollingworth visited her a lot in hospital. Then Anne managed to get to a meeting in Beacon Hill Chapel in Newark and Bob Nicholls openly encouraged her to speak and testify. In the process of this God healed her completely and filled her with joy. [10]

In Acts 19:11–12 (NASB) we read, *'And God was performing extraordinary miracles by the hands of Paul, so that handkerchiefs or aprons were even carried from his body to the sick, and the diseases left them and the evil spirits went out.'* Henri did not doubt this, but acted upon it and it worked. Some people might think this is superstition, but, there we are, it is undeniably in the Bible.

Eleven-year-old Dorothy Duncan was going deaf and her parents became very worried. The child stopped going out to play with other children. But then one day she said, 'Mum, I know I won't have to have a deaf-aid because I keep telling Jesus I don't want one and I know He will make my ears better.' 'Well, Dorothy,' her mother replied, 'if you really believe Jesus can heal you, He will.' They sent away to the Glory Office in Newark for a healing cloth. When Dorothy went to bed she lay down with her ears on it and her parents prayed that she would hear again. Next morning she went out to play with the other children and when a wrist watch was held up to her ears she could hear it ticking perfectly. [11]

Edith Lovely from near Grimsby was extremely ill with a blood disorder. She said,

My sister was a Christian and I wrote to her asking her to pray for me and she in turn wrote to her mother-in-law Mrs Clark, at Newark, who had prayed for me the night I was converted. A lovely letter came through the post and enclosed was a healing cloth. Mrs Clark told me in her letter that she had gone into the Editor's office and that they had prayed together over the healing cloth on my behalf ... As I read that letter and felt that cloth, I was quickened in spirit and picking up Henri's *Glory News* I re-read some of the testimonies. I laughed, I cried and spoke in other tongues as Jesus liberated me. Glory to His lovely name.

Eventually I was admitted to the hospital and took the healing cloth, letter and magazine with me. I did not realise it then, but for the grace of God I would never have seen my loved ones nor my home again in this life. After they had extracted my teeth I lay at death's door but God was merciful to me and when they managed to get me round I found I was praising the Lord and saying, 'Thank you Jesus'. [12]

She went home feeling groggy but, as she trusted the Lord, her strength returned and before long she decorated four bedrooms and the staircase of her house!

Mrs I. Wilson suffered from arthritis of the spine with severe pain. It occurred to her to write away for a healing cloth. She said,

Receiving this by post I placed it on my back in the name of Jesus, trusting His precious word in Isaiah 53, *'with His stripes we are healed.'* [13]

The healing gradually came, over several days, and it was complete.

Then Mrs P.P. from Ystrad Rhondda, suffering from tuberculosis, sent away for a healing cloth. 'After applying the cloth,' she said, 'I experienced as if there was a ball of fire within me and a feeling of wellbeing.' She was completely healed. [14]

There were other cases of people cured by way of healing cloths: a person with bronchial catarrh, another with phlebitis and a baby born with asthma. [15]

Then there were folk who experienced healing through the Glory tapes and *Glory News*. Their ailments may be regarded as minor ones, but their cures were surprising enough. For instance, Mrs E.P. of Thetford wrote,

My nephew, aged nine, was crazy with earache, an abscess having formed in his ear. No sleep all night, then I put the tape on and, glory to God, as Brother Henri was praying for Brother Crook to be healed, God also touched the child, his earache disappeared in a flash and so far there has been no recurrence. [16]

Mrs E.M.B. of Ilford described how her husband had a black-out at home,

> and in falling he injured his ribs. He was in bed for four days with severe pain ... But praise the Lord, while listening to the tape on Monday evening ... he felt the hand of the Lord go down his right side and the pain went straight away. He was able to move freely again and had a good night's sleep. [17]

Mr G.R.L. from Bromley wrote,

> On the Saturday after I had received your tape, I awoke and my back was full of small blisters. I felt like tearing myself to pieces. I bound this affliction in the Name of Jesus and said to my wife, 'Put that tape on. Dark and light can't stay together. I'll drive this right out of the house with the power of the Lord.' And sure enough, half an hour later, before the tape had finished, I was praising the Lord. My back was perfectly clear and I haven't had it since. [18]

From eargate to eyegate, Olive Race had this to say:

> For some time I had been suffering a lot of pain in the bottom of my back and my neighbours were quite concerned for me, as I seemed to fall ill every fortnight. Well, I want to tell you how God healed me when I was reading the *Glory News*. I felt the power of God as I read the written word and something snapped in my back and I was set gloriously free. Hallelujah! [19]

This chapter has turned into a string of case histories. Their accumulation, I feel, is overwhelming. Thank God there is such a story to tell. May it be an encouragement and not a mockery to all who read it; a quickening of faith with a sense of thankfulness to our almighty, merciful and loving God.

There is yet more that can be said. There are many tips of icebergs of what God has been doing physically in people's experience in our own lifetime. Just to take a further scanning through the *Glory News* there are a very considerable number of remarkable testimonies of healing which took place quite unconnected with the Glory movement.

One woman from Hull lay in a trance for eight weeks and saw herself laid out and her grave dug. For a week she only drank water and pins were stuck in her feet to see if there was any life in her; she was nothing more than skin and bone. An elderly lady prayed for her; the bed shook with the power of God and she was healed.

In the same way a baby was healed; he was only a few months old, and had been stricken with tuberculosis and meningitis, leaving him blind and paralysed in both legs. Also a woman suffering twenty-five years of pain following a motor accident was wonderfully healed. She had had to wear a rigid steel spinal support. A prostitute, mentally unbalanced, a slave to nicotine and bound by alcohol, demon-possessed and dying of cancer, was amazingly healed, delivered and saved. Another person 'was changed from a man who shuffled around wearing a steel corset and collar, living on scores of tablets a day, to a man who could run, bend and romp playfully with the children!' A woman was healed of blood poisoning and ulcerative colitis in an advanced state. Another woman, a sufferer of Parkinson's disease, made a heroic effort to get to an Elim prayer meeting where she was healed. A man with a fatal growth throttling him in his throat was wonderfully delivered when, in obedience to the Lord, he raised his hands above his head seven times. [20]

Surely, this all adds up to indisputable evidence that the Lord in His pity and mercy gives physical healing. Such wonders and miracles are not restricted to the New Testament.

Chapter 16

Glory News, Tapes and Cassettes

I t was obviously a great step forward in communicating the gospel when, in the fifteenth century, the printing press came on the scene. One can only wonder how the Greeks and Romans got along without it. Then our own century has seen the most extraordinary surge forward in technological inventions to broadcast the truth.

The Glory folk, in the fifties, used the simple means which came to hand of a straightforward magazine and tape recordings played on reel-to-reel machines. In the seventies these made way for the printing of a newspaper format and the playing of cassettes, with the refinement in the nineties of glossy magazine production and videos. God has used these media to bring light and joy into the lives of many people.

The ministry of magazine and reel-to-reel tape arose very naturally from the whole Glory activity. To begin with Henri encouraged the young folk around him to write letters to their friends. After a while the printed page took over from their red-hot nibs; and without a doubt the *Glory News* from its first issue in 1956 had an avid readership. Their enthusiasm was infectious. One reader from London spoke of 'your wonderful, cockles-of-the-heart warming, Spirit filled, glory bubbling magazine which some kind unknown friend got you to send me. Hallelujah! ... It made us hunger for more of the Word.' [1] What better unsolicited testimonial than that? Another man wrote, 'Praise the Lord for a paper that throbs with the message of a vital Christianity that works.' [2] And another woman said, 'Your magazine is wonderful. I read every word of it and always feel sorry when I come to the last page...' [3]. Young Ted Seymour, saved in a tent meeting at Coulsdon in Surrey, was sent a copy of the first issue by Chris Wingfield. He said,

On the bus going home that evening the pages seemed to light up and I felt such a quickening of the Holy Spirit that I laughed to myself as I scanned the pages. The joy and liberty which came from its pages and the anointed articles did something to me. [4]

The same went for a housewife in Mansfield:

After reading it for about ten minutes, I was filled with the Spirit and was quite lost in wonder, love and praise. I had a wonderful time. The Spirit seemed to come through its pages. I cried with joy, and then afterwards I got on with my work and did more than ever in a very short time. Surely the joy of the Lord is my strength. [5]

Mrs Johns in the Isle of Wight spotted an advert that Henri had put in the *Christian Herald* and sent away for the *Glory News*. 'I only seemed to glance through its pages and it lifted me into Glory, and I felt a new creature.' [6] Willie McCullough of Belfast turned to a Roy Turner chorus on the back page of another *Glory News*, 'Mighty, mighty is His Name, Jesus the great I AM,' and he said, 'Suddenly I began to sing in other tongues, while the great I AM poured His Holy Spirit upon me in great profusion.' [7]

Yes, and the pouring out of the Holy Spirit, like the precious ointment or oil on Aaron's beard (Psalm 133:2) brings unity. As another person said,

One thing I did experience while reading *Glory News* was a sense of Christian unity with all the articles. It is refreshing to read Christian literature that is free from 'denominational bias'. [8]

The magazine also had a good influence abroad. For instance, two believers in Stockholm asked for twenty-five copies to be sent regularly. They said,

We think that many people will be interested as it is something extraordinary here in Sweden. The need for a paper like this is greater than people realise. There are many looking for something to satisfy their soul but they go to the wrong places. The glory from Jesus ... is the answer. [9]

Anyone reading through these magazines will find various irrepressible comments that pop out from the pages: 'The *Glory*

News is the best Christian magazine I have ever read ... This is not a killer, it's a thriller.' [10] 'I think the *Glory News* is worth every penny of a shilling;' [11] 'The brightness and inherent sincerity of your paper impresses me deeply.' [12] 'Whoever's brainchild this *Glory News* is, it sure is a WINNER!' [13] 'I came across your magazine by accident. I work in the Post Office and someone threw it into the letterbox;' [14] 'It is a great wee book. I never saw a book like it; for when you read it, you can feel the Spirit of God go through you.' [15] 'It is just what we have been longing for. We are all for it. It is the need of the hour.' [16] 'I cannot leave them alone and the blessing seems to get into my bones.' [17] 'this marvellous *Glory News* ... I think it is glorious. I am in with it through and through.' [18]

The last enthusiastic comment which I would like to quote links me truly and firmly with the task in hand. Nine whole years before I ever met my wife Margaret and encountered the Glory Way she wrote,

> ... perhaps you will send me another dozen of the papers. I wish I had taken an armful when at Stowmarket Glory meeting the other day. The testimonies are just great and ought to convince other groups who are so bitterly opposed to you that this is of God. I am so thankful for the first day I met a 'glory' person. Praise the Lord. He has some wonderful gems in His Kingdom. [19]

As may be imagined, the readership of the *Glory News* steadily expanded. By 1963 Henri was able to say that 220,000 copies altogether of the magazine had been distributed. Up until No. 28 he had ordered 8,000 copies of every issue. He now decided to make it 12,000. Also, at this point, he took a step of faith. He decided to take away the price tag and have the magazine free of charge, as he said, 'so that it can be spread around in ever increasing quantities and bless many more folk who are hungry for more of God.' [20]

Quite apart from a magazine and its distribution, bookstalls at the back of meetings also have their part to play. They are a quiet power for good. Les and Joyce Walter always manned a varied display of books and tapes at conventions and other meetings. Then there was Ruby Sloane, who in spite of a certain lameness had been a champion swimmer. In 1978 she took over the bookstall from them and kept it going faithfully. Then finally,

Alan and Shirley with their helpers have carried on this vital role.

We now turn to the Glory reel-to-reel tapes, bringing the spontaneous immediacy of the Glory meetings. We talk about reel-to-reel. But before them there were more primitive wire recorders. Henri started with one of them. Really, Henri was a great experimenter. There was very little equipment off the peg in those days and he was right in the forefront of the business of public address systems, amplification and recording. He rigged up a whole lot of gadgets in his shop – they were not cheap – and fiddled around with them for ages until they worked together properly. Then they were fixed to the top of his car, and after that incorporated into his gospel van.

Recordings of anything – particularly if they are old – can be extraordinary. Listening to the radio one day, I was once startled by a military German voice rapping out 'Herr Brahms!' and there followed a crazy crackling recording of a Brahms piano piece played by the great man himself, in about 1890. Likewise, I find it really moving to hear an early Glory tape, say, of a Sunday evening in Mansfield Market. To begin with, I am surprised at the sound of the voices of Henri and Connie more than thirty years younger than ever I have heard them. Connie's is sharp, arresting, ringing. Her very tone throws out a challenge and her singing voice is beautifully strong, musical, unswervingly in tune. Henri is urgent, and as swift and unhesitating as a sports commentator. His broad Midland accent gives local flavour. His enunciation is good; as was said of Spurgeon, 'clear as a bell'. He hardly seems to pause for breath; yet when he does slow up a bit there is what I can only describe as a kind of compassionate caress about the way he speaks. His voice is full of acceptance and invitation.

Moreover, as the tape plays, the scene in Mansfield Market-place will come vividly to mind. In the middle, alongside the Victorian memorial, is Henri's van which he had specially made. With the curtains drawn back, there Henri stands, smile from ear to ear, nimble fingers playing the accordion; bonnie Connie by his side, singing her heart out. Around them are the supporting group of young people. The square in front of them is packed tight with a singing throng, mainly miners. Round the edge of the market square outside the pubs are others, watching, curious, moved, forgetting to drink their pints. Testimonies follow, encouragement and Henri's own special brand of open-air badinage. It all comes alive as you listen to the tape.

In the early Mansfield days the team once had a recording scoop. Someone was preaching, saying that God is intervening, the Holy Spirit is active and there are 'signs following'. At that there was a loud clap of thunder! This drama was caught on the old wire recorder and Henri loved playing it over!

As would be expected, the great majority of the tapes are of meetings under cover, in large assembly rooms and town halls, various chapels and churches, community centres, marquees. On the recording of a good meeting one can sense the anointing, the rejoicing and air of expectancy, the very presence of the Holy Spirit. Quite definitely, these tapes have a distinct ministry. I should add at this point that all the old reel-to-reel tapes have recently been transcribed onto cassettes, a labour of love of Alan and Shirley Churchill and Albert Chapman. And the whole have been meticulously documented by Albert Chapman. There is no limit then to the usefulness of these recordings. Whilst there is enough electricity to push the mechanism round, the blessing of heaven will come down. Bob Nicholls wisely said,

> The recorded tape has become a modern evangelist, a revivalist, a deliverance ministry, a missionary to thousands of people. Its scope is tremendous; that is why we urge every born-again believer to possess a tape-recorder and use it for the glory of God ... God has put the tools into our hands, so let us get on with the job. [21]

Copies of the *Glory News* bore encouraging words: 'Turn your home into a Revival Centre. Send for a Glory Tape on 21 days free loan and invite your friends and neighbours in to listen.' It certainly caught on, and as early as 1960 Bob Nicholls was able to report:

> We now have in the region of a thousand names on our tape file and the number is increasing daily. These tapes are expensive things, but even so they are much cheaper than a missionary or an evangelist and very often get in and produce results where a servant of God might find the door closed. [22]

Here is a positive flood of testimonies to the Glory tape-recorder's effectiveness. First is David Willows who, at the age of sixteen, was fascinated as he listened to Glory tapes in his grandmother's cottage in Jallands Row. His Gran was very wise.

As young David popped in for a visit she did not say much to him, but simply put a tape on. He loved electrical things and soon he was really hooked on the Glory choruses. He played them over and over again. Looking back David says, 'It was absolutely so lively and tremendous.' Other people made the following comments:

> It reminds us of the days when the Holy Ghost power first came down in this country (USA) ... My! my! When we listen to that Glory tape, it sure makes us hungry for the old-time Pentecostal power. [23]

> We put the Glory tape on and my friends sit and listen and before many minutes down comes the power and we are laughing, crying, shouting and praising God. [24]

> Thank you for sending the tape so quickly. The Lord really blessed us. We have played it hundreds of times although we have only had it one week. We would really love to have more tapes ... It's lovely to hear of happy Pentecostals that are free. [25]

> The Glory tapes have brought great joy into our home, insomuch we have danced around in the room as we have entered into the spirit of the meeting. Somebody told me some years ago that Henri's meetings did a lot of damage. Well, I think the only damage they will do is to the furniture. [26]

> Well, after listening to one or two Glory tapes we knew that here was a people who were filled with the Spirit and were free to praise God and express their love for Jesus just how they liked ... We could not get to Newark quick enough to meet you all. (300-mile journey) [27]

> There are hundreds of old people who have told me to let you know how much they appreciate your recorded Glory meetings. [28]

> Thank you for the loan of your tape ... It has drawn me closer to Jesus. I do not get out much to have fellowship with the children of God and you can guess the joy I have received. I took my tambourine and played it with you and felt I was one in the meeting with you all, and if I could have danced I would have done. [29]

It was on the 26th August (1959) that, after listening to a tape, I fell under God's power and He filled me with the Holy Ghost and I spoke in other tongues. Hallelujah! [30]

After the tape had been playing for a while something seemed to come over me and I started to tremble and could not keep still. A few of the sisters thought I had caught a chill but, thank God, it was not a chill but the fire. I got down on my knees and started to praise God and then I spoke in other tongues and the Spirit gave me utterance ... that is how God baptised me with the Holy Ghost. [31]

Then a Pentecostal friend ... invited me to hear one of your tapes. It was then my feelings changed. There was power in your meetings that I had never experienced before. There was joy, peace and above all there was love. [32]

How I praise God for the tape ministry. God did a new work in my heart. For several weeks I had asked God to help me love the unlovable and on the Tuesday evening when we were singing 'Melt my heart, precious Lord,' God broke me down and filled me with an overflowing love. I just couldn't contain it. Oh, Glory! [33]

... as I have listened I have felt the Holy Spirit upon me. I could only sit and weep when I heard the congregation singing that hymn, 'I want my life to be all filled with praise to Thee.' God really did something new in my life at that moment. It is so great to feel the moving of God's Spirit. He is *so real*. He has just changed my life completely. [34]

I was changed as I sat alone in the house listening to a Glory meeting on tape. As I listened I just entered in. When Henri said, 'All those who want more from God raise your hands,' I lifted my hands, and when he said, 'Give Jesus a clap,' I clapped, though I wasn't sure whether I agreed with this or not. I can't say I was conscious there and then of any great change, but oh, what a difference in the following days. [35]

... a word of praise and thankfulness to you dear people of God for producing such Spirit-filled, joyful tapes. It is true indeed that one cannot listen to the Glory tapes without feeling *highly uplifted* in spirit. I have now purchased a cassette recorder and can hardly wait until my next supply of tapes arrives in Belfast. [36]

As soon as the tapes arrive I put them on the machine and I am right there in the meetings with you in spirit. [37]

...a brother in our church invited us to hear one of your tapes and, praise God, it did something to me. I did not think of Henri or any other person as I listened, but I thought about Jesus and my relationship with Him ... We are on the brink of something wonderful ... Thank you Henri, even though you have not taught us a new doctrine, you have revived the one we had. [38]

What impresses me most is the *love* that is manifested in the Glory meetings and can be felt coming from the recordings we receive. [39]

I do thank God for the tape ministry. There are people in Hungary and Romania who are getting the Glory. They are beginning to clap their hands and bang their tambourines. [40]

It's terrific the way the Lord can bless just through a tape recording. [41]

Oh, for a thousand tongues to thank you for this anointed tape. [42]

Chapter 17

Glory Choruses

M usic touches us at a deep level. It stirs our emotions and strongly affects our imaginations. God meant it that way.

In the Old Testament the Israelites certainly proved themselves to be a musical people. After their great deliverance at the Red Sea they sang in exultation while Miriam led the women in timbrel playing and dancing. Under King David there was a great upsurge of music making in praise to God. It was highly organised. Encouraged by David, the Levites arranged *'singers with instruments of musick, psalteries and harps and cymbals, sounding, by lifting up the voice with joy'* (1 Chronicles 15:16). A great hymn book was written, the Book of Psalms.

As already mentioned, Henri had the conviction that music was the secret hidden weapon of the gospel. It is glorifying to God to sing the gospel as well as preach it. The experience of the Glory team in Mansfield Market went to prove it. The truths of the Bible were soon being sung by the miners in their shifts underground.

What then has been the particular mix of the Glory Way's music? This is an important question, particularly these days, when in the English language alone a positively overwhelming variety of Christian music is being sung. We can say that the Glory music has been both old and new, ancient and modern, and this is healthy. Jesus spoke of *'a householder who brings out of his treasure things new and old'* (Matthew 13:52 NKJV). There are hymns in our *Glory Revival Song Book* which quite simply are old evangelical and Pentecostal favourites, much sung in church and chapel, evangelistic meeting and in the open air. These are hymns from the eighteenth century or earlier, the classic age of Isaac Watts, Charles Wesley, William Williams, John Newton and William Cowper, such as 'When I survey the wondrous cross', 'Oh, for a thousand tongues to sing', 'Guide me, Oh thou great Jehovah', or 'Amazing Grace!' Then there are old favourites from the no less classic nineteenth century: 'Blessed assurance, Jesus is mine!' 'Crown Him with many crowns', or 'Onward, Christian soldiers'.

Then we can say that there are also certain hymns which are well known because they contain popular choruses. One can set it out like this:

> To God be the glory, great things He hath done,
> [Chorus]: *Praise the Lord ... Let the earth hear His voice.*

> When upon life's billows you are tempest-tossed,
> [Chorus]: *Count your blessings, name them one by one.*

> Who can cheer the heart like Jesus...?
> [Chorus]: *All that thrills my soul is Jesus.*

This leads on to thinking carefully about that speciality of twentieth-century Christian singing: the chorus. This is quite simply a one-verse hymn. The apostle Paul twice speaks of 'psalms, hymns and spiritual songs,' and choruses clearly come in the spiritual song category. (In their brevity they have their equivalent in many lyrics and catchy folk songs.) Ideally the chorus is a composition of one idea, expressed simply and pointedly.

Choruses have been composed steadily throughout this last century. Initially many of them, as shown above, were the recurring refrain of a hymn. The classic Pentecostal hymn books, *Redemption Songs* and *Redemption Hymnal*, are full of them. And evangelistic open-air meetings in street, park and market place up and down the country must have popularised them. The Salvation Army, various Pentecostal groups, the Brethren and evangelical chapels and missions have stood on the kerbside and played and sung them lustily and so these refrains took off and had a life of their own.

My own first encounter with this musical art form was on the beach at Westward Ho! in Devon in the 1950s. With a strong sea breeze fluttering the pages of the CSSM chorus book, held firmly back with elastic bands on the collapsible harmonium, we sang and sprang about on the sand in front of a jolly bunch of children. 'Wide, wide as the ocean,' and everyone's arms would fling out. The adults in deck chairs with their sun hats and magazines would glance up and smile.

One of the virtues of the chorus is that, once learnt, one can forget about the printed page and sing it over and over again with free gesture and abandon. This certainly loosens people up and enables them to express themselves spontaneously in praise. Also there is a strong aural transmission element about choruses. One imagines that many of them have been written and composed quickly on the spur of the moment and sung to a ready audience at the next meeting. Like children's skipping rhymes, which have flitted from playground to playground, a newly composed chorus has burst out of its chrysalis and flown from one delighted fellowship group to another. Often enthusiasts adroitly translate them, and if one is abroad it is delicious to sing a familiar chorus in new dress and in a totally unfamiliar context. I once found myself with some friends on the streets of Lourdes, in south western France, singing 'Vivant! Vivant!' (Alive! Alive! My Saviour is alive!)

The early chorus impetus, no doubt with the publication of many pamphlets and booklets, finally channelled into two main streams: *Elim Choruses* for the Pentecostals and *CSSM Choruses* (Children's Special Service Mission) for other evangelical churches. A good example of an Elim chorus is:

> *Just a little longer, and the trump of God shall sound,*
> *Just a little longer, and we'll all be Glory bound.*
> *Look away to Jesus, your redemption draweth nigh,*
> *Just a little longer, and we'll meet Him in the sky.*

While the CSSM might have:

> *All your anxiety, all your care,*
> *Bring to the mercy-seat, leave it there;*
> *Never a burden He cannot bear,*
> *Never a friend like Jesus.*

And both chorus streams could share the classic salvation statement:

> *Living, He loved me; dying, He saved me;*
> *Buried, He carried my sins far away;*
> *Rising, He justified freely for ever;*
> *One day He's coming – Oh, glorious day!*

New choruses keep popping up. Certainly in our own English-speaking catchment area there has been a cornucopia. Since the beginning of the sixties we have been positively inundated with choruses; it has been a floodtide surge. Some choruses have their little day, do the rounds a bit and then fade away. It must always have been so with hymns. Time inexorably weeds them out. But once a chorus has proved its worth, it becomes part of the repertory and finally gains 'old favourite' status.

Coming back to the Glory Way, the choruses sung sprang naturally out of the Elim tradition and *Redemption Songs*. Then before long they, the Glory folk, were joined by the Jamaicans with their vigorous tambourine playing. They brought with them a new characteristic nexus of choruses, like 'Cry out and shout, thou inhabitant of Zion,' which had very distinctive Caribbean rhythms. Then after a short while the Glory folk began their own spell of creativity.

Sally Bills wrote at least ten choruses. Besides those already mentioned, she was the authoress of 'I've crossed over Jordan and the Lord has led me through,' as well as, 'Whatsoever you desire when you pray,' and 'Are you thirsty, brother, are you thirsty, sister?' Particularly memorable, with its tripping, dancing melody, is Sally's 'Whatsoever things are lovely, whatsoever things are true...'

Besides her we have George Kinley with 'The Lord of life died on Calvary's tree,' and Arthur Warren with 'Taste and see how good the Lord can be,' and 'Glory to Jesus ... Blessed be His lovely Name.' While Phyllis Preudhomme wrote, 'It is Love, Joy, Peace in the Holy Ghost...' Behind the scenes, musically, were Mavis Johns, Norman Wicker, Connie Wingfield and Walter Eden who did a very good job with piano arrangements.

Attractive choruses can arrive from any direction. Here is one written recently by Izzie Waller, whom my wife and I met at Arthur Burt's fellowship in North Wales. The melody has such a folksy rhythm, and we have found that when people are introduced to it, there is always an element of surprise and discovery:

> *Our God is the God of much more,*
> *Our God is the God of plenty,*
> *Our God is the God of much more,*
> *He gives to all of His abundance!*
> *The flowers of the field, the fruit of the trees,*
> *The berries on the bush, He gives us all these.*
> *The water that we drink, the air that we breathe,*
> *The food that we eat, He gives us these!*

As already explained, Roy Turner brought something altogether unusual to the Glory musical scene. There is a peculiar lilt and flow about his compositions which is unmistakable. Here are a few more:

> *Gone are my burdens, oh, Hallelujah,*
> *I came to Jesus, I felt them go.*
> *Happy I now abide, down by the riverside,*
> *Living for ever where the blessings flow.*

> *God is moving on, by His mighty power,*
> *This is latter rain, the visitation hour,*
> *Glory all divine, coming from above,*
> *God is moving, I am moving, in His love.*

> *Roll your burden on Jesus, He'll give you a song,*
> *When nothing seems to go right*
> *And everything seems to go wrong,*
> *When the road is rugged*
> *And the way seems hard and long,*
> *Just roll your burden on Jesus, He'll give you a song.*

> *I'm going to thank Him in the morning,*
> *I'm going to thank Him through the day,*
> *I'm going to thank Him in the evening,*
> *When the blue skies turn to grey.*
> *I'm going to thank him every moment,*
> *For all around I see*
> *The very many wonderful blessings*
> *God has bestowed on me.*

If the expression 'anointed choruses' has any real meaning, then surely it has with these compositions of Roy's. Words and music fuse together, it seems, in an almost inevitable way. Perhaps his most memorable chorus, certainly the one which has got around most, is:

> *All over the world the Spirit is moving,*
> *All over the world, as the prophet said it would be.*
> *All over the world there's a mighty revelation*
> *Of the glory of the Lord, as the waters cover the sea.*

I think it can be classed as a classic example of aural transmission. People find themselves singing it without having a clue where it has come from and so Roy Turner simply becomes 'anon' as though he lived on another planet. However, it is good to see that Mission Praise gives him full acknowledgement. *All over the world* has been sung on BBC television *Songs of Praise*. And one year thousands sang it on the last night of the Edinburgh Festival.

There is another chorus of Roy's which has really caught on in a general way across the denominations:

> *By the anointing Jesus breaks the yoke,*
> *By the Holy Ghost and power, just as the prophet spoke.*
> *This is the day of the latter rain,*
> *God is moving in power again,*
> *And the anointing will break the yoke.*

Roy believes that the words of one of his songs sums up his approach to Spirit-filled music perfectly:

> *Man was made to be His music,*
> *People to be His praise,*
> *All living things sing a song of love*
> *Lifting their voices to God above;*
> *Tune your heart to the melody*
> *Of creation as it rolls along;*
> *Man was made to be His music,*
> *People to be His song.*

Currently Alan Churchill is transcribing recordings of upwards of two hundred of Roy Turner's choruses on CD and the Glory Office is re-releasing them for sale to promote them to a whole raft of new people.

North of the Border at Peterhead an independent native school of Glory song writing flourished. To begin with, there was that glory ditty that John Cameron sang spontaneously to Simon on a lay-by near Huddersfield: 'This Glory Way... has been revealed. It's for today.' Back in Peterhead a number of them started writing Glory choruses. Simon Cameron said: 'We seemed to hit a seam of song. We were always writing and singing new songs.' One of them was his son Philip, and another Aunt Janet Ross. She wrote, 'Oh, I never can tell what He's done

BY THE ANOINTING

Composed by
ROY TURNER

Arr. by
NORMAN WICKER

By the a - noint - ing Je - sus breaks the yoke.

By the Hol - y Ghost and pow'r just as the proph-et spoke.

This is the day of the lat - ter rain. God is mov-ing in

pow'r a - gain. And the a - noint-ing will break the yoke.

for me,' and 'I've found it, I've found it, I've found the Glory joy.'
Charles Stevens in real gratitude to the Lord wrote:

> *He set me free, my lovely Jesus set me free.*
> *I thank you, Jesus, for this glorious liberty.*
> *When I was bound with no one to deliver me,*
> *My lovely Jesus came and He has set me free.*

If this seems a little over the top, remember that God is the
Heavenly Lover, and that 'He is altogether lovely' (Song of
Solomon 5:16).

Once, after a Zion convention at Peterhead, several people put
their heads together and, twanging their guitars, collected up a
number of unrhymed catch phrases from the preaching of the
Cameron brothers. They wove them together like this:

> *Precious moments, privileged people,*
> *When we realise the good things God has done.*
> *Lift your hands up, shout 'Amen!' friends,*
> *To a thankful heart a double portion comes.*

Roy Turner became a close friend of the Camerons, and Simon
and he sparked off something in one another. Once, at a Glory
Banquet, Simon, like a Highland chieftain, pushed his chair back
from the table and cried, 'I'm satisfied, fully satisfied!' At which
Roy reached for his accordion and broke into song:

> *I am satisfied, satisfied with Jesus,*
> *I am satisfied, satisfied with Him.*
> *Every need has been supplied,*
> *Praise the Lord, I'm satisfied,*
> *Fully satisfied, satisfied with Him.*

When they were in the United States, on at least three occasions
Simon made a punchline in his preaching, which was immediately seized on by Roy and improvised into a chorus: 'I fell in love
with the Nazarene,' 'Hallelujah! I want to sing all about it!' 'I'm
going to thank Him in the morning.'

Now let us look away from the Glory Way to the Christian
scene at large. In the decade from about 1975 to 1985 there was a
remarkable outpouring of spiritual songs. This has gone on to the
present day, but this burst of creativity was particularly marked
in the years just before and after 1980. If one could get it all

I FELL IN LOVE WITH THE
NAZARENE

Composed by
ROY TURNER

Arranged by
WALTER EDEN

I fell in love with the Naz – a-rene   I fell in love with Him _____ I fell in love with the Naz – a-rene He took a-way my sin. _____ He gave me beauty for ash – es here Glo-ry for all my shame _____ I fell in love with the Naz – a-rene and Je - sus is His name. _____

5

together it would be very interesting to know, right across the world, how many writers in how many cultures and countries have been involved and in how many languages.

This outpouring of chorus and hymn writing has been surprising and, one should say, enriching. It is certainly a good thing that new praise and worship music is continually being written and composed; otherwise we would never have the hymns and so on that we do possess. We crush creativity at our peril. Writers and musicians are bound to have new inspirations. Take Isaac Watts, for instance. In his day most churches only sang psalms and Scripture paraphrases, and this gifted poet broke out from this limitation and started writing hymns as we know them. He was criticised for this, but his hymns were of good mint. They really proved themselves and they ushered in, as I have mentioned, a classic age of Christian poetic composition of a high order to the accompaniment of wonderfully tuneful and harmonious music. This recent spate of chorus and hymn composition has brought a mixture of battles and blessings, of joys and snags. On the positive side, a good number of choruses are pure Scripture put straight into music, such as:

> *Whoso offereth praise glorifieth Me: and unto him that ordereth his conversation aright will I shew the salvation of God.*
> (Psalm 50:23)

> *The* LORD *liveth; and blessed be my rock; and let the God of my salvation be exalted.*   (Psalm 18:46)

However, I would like to pinpoint four problems or snags. To begin with, I cannot help noticing that very often these new 'charismatic' choruses and hymns are not crafted as those of the previous generation were. (I use the word 'charismatic' advisedly. For the most part, this upsurge of new choruses was a result of the charismatic renewal of the Holy Spirit, which began some time during the sixties.) For one thing, the rhyming of these choruses appears to be slipshod. In this way they are no different from Country and Western songs and many modern lyrics and pop songs. It seems that this way of writing is in the air. Also it must be said that a very great deal of serious poetry during much of the twentieth century has been very free in construction. I imagine that it is the assonance of the vowels which matters and the precise repetition of the consonant sounds is not required. This is not new in the history of poetry. But I just find that the result grates on my old-fashioned ears and I must admit I have an urge to tidy up many choruses. For instance, I feel that to rhyme 'Spirit' and 'limit' is just about the limit! I would hasten to add that Glory choruses are not immune from this rather slapdash approach. Anyhow, as I have already said, time will ruthlessly weed out what is not up to scratch.

Secondly, I would add, with certain of the 'charismatic' choruses, that they are not all that easy to sing: in other words, they are not very congregational. They have syncopations, pauses and sudden hurryings where least expected. Some melodies don't come up to a climax, but wander on. As Simon Cameron expresses it: 'There are too many words in one line. And when you expect the tune to go up, it goes down, and vice versa.' He said again to me, 'To this day I don't know of any "charismatic" chorus which really grabs me.'

In the third place, there is a certain harshness about the music of these choruses which is often hard to take. It is a question of decibels. In a sense, with the march of technology, I suppose, it was bound to come in at some moment. The pop scene has provided the format; it has been around for years. So it is argued, why should the Lord's people lag behind and not use the same electronic expertise to the glory of God? It attracts the young people. It is their idiom, it is what they understand. Maybe. If so, then we plead, play the music judiciously and with real musicianship. Avoid harshness and brashness. If you are going to make a loud noise, then *'play skilfully with a loud noise'* (Psalm 33:3).

And fourthly, I do not for the life of me understand why the old, time-honoured hymns in some instances have dropped out of existence. It seems to be a complete replacement job. It is hard to get the overall picture and one must guard against uninformed sweeping statements. But I have the impression that in some Christian gatherings these days the old hymn has been totally pushed aside. We have a colossal heritage of magnificent hymns, anointed compositions if ever there were, full of saving doctrine, praise and confident affirmation. We must guard against being robbed.

Cooling off from this, let us now take a calm look again at the modern chorus scene – the Glory ones and what we are calling the 'charismatic' ones. Occasionally the Glory folk will sing 'When I feel the touch of Your hand upon my life...' There are, in fact, fourteen choruses common to *The Source* (edited by Graham Kendrick) and *Glory Revival Song Book*, including 'I give glory to Your Name, O Lord' and 'Lord, I lift Your Name on high.' In turn, people who use *The Source* will sing 'Spirit of the living God, fall afresh on me,' which is a golden oldie from *Elim* (though with an alternative tune). It is also good to see that Kendrick and his team have included a basic sprinkling of well-known hymns.

When we turn to the 'charismatic' *Songs and Hymns of Fellowship* published in 1985, then we find a very considerable overlap with Glory choruses. I have counted at least 49 which are in our *Glory Revival Song Book*, including:

> *'Come bless the Lord, All ye servants of the Lord'*
> *'I saw the Lord ...*
>   *He was high and lifted up, and his train filled the temple'*
> *'Jesus, name above all names'*
> *'Praise Him on the trumpet, the psaltery and harp'*

There are also a number which we sing which are not in our book, such as:

> *'Emmanuel, Emmanuel, We call Your name Emmanuel'*

Mission Praise also has a similar number of choruses which are familiar to the Glory people. There are, for instance:

> *'Because He lives I can face tomorrow'*
> *'Blessed be the name of the Lord ...*
>   *The name of the Lord is a strong tower'*
> *'Worthy of honour and worthy of glory and*
>   *worthy of praise is He'*

Now, it may come as a real surprise to some Christians in the 'charismatic' camp to know that there is in existence another whole live body of choruses alongside their own. We invite you, 'Come, taste and see!' That is, if you can find us and our music. The snag is that, from the word go, the 'charismatic' choruses have been strongly organised and promoted, while the Glory choruses, on the other hand, are in a much more fluid aural state. The 'charismatic' choruses are now encoded in a scholarly and well produced publication, *The Source*, which appeared in 1998. The *Glory Revival Song Book*, though attractively printed, is only in a words copy. We have no music written down. Improvisation has always been the order of the day. So all I can say is, 'Come to one of our meetings. Borrow one of our cassettes or videos from the Glory office.'

In closing, I will round off this chapter with some words of testimony about the character and quality of Glory choruses:

> I am choked with tears of happiness. So natural, so unstarched, so wonderfully *free* and full of *praise* to God ... one's heart *sings* with sheer delight at the beautiful, lilting swing-along music. [1]

> When I saw you all on the platform with your musical instruments and when I heard the singing, I was amazed and felt that we had surely turned into the wrong place, but after being there a short time I began to feel at home and joined in the singing of those lovely choruses. [2]

> By the way, the Glory choruses are being sung by folk of all denominations over here (in Pennsylvania) including Jews and Catholics of all ages. [3]

> In my ministry in the various denominations (in Los Angeles) I get the people to sing all the wonderful songs we sang in the meetings in Newark. They have been implanted on my heart for the rest of my life... [4]

> The thing that first impressed me was the joy that was evident among the believers and then there is the music. There is something about this side of it that is characteristic to Newark and Newark only. [5]

The best of the Glory choruses – and that is a large proportion of them – have an unmistakable dynamic quality. They are full of praise to Almighty God, full of personal testimony. They get the very foundation of our faith into the spiritual bloodstream. Each chorus has a rhythmic lilt and tunefulness and a well-rounded climax. They liberate the spirit. They make the face shine!

Chapter 18

Glory Glimpse

We have a few snapshots of Henri at the end of his life. Riverside Cottage at Fiskerton is an attractive wooden bungalow on the grassy edge of the bank of the River Trent, half-a-mile downstream from the village. Many miles up the river from there the Trent gathers in the waters of the Dove and the Derwent, which drain the high fells of the Peak District, and by the time it passes Fiskerton, it is a purposeful flow of water as it swishes past the dwelling of Henri and Connie on its way down to Newark. The Trent is a fickle neighbour and after heavy rains can rise alarmingly. Opposite the bungalow, clinging to the further bank, is a tangle of trees. A couple of herons can be seen flying up and downstream with lazy wingbeats, or standing motionless in the water ready to strike a fish.

Below the bungalow is a little jetty and tied up to it is Henri's neat motorboat *Born Again*. More than once passers by have asked why it is called that. Henri loved tinkering about with the boat; in fact, he liked making things. Roy Hollingworth gives us a glimpse:

> Henri spent all his days bodging and making things right. He loved it. He was quite clever and made a large area by his bungalow where he could do all his jobs, which was completely covered in. He was thrilled with it when it was done, and used to get up every morning and walk up and down in it saying, 'Bye, this is lovely, this is!'

Roy, as you remember, was one of the young stalwarts who stood with Henri and Connie on Mansfield Market. Now, forty years later, he and Henri could be seen walking along the towpath together, talking over many things. As a holiday boat cruised up the river the two men would give it a Glory wave!

Violet Cowling, another of Henri's faithful evangelistic youngsters from those early days, gives us another touching snapshot:

> About a fortnight before Henri died, I was walking through the precinct in Newark and I heard Henri say to the woman in an ice cream kiosk, 'I'll have a chocolate one, me duck.' And I put my arm on his shoulder and said, 'Make that two!' We sat on a seat near the supermarket for well over an hour eating our ices, chatting and laughing. Henri said, 'Every time those doors open and people come by they say, Look at those two, aren't they in love?' Henri talked of the love God had given him for people at the beginning. He said that he had had one of the most understanding wives who knew he loved her, but that he had never had any love in his life like his love for Jesus. He spoke of sacrifices they had made regarding family and such like, 'but,' he said, 'my love has been Jesus, and that has been fulfilled. I'm getting on a bit, duck, but I'll tell you something, You haven't seen anything yet. I know I shan't see it, but I tell you what, duck, you're going to see it.'

All the years Violet had known Henri, she had simply never met him and sat and had an ice cream with him on the market. After Henri's promotion to Glory, on 12 December 1992, she felt the preciousness of those moments when he had shared his vision.

'You haven't seen anything yet.' What did Henri mean? As he looked back in thankfulness, there was yet a yearning in his heart for what lay ahead. The Apostle Paul himself was eager to forget those things which were behind and reach forward to the future (Philippians 3:13). Without any doubt the great overwhelming event is the return, the second coming of the Lord Jesus Christ, which will be nothing less than the end of human history as we know it and a completely new beginning of the unfolding of God's further plans. However, amongst believing people there is a great expectancy of the fulfilment of other prophecies beforehand. It would appear to be in the nature of absolutely marvellous worldwide revival, mixed in with fierce persecution and acts of God's judgement. Arthur Burt, in recent conferences, has touched on it with the expression, 'the greatest thing that has ever hit this planet'.

How soon could this be? Well, the Jewish nation is the key to these prophecies. They have already, for over fifty years, been established as a sovereign independent nation in the land which God has given them. The Lord's time clock started ticking in 1948.

Smith Wigglesworth, towards the end of his life, once said to some young men gathered round him:

> I envy you. I envy you. You are going to see a great visitation of God such as the world has never seen. I won't see it, but you are going to live to see it. [1]

Now, this Pentecostal pioneer died in 1947. That means to say that the young men he was talking to must now, in the year 2000, be in their mid-seventies. Wigglesworth's statement has been interpreted by some as already fulfilled. But I cannot help feeling it still lies in the future.

Finally, let's ask again, What has this Glory Way really been? What, under God, has it achieved? As I was reading old copies of the *Glory News* I plotted on a map of the British Isles the various meetings and rallies as I came across them. While gathering this information a vivid image came to my mind. I saw, as it were, a huge sea wave. It has been travelling along in the deep swell of mid-ocean for a long way. Now as the wave approaches a distant shore it begins to heave up from a smooth trough, gathering momentum, a massive shoulder of deep greeny blue translucent water. The crest mounts up, pauses a moment. A stiff wind whips at the top and sends a sheet of horizontal spray flying. Then the crest curls over and crashes down with all its force, a deluging plunging cascade of relentless foam. The surge of the wave sweeps on, powerfully and inexorably. It has gained a great impetus and keeps charging forwards.

How does this fit the Glory Way? In 1948 Henri receives his unusual anointing from the Lord, falling off the piano stool. Not long after this he and Connie start witnessing locally and begin their open-air meetings in Mansfield Market. The swell of the ocean is moving along. They gather together a young enthusiastic team. The surge of water starts mounting up. Then in the late fifties they begin to get invitations for meetings from further afield and they break out from the local scene. Word gets round; the bush telegraph begins to work overtime. The greeny blue translucent wave is gaining momentum as it rises: Hull, Brixton, West Auckland, Gillingham, Leeds, Barrow-in-Furness, Lambeth, Stockport, Stockton-on-Tees, Hawick in the Scottish Borders, Ringwood in the New Forest. The crest of the wave is forming.

Glory meetings, Glory weekend rallies, then seaside Glory holi-days: the Isle of Wight, Blackpool, Southend-on-Sea. We are now into the mid-sixties: far northern Peterhead gets wind of some-thing happening, so do Willesden and Norwich, South Wales and Northern Ireland. The blessing reaches out to Holland and Scandinavia, and then the United States, Africa and the wave crashes down in a dazzling flurry of foam and spray. The Glory Way is blazing a trail for a mighty revival. Glory cassettes and copies of the *Glory News* are flying out in all directions. The meetings, the rallies, the various get-togethers and holidays are affecting a broad spectrum of believing people. Burning heart kindles burning heart. Spray from that breaking Glory wave spontaneously refreshes, invigorates, empowers many lives. The Holy Spirit, moving where He wills, blows and breathes into many situations. Henri and Connie have been faithful to the vision that God gave them. The Glory Way has been fulfilling its mission. It has been a spearhead, a vanguard. It has been at the cutting edge.

The great wave surges powerfully along. Then at either side we can see other breath-taking waves too, riding forward, mounting up, cresting over, pounding, crashing down and sweeping on. What colossal ocean swell. The green translucent water drops away, down, down and then inexorably wildly wells up again. 'We're into something big!' God has wonderful overwhelming purposes. He is working something out, with all its ramifications, which is way beyond all that we could possibly ask or think.

Look to the left and right as far as the eye can see, across the wide expanse of surfing ocean and flying spray to the widest horizon. These great waves, what are they all? They are nothing less than awakening and revival in every land and every continent, transformations of whole communities, evil and wickedness thrown back, the Bible translated into every remote tribal tongue, pulling down of the strongholds of the old false religions and pagan thraldoms, setting millions of captives free, the Cross of Jesus lifted high and the Holy Spirit bringing to birth and vitalising on a tremendous scale. And God's key nation, His special people, the Jews; here they are flocking home to Israel from north, south, east and west, in readiness – whether they realise it or not – for that great moment when their Messiah will return, His feet touching the Mount of Olives. And *'the earth shall be filled with the knowledge of the glory of the* Lord, *as the waters cover the sea'* (Habakkuk 2:14).

Chapter 19

Glory Yesterday, Today
and Tomorrow

By Alan Churchill

T he wonderful thing about this book is that it enables us to clearly see the hand of God at work.

In what way?

In bringing the Glory Way to birth. It was a sovereign move of the Holy Spirit. We were the onlookers as He influenced and breathed through the lives of many people.

The past always bears record to God's faithfulness in those who were willing to step out in faith and who dared to do what God was prompting them to do. The future of any work started by God can only be seen by faith through the eyes of the Holy Spirit. All those touched by the Glory wave of revival know that there is so much more to be revealed to us and we are all hungry for that. The Word of God reveals the milestones of the prophecies concerning the return of Jesus, the majority of which have already been fulfilled. We are all convinced His coming cannot be long delayed. The following is a pointer to what we believe awaits us as we reach out by faith into the future.

Looking back we can now see that one of the most formative events setting the direction of Henri and Connie's ministry after he fell off the piano stool was the rejection of Henri's experience by the Pastor at Newark. As Henri said to him, 'You get what I've got Brother Ernest and see if you can stand still.' That must be a significant pointer to us. More rejection is bound to come our way – for all of us – as we press into a greater revelation of the Glory. It's not surprising that the church at that time didn't know how to accommodate all the exuberance Henri displayed.

But in throwing Henri out they did what God had already planned, made him go to his customers with the gospel.

He went to the common people in his shop with the good news just as Jesus did. He would read to us often in the meetings, from the books of Isaiah or Luke, putting his and other people's names wherever it says 'me'. Henri did this to stir us up and to make us aware of the high calling we have in Jesus, under His anointing. In fact, he dared to put himself and us in the same place of anointing!

> *The Spirit of the Lord is upon* [Henri], *because he hath anointed* [Henri], *to preach the gospel to the poor; he hath sent* [Henri] *to heal the broken-hearted, to preach deliverance to the captives, and recovering of sight to the blind, to set at liberty them that are bruised, To preach the acceptable year of the Lord.*
>
> (Luke 4:18–19)

Wherever he preached God honoured his faith, and people caught the vision, that is to say an awareness of the presence of God within one's personality. To put it another way, Jesus dwells within the believer's inner consciousness. Henri used to say 'It's in you!'

God showed Henri and Connie many scriptures at this time, one of which is very relevant here for us all today.

> *But ye shall receive power, after that the Holy Ghost is come upon you: and ye shall be witnesses unto me both in Jerusalem, and in all Judaea, and in Samaria, and unto the uttermost part of the earth.*
>
> (Acts 1:8)

Henri first concentrated on his *'Jerusalem'*, his shop and customers; God showed him *'Jerusalem'* is where you are daily at home or at work. Then God gave him Christians drawn to them by the Holy Spirit, coming to the Glory Room in his house, his *'Judaea'*. This was followed by the meetings in the open air at Mansfield Market Place, his *'Samaria'*. As the move of the Spirit grew many were drawn to the market place and the vision expanded to the whole world, *'unto the uttermost part of the earth'*, just as Jesus said it would.

The church that rejected Henri at Newark is today a thriving community, flowing in much of what Henri pioneered in his exuberance. This illustrates the fact that even though the then pastor rejected what God was doing in Henri, God's blessing was still manifest upon this church with which Henri's family were so closely associated during its early years. God took him out to go elsewhere. Many of us had this experience with God in some way, as we have grown in the Spirit and will continue to do so as God's vision expands.

In a similar way God took Shirley and me out of a Brethren-style church soon after we were filled with the Spirit. What a shock the Glory Way was to us then when we first came into contact with the Holy Spirit in the meetings. The Glory immediately changed our vision of Jesus and all our horizons were opened up. We were made so hungry that the changes that God needed in our thinking weren't a problem as His Glory was revealed. We are still as hungry today for more. I believe that's part of the secret of what will continue to happen for all those touched by the Holy Spirit in the future. Once people have really been touched by His Glory they will be continually hungry for more of His presence in their lives.

If we look back to New Testament times we see that God used persecution and the destruction of Jerusalem to spread the Gospel world-wide as it is today. This uprooting of the church systems seems to be a continuing process throughout church history. Oral Roberts who was anointed in America about the same time as Henri in 1948 has a famous sermon that has blessed me greatly entitled 'Don't Camp Here'. We must keep following the Holy Spirit's leading! We must not settle down, but continue to keep focused on the prompting from that indwelling presence in our lives if we are to fulfil our destiny.

The *real* Gospel has a continuously expanding theme. Even today we see world evangelism proliferating as a result of a new move of the Holy Spirit. Millions are being saved each month! More than ever before in the history of the world!

During the thirty years in which Henri travelled extensively there was hardly a town in the UK that wasn't touched with the Glory of God. Roy and the Camerons travelled to North America. Others travelled as far as New Zealand, Australia and the Far East with the Glory message. So God fulfilled Henri's vision by using others touched by the Glory to reach, *'unto the uttermost part of the earth'*. The work continues today in many areas world-wide. Many are second-generation ministries.

In later years, when Henri reached seventy years and was not able to travel regularly, God started a move in his own village. He was asked to speak at a Methodist ladies meeting and they were so touched that they asked him to hold a Revival meeting in the local Fiskerton Methodist church on just one Saturday.

Henri invited many of those who had travelled with him and spontaneously a regular meeting was started only a mile from his home. Henri, being Henri, used these meetings as a focus for country-wide evangelism. Using tapes he travelled to homes all over the UK. The message was the same. He would phone you up and ask, 'Are you enjoying it, lad? Why not come up to Fiskerton again this weekend?'. It was this encouragement that was the hallmark and still is today. Our message is still 'It's in *you!*'

This book has been focused mainly on the period between the 1920s and the 1970s because there isn't room in one book to begin to include what has happened in the last thirty years.

Many of those touched by God during the fifties and on through to the seventies now have their own churches. Many started through the moving of the Holy Ghost during Glory meetings. It can be truly said that the Glory has gone world-wide. Philip Cameron and Robert Cameron are still evangelising in America, and Robert has written some really wonderful Glory choruses over the last few years. There are churches all over this country and the world that have been founded by people touched during this period.

We have lost contact with so many over the years, but every now and then someone rings us and says, 'Do you remember me?' and then goes on to tell us how their lives were touched and changed by the Glory.

Ecclesiastes 11:1 says,

> *Cast thy bread upon the waters: for thou shalt find it after many days.*

It's very true there are still so many testimonies coming our way day-by-day telling of the change that was wrought in people's lives through the touch of the Glory. Once people have been touched by God there's a permanent change in them, just like it was with Jesus and the woman with the issue of blood. Often, many years later, we continue to hear how people were greatly blessed in a meeting.

What is the Glory we keep talking about so much?
Henri and Connie used to say, 'The Glory's the oldest thing in the world.'

John's Gospel 17:5 says,

> *And now, Father, glorify Me in your presence with the Glory I had with you before the world began.*

So the Glory is not of this world. It's the supernatural manifestation of God's love and presence to His blood-bought sons and daughters.

Connie says that it will go on manifesting itself while there are people who are open to receive it in all its fullness. She emphasises that the Glory will always have a people to manifest this love, joy and peace in. It's not dependent on a man, but only on God. As Elijah was told, God always has a remnant of people who are willing to let Him flow unconditionally through them.

What has happened since Henri was called home to Glory?

After Henri died in December 1992 we were all challenged by the loss of such a mighty man of God, who had given the whole Glory Family so much support, direction and encouragement.

In June 1992 God worked a miracle and made it possible for me to be able to take paid early retirement, seven-and-a-half years early. Even though as a manager I wasn't on the management's eligibility list, I believe God arranged for me to be included. I believe it wasn't an accident that God chose this time to set me on as a 'full-time' minister from the Glory Office and for the Basildon Glory Fellowship meetings. I well remember soon after, as we travelled to Methil in Scotland to take an outreach weekend of meetings with Pastor Keddie, it seemed as if God poured out a fresh anointing on us all. As we ministered, the power fell and spontaneous laughter and joy broke out among us. We were filled with joy as we prayed over people and that joy was transferred to others. It was special and it seemed thereafter that our outreach meetings shifted up a gear. The power was manifest with people being saved, healed and delivered.

Not connected with this but at about the same time, Doug Aistrup was invited to speak at a Full Gospel Businessmen's dinner and he felt the impact of this new move there. His testimony of that event and what followed is related in Chapter 13. It was then that he started to link together with us at different venues throughout the country including the Glory Conventions, where the Holy Spirit did some remarkable things. Starting in 1993 at the Summer Convention at Bridlington, God brought a greater focus among those of us hungry for more of His Holy Spirit. We were blessed that year to have the folk from Faith Acres with us for a couple of the days during the convention. There seemed to be a new unity springing up among the various groups which make up the Glory Family.

Not withstanding all this, the beginning of 1993 with the loss of Henri was a challenging time for us at the office. But it seems as if God moved to compensate us with a new wave of joy and gave many of us a fresh baptism of Glory. When we took over the Glory work in the office in 1978, I agreed with Henri that we would do it for ten years only. Some fourteen years later the ministry was part of us, our passion, and our lives. It wasn't a job, or a hobby for retirement, it was a twenty-four-hour challenge; our home being the spring board for revival.

I was so challenged at this time, I said to Ron Wray on the phone one night, 'If we don't go for it now, it will pass us by and the Glory people will just be another group that have been and gone.' I continued, 'Ron, I have made up my mind! If we don't go for what God is showing us now we will be left behind.' Praise God He heard my cry and we are still by His grace going for it. As long as God gives us strength we will continue to reach out for the new things He has promised us. Thank the Lord at that time, we all began to feel the impact of a new and greater hunger within us for a fresh awareness of the presence of the anointing as we came together. Doug wrote of this time,

> God showed me my job was one of enablement, setting the scene – so to speak – and orchestrating the proceedings, allowing the Holy Spirit to move as He so wished in and through whosoever He wills. This causes a great variety in the meetings. Terms I often use are 'spontaneous combustion', 'first within then without'. When the heart wells up with His joy always use 'first thought' and obey the command.
>
> Many have often asked me, 'How do you dare to handle a meeting with no preparation as to how it should proceed?' My answer is, 'We walk by faith.' God told me to follow His promptings from within, but that is not to say that I feel, of myself, full of confidence. Many times I go in fear and trembling often thinking, 'What better right have I to minister to those who come?' But as I open my mouth in faith, He never fails to fill it, and tell me how to proceed. Continually I stand amazed at what He, the Holy Spirit does, and the privileged ministry of inclusion, giving us a platform, so that He can use us as He sees fit, to include the people His body.

A refining was taking place in all our lives. We had been persecuted by the religious fraternity for many years and in some

ways had become protective of our experience. Our freedom and
exuberance had mistakenly been interpreted as happy-clappy
and unspiritual by many. The danger in this situation was for us
to become inward looking, putting up the shutters and to be
defensive, not sharing and reaching out to new contacts. It
seemed as if God opened new doors to our ministry country-
wide from the office at Basildon. There is another scripture that
describes how we felt. It says,

> *So that we may boldly say, The Lord is my helper, and I will not
> fear what man shall do unto me.*   (Hebrews 13:6)

It reminds me of the statement at the beginning of *Star Trek*
which says, 'To boldly go where no man has gone before.' That
was our calling. It seemed we had suddenly found a new boldness
to go out with this Love-Joy-anointed message country-wide. We
were suddenly opened up in our spirits, able to come alongside
anyone who was reaching out for more, of whatever persuasion.
Henri had always said, 'You can take this Glory anywhere and it
will take you anywhere.' We found the truth of that. Since that
time God has given us many new opportunities to engage with
other Christians and churches in a new way. Many of those new
contacts have been touched and found the depth of the experience of being filled with the Glory.

During the year 1993 the outreach team which travelled to
take meetings country-wide began to expand and the meetings
became more focused. New ministries came to birth. We received
more invitations to church groupings and there was a greater
oneness among those who ministered. Proverbs 27:17 says,

> *Iron sharpeneth iron; so a man sharpeneth the countenance of
> his friend.*

That is certainly true. As we came together God spoke to us and
moulded each of us to be a spearhead for revival. There was no
lack in our ministry wherever we went.

> *And they went forth, and preached every where, the Lord working
> with them, and confirming the word with signs following.*
>   (Mark 16:20)

Coincidentally, later that year, we believe as part of God's
plan, a new impetus was given to the Glory move world-wide

when Philip Cameron met up with Rodney Howard-Browne in Florida and invited him to Peterhead.

I well remember a tape that Simon and Wendy Cameron sent to many of us soon after. Shirley and I played it in our car one morning for the first time and we had to stop as we were having difficulty driving. We started to get drunk because of the anointing.

Rodney came later in 1993 to visit Simon and Wendy Cameron's church at The New Hope Christian Centre at Faith Acres, in Peterhead, on his way to a revival campaign in Russia.

Through Rodney's ministry, as he toured the United Kingdom over the next few years, many of the Glory People who had been filled with the Glory under Henri's ministry received a fresh touch. At one of Rodney's meetings in London, Don Double (who we at Basildon were in contact with via the Surrey Group in meetings at Ipswich in the late fifties and early sixties) said to me, 'He's like Henri reincarnated.' He could see in Rodney's meetings much of what Henri had pioneered all those years before.

It was certainly uncanny to hear many of Henri's sayings and the laughter and to see people who had been set free running around the meeting, just as it had happened time and again in Henri's meetings. It wasn't so much that Rodney came with a new outpouring; more that he confirmed for us all, that what we were flowing in was still at the cutting edge – still at the forefront of what God's Spirit was doing for today.

The next year's convention at Christchurch was especially anointed as all the ministries within the fellowship came together, the Holy Spirit directing and challenging us as we entered into His presence.

Our emphasis today is still on evangelism. We take meetings all over the UK. We have teams of leaders and musicians who come from all parts of the country. We still minister to a wide audience, from different denominations under the same powerful anointing.

The Glory Holiday Convention is still the highlight of our calendar, when hungry people come from all over the country to spend a week together in the Spirit. These meetings have had an increasingly special touch of God's Glory in recent years, with many touched, set free and delivered. A new deeper dimension has also been evident in our praise and worship.

Glory Praise and Worship is more than just excitement. It's an expression of heartfelt Thanksgiving and surrender to the Holy Spirit.

As Bruce has so eruditely expounded, some of our choruses and our hymns might at first appear dated when compared to the contemporary scene. Music is so important, as can be seen for example in Benny Hinn's meetings, where the anointing on the music brings many spontaneous miracles in the congregation. Pastor Benny's meetings use many of the choruses and hymns that we do, with astonishing impact.

From the earliest days after Henri was filled with the Glory in 1948, the anointing and the spontaneity of the Glory Music was, as Henri said, 'God's secret weapon'. Much of the current new music that predominates in churches today copies the latest trend in the Pop Music scene, poor repetitive lyrics, with a limited musical harmony and rhythm. As we see it from the Glory standpoint, much of this music fails to lead into a deeper spiritual experience, focusing on excitement rather than the anointing. Of course it does have its place, providing a bridge for the younger generation. But it cannot be a substitute for real Spirit-filled Praise and Worship which brings the spiritual breakthrough. We certainly can't change the format that God has given us to conform to the current trend, as many seem to think we should. We are blessed so often when people ring or write to tell us how refreshing it is to have such spontaneous and joyful singing in our meetings. An anointing on the singing is the most precious commodity that God has given us for the Glory Move. New anointed choruses are still coming our way each year: some from Robert Cameron in the USA, many from within the fellowship, but for the most part we don't have any idea who wrote them. Much anointed music is being written today and reaches us from many directions to become incorporated into our praise and worship.

What the Church needs is anointed men and women who are able to let this Praise and Worship become part of them and provide a vehicle for others to enter into the Shekinah Glory, beyond the veil, one on one with God. Music is a vehicle to bring people into a heavenly harmony with Him and one another.

What of the future?

What then do we conclude will happen in the future? Will this Glory move just fade away with the generation who received the vision, or will it continue into future generations until Jesus comes back for His Church? Glory meetings have always been at the cutting edge of what God is doing. Many think they are old fashioned, but miss the whole point, failing to enter into the special anointing God has put in this ministry. Once people enter in, something special happens inside which brings a release, and you're then spoilt for anything less than a personal one on one with God.

We will continue to grasp all the tools available to us as Henri did. He first recorded meetings in the open air at Mansfield Market Place on a wire recorder, before recording tape was invented. He pioneered PA in the open air taking advantage of having his own engineers in his radio shop to design and build 12-volt amplification. He also pioneered the country-wide use of reel-to-reel tape in a free loan library, with the slogan, 'A tape recorder is more important than a washing machine', much to the chagrin of some of the sisters.

Now the Internet is an emerging tool for world-wide evangelism. We have started in a small way with our Web Site glorypeople.org, but will expand this area as the new technology unfolds into online music, speech and video. Christian Television is in its infancy, bringing much benefit to Christians nation-wide. We have started to advertise on the God Channel and will use this media as the fellowship continues to grow. The Glory has been God's best kept secret for too long and it's time to start the final reaping that the prophets have prophesied would happen before Jesus comes again.

We continue to develop meeting tapes, music tapes, CDs and videos. We are currently reviving all of Roy Turner's choruses and putting them onto CD with the object of sharing them with a wider audience. We look to the future of DVD (Digital Versatile Disk) which will evolve over the next few years. We will use whatever tools we can to manifest the Glory of Jesus to this world. As we lift up Jesus with the multitude of witnesses around the world who knows but that we will hasten His return.

What are we talking about when we express ourselves in this way – the return of Jesus? This is nothing less than the finish of human history as it has been unfolding over the centuries. When the Lord Jesus ascended to heaven from the Mount of Olives, the disciples were asked by the two men in white clothing standing by why they were gazing upwards as they were. The two men said that this same Jesus will come again in the same way that they saw Him go into heaven (Acts 1:11). The Church has certainly been waiting a long time for this moment. How can we know perhaps that it is nearly here? We believe that when the Jewish nation of Israel was established in 1948, when the nation was born (Isaiah 66:8), that a new era of prophecy began, and that the fulfilment of many things foretold in the Bible are coming hard on the heels of this remarkable event. We must keep our eyes on what God is doing with His ancient covenant people. Remember the gospel came to the Jew first, and God deals with the Jew first (Romans 1:16, 2:9–10).

Will this Glory transfer to the next generation?

I believe it has already. We were blessed to be the forerunners of this end-time move of the Glory, and it's widespread now! We are now no longer ostracised for being outgoing and are now able to come alongside virtually any of the new breed of churches springing up.

We are now still pioneering the love and joy, but we find that God is bringing us into contact with more and more people of like mind, even within main stream churches. We don't need a new format. We cannot force what God has planned. We need to just go with the flow and flow into it. God has said He will do a new thing and He is.

> *Behold, I will do a new thing; now it shall spring forth; shall ye not know it? I will even make a way in the wilderness, and rivers in the desert.*   (Isaiah 43:19)

The 'way' this verse talks about is the Glory Way. This end-time outpouring we are beginning to see is The Glory, being revealed in a more dynamic way than ever before. Every one in Christian circles is talking about The Glory being revealed. Books are being written. It's a wonderful confirmation of what we have all been reaching out for all this time.

What will be the Hallmark of this end-time move?

I believe it will be an outpouring of God's love into His Church, without spot or wrinkle. Jesus is coming back to rapture His Church without spot and wrinkle.

> *That he might present it to himself a glorious church, not having spot, or wrinkle, or any such thing; but that it should be holy and without blemish.*   (Ephesians 5:27)

What are the spots and wrinkles but lack of love and purity of motives among God's people?

The final mighty outpouring of God's Spirit before Jesus comes will bring total unity among God's people denominationally-wide. The wise virgins will have this oil in their vessels and lamps.

This oil of the Spirit will burn as a fire in the bellies of God's people, consuming the dross, bringing forth a real love and purity. This coming together of the Body of Christ will not come from ecumenical activity, but will come to spiritual birth by an outpouring of Spiritual Glory. Unfortunately much of today's ecumenical activity is not spiritually based. Those without a real spiritual experience when Jesus comes will lack the oil in their vessels and miss out. The challenge is to keep being continually filled by the Holy Spirit day by day. That's the way God planned to keep us until Jesus comes.

Denominational barriers are breaking down, bringing all born-again Christians into the oneness of His Glory.

> *And the glory which thou gavest me I have given them; that they may be one, even as we are one.* (John 17:22)

If there is anything we are striving for in this New Millennium, it is oneness of heart and spirit, where we can lay down our own private agenda and take up God's glorious agenda together.

To conclude let us look at the beginning of Isaiah chapter 60, so often quoted and used in our meetings. It is a great pointer to what we can all look forward to in the future.

> *Arise, shine; for thy light is come, and the glory of the Lord is risen upon thee.* (Isaiah 60:1)

Let us be diligent with the calling that God has given us. Let us arise and let this Glory shine out to all those we come into contact with day by day. There's a harvest to be reaped. Jesus put it like this in Mathew 5:16:

> *Let your light so shine before men, that they may see your good works, and glorify your Father which is in heaven.*

God has made us stewards of His Glory and we make choices every day as to whether we will let The Glory shine out before our fellow men. When we do so in a genuine way we glorify God. People are drawn to Him through us. We don't have to be a nuisance with religious talk. We need to show forth the reality of our relationship with God and a willingness to do what the Holy

Spirit prompts us to do. He has a total insight into people's needs at a higher level than we can ever comprehend. A word in season can bring release to many.

> *For, behold, the darkness shall cover the earth, and gross darkness the people: but the Lord shall arise upon thee, and his glory shall be seen upon thee. And the Gentiles shall come to thy light, and kings to the brightness of thy rising.*   (Isaiah 60:2–3)

There's no doubt that there is darkness all around us on every side. But God will use this to emphasise the contrast between His light in us and the darkness in people's lives. Let us not compromise and hide our light under a bushel. We can impact the whole spectrum of society, even kings and those in authority over us. Let us dare to be like Daniel, having a spirit of excellence in everything we do in both word and deed. The king acknowledged that Daniel was different. People will do the same with us if we dare to stand for this reality. God doesn't do things half-heartedly and neither should we. I praise God that our motives are totally clean when we truly get the Glory inside. Yes, we get challenged. But look at it this way; when they challenge us they are challenging God in us, and we all know that God always has the last word in every situation. It is good to be able to leave all our justification in every circumstance to a just and faithful God.

> *Lift up thine eyes round about, and see: all they gather themselves together, they come to thee: thy sons shall come from far, and thy daughters shall be nursed at thy side.*   (Isaiah 60:4)

Let us learn to lift our eyes above the natural every-day existence into the Spiritual realm. It is then that we begin to see things as they really are and start to live in the Spirit. God sends people to us every day if we can but see it. We need to learn to see everybody we meet as an opportunity for God to move by His Spirit. Everyone has a deep need which only God can satisfy. If we are sensitive to the Spirit, He will give us insight where we need it. People used to say to Henri, 'Hey, you've done something to me.' it wasn't Henri, it was God within him. I believe we've all had this experience at some time. We can affect people without them knowing how or why, by speaking truth and love into every situation that people face, without even mentioning God. People will draw God's presence out of us. That's why God put a well within each one of us and, as Jesus said,

> *But the water that I shall give him shall be in him a well of water*
> *springing up into everlasting life.*   (John 4:14)

People will travel to receive the real thing. We are amazed that
people travel hundreds of miles just to get a drink of this New
Wine. People are drawn by the Spirit even before they know Him.
God has given us the privilege to reap a harvest that we didn't
sow. Yes! our family will be affected by this Glory. They, like the
prodigal, instinctively know of the blessing of Father's House and
where it is. It's a matter of coming to the end of their resources
and for them to be willing to surrender to God. We have such
wonderful promises for the future of all our families. Let us press
in and claim them. They don't come by observation but by
intercession.

> *Then thou shalt see, and flow together, and thine heart shall*
> *fear, and be enlarged; because the abundance of the sea shall be*
> *converted unto thee, the forces of the Gentiles shall come unto*
> *thee.*   (Isaiah 60:5)

The Glory is a flow. It brings us together as John 17:22
indicates. It will bring oneness between born-again Christians.
No Glory! No oneness! As we have said to so many, 'You can't
join us.' There is no membership. There are no cliquey groups. If
God touches your life with His Glory you will be complete in
your experience and one with us. Division in God's body comes
mainly from a sense of insecurity and lack of self-worth, that
causes people to have their own agenda rather than God's. One
of the aspects of the Glory is the security that it gives to each one
in the knowledge that God's love has been poured into our souls
and our hearts enlarged. Suddenly we get a new perspective of
compassion for the lost and we see the worth of what God has
put into our lives. Philippians 2:5 says,

> *Let this mind be in you, which was also in Christ Jesus.*

Let us not look to further our reputation or a selfish life style, but
let us be willing to be used fully in the service of those God draws
to us in the coming days; that in all things God may be Glorified.

One of the major motivations for me in getting this book
published has been to bring people together and to inspire us
all to break every barrier down. The Glory over the years has
brought to birth many new ministries and we pray that this book

will be an influence for good in bringing those touched closer together. This book has been a long-term project. It's been on my 'to do' list for thirty years and even now can only give us a flavour of what God did among us all during the Glory outpouring. We believe one of the greatest hindrances to the growth of this mighty outpouring of God's Spirit is the smallness of vision so prevalent today among Christians in general. The Glory Move right from the start had a global vision, as Henri always said so often:

> *Let the whole earth be filled with his Glory; Amen, and Amen.*
> (Psalm 72:19)

Today many of us are so pressed by circumstances and time constraints, even in our ministries, that the big picture of the Glory of what God is doing seems to get lost. The word well says in Luke 21:28,

> *And when these things begin to come to pass, then look up.*

Let us look up to God together for a mighty outpouring of the Holy Ghost. Let us encourage each other. Let us join our hands together and go forward promoting this wonderful Glory-oneness and love. Let us take time, as Henri did so often, to encourage one another and, as Jesus said in Luke 10:42,

> *But one thing is needful: and Mary hath chosen that good part, which shall not be taken away from her.*

May we take time away from our own patch for a little togetherness with others in the coming days – maybe just a letter or phone call to show our love to all those brothers and sisters that Jesus has established in this Glory Way.

Let me end with the words of the apostle John:

> *I suppose that even the world itself could not contain the books that should be written. Amen.*

Maybe in the future someone will write a sequel to this book. Thank you Bruce, Margaret and Ruth for all your hard work and to all the others, too numerous to list here, for all your help in preparing this book.

God bless you all. Come and visit us soon as we travel, or here at the Basildon Fellowship. Until we meet again.

May the Joy of the Lord be your strength

The Blood of Jesus your total protection, for body, soul and spirit

And may the Love of God that passes all understanding guard your hearts and minds.

'I pray, Jesus, that You will do a new thing in the life of all who read this book, bring hunger and change, that Your Name Lord Jesus may be Glorified. Amen.'

References

Chapter 1: Beginnings

1. *The World Aflame*, 1993, p. 7, 11
2. 'Conversation with Michael Harper' in Whittaker, *Seven Pentecostal Pioneers*, p. 10
3. Edward Jeffreys, *Stephen Jeffreys*, p. 92
4. Jack Hywel-Davies, *The Kensington Temple Story*, 1998, p. 48
5. Edward Jeffreys, *Stephen Jeffreys*, p. 82–3

Chapter 2: Transformation

1. GN 1988, p. 8
2. GN 1995, p. 7.
3. GN 1st Issue, p. 6
4. GN 1984, p. 3
5. GN 1988, p. 5
6. GN 1995, p. 7 and cassette
7. GN 1st Issue, p. 6
8. GN 1984, p. 5
9. GN 1995, p. 7 and cassette

Chapter 3: Standing for God

1. GN 1996, p. 3
2. GN 1997, p. 9
3. GN 17, 1961, p. 10
4. GN 4th Issue, 1957, p. 8–9
5. GN 1986, p. 6
6. GN 1997, p. 8
7. GN 1st Issue, 1956 p. 7
8. GN 1996, p. 3
9. GN 1996, p. 3
10. GN 1st Issue, 1956, p. 7
11. GN 1996, p. 3
12. GN No. 46, 1969, p. 16
13. GN No. 19, 1961, p. 5

Chapter 4: Young Glory Warriors

1. GN 1st Issue, 1956, p. 9
2. GN Newspaper No. 16, 1975, p. 3
3. GN 1st Issue, 1956, p. 9
4. GN Newspaper No. 16, 1975, p. 3
5. GN No. 5, 1958, p. 13
6. *Encyclopaedia Britannica*
7. GN No. 9, 1959, p. 2
8. GN No. 6, 1958, p. 14
9. GN Newspaper No. 12, 1974, p. 3
10. GN Newspaper No. 12, 1974, p. 3
11. GN Newspaper No. 12, 1974, p. 3
12. GN 3rd issue, 1957, p. 14

Chapter 5: Wider Horizons

1. GN No. 39, 1965, p. 3
2. GN No. 39, 1965, p. 3
3. GN No. 21, 1961, p. 5

Chapter 6: Rhythm and Song

1. GN 4th Issue, 1957, p. 16 and GN Newspaper No. 7, 1973, p. 1
2. GN 4th Issue, 1957, p. 16
3. GN 3rd Issue, 1957, p. 16
4. GN No. 22, 1962, p. 12
5. GN No. 5, 1958, p. 20
6. GN 4th Issue, 1957, p. 12
7. GN 1996, p. 8
8. GN 1996, p. 8
9. GN 1996, p. 9

Chapter 7: Behind the Scenes

1. GN No. 28, 1963, p. 2
2. GN No. 5, 1958, p. 2
3. Newsletter, January 1979

Chapter 8: Dramatic Expansion

1. GN No. 47, 1970, p. 18
2. GN No. 14, 1960, p. 6
3. GN No. 26, 1962, p. 10
4. GN No. 21, 1961, p. 8
5. GN No. 35, 1964, p. 10–11
6. Newsletter, February 1966
7. GN No. 11, 1959, p. 18
8. GN No. 37, 1965, p. 9
9. GN No. 32, 1963, p. 3
10. GN No. 15, 1960, p. 10
11. GN No. 25, 1962, p. 10
12. GN No. 44, 1968, p. 12

Chapter 8: Dramatic Expansion (*cont.*)

13. GN No. 17, 1961, p. 16
14. GN No. 42, 1967, p. 7
15. GN No. 40, 1966, p. 10–11
16. GN No. 15, 1960, p. 8
17. GN No. 29, 1963, p. 8
18. GN Newspaper No. 7, 1973, p. 7
19. GN No. 18, 1961, p. 17
20. Roy Turner: Newsletter, May 1966
21. GN No. 23, 1962, p. 4
22. GN No. 15, 1960, p. 6
23. GN Newspaper No. 13, 1974, p. 4–5
24. GN No. 32, 1963, p. 10–12
25. GN 1992, p. 6
26. First and Last Loves, p. 24
27. GN No. 33, 1963, p. 13
28. GN No. 36, 1965, p. 19
29. GN No. 37, 1965, p. 4
30. GN No. 40, 1966, p. 8

Chapter 9: Glory Friends

1. A. Burt and N. Snyder, *Around the World in 80 Years*, p. 35
2. A. Burt and N. Snyder, *Around the World in 80 Years*, p. 111
3. GN No. 15, 1960, p. 6
4. GN No. 19, 1961, p. 10
5. The Oasis, Ysguborwen Road, Dwygyfylchi, Conwy, North Wales LL34 6PS
6. GN Newspaper No. 1, 1972, p. 4
7. GN Newspaper No. 11, 1973, p. 3
8. GN No. 27, 1962, p. 8
9. GN Newspaper No. 1, 1972, p. 5
10. GN No. 40, 1966, p. 11
11. GN No. 40, 1966, p. 11
12. GN 1988, p. 2
13. GN 1990, p. 2

Chapter 10: Glory World

1. GN No. 28, 1963, p. 2
2. GN No. 17, 1961, p. 8
3. GN No. 18, 1961, p. 19
4. GN No. 36, 1965, p. 4
5. GN No. 36, 1965, p. 5
6. GN No. 36, 1965, p. 6
7. GN No. 36, 1965, p. 6
8. GN No. 36, 1965, p. 8
9. GN No. 36, 1965, p. 7
10. GN No. 36, 1965, p. 7
11. GN No. 38, 1965, p. 15

Chapter 10: Glory World (*cont.*)

12.   GN No. 47, 1970, p. 12

13.   GN Newspaper No. 8, 1973, p. 3

14.   GN No. 12, 1959, p. 10

15.   GN No. 12, 1959, p. 10

16.   GN No. 12, 1959, p. 14

17.   GN No. 12, 1959, p. 15

18.   GN No. 13, 1960, p. 3

19.   GN No. 12, 1959, p. 12

20.   GN No. 12, 1959, p. 15

21.   GN No. 14, 1960, p. 3

22.   GN No. 11, 1959, p. 4

23.   GN 48th Edition, 1971, p. 9

24.   GN Third Issue, 1957, p. 13

25.   GN No. 27, 1962, p. 14

26.   GN No. 31, 1963, p. 8

27.   Michael Cameron, *By the Anointing*, p. 98–99

28.   GN 48th Edition, 1971, p. 15

29.   GN Newspaper No. 5, 1972, p. 5

30.   GN Newspaper No. 2, 1972, p. 5

31.   GN Newspaper No. 7, 1972, p. 1

32.   GN No. 7, 1958, p. 15

33.   GN No. 32, 1963, p. 3

34.   GN No. 39, 1965, p. 2

35.   GN No. 39, 1965, p. 2

36.   GN No. 18, 1961, p. 16

37.   GN No. 15, 1960, p. 15

38.   GN No. 24, 1962, p. 10

39.   GN 48th Edition, 1971, p. 17

40.   GN No. 34, 1964, p. 5

41.   GN Newspaper No. 7, 1972, p. 6

42.   GN Newspaper No. 13, 1974, p. 3

43.   GN Newspaper No. 5, 1972, p. 3

44.   GN Newspaper No. 10, 1973, p. 5

45.   GN Newspaper No. 9, 1973, p. 6

46.   GN No. 9, 1959, p. 10

47.   GN No. 19, 1961, p. 17

48.   GN No. 16, 1960, p. 12

49.   GN Newspaper No. 12, 1974, p. 7

50.   GN No. 31, 1963, p. 13

51.   GN Newspaper No. 12, 1974, p. 6

52.   GN Newspaper No. 12, 1974, p. 1

53.   GN Newspaper No. 14, 1974, p. 3

54.   GN No. 35, 1964, p. 13

55.   GN Newspaper No. 13, 1974, p. 7

56.   GN Newspaper No. 13, 1974, p. 7

Chapter 11: Glory Reality

1. J.I. Packer, *Keep in Step with the Spirit*, 1984, p. 253–4
2. GN No. 40, 1966, p. 17; Alan Britten
3. GN Newspaper No. 11 1973, p. 2; Michael Lewis
4. GN No. 39, 1965, p. 7; Audrey Cameron
5. GN No. 43, 1967, p. 3; Riden Morris
6. GN No. 39, 1965, p. 9; Joy Heasty
7. GN No. 40, 1966, p. 9; Dora Breakley
8. GN Newspaper No. 13, 1974, p. 5; Jean Foster
9. GN No. 39, 1965, p. 9; Elizabeth McChesney
10. GN No. 9, 1959, p. 16; Lena Burke
11. GN No. 15, 1960, p. 10; Brenda Young
12. GN Newspaper No. 14, 1974, p. 6; Elizabeth Crawford
13. GN No. 14, 1960, p. 15; Leslie Dacre
14. GN No. 43, 1967, p. 7; Mrs D. Collins
15. GN No. 46, 1969, p. 12; Deidre Collins
16. GN Newspaper No. 9, 1973, p. 3; Elaine Eaton
17. GN No. 43, 1967, p. 14; Glenys Philips
18. GN No. 22, 1962, p. 3; Molly Perry
19. GN No. 43, 1967, p. 7; Mr J.C.R.C., Chesham
20. GN No. 9 1959, p. 4; Elizabeth Clark
21. GN No. 40, 1966, p. 17; Alan Britten
22. GN Newspaper No. 11, 1973, p. 2; Michael Lewis
23. GN No. 39, 1965, p. 7; Audrey Cameron
24. GN No. 43, 1967, p. 3; Riden Morris
25. GN No. 39, 1965, p. 9; Joy Heasty
26. GN No. 40, 1966, p. 9; Dora Breakley
27. GN Newspaper No. 13, 1974, p. 5; Jean Foster
28. GN No. 39, 1965, p. 9; Elizabeth McChesney
29. GN No. 9, 1959, p. 16; Lena Burke
30. GN No. 15, 1960, p. 10; Brenda Young
31. GN Newspaper No. 14, 1974, p. 6; Elizabeth Crawford
32. GN No. 14, 1960, p. 15; Leslie Dacre
33. GN No. 43, 1967, p. 7; Mrs D. Collins
34. GN No. 46, 1969, p. 12; Deidre Collins
35. GN Newspaper No. 9, 1973, p. 3; Elaine Eaton
36. GN No. 43, 1967, p. 14; Glenys Philips
37. GN No. 22, 1962, p. 3; Molly Perry
38. GN No. 43, 1967, p. 7; Mr J.C.R.C., Chesham
39. GN No. 9, 1959, p. 4; Elizabeth Clark
40. GN No. 42, 1967, p. 10
41. GN No. 41, 1966, p. 8
42. GN No. 47, 1970, p. 19
43. GN No. 24, 1962, p. 16
44. GN No. 21, 1961, p. 3; Brenda Hargreaves
45. GN No. 44, 1968, p. 3; Jim Cargill
46. GN No. 16, 1960, p. 17
47. GN No. 10, 1959, p. 10–11

Chapter 11: Glory Reality (*cont.*)

48. GN No. 36, 1965, p. 19
49. GN No. 39, 1965, p. 3
50. GN No. 24, 1962, p. 3
51. GN No. 15, 1960, p. 2, 14
52. GN No. 17, 1961, p. 12
53. GN No. 13, 1960, p. 10
54. GN Newspaper No. 7, 1972, p. 1
55. GN No. 7, 1958, p. 11
56. GN No. 10, 1959, p. 10–11
57. GN 1st Issue, 1956, p. 2
58. GN No. 7, 1958, p. 2
59. GN No. 27, 1962, p. 2
60. GN Newspaper No. 11, 1973, p. 2
61. GN No. 6, 1958, p. 14
62. GN No. 38, 1965, p. 5
63. GN No. 27, 1962, p. 12
64. GN No. 13, 1960, p. 6; Peggy Hewitson
65. GN Newspaper No. 14, 1974, p. 6; Elizabeth Crawford
66. GN No. 42, 1967, p. 3; Sidney Warrington
67. GN No. 25, 1962, p. 17; Ivor Owen
68. GN No. 19, 1961, p. 5; Pastor G. Hadley
69. GN No. 41, 1960, p. 13; Tom Price
70. GN No. 40, 1966, p. 17; Diane Quantrill
71. GN No. 21, 1961, p. 19; Margaret Stobie
72. GN No. 40, 1966, p. 9; Dora Breakley
73. Louis Berkhof, *Systematic Theology*, p. 96
74. GN Newspaper No. 15, 1975, p. 7
75. GN 48th edition, 1971, p. 23
76. GN Newspaper No. 3, 1972, p. 1
77. GN No. 37, 1965, p. 7
78. GN No. 13, 1960, p. 11
79. GN 48th edition, 1971, p. 5
80. GN No. 8, 1958, p. 9
81. GN No. 34, 1964, p. 12
82. GN Newspaper No. 7, 1972, p. 4
83. GN No. 41, 1966, p. 13
84. GN No. 10, 1959, p. 19
85. GN Newspaper No. 13, 1974, p. 4
86. GN No. 25, 1962, p. 13
87. GN No. 24, 1962, p. 9
88. GN No. 26, 1962, p. 3
89. GN No. 7, 1958, p. 17
90. GN No. 19, 1961, p. 7
91. GN No. 33, 1963, p. 3
92. GN No. 19, 1961, p. 13
93. GN No. 6, 1958, p. 18
94. GN No. 5, 1958, p. 14

Chapter 11: Glory Reality (*cont.*)

95. GN No. 44, 1968, p. 13
96. GN Newspaper No. 12, 1974, p. 7
97. GN No. 6, 1958, p. 14
98. GN No. 39, 1965, p. 17
99. GN No. 40, 1966, p. 18
100. GN No. 37, 1965, p. 12
101. GN No. 41, 1966, p. 10
102. GN No. 41, 1966, p. 14
103. GN No. 15, 1960, p. 19
104. GN No. 8, 1958, p. 8
105. *William Tyndale,* Select Works Religious Tract Society/Focus Christian Ministries Trust, 1986, p. 110
106. GN Newspaper No. 11, 1973, p. 7
107. GN No. 17, 1961, p. 16
108. GN No. 37, 1965, p. 3
109. GN No. 39, 1965, p. 19
110. GN No. 17, 1961, p. 17
111. GN No. 27, 1962, p. 6
112. GN No. 38, 1965, p. 12
113. GN No. 13, 1960, p. 11
114. GN No. 13, 1960, p. 8
115. GN No. 21, 1961, p. 19; Margaret Stobie
116. GN Newspaper No. 3, 1972, p. 1; Ann Scarbrow
117. GN No. 43, 1967, p. 14; Mrs F. Lockyer
118. GN No. 9, 1959, p. 16; Wilfred Burke
119. GN Newspaper No. 7, 1972, p. 3; Laurie James
120. GN No. 39, 1965, p. 2; Mrs J. of Sandown
121. GN 48th edition, 1971, p. 24; Mr A.P. of Barnstaple
122. GN Newspaper No. 3, 1972, p. 4; Sharon Wingfield
123. GN No. 39, 1965, p. 12; David Vautier
124. GN No. 35, 1964, p. 11
125. GN No. 19, 1961, p. 5
126. GN No. 21, 1961, p. 19
127. GN Newspaper No. 5, 1972, p. 3
128. GN No. 19, 1961, p. 3
129. GN No. 40, 1966, p. 9; Mrs A.M. Heasty
130. GN Newspaper No. 7, 1972, p. 6; Dorothy Schalcher
131. GN No. 5, 1958, p. 13; Ben Davies
132. GN No. 6, 1958, p. 14; Joan Chadwick
133. GN Newspaper No. 4, 1972, p. 1; Ethel Adams
134. GN No. 39, 1965, p. 3; John Richardson
135. GN No. 34, 1964, p. 13; Bill Kirkham
136. GN No. 24, 1962, p. 16
137. GN Newspaper No. 7, 1972, p. 7
138. GN No. 35, 1964, p. 16
139. GN No. 17, 1961, p. 16
140. GN No. 17, 1961, p. 17

Chapter 11: Glory Reality (*cont.*)

141. GN No. 26, 1962, p. 12
142. GN No. 22, 1962, p. 6
143. GN No. 10, 1959, p. 19
144. GN No. 29, 1963, p. 8; Jane Stephen
145. GN No. 19, 1961, p. 5; Pastor G. Hadley
146. GN No. 6, 1958, p. 15; Mr Johns
147. GN No. 41, 1966, p. 8; Julie Jeffries
148. GN No. 36, 1965, p. 19
149. GN No. 34, 1964, p. 13
150. Watchman Nee, *A Table in the Wilderness*, Kingsway, 1969/1983, page for November 28th

Chapter 12: Glory Link

1. GN No. 18, 1961, p. 4; David Fuller
2. GN No. 36, 1965, p. 13
3. GN No. 11, 1959, p. 15
4. GN No. 9, 1959, pp. 3, 19
5. GN No. 11, 1959, p. 3
6. GN No. 15, 1960, p. 16
7. GN No. 10, 1959, p. 13
8. GN No. 9, 1959, p. 19

Chapter 13: Glory Testimonies

1. GN No. 7, 1958, p. 3
2. GN No. 16, 1960, p. 5
3. GN No. 43, 1967, p. 13
4. GN No. 37, 1965, p. 8
5. GN No. 5, 1958, p. 13
6. GN No. 8, 1958, p. 14
7. GN No. 9, 1959, p. 12
8. GN No. 37, 1965, p. 17
9. GN No. 29, 1963, pp. 3, 13
10. GN No. 15, 1960, p. 4
11. GN 1996, p. 7
12. GN Newspaper No. 1, 1972, p. 7

Chapter 14: Glory Word

1. GN No. 10, 1959, p. 10
2. GN No. 38, 1965, p. 8
3. GN No. 2, 1957, p. 6
4. Richard Wurmbrand, *Reaching Toward the Heights*, 1977, page for July 15
5. GN No. 24, 1962, p. 3
6. GN No. 41, 1966, p. 13
7. GN Newspaper No. 3, 1972, p. 1
8. GN No. 25, 1962, p. 3
9. GN No. 15, 1960, p. 18
10. GN No. 9, 1959, p. 5

Chapter 14: Glory Word (*cont.*)

11. GN No. 29, 1963, p. 2
12. GN No. 46, 1969, p. 2
13. GN No. 12, 1959, p. 2
14. GN No. 18, 1961, p. 8
15. GN No. 45, 1968, p. 4
16. GN No. 6, 1958, p. 9
17. GN No. 34, 1964, p. 17
18. GN Newspaper No. 11, 1973, p. 6

Chapter 15: Glory Healings

1. GN 1990, p. 3
2. GN 1st Issue, 1956, p. 9
3. GN No. 6, 1958, p. 4; GN No. 10, 1959, p. 17; GN No. 15, 1960, p. 15; GN No. 37, 1965, p. 2; GN No. 47, 1970, p. 4; GN Newspaper No. 1, 1972, p. 3 and cassette, Warrington, April 1989
4. GN 3rd Issue, 1957, p. 10
5. GN No. 10, 1959, p. 17
6. GN No. 16, 1960, p. 3
7. GN No. 25, 1962, p. 13
8. GN 48th edition, 1971, p. 3
9. GN Newspaper No. 1, 1972, p. 3
10. GN Newspaper No. 9, 1973, p. 1
11. GN No. 6, 1958, p. 5
12. GN No. 11, 1959, p. 5
13. GN No. 7, 1958, p. 16
14. GN No. 7, 1958, p. 7
15. GN No. 9, 1959, p. 9; GN No. 10, 1959, p. 16; GN No. 46, 1969, p. 18
16. GN No. 25, 1962, p. 18
17. GN No. 47, 1970, p. 8
18. GN No. 47, 1970, p. 8
19. GN No. 46, 1969, p. 16
20. GN No. 6, 1958, p. 5; GN No. 15, 1960, p. 17; GN No. 17, 1961, p. 15/ 48th edition, 1971, p. 22/newspaper No. 10, 1973, p. 2; GN Newspaper No. 11, 1973, p. 4; GN Newspaper No. 14, 1974, p. 1; GN Newspaper No. 15, 1975, p. 2

Chapter 16: Glory News, Tapes and Cassettes

1. GN No. 8, 1958, p. 2; Mr A.C. of London
2. GN No. 6, 1958, p. 8; Mr A.H. of Nottingham
3. GN No. 6, 1958, p. 8; Miss I.B. of Droylsden, Manchester
4. GN No. 10, 1959, p. 15
5. GN 3rd Issue, 1957, p. 11; Mrs M., Mansfield
6. GN No. 6, 1958, p. 15
7. GN No. 36, 1965, p. 16
8. GN Newspaper No. 4, p. 7; Mr E.G.S. in Cheshire
9. GN Newspaper No. 4, p. 7
10. GN No. 27, 1962, p. 2; Mr E.T. of Newport, Monmouthshire
11. GN No. 36, 1965, p. 14; Miss J.N. of London

Chapter 16: Glory News, Tapes and Cassettes *(cont.)*

12. GN Newspaper No. 5, 1972, p. 7; Mr P.L.B., Blackpool
13. GN Newspaper No. 4, 1972, p. 7; Mrs D.B. of Yorkshire
14. GN No. 42, 1967, p. 12; Mr W.H. of Ballymoney, N. Ireland
15. GN 48th edition, 1971, p. 16; Mr S.P. of Carrickfergus, N. Ireland
16. GN No. 8, 1958, p. 2; Mr and Mrs C.C. of Cardiff
17. GN No. 9, 1959, p. 10; Mrs K. of Nottingham
18. GN No. 9, 1959, p. 10; Mrs M.C. of Stornaway, Hebrides
19. GN Newspaper No. 16, 1975, p. 8; Margaret Jacob of Saffron Walden
20. GN No. 28, 1963, p. 2
21. GN No. 23, 1962, p. 2
22. GN No. 14, 1960, p. 19
23. GN No. 35, 1964, p. 4; Pastor Elizabeth Wallace Davenport of Vicksburg, Michigan
24. GN No. 19, 1961, p. 7; Mr G.W. of Evesham
25. GN 48th edition, p. 16; Mr and Mrs D.S. of Umberleigh, Devon
26. GN 48th edition, p. 18; Barry Colley of Leeds
27. GN No. 16, 1960, p. 17; Doreen and David Irvine of Gunnislake, Cornwall
28. GN No. 9, 1959, p. 11; Mr R.P. of Liverpool
29. GN No. 39, 1965, p. 2; Mrs E.W. or Workington, Cumberland
30. GN No. 13, 1960, p. 6; Paula Smith of Hereford
31. GN No. 15, 1960, p. 19; Jennifer Wright of Bradford
32. GN No. 43, 1967, p. 7; Mr J.C.R.C. of Chesham, Buckinghamshire
33. GN No. 47, 1970, p. 8; Miss E.F. of Birmingham
34. GN Newspaper No. 15, p. 8; J.B. of Dundee
35. GN No. 42, 1967, p. 4, Emily Crossley of Fleetwood, Lancashire
36. GN Newspaper No. 12, 1974, p. 7; Mr S.M. of Belfast
37. GN Newspaper No. 14, 1974, p. 8; M.C. of Brixton Hill, London
38. GN No. 11, 1959, p. 5; Mr P. Rowe, of Ryde, Isle of Wight
39. GN Newspaper No. 7, 1972, p. 6, Dorothy Schalcher of Brisbane, Australia
40. GN 1988, p. 2; William and Audrey Leadbeater
41. GN No. 19, 1961, p. 7; Mr G.D. of Yeovil
42. GN No. 6, 1958, p. 8; Mr G.M. of Gillingham

Chapter 17: Glory Choruses

1. GN Newspaper No. 5, 1972, p. 7; Mrs R.M., Yorkshire
2. GN No. 43, 1967, p. 14; Mrs F. Lockyer, Aberkenfig nr. Bridgend, S. Wales
3. GN Newspaper No. 4, 1972, p. 7; Mrs L.H.M., Pennsylvania
4. GN No. 27, 1962, p. 14; Ted Seymour, English evangelist, Youth for Christ, Los Angeles
5. GN No. 7, 1958, p. 16; Nessie Colvin, Angus

Chapter 18: Glory Glimpse

1. GN No. 12, 1959, p. 9, quoted by David Greenow

Further Information

Sayings of Henri

This gospel works!
We're blazing a trail for a mighty revival!
You'll never be the same again!
You will feel better for coming here!
It's in you, brother. It's in you, sister!
It's more infectious than measles!
We're into something big!
We're not here to play chapels and churches.
We're setting the captives free!
You can't mix it!
God has no favourites. He loves everybody.
If we love one another, everything else will work out all right!
Get right with God. It's later than you think!
The Glory Way is a filling station. Fill up and feel the difference.
If there were more happy Christians, there would be more
    Christians!
Once you've been to a Glory meeting it spoils you for any other
    meeting.
Get the man out of the sea. Then get the sea out of the man!
You can get delayed action, you know.
Never have a critical spirit. It will rob you.
Follow us home to know us.
The first thing God does with you is to take you into His Beauty
    Parlour.

The spelling of Henri's name

This puzzles many people and it was always meant to. It was Henri's
intention! The spelling on his birth certificate was *Henry* and this
evidently was how his name was spelt right up until the moment
when he set up in business on his own in Newark, at the age of 31. No
one quite knows whether all along he had had an eccentric hankering

after the French spelling, or whether he changed it on a sudden whim at the suggestion of a friend or family member.

What's in a name? More than might be expected. Certainly it was as an entrepreneur that he made the change, and one must admit that the French spelling is distinctive and sticks in the mind.

In this book, for simplicity's sake, I have called him Henry in the section on his boyhood, 'Express Trains'. And thereafter he is Henri.

What the Newspapers said

The Newark Herald

Henri took full advantage of the local press. The Glory Way was news. It was good news. Here are extracts from the 1950s:

> I walked into the Corn Exchange on Sunday afternoon and met a happy band of people. And I mean REALLY HAPPY. They were singing, laughing and even shouting...
>
> But they were doing it with a difference because I had not stumbled upon just any meeting. It was a meeting to sing praises to Jesus and to ask him for deliverance.
>
> It was, in fact, Newark's own Gospel Revival Group led by Mr. W.H. (Henri) Staples, and the people there had found that by giving themselves to God in a happy way they had discovered the greatest thing in life.
>
> You have only to listen to the testimonies of people who have found deliverance to know that Henri and his happy band are doing wonderful work in encouraging people to re-build their lives around the Saviour. Their members are undenominational and it is stressed that by their endeavours more people will find 'the right path.' By that, it is meant that the Revival Group is out to help the accepted Churches by bringing converts back into the churches.
>
> From a small beginning Henri, with meetings above his premises in Appletongate, Newark, has built up his crusading on the teachings of America's Oral Roberts, foremost evangelist in the devotion to deliverance in that country and now world famous.
>
> The atmosphere is to be found at Henri's revival meetings. When I talked to people on Sunday they radiated happiness. There was no gloom ... even though many of the people had known hardship, poverty and long suffering in the past.
>
> Like the local business man who was once in the depths of despair and is now fully alive to the fact that life is really worth living. He told me that a serious illness almost shattered his existence. His self-confidence, which had brought him success went when he suffered ill-health. He found that he was 'going to pieces.'

'Then I came to Henri's meetings,' he said. 'The result was astounding. I found God and since then He has been with me. God changed my state of mind.'

Jamaican Finds New Hope at Revival Meetings

In a recent edition of the *Newark Herald* ... Mr ... Henry Staples, organiser of 'Henri's Revival Meetings', said that a number of Jamaicans were trying to get work in the Newark district in order to attend his meetings regularly.

The following account is that of a Jamaican, Mr W.S. Faulkner of 2 Crown Street, Newark, as told to a *Herald* reporter:

I would like through the medium of your paper, to express my gratitude and appreciation for the privilege of being able to reside in Newark.

I am a Jamaican and was a minister of the Church of God in Jamaica. I have been living in Nottingham for about 6 months and during that time I have tried to find a place of worship where men and women really worship God in spirit and in truth, and enjoy a rich pentecostal experience.

Such a meeting and experience was what I was used to back home. I was sadly disappointed...

You can imagine my joy, however, when a fellow Jamaican told me of a real live Holy Ghost meeting at Newark, led by brother Henri.

I came over at the first opportunity and found just what I had been seeking. Here was a man of God who not only believed but also put into operation this wonderful pentecostal experience and for the first time since landing in England I had fellowship with people who were rejoicing in the possession of life so rich and abundant.

Signs and wonders accompany the ministry of Bro. Henri, and I have decided to back him up one hundred per cent.

That is why I have come to live in Newark. I am so grateful to be here for I feel there is nothing like this in all England.'

Bob Nicholls was given a regular column to write called 'Revival Time'. He seized the opportunity. We quote from one which was subheaded:

Have You Felt It Yet?

We were over in Mansfield Market Square with the gospel caravan, having our usual Sunday night open-air meeting. There were about five to six hundred attentive listeners enjoying the good news of salvation put over in the glory way.

At the close of the meeting a man pushed his way to the front and said: 'Henri, can I have that there what's coming off that van?'

What 'that there' was he could not see, except that it was something that lifted his spirits and made him feel good inside. It was not something that he could see, but it was certainly something he could feel and it didn't make him feel miserable or condemned. 'That there' had penetrated deep down into his heart and made him feel happy and contented. It had held him like a magnet and had given him a little taste of that wonderful peace, love and joy all enjoy in Henri's meetings.

Of course, we knew just what 'that there' was and we were pleased to tell him that he could certainly have it, for it was freely given by God and He has no favourites, but is rich unto all that call upon Him (Romans 10:12).

Another of the columns contained the following:

Are You TB?

It is now an established that a new type of TB has broken out in Newark. It appears to be of a very infectious nature and every week more cases are coming to light. Mild forms of this TB have been reported from various parts of the country, but Newark seems to be the main source of infection.

We are happy to tell you, however, that this is not a matter for the sanitoriums of our land, for if such were the case they would soon be filled to overflowing and could never hope to cope with this new epidemic. No man can stop it, although some have tried, and we expect it to sweep through the land from Land's End to John o'Groats. It is affecting old and young alike and particularly our Jamaican visitors. Unlike the hard-boiled Englishmen they appear to offer no resistance against it whatsoever.

Having by this time gained considerable experience regarding this new kind of TB, we have found that it is very deep seated: first of all it affects the heart. The early symptoms are very often tears which quickly change to an expression of heavenly joy and peace and a fervent desire to love everybody, everywhere. Sorrow and disappointment vanish. Nervous tension disappears. A feeling of ease and contentment takes possession of the soul. One wonders if they are still in Newark or whether by some wonderful means they have been transported to heaven.

Strange to relate this TB results in a greater measure of health and strength, and many are finding a new lease of life, with a happier outlook on life altogether. In fact many who have suffered ill health and disease have been marvellously healed as a result of this TB.

On tracing it to its source we find ourselves in Henri's glory meeting and discover that this TB is not a physical affliction but a 'Tremendous Blessing.'

Billy Bray

Thinking back on his life in 1985, Henri wrote:

> I had something come upon me. My mother said, 'This is
> wonderful. Henri, you are just like Billy Bray.' I said, 'I don't
> know about Billy Bray, but I know God's behind me like a
> bulldozer pushing me.' All I could do was to say, 'Praise the
> Lord,' and tell folk what had happened to me.
>
> (GN, January 1985, p. 3)

Gran Staples certainly hit a bull's eye with this remark, and she was
not the only one to notice this striking similarity between her son and
the Cornish tin miner and Methodist preacher.

Who was Billy Bray? He was certainly a one-off character, one of
those rugged individualists whom people never forget. He was born in
1794 in the village of Twelveheads, midway between Redruth and
Truro, and he spent all his life at the sweated labour of mining tin
which, like any other kind of mining, was fraught with danger. Once
as a young man he heard a loud crack overhead; he ran out of the way
and forty tons of rock crashed down where he had been. He was a
bright quick-witted young man, always ready for a good laugh, the life
and soul of the party, particularly when he was drunk. And that was
his big problem; he took to the bottle. He was always knocking it back
with his mates and he became an alcoholic, to the great distress of his
young wife Joey. Drink sent him crazy. 'He was the wildest, most
daring and reckless of all the reckless, daring men...'

But about the age of twenty-nine he came under great conviction
of sin, 'his conscience tormented him by day, and dreams terrified him
by night.' He read Bunyan's *Visions of Heaven and Hell* and began to
seek the Lord. For about a week he cried to God for mercy. When he
was not working at the mine he spent the whole time alone reading his
Bible and hymn book. He ate, drank and slept very little, he was so
desperate to get right with God. Then once he was through, he was
filled with 'joy unspeakable and full of glory'. He said,

> In an instant the Lord made me so happy that I cannot express
> what I felt. I shouted for joy. I praised God with my whole heart
> for what he had done for a poor sinner like me; for I could say,
> The Lord hath pardoned all my sins ... I remember this, that
> everything looked new to me, the people, the fields, the cattle,
> the trees. I was like a man in a new world. I spent the greater part
> of my time in praising the Lord.

It was really very wonderful the way his life was completely transformed, from drunkard to witnessing evangelist in one week.

> His was no ordinary struggle, but it ended in perfect liberty of
> soul. He could say, 'No condemnation now I dread.' The conflict

was terrible, but the victory was all the more glorious. The trial of his faith was sharp, but the reward was sweeter ever afterwards. He knew more certainly, how inconceivably great and glorious was the salvation which is by faith in Christ Jesus with eternal glory. He was filled with a holy rapture of soul, which nothing could restrain. His words, his tones, his looks, had a magnetic power. He was, so to speak, charged with a divine electricity ... He could no more help speaking of Christ and His Salvation than the sun can help shining, or the trees in spring can help budding and blossoming into beauty and life.

Understandably it did not take long for Joey, who as a girl had been saved but then had backslidden, to be restored to full joy as well.

It is not surprising that Billy Bray soon lived to be an outstanding witness for the Lord Jesus throughout his native Cornwall. His natural ability to tell a racy yarn and gain a laugh was turned to good effect when he spoke about his Lord. His droll ironic sense of humour quickly seized the attention of his hearers and he pressed the advantage home; scriptures which flew from his lips went like arrows to their target. He proved to be a gripping and dynamic evangelist. For forty years he preached on the Methodist circuits, drawing crowds wherever he went. But this never went to his head. He was always a relatively poor man, labouring in the tin mines, his 'tent making', and tirelessly preaching, visiting, exhorting. He was most solicitous about the welfare of his locality, building more than one chapel with remarkably few resources, praying and interceding for houses, families, hamlets as he walked the twisting country paths and went about his business.

Henri was not unlike Billy Bray in physique. They were both short, spare, wiry, jack-in-a-box men. But the similarity did not end there. We read that Billy was always dancing, shouting and praising God. Both men were irrepressible. I remember one of the first times I went to Fiskerton Chapel, Henri, nigh on eighty years of age, sprang off the platform at me and squeezed the breath out of me in a great bear hug. I was stunned. Likewise Billy Bray showed his affection for the Lord's people in a most extraordinary way. On one occasion, at the end of a meeting after a certain Mr Maynard had been preaching,

> Billy did not exactly carry the preacher, but he dragged him round the pulpit pew to the amusement of the people, shouting and jumping all the time. When he let the preacher go, he asked him whether he could stand that or not. 'Yes, much more than that,' was the answer. 'All right, friend Maynard, praise the Lord!'

Allowing for differences of broad Cornish accent and broad Nottinghamshire, one can just imagine Henri saying this and indulging in the same heavenly horseplay!

Both men had no inhibitions about letting off steam and dancing before the Lord. Billy Bray once exclaimed (I can almost hear an echo from Newark a century later),

> Well, I dance sometimes. Why shouldn't I dance as well as David? David, you say, was a king; well, bless the Lord! I am a King's son! I have as good a right to dance as David had. Bless the Lord! I get very happy at times; my soul gets full of the glory, and then I dance too! I was home in my chamber t'other day, and I got so happy that I danced, and the glory came streaming down upon my soul and it made me dance so lustily that my heels went down through the planchen (floor boards).

Billy Bray is famous for other sayings. For instance, when people opposed him and tried to bring him to task for singing and shouting so much, he would say,

> If they were to put me into a barrel, I would shout glory out through the bunghole! Praise the Lord!

Again,

> They said I was a *mad*-man, but they meant I was a *glad*-man, and, glory be to God! I have been glad ever since.

And again,

> I can't help praising the Lord. As I go along the street I lift up one foot, and it seems to say 'Glory!' and I lift up the other, and it seems to say 'Amen', and so they keep on like that all the time I am walking.

It is recorded that, in May 1868 on his death bed, Billy Bray's last word was 'Glory!' (F.W. Bourne: *Billy Bray*, pp. 17, 16, 19–20, 21, 28, 46, 47, 20, 44, 121). A glory man indeed. And can we imagine that it has been with particular relish, 124 years later as Henri entered heaven, that the angels or the Lord Himself have introduced these two kindred glory men to one another?

There is a postscript to the twinning of these two men, for Henri and Connie went on holiday a good number of times to Cornwall. On one occasion they made a point of going to the Methodist chapel where Billy Bray was buried, in the village of Baldhu, which is the next village to Twelveheads where he was born. Henri was the first to explore. To his surprise he found the door to the chapel open, so he went in and saw an old man sitting there on his own. Henri sat down beside him and said characteristically, 'Now then, brother, praise the Lord.' The elderly man looked up, 'I'll praise the Lord when my wife is better.' He explained that she could not walk; she had had very bad legs for a long while. Henri asked if he could see her, and the elderly husband replied, 'I don't know whether I'm doing right by taking you.

I might get turned out. But, anyhow, we'll risk it.' So he took Henri home, and his wife grudgingly let Henri pray for her.

Two days later on the Sunday evening Henri and Connie went again to the Billy Bray chapel to see if there was a service. Yes, a few people were meeting there and, lo and behold, there was the old lady walking about. They were amazed. She said to everyone, 'I'm praising God today because somebody prayed for me and I can walk. Let's praise the Lord, if it's only for what He's done for me!' After the service she invited Henri and Connie back home for a cup of tea. There was much rejoicing. They had a small organ in the house. Henri sat down and began playing, and they had a grand time of singing and praise.

The wife's name was Ida. She continued as a good witness in the chapel. After a time the husband died. On another occasion, when Henri and Connie visited her, there was a drought. They had not had rain for months. Now Ida had a small-holding with lots of chickens and other livestock, and she had a huge rainwater tank which filled up from the catchment area of her roofs. She used this tank to give drink to all her birds and water her vegetables and flowers. By now it had run dry. She remarked ruefully to Henri, 'I'll praise the Lord if that tank gets full of water for me kettle.' He immediately took the matter to the Lord and prayed for rain, and that night there was an absolute downpour, filling the great tank to the brim. This strengthened her faith, and again their hearts overflowed with rejoicing.

On another occasion Alan and Shirley Churchill were on holiday in the area when Henri and Connie were also there and the four of them went to see Ida. There she was, in her cottage at Boldhu, surrounded by lots of cats and their kittens – as well as her chickens – praising the Lord.

Notes on Central Nottinghamshire

The Midland counties of England suffer from being corridors that people rush through to get to other places. But they have in themselves a very sterling interest and are fascinating for sight-seeing. Nottinghamshire has much agricultural countryside: a patchwork of rich pastures, meadows and fields of grain with woods and nestling villages. To the north lies the ancient Sherwood Forest, where four hundred acres have been made into a country park.

Mansfield

This is a medium-sized town with a population of about 55,000 and is the administrative centre for Sherwood Forest. In the old Moot Hall the forest courts were held.

Mansfield strikes one as being a backbone-of-the-nation place; something of an unsung hero of a town, where hard-working people have got on with life, come what may, and have more than done their bit towards the general economic stability of the country.

To begin with, the town had a medieval market. Then in the eighteenth century the little River Maun, cheerfully tumbling down its rocky bed, was harnessed to drive cotton mills. At one time there were eighteen of them. (Also about a dozen windmills could be seen at work grinding corn.) A process called cotton-doubling was developed; strands were twisted together to make a thicker thread. Then there was the framework knitting industry for making stockings and shawls. (Roy Turner's great-grandfather Rowland, from nearby Sutton-in-Ashfield, was known as 'The Royal Knitter,' working a stocking-frame from the age of eleven and eventually making silk stockings for Queen Victoria and other royalty.) The first power-driven knitting machine was invented and set up in 1864. This is very interesting because we know that, at some point, one of Connie's grandfathers invented some important knitting machinery.

When one looks at the pleasant light creamy colour of the stone buildings it is not a surprise to know that there have been limestone and sandstone quarries there from the Middle Ages onwards. The lower courses of the Westminster Houses of Parliament are built of Mansfield stone.

There is a solid dignity about the centre of the town. It is pleasant to walk down pedestrian West Gate, where the medieval market was held. One passes the Old Market Cross, a pillar with four sundials standing on its square sandstone base. Beside an old pump a plaque tells us that a Methodist preacher, John Adams, walked over from Nottingham in 1788 and preached the gospel here. (That was one year before the start of the French Revolution. It has been said that if it were not for the grace of God poured out in the great Methodist revival, Britain might very well have suffered a terrible revolution like the one in France.) Then, only a short distance from this pump and market cross one notices Curry's shop. Ah, so that's where Henri started work!

West Gate opens out into the Market Place, the scene of those remarkable open-air meetings, the first Glory witness. Ahead looms a high railway viaduct that strides over the top of the town. Down a hill through one of its arches one glimpses the sturdy tower of a medieval church. Originally the Market was a mass of tiny streets, shops and pubs; these became so congested that horses and carts could barely pass through. In the 1840s these higgledy piggledy buildings were cleared away to make a square and in 1849 the large gothic cross was built, on which exactly a century later the Glory team were to hang their microphones. The Lord's provision!

On the other side of the viaduct one can still see remains of rock houses dug out of a sandstone cliff. They were inhabited by besom makers who used the heather on the surrounding heathland to make brooms. Rock Valley, where Connie was born, is quite close to the city centre. There, at the bottom of that road, is the Metal Box Factory, with its elegant little green dome, where teenage Connie worked; now part of a huge American multinational company. A man working there, Charles Fletcher, designed the well known *Quality Street* tins. He died recently aged 104.

Finally we come to coal mining. The coal measures of Derbyshire and Nottinghamshire dip steeply from west to east. In the area round Mansfield the seams are deep and for a long time it was not thought worthwhile digging shafts. As a result, coal mining did not really get going until the late 1800s. In retrospect, it is tragic that ever the government of a country and its mining industry should be at logger-heads. If ever there were workers who deserved good pay and conditions it is miners, because of the deprivation of daylight, the dust and the danger. For instance, in 1913 at Rufford Colliery, four miles east of Mansfield, a huge barrel of water, being hoisted up a shaft, suddenly toppled back down, killing fourteen men. Then there was a terrible fire which swept through Creswell Colliery, about eight miles to the north, in which no less than eighty people died. That was in 1950, just after Henri and Connie had started the Mansfield Market meetings. No wonder the miners hung on their words.

Southwell

Between Mansfield and Newark-on-Trent you come across the little cathedral town of Southwell. Sir John Betjeman said, 'there can be so few small towns as unspoilt as Southwell.' It is a pleasure to walk through the quiet alleyways, to catch glimpses of leafy gardens, solid eighteenth-century houses, and old coaching inns. The Minster, or cathedral, has a Norman nave, a gothic choir and two distinctive square towers at the west end with spires like great dunce's caps. In the Chapter House, of about 1300, are exceptional stone carvings of leaves, flowers, fruit and animals.

Three miles to the south-east of Southwell lies the village of Fiskerton, where Glory meetings have been held in the Methodist chapel for over twenty years. Nearby is the isolated bungalow of Connie Staples, perched on the river bank of the Trent.

Newark

Eighteen miles to the east of Mansfield, and about half its size, is the historic market town of Newark-on-Trent, built at the intersection of the Great North Road, A1, with the Roman Fosse Way, A46.

The castle was built in the early twelfth century, with later additions, and came into its own in the Civil War when it was a stalwart stronghold of the Cavaliers, who withstood three prolonged sieges of the Roundheads, or Parliamentarians. In the second of these the dashing Prince Rupert, nephew of King Charles I, scattered the enemy's cavalry. However, a year later, in 1645, Charles I lost the war in the Battle of Naseby, about fifty miles to the south. A last Cavalier stand was made at Newark and the Roundhead and Scottish armies closed in. King Charles spent a last night of freedom in Southwell and then gave himself up to the Scottish army, at Kelham two miles to the west of Newark, sending orders to the governor of Newark to surrender the town to the Roundheads. With great reluctance the governor did so. Newark was in a frightful state; the buildings had been knocked about by bombardment and the citizens were half-starved and wracked by disease. They were ordered to destroy the castle. Happily they were too ill to make a thorough job of it. The imposing curtain wall still remains, reflected in the River Trent.

The centre of Newark is dominated by the 242 foot spire of the large medieval church. Many other buildings in the middle of the town have great character. The White Hart, in the Market Place, begun in the fourteenth century, is a striking example of timber framed building; it has a beautifully restored painted front. The Governor's House, in Stodman Street, is another picturesque building, timber framed and with a double overhang. It was here, in October 1645 with defeat hanging over him, that King Charles had a bitter quarrel with his nephew Prince Rupert.

Henri's shops, with the Glory Room, the Glory Office and the Staples's flat and with Jallands Row behind, were close to the centre of the town. They can be found on the north-west side of Appleton Gate, right next door to a car park, a stone's throw away from the junction with Magnus Street.

Glory Holidays

Down the years holidays by the seaside have provided a natural opportunity for many people to enjoy fellowship together. On the whole, the numbers who have gathered together at these times have been considerably greater than in the other meetings up and down the country; they have been gatherings of the Glory clan.

To date there has been a continuous series of these holidays for nearly forty years. Folk stay in chalets, caravans and bed and breakfast. Usually the days are kept free for swimming, walking, boating, sight-seeing. Sometimes an excursion by coach or boat is arranged. At some point in the week everyone enjoys a barbecue. Often, on a Sunday, the fellowship witness, in the open air on the sea front. One main meeting per day is held in the evenings. Sometimes there are morning meetings. A week spent in this way has been wonderfully beneficial: a physical relaxation, a time for renewing friendships in the Lord, and an occasion of invigorating praise to God and spiritual refreshment.

There has been specific evangelism too, particularly in Ireland. Cecil Stewart, with the support of his brother Victor, set up a team who held tent camps and campaigns in Portglenone, Enniskillen,

Ballymena, Monaghan and at Douglas on the Isle of Man. Sometimes Henri and Connie or Roy Turner and other members of the Glory team have come in for a few days of meetings at the end of the campaign.

Two evangelistic tent missions, on the initiative of Bob Searle, have also been held in Southsea on the outskirts of Portsmouth, and once on home ground in Southwell.

Another fruitful occasion for gathering Glory folk together has been a three-day (or even four-day) convention at a weekend, usually a bank holiday at Easter, Whitsun, August or New Year. As already described, outstanding were the Whitsun conventions at Newark. There have been others at Blackpool, Bedlington, Bolton, Bradford and Bristol, to name a few. For some an annual trek up north to Peterhead for the New Year has been a real event. Instead of hogmanay carousals, the Glory folk seize the moment to have 'a fill-up of the Holy Ghost wine', in sober joyful energetic bursts of praise as only the the true kilted Scots can do it; not being drunk with wine, wherein is excess, but being filled with the Spirit (Ephesians 5:18).

In 1975 Henri made an agreement with the local Methodist Chapel in the village of Fiskerton, where he and Connie lived near Newark, to hold Glory meetings there on Saturday evenings and bank holiday Mondays. This has made Fiskerton a veritable Glory centre and eventually, in 1998, the chapel was bought from the Methodists.

Glory Holiday Conventions

1962   Ryde, Isle of Wight
        Southend-on-Sea
1963   Ryde, Isle of Wight
        Southend-on-Sea
        Portglenone (2-week campaign)
1964   Ryde, Isle of Wight
        Southend-on-Sea
        Portglenone (1-week campaign)
1965   Ryde, Isle of Wight
        Cleethorpes
        Southsea
        Bangor, Co. Down
1966   Ryde, Isle of Wight
        Cleethorpes
        Lisburn
        Southsea (2-week campaign)
        Enniskillen (1-week campaign)
        Ballymena (1-week campaign)
1967   Ryde, Isle of Wight
        Southend-on-Sea
        Scarborough

1968	Ryde, Isle of Wight
	Scarborough
	Monaghan (3-week campaign)
1969	Llanfairfechan
	Scarborough
	Douglas, Isle of Man
1970	Fleetwood
	Boscombe
1971	Fleetwood
	Boscombe
	Douglas, Isle of Man
1972	Fleetwood
	Walton-on-the-Naze
	Porthcawl
1973	Margate
1974	Margate
1975	Clacton
1976	Clacton
1977	Colwyn Bay
1978	Clacton
1979	Clacton
1980	Lowestoft
1981	Lowestoft
1982	Swanage
1983	Swanage
1984	Hunstanton
1985	Hunstanton
1986	Bridlington
1987	Bridlington
1988	Bridlington
1989	Bridlington
1990	Bridlington
1991	Bridlington
1992	Bridlington
1993	Bridlington
1994	Bridlington
1995	Christchurch
1996	Christchurch
1997	Walton-on-the-Naze
1998	Walton-on-the-Naze
1999	Lowestoft
2000	Hunstanton
2001	Walton-on-the-Naze
	Penmaenmawr

Contacts

For further information please contact:

The Glory Office
PO BOX 10
Basildon
SS16 5SX
United Kingdom

Alan and Shirley Churchill, Basildon

Tel: +44(0) 1268 544526
Fax: +44(0) 1268 453433
Email: ac@glory-people.org
Web site: www.glory-people.org

Do you know Jesus?

If you don't know Jesus as your personal Lord and Saviour, pray this prayer now. Confess Jesus with your mouth and believe it in your heart, and you will be born again into the family of God!

> Lord Jesus, I need You in my life. I believe You are the Son of God and that You died on the cross for me. I repent of all my sins. Please forgive me as only You can. Come into my life Holy Spirit and create in me a new heart full of love. Teach me to hear Your Voice and to follow You. I confess Jesus You are my Saviour and Lord. I've been ***born again***!

Praise the Lord ***you are now a child of God***, part of His family. You need to do four things now:

- Get a Bible and read it daily.
- Pray daily and ask Jesus to help you.
- Find a church and attend regularly.
- Let us know what you have done.